RSF: The Russell Sage Foundation Journal of the Social Sciences

The U.S. Labor Market During and After the Great Recession

VOLUME 3 · NUMBER 3 · APRIL 2017

RSF: The Russell Sage Foundation Journal of the Social Sciences   ISSN 2377-8261

The Russell Sage Foundation

The Russell Sage Foundation, one of the oldest of America's general purpose foundations, was established in 1907 by Mrs. Margaret Olivia Sage for "the improvement of social and living conditions in the United States." The foundation seeks to fulfill this mandate by fostering the development and dissemination of knowledge about the country's political, social, and economic problems. While the foundation endeavors to assure the accuracy and objectivity of each book it publishes, the conclusions and interpretations in Russell Sage Foundation publications are those of the authors and not of the foundation, its trustees, or its staff. Publication by Russell Sage, therefore, does not imply foundation endorsement.

Mission Statement

RSF: The Russell Sage Foundation Journal of the Social Sciences is a peer-reviewed, open-access journal of original empirical research articles by both established and emerging scholars. It is designed to promote cross-disciplinary collaborations on timely issues of interest to academics, policymakers, and the public at large. Each issue is thematic in nature and focuses on a specific research question or area of interest. The introduction to each issue will include an accessible, broad, and synthetic overview of the research question under consideration and the current thinking from the various social sciences.

Opinions expressed in this journal are not necessarily those of the editors, editorial board, trustees, or the Russell Sage Foundation.

We invite scholars to submit proposals for potential issues through the *RSF* application portal: https://rsfjournal.onlineapplicationportal.com/. Submissions should be addressed to Suzanne Nichols, Director of Publications.

To view the complete text and additional features online please go to **www.rsfjournal.org**.

Russell Sage Foundation
112 East 64th Street
New York, NY 10065

ISSN (print):	2377-8253
ISSN (electronic):	2377-8261
ISBN:	978-0-87154-741-5

RSF: The Russell Sage Foundation
Journal of the Social Sciences

VOLUME 3 NUMBER 3
APRIL 2017

The U.S. Labor Market During and After the Great Recession

ISSUE EDITORS
Arne L. Kalleberg, University of
North Carolina at Chapel Hill
Till M. von Wachter, University of California,
Los Angeles

CONTENTS

The U.S. Labor Market During and After the Great Recession: Continuities and Transformations

ARNE L. KALLEBERG AND TILL M. VON WACHTER

The Great Recession of 2007–2009 created the largest economic upheaval in the United States since the Great Depression of the 1930s. Although economic downturns are a recurring phenomenon, the most recent recession was exceptional in its duration and depth. It was the longest recession since the Great Depression. At eighteen months, from December 2007 to June 2009, it exceeded the sixteen-month recessions of 1973–1975 and 1981–1982; the average period from peak to trough of post–World War II recessions was 11.1 months. The Great Recession was also especially severe; both GDP and number of jobs declined by about 6 percent and median family incomes declined by about 8 percent. The Great Recession was particularly worthy of its name because of the protracted slump in employment that followed even after the recession was of-ficially over, as assessed on the basis of the dating procedure of the National Bureau of Economic Research.[1]

As a result, during the Great Recession unemployment rates skyrocketed, housing prices and stock portfolios plummeted, and the lives of millions were disrupted. By some measures, over 30 million individuals lost their jobs, and the rate of long-term unemployment doubled its historical high (Song and von Wachter 2014). Household net worth dropped by 18 percent, or more than $10 trillion, the largest loss of wealth in the fifty years since that the federal government has collected data on wealth accumulation (Jacobsen and Mather 2010). The Great Recession did not affect all subgroups within the population equally; rather, the impacts of the economic downturn differed for different groups, according to their members'

Arne L. Kalleberg is Kenan Distinguished Professor in the Department of Sociology, University of North Carolina at Chapel Hill. Till M. von Wachter is associate professor in the Department of Economics at the University of California, Los Angeles.

© 2017 Russell Sage Foundation. Kalleberg, Arne L., and Till M. von Wachter. 2017. "The U.S. Labor Market During and After the Great Recession: Continuities and Transformations." *RSF: The Russell Sage Foundation Journal of the Social Sciences* 3(3): 1–19. DOI: 10.7758/RSF.2017.3.3.01. Direct correspondence to: Arne L. Kalleberg at arnekal@email.unc.edu, CB#3210 Hamilton Hall, University of North Carolina, Chapel Hill, NC 27599; and Till M. von Wachter at tvwachter@econ.ucla.edu, Department of Economics, 8283 Bunche Hall, Mail Stop: 147703, Los Angeles, CA 90095.

1. Recessions, as defined by the Business Cycle Dating Committee of the National Bureau of Economic Research (2010), are periods of a "significant decline in economic activity . . . [that] can last from a few months to more than a year." The committee's definition of what constitutes a recession is not fixed, but rather is based on its judgment of the behavior of various indicators of economic activity, such as declines in real gross domestic product (GDP), real income, employment, and industrial production and wholesale-retail sales. Since World War II, the NBER has declared eleven recessions (1948–1949, 1953–1954, 1957–1958, 1960–1961, 1969–1970, 1973–1975, 1980, 1981–1982, 1990–1991, 2001, and 2007–2009). There have been twenty-two recessions and recoveries since 1900.

gender, race, and ethnicity. Men, the less-educated, and African Americans were especially hard hit.

The profound impact of the Great Recession has prompted numerous studies by social scientists of its causes and consequences for individuals, their families, communities, and society more generally (see, for example, Grusky, Western, and Wimer 2011; Danziger 2013; Card and Mas 2016). This research has tracked economic outcomes such as the impacts of unemployment on poverty, economic inequality, and earnings growth, as well as social outcomes such as marriage and fertility, education, health, politics, and child development, throughout the recession and the immediate recovery. From these and other studies we have made important progress in understanding some of the consequences and mechanisms of the Great Recession. Yet many questions remain as to the nature and consequences of the Great Recession and its aftermath.

The passage of nearly ten years since the NBER declared the official beginning of the Great Recession in December 2007 puts us in a better position than we were earlier to undertake deeper analyses of the sources and consequences of the protracted recovery on workers, families, and communities. We can thus begin to assess with greater confidence the extent to which the changes wrought by the Great Recession represent structural and transformative changes, whether these are continuations of the kinds of structural changes that began in the mid-1970s, or whether these are relatively temporary features associated with business cycles.

Like the collections of studies about the Great Recession cited above, this issue of *RSF: The Russell Sage Foundation Journal of the Social Sciences* is also devoted to understanding some of the characteristics of the U.S. labor market during and after the Great Recession. The articles in this issue deal with several important questions about the nature as well as economic and noneconomic consequences of the Great Recession. Despite much work, ongoing controversy reigns as to the potential causes of the Great Recession and the protracted weakness in the labor market that followed. With the benefit of having access to data spanning the long recovery, several articles in the volume contribute new empirical findings that inform our understanding of alternative economic channels. The article by Jesse Rothstein studies how the role of mismatches and wage growth evolved before and during the Great Recession and has continued to evolve since its official end. Brian L. Levy, Ted Mouw, and Anthony Daniel Perez examine the role of regional mobility in the adjustment process. Erling Barth, James Davis, Richard Freeman, and Sari Pekkala Kerr study the role of establishments in job destruction during the Great Recession and the job creation that followed. In the final article, Henry S. Farber, Dan Silverman, and Till von Wachter provide new evidence on the extent of hysteresis in the U.S. labor market during the recovery. By helping to assess the nature of the Great Recession, these studies also inform other important yet understudied issues: the mechanisms behind the protracted and costly losses in earnings and long-term unemployment following widespread job destruction during the Great Recession.

Several articles in this volume also examine the direct impact of job loss and unemployment on workers. Although this question has received more attention in the literature than some others, several open questions remain. William Dickens, Robert Triest, and Rachel Sederberg contribute to the complex but crucial question as to the extent to which workers are able to self-insure against income losses during job loss. In three separate articles, Kelsey O'Connor; Gokce Basbug and Ofer Sharone; and Daniel Schneider further examine the social consequences of unemployment on the social outcomes (on happiness, mental health, and teenage fertility, respectively), other important but understudied areas. This volume of the journal also takes up the impact of the Great Recession on the institutional environment in the labor market, a subject neglected so far in the literature. The political storm around public sector unions in the aftermath of the Great Recession has shown that economic conditions can interact with and affect political and institutional landscapes. Ruth Milkman and Stephanie Luce take up this question in their study of the evolution of unions in the context of the Great Recession.

THE GREAT RECESSION IN ECONOMIC, POLITICAL, AND SOCIAL CONTEXTS

We begin by putting the Great Recession in historical perspective by comparing it to previous recessions on a variety of dimensions and situating it in relation to broader social and economic trends. We also briefly summarize the current understanding of the mechanisms behind the Great Recession, thus indicating how the contributions in this volume help to address ongoing debates.

Taking Stock of the Great Recession and Its Aftermath

Apart from its intensity, the Great Recession initially resembled in many ways a large postwar recession, such as the downturns in 1975 or 1982. For example, while the decline in GDP and the rise in unemployment were unusually steep, the unemployment rate at its peak was about the same as in the 1982 recession. The canonical relationship between unemployment rates and GDP growth, termed Okun's Law, held in the Great Recession, consistent with it being a large, demand-driven downturn (Ball, Leigh, and Loungani 2012). In accordance with this view, the Great Recession was broad, and ultimately led to large employment declines in all sectors of the economy and among all demographic groups.

Over time, it quickly became apparent that perhaps the most unusual and unexpected feature of the Great Recession was the persistence of weak economic conditions in its aftermath. Despite the fact that the Great Recession officially ended in December 2009, GDP remains well below its potential level even at the date of publication of this volume. Moreover, since the start of the Great Recession, estimates of potential GDP itself have been revised downward substantially (Congressional Budget Office 2014). Hence,

some fraction of the recovery that did occur was a result of the reduction in the target rather than due to actual growth.

At the same time, recovery in the labor market has been slow. Although the rate of unemployment has fallen close to pre-recession levels, it has taken nearly ten years after the start of the Great Recession to do so, by far exceeding the period of recovery after previous downturns. Moreover, the gradual but steady decline in the official unemployment rate masks several related phenomena that signal continued weakness in the labor market. The number of marginally attached and discouraged workers during the Great Recession rose substantially, and the labor force participation rate declined. The fraction of workers reporting involuntarily working part-time for economic reasons remains high. For example, as of March 2016, the fraction of individuals among the total labor force that is unemployed, discouraged, marginally attached, or involuntarily working part-time is 9.8 percent. At the trough, the rate was 17 percent.[2] This number does not include workers who permanently left the labor force because of the economic downturn, and hence would not be counted as marginally attached in official statistics, but may still work if the opportunity came along. One measure that includes these workers, the employment-to-population ratio, has fallen substantially and has not recovered since the beginning of the Great Recession. The employment of both men and women decreased during the Great Recession, but the drop was especially sharp among men: in November 2010, about 80 percent of working-age men were employed, down from about 88 percent before the Great Recession (in April 2015, the figure was 84.5 percent; see Donovan 2015, figure 4). This is lowest since 1948, and it has never fallen as much during a recession. The decrease among women's em-

2. See Bureau of Labor Statistics, Economics News Release, "Table A-15. Alternative Measures of Labor Utilization," www.bls.gov/news.release/empsit.t15.htm (accessed April 5, 2016). The Bureau of Labor Statistics defines persons marginally attached to the labor force as those who currently are neither working nor looking for work but indicate that they want and are available for a job and have looked for work sometime in the past twelve months. Discouraged workers, a subset of the marginally attached, are those who give a job-market-related reason for not currently looking for work. Persons employed part-time for economic reasons are those who want and are available for full-time work but have had to settle for a part-time schedule (Bureau of Labor Statistics 2009).

ployment was not as great, though it reversed a long-term upward trend (Hout and Cumberworth 2012).

Not only the labor market has been exceptionally sluggish after the Great Recession. Capital investment, too, has been low, and a projected decline in investment has contributed substantially to the reduction in predicted potential output. This is noteworthy, since business profits have rebounded and companies have substantial reserves of cash, indicating a potential lack of profitable investment opportunities. Measures of productivity growth have declined as well. Perhaps not surprisingly, given the state of investment, productivity, and labor supply, wage growth was minimal for many years after the recession, only picking up in the course of 2016.

The Great Recession and Preexisting Trends

Some important consequences often associated with the Great Recession may have their roots in events beginning in the United States in the mid-1970s. The Great Recession is likely to have interacted with or exacerbated several preexisting trends in the U.S. economy, some of which may have been masked by the dot.com and housing bubbles.[3] During the past decades, there was a confluence of events that gained traction, such as the rise of global competition, technological advances such as the invention of the microprocessor, the spread of neoliberal policies that emphasized the deregulation of markets, the continued expansion of the service sector, and the sustained decline of unions with the associated reduction in institutional protections for workers.

The Great Recession also occurred against the backdrop of significant changes in the composition of the labor force since the 1970s. For example, the number of dual-earner families increased, as did the share of the workforce made up of women. The U.S. economy and society also experienced other profound changes over the last several decades, including an aging workforce, stagnating or even declining

educational attainment among men, and a growing proportion of nonwhite and immigrant workers, who tended to be concentrated in the most insecure and low-quality jobs.

It is likely that many of the changes in American society that began in the mid-1970s reflect structural changes and were not merely temporary features of the business cycle that corrected themselves once economic conditions improved—as was the case in the recessions of 1973–1975 and 1981–1982. These structural changes are likely to have influenced the path and effects of the Great Recession. For example, the strong rise in women's labor force participation in the 1980s masked a persistent decline in the employment rate of men during the 1970s and 1980s recessions; this counteracting channel was absent in the Great Recession, bringing out more clearly a pattern of declining labor force participation for men over a longer horizon.

Similarly, the economic restructuring and removal of institutional protections since the 1970s may have affected the impact of the Great Recession. For example, much has been written about the rise of low-wage, insecure jobs that are now a central, and in some cases growing, portion of employment in the United States (Kalleberg 2011). While many economists have put emphasis on secular shifts involving long-term changes in methods of production, including a reduction in manual routine work (Acemoglu and Autor 2014), recent research suggests that part of these changes may have occurred during recent business cycle downturns (Jaimovich and Siu 2012). This research is ongoing but implies that the Great Recession may have accelerated the replacement of routine work with computers and machines. Similarly, recent studies indicate that another trend already in existence before the Great Recession is the secular decline in labor market dynamism in the U.S. (Davis and Haltiwanger 2014). A secular decline in the exit rate from unemployment implies that the same amount of job destruction can lead to a substantially more persistent rise in unemployment rates (Song and von

---

3. It is a classic hypothesis that recessions help to reallocate factors of production to more productive uses in sectors that are growing, at the expense of secularly declining industries. Edward Leamer (2007) and Kerwin Charles, Erik Hurst, and Matthew J. Notowidigdo (2015) assess the extent to which the housing bubble masked the effect of the long-term decline of manufacturing.

Wachter 2014), underscoring how the Great Recession may have interacted with preexisting trends in the labor market.

Explanations of the Great Recession and Its Aftermath

The initial efforts to understand the sources of the sudden and large downturn associated with the Great Recession focused on several partly intertwined areas. The main suspects were the bursting of the housing bubble and the financial crisis that began with the collapse of Lehman Brothers in September 2008, which led to a substantial contraction in the availability of credit and the need for protracted deleveraging among households (Hall 2014). Others emphasized the potential role of structural mismatches in the labor market (Kocherlakota 2010; Şahin et al. 2014), high implicit disincentives to work created by government programs (Mulligan 2010), or the uncertainty created by economic events and public policy (Bloom 2009; Taylor 2010).

The absence of a full recovery in employment and output to pre-recession levels has raised the question of whether the Great Recession was indeed substantially different from prior downturns. It became apparent that none of the macroeconomic approaches that were initially used to explain the onset of the Great Recession are able to explain the high degree of persistence of dislocation that followed (Hall 2012; Ohanian 2010). The question of the sources of the continuing economic slump in the aftermath of the Great Recession may well be the most important one in macroeconomics today. The ongoing search for explanations drew comparisons to prior episodes of high and persistent unemployment, chiefly in continental Europe in the early 1980s and following the Great Depression.

One explanation of the high degree of persistence of the after-effects of the Great Recession in the labor market is that high rates of unemployment, especially high rates of long-term unemployment, led to a lasting increase in the equilibrium unemployment rate, a pattern sometimes called hysteresis. By permanently reducing the quantity and possibly the quality of labor output, hysteresis in the labor market can also reduce aggregate output. A key feature of the labor market in the aftermath of the Great Recession was indeed the staggering increase in the proportion of unemployed that had spells of unemployment longer than twenty-six or fifty-two weeks, which at the trough of the Great Recession stood at more than double its historical value. This led to the concern that the United States may be experiencing a similar phenomenon as that observed in several European countries that endured lasting increases in equilibrium rates of unemployment after a steep rise in unemployment and unemployment duration in the early 1980s (Ball 2009).[4]

Another popular view of the persistent rise in European unemployment was that rigid labor market institutions and high social benefits prevented the necessary labor reallocation following a set of economic shocks (Blanchard and Wolfers 2000; Ljungqvist and Sargent 1998). This view of unemployment has received substantial attention during the Great Recession because it combined the hypothesis of structural mismatch with the notion that substantial social benefits may reduce work incentives, especially for those at the bottom of the labor market (Glaeser 2014). However, the evidence of mismatch in the labor market was mixed (Lazear and Spletzer 2012; Rothstein 2012), leading some supporters to revise their views (Kocherlakota 2012). A related hypothesis is that

---

4. There are several hypotheses as to how such hysteresis might arise. The most straightforward view is that a cohort of unemployed workers becomes permanently less employable, perhaps because their skills or their motivation declines during unemployment. Although this channel could play a potentially important role for given estimates of unemployment persistence (see Kroft et al. 2016), the effect depends on the number of people directly affected by hysteresis (Song and von Wachter 2014). Even though the cohort-specific effect would necessarily fade over time, the original hypothesis posited that an increasing set of "outsiders" would lead to a rise in wage demands by "insiders," thus leading to a rise in equilibrium unemployment (Blanchard and Summers 1986). Although such a channel may not be directly relevant for the U.S. labor market because of the absence of widespread collective bargaining, the permanent withdrawal of workers from the labor force may have a similar effect, in terms of wages and employment if wages of existing workers are downwardly rigid.

the high duration of unemployment insurance (UI) benefits in the Great Recession—UI duration reached ninety-nine weeks in the Great Recession, compared to fifty-two weeks in the early 1980s recession—explains part of the rise and persistence in unemployment. Although there is some evidence that supports this explanation (Hagedorn et al. 2013), other studies suggest high UI benefits are unlikely to be a cause of persistent unemployment in the United States (Rothstein 2012; Marinescu 2015).

The unusual depth and duration of the Great Recession has prompted comparisons to the Great Depression of the 1930s (Summers 2014; Eichengreen 2015). The Great Depression was substantially larger, involving a decline of over 20 percent of GDP and a rise in unemployment rates of about twenty percentage points, to approximately 30 percent. Yet, the Great Depression also began with a financial crisis and was followed by a prolonged slump. Some have taken the parallels further, noting that both economic downturns occurred in an environment of slowing population growth and increasing savings. If these and other concurrent developments were associated with a persistent decline in real interest rates, this may contribute to what has been called "secular stagnation" (Summers 2014). One view is that only a large government stimulus can return the economy to a higher path of growth, such as occurred with the New Deal and World War II after the Great Depression. Another, complementary view is that the cyclical slack in the U.S. economy is in fact subsiding, and that secular stagnation began well before the Great Recession (Hall 2014).

Several articles in this volume contribute further to our understanding of the potential explanations of the Great Recession and the protracted recovery that followed. The article by Rothstein disputes the idea that the Great Recession has produced a "new normal" characterized by structural unemployment. He convincingly shows that wages have not been increasing, holding the composition of employment constant. Such a finding is inconsistent with the view that a lack of appropriate workers prevented employers from creating jobs, a mechanism that would have eventually led to a rise in wages. Hence, Rothstein's find-

ing points to a demand-based explanation of the recent recession and the ensuing weakness in the labor market lasting into 2016. Levy, Mouw, and Perez examine the incidence and patterns of regional mobility, another debated aspect in the context of potential spatial mismatch between unemployment and jobs during the Great Recession (see also, Yagan 2014).

Barth, Davis, Freeman, and Kerr (this volume) provide a new set of facts regarding an understudied but presumably crucial set of players during the Great Recession—employers. Their findings on job creation and destruction, further discussed later, sharpen our understanding of the process of renewal in the labor market during recessions. In addition, they show that the degree of labor hoarding, and ensuing productivity changes was substantially different in the United States than in other countries, but also heterogeneous within the United States itself. Their numerous findings challenge standard models of labor market adjustment.

Farber, Silverman, and von Wachter also identify potentially important heterogeneity in the adjustment processes in the U.S. labor market. Their article addresses the question of whether hysteresis of unemployment is likely to be a widespread phenomenon. In contrast to recent work, they conclude that hysteresis from unemployment duration appears not to be present among the mature women they study. Hence, the effects of long-term unemployment in reemployment rates may be concentrated among younger workers, but may be less devastating for the economy as a whole.

ECONOMIC CONSEQUENCES OF THE GREAT RECESSION

The Great Recession had profound and potentially long-term economic consequences; we provide a brief overview of these economic consequences in the next section.

Effects of Job Loss and Unemployment on Income and Consumption

The workers most immediately affected by the Great Recession were those who lost their jobs. A growing literature shows how a job loss during a recession can have profound consequences for workers and their families. In particular, workers losing stable jobs with good employers can experience substantial losses in wages and earnings in the immediate aftermath of a job loss (Farber 2011; Couch and Placzek 2010; Jacobson, Lalonde, and Sullivan 1993). These large initial losses fade only somewhat, and translate into annual earnings disadvantages lasting beyond twenty years (Davis and von Wachter 2011). The large declines in earnings are certainly telling, but economists often also use measures of income or consumption to measure the welfare consequences of shocks. Such measures better reflect the actual change in well-being if workers are able to supplement their earnings, for example, by earnings from other family members, savings, or social insurance programs. It is not easy, however, to estimate the effects of job loss on consumption and income.

Nevertheless, there is some evidence on the role of transfer programs and private insurance mechanisms, such as dissaving or spousal labor supply. Existing evidence suggests that the take-up of social programs rose in the Great Recession. Clearly, an increasing number of workers have received and are increasingly dependent on unemployment benefits, owing to a rise in unemployment, its long duration, and a substantial expansion of the program (Rothstein and Valletta 2014). In addition, especially in the aftermath of the Great Recession, the importance of food stamps (the Supplemental Nutrition Assistance Program, or SNAP), the earned income tax credit (EITC), and Supplemental Security Income (SSI) increased (Moffitt 2012). At the same time, more workers claimed Social Security benefits and Social Security Disability Insurance (Mueller, Rothstein, and von Wachter 2015).

Moreover, workers have means to temporarily offset some of their lost earnings by borrowing, reducing their savings, increasing labor supply of other family members, and family transfers. William T. Dickens, Robert K. Triest, and Rachel B. Sederberg (this volume) examine in detail families' ability to weather the earnings declines due to job loss in the Great Recession by relying on their own financial resources. Their conclusion is pessimistic, since, as they note, most families did not possess sufficient wealth to buffer the large and extended earnings losses for more than a short period of time. More generally, borrowing and saving may simply postpone or redistribute the realization of lost income over time. In contrast, family labor supply and transfers can present a real buffer, albeit not without costs in terms of lost leisure or household production (Pistaferri, Blundell, and Saporta-Eksten 2016).

Although transfer programs often mitigate the loss of earnings resulting from job displacement, the replacement amounts are quite modest compared with estimates of present-value earnings losses. The few studies that estimate the effects of job loss or unemployment directly on consumption typically find sizable near-term declines in consumption expenditure but lack evidence on long-term consumption responses (see, for example, Gruber 1997; Stephens 2004). The consumption responses tend to be concentrated at the lower end of the income distribution (Browning and Crossley 2001; Congressional Budget Office 2004). Even the generous, long-lasting benefits available under the German unemployment insurance system replace only a modest share of the earnings loss associated with job displacement (Schmieder, von Wachter, and Bender 2009).

Differences by Gender
At the onset of the Great Recession, the unemployment rate increased more for men than women, suggesting that the Great Recession was more of a "man-cession" (Hout and Cumberworth 2012).[5] However, this gender dynamic was reversed as the economy started gaining jobs: between February 2010 and June 2014, men gained 5.5 million jobs while women gained 3.6 million jobs. This recovery differs from recent recoveries from recessions, as this

5. The kinds of occupations and industries in which men were more likely than women to work (such as construction and the building trades) were especially hard hit. By contrast, women are more likely to work in the public sector and in occupations such as nursing, child care, and food preparation, which were less affected (at least initially) by the Great Recession and which benefited more from the stimulus spending (until the Spring of 2010), whose aim was to alleviate the impacts of the economic downturn.

was the first time since 1970 in which men have gained more jobs than women in the first two years of a recovery. That the unemployment rates for men have fallen but risen for women underscores the unique nature of the current recovery (Kochhar 2011), leading some to term it a "he-covery" (Rampell 2011). Nevertheless, the Great Recession was harder on men overall: men have not outperformed women in the recovery nearly as much as men underperformed women in the recession.

Differences by Race and Ethnicity
The Great Recession hit nonwhites especially hard. For example, African American and Latino homeowners were more likely than whites to default on their mortgages or to experience foreclosures of their homes (Pfeffer, Danziger, and Schoeni 2013; Wolff, Owens, and Burak 2011). Younger, less-educated, and minority workers were also more likely than whites to lose their jobs (Hout, Levanon, and Cumberworth 2011). Latino immigrants managed to gain jobs in the recovery, but also experienced large drops in wages, suggesting their greater vulnerability in the labor market (Kochhar, Espinoza, and Hinze-Pifer 2010). The consequences of the fallout from the Great Recession for individuals and communities of color remain important issues to study.

Effects on Labor Market Entrants and Youth Unemployment

How young workers have fared during and after the Great Recession is another understudied question. Young workers are particularly vulnerable to adverse labor market conditions.[6] Existing studies based on past recessions show that beginning to work in a recession leads to lasting reductions in earnings—a "typical" recession would have led unlucky labor market entrants to have lower earnings for approximately ten years (Kahn 2010; Oreopoulos, Heisz, and von Wachter 2012). Not surprisingly, the losses of labor market entrants were particu-

larly severe during the Great Recession (Altonji, Kahn, and Speer 2016). Besides having lowered earnings, workers entering the labor market during a recession are more likely to have worse jobs and occupations and also experience lasting reductions in health and a change in attitudes. For example, Paola Giuliano and Antonio Spilimbergo (2014) found that individuals who experienced a recession during their formative years were more likely to believe that success in life depends more on luck than on effort, to support more government redistribution, and to have decreased confidence in public institutions.

Mechanisms Explaining the Incidence and Effects of Job Loss

Several mechanisms have been suggested for explaining the lasting effects of job loss and the sluggishness in the labor market after the Great Recession. A popular view is that recessions involve structural changes and require workers to adjust to new skill demands (or to skill demands appearing in other regions). As previously mentioned, there have been contrasting findings as to the role of structural change, mismatch, and reallocation during recessions in general and the Great Recession in particular. On the one hand, Nir Jaimovich and Henry E. Siu (2012) document that a substantial portion of the secular decline in routine manual employment occurred during recessions. This view is consistent with the notion that part of the earnings losses for job losers arise because they are forced to switch occupations or industry (Jacobson, Lalonde, and Sullivan 1993; Neal 1995). On the other hand, studies have found little in terms of shifts of employment between sectors during recessions (Aaronson, Rissman, and Sullivan 2004). An analysis of a range of standard labor market indicators also speaks against mismatch, and hence against an important role for structural changes (Rothstein 2012).

Another classic hypothesis is that job qual-

---

6. Young workers tend to have entered their job later than older workers, and thus are often the first to be let go. Many of them look for a job for a first time, and thus experience the full brunt of reduced wages and job opportunities. The lack of opportunities risks holding them back during a crucial state of the career—earnings for the average worker typically double over the first ten years in the labor market due to productive job mobility and increasing experience.

ity is reduced in recessions, leading to what has been termed "cyclical downgrading" of job seekers into lower-quality jobs (Reynolds 1951; Okun 1973). A growing body of evidence suggests that the distribution of net job creation shifts toward lower-paying jobs in recessions (Kahn and McEntarfer 2014). As a result, Johannes Schmieder, von Wachter, and Stefan Bender (2015a) show that a substantial fraction of earnings losses of job losers in recessions arises because of a persistent decline in job quality.

The literature has also examined various ways in which workers respond to adverse economic conditions during recessions. This includes such disparate but related outcomes as mobility between regions, mobility between occupations and sectors, retraining, borrowing, or withdrawal from the labor force. For example, despite the depth of the recession, there was sufficient geographical variation among U.S. states such that workers had opportunities to improve their employment situation by moving. Yet, as documented by Levy, Mouw, and Perez (this volume), regional mobility rates have declined slightly during the Great Recession, and workers were about as likely to move for economic reasons as before. In the aftermath of a job loss, mobility between jobs and industries tends to increase (von Wachter, Song, and Manchester 2011; Stevens 1997). These movements are associated with further wage declines. In fact, job-to-job transition rates typically decline in recessions and new jobs formed in recessions are typically less stable than jobs formed in expansions. Hence, although job mobility may be important in the recovery process, this is an option typically available only further into the recovery. The fact that earnings losses after job loss are so persistent suggests that this job mobility comes too late for many workers, who by then have settled into new jobs at permanently lower earnings.

Barth and his colleagues (this volume) provide an important additional piece of evidence on the mechanisms of labor adjustment during recessions. They show that most of the job creation during and after the Great Recession occurred at new establishments. In contrast, most of the job loss occurs at existing, continuing establishments. Hence, part of the reallocation

process in recessions might occur through workers moving from older, higher-paying, to younger, lower-paying enterprises. If older firms pay more on average, then the shift to younger firms could help to explain the substantial earnings losses of job losers.

Earnings reductions can also result from a decline in hours worked or a rise in long-term unemployment. Many observers noted the stark rise in the fraction of workers reporting that they worked involuntarily part-time during the Great Recession. In fact, a substantial portion of short-run earnings losses can be explained because workers take part-time or other nonstandard jobs (Farber 1999). Although the long-term effect of job loss appears to be driven mostly by a decline in wages, Schmieder, von Wachter, and Bender (2015b) show that prolonged unemployment can have substantial consequences for reemployment wages. Identifying the causal effect of unemployment duration on reemployment probabilities in observational data is notoriously hard. One way to credibly identify the causal effect on long-term unemployment is by means of an audit study. One of the few such audit studies is by Kory Kroft, Fabian Lange, and Matthew J. Notowidigdo (2013), who show that longer unemployment duration on fictitious résumés sent in response to real job advertisements leads to a significant reduction in callback rates for job interviews for younger workers. In contrast, Farber, Silverman, and von Wachter (this volume), using a similar research design, do not find such a relationship for mature and older workers. Instead, for this demographic group they find substantial penalties for age and for having held a low-quality, interim job. This suggests that some of the increased job churning occurring in recessions may be self-perpetuating as an increasing number of workers experience sequences of short-lived job spells or unemployment.

Effects on Employed Workers

Clearly, the Great Recession also had effects on individuals who did not lose their jobs. A large number of families saw the values of their homes decline, and many found themselves under foreclosure as a result. Homeownership rates increased slightly from 2000 to 2007 (66 to 67.2 percent), then declined to 66.8 percent in 2008 and 65 percent in 2010. The median home value of owner-occupied units in the United States declined from $202,000 in 2007 to $198,000 in 2008 and $179,900 in 2010, after rising steadily from 2000 to 2007 (it decreased 16 percent each in California and Nevada, almost 9 percent in Florida). The shocks to wealth and living situation and stress may have had important consequences for families. For example, Janet Currie and Erdal Tekin (2015) show that foreclosures led to reductions in health, at least over the short run. In addition, workers with substantial savings saw at least temporary declines in the value of their wealth as a result of lower stock prices, and this may have led to a postponement of retirement among some workers. Even absent effects on house prices or wealth, employed workers may have seen reduced chances to further their careers, and may have had to work harder to maintain their jobs. Edward Lazear, Kathryn Shaw, and Christopher Stanton (2016) document for single firms that workers increased their efforts and hence increased the firm's overall productivity.

SOCIAL CONSEQUENCES OF THE GREAT RECESSION

The Great Recession was also a social recession in the sense that it affected individuals, their families, and their communities in ways that went beyond matters of employment and finances. These social outcomes of the Great Recession were of course closely linked to concerns about job and income loss, as discussed earlier. The difficulties experienced by young people in establishing themselves in the labor market and forming a family led to concerns about a "lost generation" (Coy 2009), although the extent to which young people are able, despite the knock-on effects of the Great Recession, to make successful transitions to adulthood is still an open question at this point. Moreover, studies have shown economic instability, uncertainty, job loss and residential moves experienced by parents are likely to have negative effects on their children's development (Kalil 2013). At the other end of the life cycle, older workers who become unemployed but who are unable to retire as a result of financial concerns may well lack the skills to adapt to the technological requirements of the new economy.

Thus, the negative consequences of job loss go well beyond earnings; the insecurity generated by the duration and depth of the economic downturn had pervasive consequences for individuals' well-being and their family lives. These effects of the Great Recession have exacerbated the insecurity that has been building for a number of years. Panel analyses of U.S. workers (from the General Social Survey) show that people were more likely after the Great Recession than they were before it to be pessimistic about their finances and to identify with being in the lower class (Hout and Hastings 2014). The pessimism engendered by the Great Recession is reminiscent of the powerful sense of uncertainty that was associated with the Great Depression (Schwarz 2009).

To be sure, there are some things that either were unaffected or were not made worse by the Great Recession. For example, crime decreased between 2007 and 2010 (Uggen 2012), as it did during the Great Depression, and there was not much change in voting patterns (Bartels 2013), although politics did affect perceptions, as reflected in Democrats being more likely to have an optimistic view of their standard of living during the Great Recession than Republicans (see Morgan, Cumberworth, and Wimer 2011). Moreover, undocumented migration to the United States slowed significantly during the Great Recession, which reflects in large part the slowdown in economic growth in the United States (Massey 2012).

Effects of Job Loss and Unemployment on Individuals' Health and Well-Being

Studies summarized by Jennie Brand (2015) and von Wachter (2015) find that there are short-run consequences of job loss on a range of physical and mental health outcomes, including increases in mortality. In extreme cases these health effects can be long-lasting, increasing mortality rates even several decades after job loss (Sullivan and von Wachter 2009), though the longer run impacts of the Great Recession on health and mortality are still open questions. A smaller number of studies document that job losses can also affect the outcomes of children of job losers over the short and long run. Research on the exact magnitude of these studies is ongoing; the current evidence suggests job loss can have at least some adverse consequences for children's birth weight, test scores in schools, and earnings as adults (von Wachter 2015).[7]

The effects of long-term unemployment are pervasive, affecting men and women and members of all racial and ethnic groups as well as those with differing amounts of education. Basbug and Sharone (this volume) summarize much of the literature that describes the tolls of being unemployed for long periods of time on persons' mental and physical health. They also show that marriage is a source of emotional support for both men and women. For men this was mainly due to marriage being associated with a higher household income. For women, marriage provides a buffer that goes beyond the effect from increased household income. Overall, these findings demonstrate that the large amount of job loss and unemployment typically associated with recessions is consequential for workers and their families.

The adverse effects of recessions are also felt by those not directly affected by job loss and unemployment. Workers and the public at large express substantial concerns about the state of the economy, the rate of unemployment, and the risk of job loss (Davis and von Wachter 2011), and job and financial insecurity have been shown to be related to psychological outcomes such as anger, stress, depression, anxiety, and pessimism (De Witte 1999). Studies have also demonstrated a clear correlation between suicide rates and the business cycle among young and middle-aged adults (Carey 2011).

It is thus not surprising that economic crises such as the Great Recession are associated with declines in subjective feelings of well-being and happiness (Arampatzi, Burger, and Veenhoven 2015). Indeed, Kelsey J. O'Connor (this volume) finds that 2010 marked the lowest level of reported happiness in the United States since the 1970s. The decline in happiness in 2010 was smaller than in the early 1980s, although the decline after the Great Recession, unlike that of the early 1980s, was due more to declining income and rising unemployment. The happiness of all population groups was negatively affected in 2010, but some reported greater declines than others, especially men, older people, and Hispanics (O'Connor, in this volume). The paucity of comparable time-series data makes it more difficult to draw firm conclusions about whether the effects of the Great Recession on such subjective social outcomes differed from previous downturns, however.

Families

Major weaknesses in the labor market and severe job disruptions such as the Great Recession are likely to affect family structures and household formation such as timing of marriage, divorce, cohabitation, and childbearing. Recessions can affect family life in two main ways (Cherlin et al. 2013). Financial hardship and uncertainty may limit the choices people are able to make about their family lives, such as making it more difficult to afford to get married or children. In addition, families may be activated as "emergency support systems" to help lessen economic impacts, as when adult children move back with their parents during periods of unemployment.

A recent study by Andrew Cherlin et al. (2013) found evidence that both of these familial responses have occurred and have lasted beyond the official end of the Great Recession in 2009. For example, there was a 9 to 11 percent drop in fertility from 2007 to 2011, which was a return to the lowest level since 1987. This decline was greater among younger women, suggesting a postponing of births (as opposed to averting fertility permanently), which is similar to the effects of recessions in other Western countries. Recession-induced declines in fertility have also been shown to lead to reductions in women's total fertility rate, mainly driven by an increase in the fraction of women remaining childless (Currie and Schwandt 2014). The drop in birth

7. Some of these outcomes may themselves arise from a behavioral response of individuals to the reduction in earnings. Such behavioral responses to the earnings loss should not be counted as additional costs of job loss in their own right. Yet, many of these outcomes are not simply consequences of earnings reductions, or at least not from a behavioral response to the earnings shock.

rates was greater among the poor and near poor and among Hispanics (see also Cohen 2015), due to a substantial decline in Mexican immigration (recent Hispanic immigrants have the highest fertility rates in the country). The decrease in fertility was also greater in red states than blue states, which may reflect differences in perceptions about the severity of the Great Recession (Morgan, Cumberworth, and Wimer 2011).

This drop in fertility is likely due to the duration and depth of the Great Recession, although fertility is procyclical and negatively related to the unemployment rate: total fertility rates consistently decline (or increases are halted) in response to recessions, but these changes are generally modest and occur in a relatively narrow range. One reason for this stability is that 49 percent of all pregnancies in the United States are unintended—over 38 percent of births are to unmarried women—so the extent to which uncertainties associated with economic disruptions actually change couples' fertility decisions in the United States is not clear (Morgan, Cumberworth, and Wimer 2011).

The Great Recession was also associated with lower rates of nonmarital and teen fertility. Daniel Schneider (in this volume) finds that this is partly due to the increased use of contraception—and the use of more effective means of contraception—which suggests that these groups consciously changed their fertility avoidance behavior in response to uncommonly large economic shocks. In past recessions, this type of avoidance behavior has differed by demographic groups: during periods of high unemployment, more highly educated black women become mothers, as do less-educated white women (Dehejia and Lleras-Muney 2004).

During the Great Recession not only fertility but also marriage and divorce rates declined and cohabitation increased. These trends, too, are typical of past economic downturns: since marriage and divorce are expensive, they decline during recessions and increase during expansions. But although the Great Recession may have exacerbated these trends somewhat, both marriage and divorce rates were already declining prior to 2007 (Morgan, Cumberworth, and Wimer 2011). In fact, the decline in marriage rates has been going on for some time, as technological and cultural changes have helped to increase women's labor force participation and to diminish the economic basis for marriage. The increase in cohabitation during the Great Recession, too, was a continuation of longer-term trends, as was the greater likelihood of both unmarried and married young adults living with their parents (Morgan, Cumberworth, and Wimer 2011).

A possible consequence of the Great Recession that has been little studied is the increase in domestic violence: a spike in intimate-partner violence coincided with the abrupt increase in men's unemployment rates. Philip N. Cohen (2015) suggests that the economic shocks associated with unemployment increased family stress and violence, such as spankings and, presumably, striking that caused an increase in abusive head traumas.

Overall, Andrew Cherlin et al. (2013) conclude, "The Great Recession had a moderate effect on family life. It brought about some changes in behavior but did not constitute a major disruption on the order of the effects of the Great Depression. . . . Our analysis suggests that the Great Recession did not weaken family life. . . . It heightened the importance of intergenerational exchanges of shelter and support. In doing so, we would speculate, the Great Recession may have strengthened, rather than weakened, the family as a social institution" (228–30).

Unions

The Great Recession further damaged organized labor, continuing a declining trend in union density that began a half century ago that saw a decrease in the percentage of unionized U.S wage-earning and salaried members in the public and private sectors combined from 24 percent in 1973 (the union density in the private sector was 24.2 percent) to 11.2 percent in 2012 (6.6 percent in the private sector). By contrast, union density in the public sector is fairly high, at 35.9 percent in 2012. There has also been a decline in large-scale strikes in the period 2001–2010, continuing a downward trend since the 1970s (Milkman 2013). This suggests that unionization rates do not fluctuate all that much in response to movements in the business cycle (Milkman and Luce, this volume). Steven Greenhouse (2011) reported that union density dropped in 2009 to the lowest level in more than seventy years, after a two-year growth spurt before the Great Recession.

The decline in union membership has been accompanied by a backlash against labor generally. In 2009 support for unions in the Gallup poll dipped below 50 percent for the first time ever: support went from a high of 75 percent in the 1950s, to 55 percent in the early 1980s recession, 65 percent in 2003, 59 percent in 2007, and 48 percent in 2009 (Madland and Walter 2010). In a 2010 Pew Research poll, only 41 percent of respondents said they had a favorable view of unions; the percentages holding a "mostly" or "very favorable" view fell from 58 percent in January 2007 to 41 percent in February 2010 (Surowiecki 2011).

This reduction in support for unions is likely due to the weakness of the economy during the Great Recession. Historically, there has been a negative correlation between the unemployment rate and the popularity of unions: for example, since the late 1940s, when the unemployment rate has been low, approval of labor unions has been high, and vice versa; every percentage-point increase in the unemployment rate lowers the approval rate for unions by 2.6 percentage points (Madland and Walter 2010). Disapproval of unions is likely to be magnified by the fact that so few people now belong to unions. Hence, nonmembers are increasingly resentful of union advantages, seeing unions as another interest group that gets perks for their members, often at others' expense (Surowiecki 2011).

More generally, approval ratings for powerful institutions of all kinds (government, unions, business) and their leaders decline in bad economic times such as the Great Recession (Lipset and Schneider 1987). Similarly, Lindsay A. Owens and Karen S. Cook (2013) argue that individuals in counties that were more affected by the Great Recession were more likely to decrease their support for organized labor and the federal government. To put union disapproval in context, though, David Madland and Karla Walter (2010) note that a March 2010 Pew Survey found that the percentage of re-

spondents who view unions positively (32 percent) was greater than the percentage who have a positive view of banks and financial institutions (22 percent), of Congress (24 percent), of the federal government (25 percent), and of large corporations (25 percent).

The falling-off in approval of unions and the continued decrease in union density and strike activity are undoubtedly a reflection of the impact of the economic downturn on the inability of workers to exercise collective power. But there were also other factors at work in the Great Recession and its aftermath that contributed to the weakening of organized labor. Milkman and Luce (in this volume) argue that employers' hostility toward unions during the previous three decades, especially in the private sector, was much more consequential than the short-term effects of the Great Recession on the reduction of support for unions. For example, public disapproval of auto bailouts linked the financial problems of automakers to high wage and insurance costs that were included in union contracts. In addition, the emergence of Republican governors and legislative majorities after the midterm elections of 2010 in traditionally unionized Midwestern states such as Wisconsin and Indiana fueled assaults on public sector unions by conservatives—assaults that were powered by claims that public employees' compensation practices were largely responsible for budget deficits. Further evidence of the weakening of labor is reflected in the passage of right-to-work laws in traditionally strong union states such as Indiana and Michigan (Milkman 2013).

CONCLUSIONS

The depth and duration of the Great Recession produced widespread economic and social impacts on the U.S. labor market. Some of these effects represent continuations of trends that started well before the onset of the Great Recession in 2007, some are consequences that tend to occur during all recessions (though they might have been more severe due to the greater depth and duration of the Great Recession), and some might conceivably be regarded as relatively unique to the Great Recession.

With the advantage of almost a decade's passing since the last business cycle peak, the papers in this volume contribute to our understanding of core questions pertaining to the Great Recession and its aftermath. This includes such complex questions as the causes of the protracted downturn and the mechanisms behind the consequences of job loss and unemployment (Rothstein on the stagnation of wages; Barth, Davis, Freeman, and Kerr on job destruction and creation at the establishment level; Levy, Mouw, and Perez on patterns of regional mobility; Farber, Silverman, and von Wachter on hysteresis in the labor market); open questions regarding the economic and social consequences of job loss and unemployment (Dickens, Triest, and Sederberg on the lack of the ability of self-insurance among the unemployed; Basbug and Sharone on the mental health costs of long-term unemployment); and broad questions on the social and institutional effects of the Great Recession (O'Connor on the effect of the Great Recession on happiness; Schneider on its effect on teen fertility; Milkman and Luce on union activity during the Great Recession).

The extent to which—and for what outcomes—the Great Recession was a transformative event are still unresolved issues. One view is that, as in past recessions, a limited fraction of workers experienced large losses, whereas the majority of workers bounced back as the economy recovers. Another view is that a sufficiently large number of individuals were affected so as to lead to a transformation of society more broadly. Definitive answers to these questions await the further passage of time and the collection and analysis of additional data.

REFERENCES

Aaronson, Daniel, Ellen R. Rissman, and Daniel G. Sullivan. 2004. "Can Sectoral Reallocation Explain the Jobless Recovery?" In *2Q/2004, Economic Perspectives*. Chicago: Federal Reserve Bank of Chicago.

Acemoglu, Daron, and David Autor. 2014. "Skills, Tasks and Technologies: Implications for Employment and Earnings." *Handbook of Labor Economics*, edited by David E. Card and Orley Ashenfelter. Amsterdam: Elsevier.

Altonji, Joseph G., Lisa B. Kahn, and Jamin D. Speer. 2016. "Cashier or Consultant? Entry Labor Market Conditions, Field of Study, and Career Suc-

cess." *Journal of Labor Economics* 34(S1): S361–401.

Arampatzi, Efstratia, Martijn Burger, and Ruut Veenhoven. 2015. "Financial Distress and Happiness of Employees in Times of Economic Crisis." *Applied Economics Letters* 22(3): 173–79.

Ball, Laurence. 2009. "Hysteresis in Unemployment: Old and New Evidence." NBER Working Paper No. w14818. Cambridge, Mass.: National Bureau for Economic Research.

Ball, Laurence, Daniel Leigh, and Prakash Loungani. 2012. "Okun's Law: Fit at 50?" International Monetary Fund Working Paper 13/10. Washington, D.C.: International Monetary Fund.

Bartels, Larry M. 2013. "Political Effects of the Great Recession." *Annals of the American Academy of Political and Social Science* 650(1): 47–76.

Barth, Erling, James Davis, Richard Freeman, and Sari Pekkala Kerr. 2017. "Weathering the Great Recession: Variation in Employment Responses, by Establishments and Countries." *RSF: The Russell Sage Foundation Journal of the Social Sciences* 3(3): 50–69. DOI: 10.7758/RSF.2017.3.3.03.

Basbug, Gokce, and Ofer Sharone. 2017. "The Emotional Toll of Long-Term Unemployment: Examining the Interaction Effects of Gender and Marital Status." *RSF: The Russell Sage Foundation Journal of the Social Sciences* 3(3): 222–44. DOI: 10.7758/RSF.2017.3.3.10.

Blanchard, Olivier J., and Lawrence H. Summers. 1986. "Hysteresis and the European Unemployment Problem." *NBER Macroeconomics Annual*, vol. 1 (Fall), edited by Stanley Fischer. Cambridge, Mass.: MIT Press.

Blanchard, Olivier J., and Justin Wolfers. 2000. "The Role of Shocks and Institutions in the Rise of European Unemployment: The Aggregate Evidence." *Economic Journal* 110(March): 1–33.

Bloom, Nicholas. 2009. "The Impact of Uncertainty Shocks." *Econometrica* 77(3): 623–85.

Brand, Jennie E. 2015. "The Far-Reaching Impact of Job Loss and Unemployment." *Annual Review of Sociology* 41: 359–75.

Browning, Martin, and Thomas F. Crossley. 2001. "Unemployment Insurance Benefit Levels and Consumption Changes." *Journal of Public Economics* 80(1): 1–23.

Bureau of Labor Statistics. 2009. "Ranks of Discouraged Workers and Others Marginally Attached to the Labor Force Rise During Recession." Issues in Labor Statistics, Summary 09-04. Washington: Bureau of Labor Statistics.

Card, David, and Alexandre Mas. 2016. "Introduction: The Labor Market in the Aftermath of the Great Recession." *Journal of Labor Economics* 34(S1): S1–S6.

Carey, Benedict. 2011. "Study Ties Suicide Rate in Work Force to Economy." *New York Times*, April 15, p. A13.

Charles, Kerwin, Erik Hurst, and Matthew J. Notowidigdo. 2015. "Housing Booms and Busts, Labor Market Opportunities, and College Attendance." NBER Working Paper No. 21587. Cambridge, Mass.: National Bureau for Economic Research.

Cherlin, Andrew, Erin Cumberworth, S. Philip Morgan, and Christopher Wimer. 2013. "The Effects of the Great Recession on Family Structure and Fertility." *Annals of the American Academy of Political and Social Science* 650(1): 214–31.

Cohen, Philip N. 2015. "How the American Family Was Affected by the Great Recession." *Pacific Standard*, February 5, 2015.

Congressional Budget Office. 2004. "Family Income of Unemployment Insurance Recipients." Washington: Congressional Budget Office.

———. 2014. "Revisions to CBO's Projection of Potential Output Since 2007." Washington: Congressional Budget Office.

Couch, Kenneth A., and Dana W. Placzek. 2010. "Earnings Losses of Displaced Workers Revisited." *American Economic Review* 100(1): 572–89.

Coy, Peter. 2009. "The Lost Generation." *Bloomberg Business Week*, October 19, 2009, pp. 33–35.

Currie, Janet, and Hannes Schwandt. 2014. "Short- and Long-Term Effects of Unemployment on Fertility." *Proceedings of the National Academy of Sciences of the United States of America* 111(41): 14734–39.

Currie, Janet, and Erdal Tekin. 2015. "Is There a Link Between Foreclosure and Health?" *American Economic Journals: Economic Policy* 7(1): 63–94.

Danziger, Sheldon. 2013. "Evaluating the Effects of the Great Recession." *Annals of the American Academy of Political and Social Science* 650(1): 6–24.

Davis, Steven J., and John Haltiwanger. 2014. "Labor Market Fluidity and Economic Performance." NBER Working Paper No. 20479. Cambridge, Mass.: National Bureau of Economic Research.

Davis, Steven J., and Till von Wachter. 2011. "Recessions and the Cost of Job Loss." *Brookings Papers on Economic Activity* 43(2): 1–72.

De Witte, Hans. 1999. "Job Insecurity and Psychological Well-Being: Review of the Literature and Exploration of Some Unresolved Issues." *European Journal of Work and Organizational Psychology* 8(2): 155–77.

Dehejia, Rajeev, and Adriana Lleras-Muney. 2004. "Booms, Busts, and Babies' Health." *Quarterly Journal of Economics* 119(3): 1091–1130.

Dickens, Williams T., Robert K. Triest, and Rachel B. Sederberg. 2017. "The Changing Consequences of Unemployment for Household Finances." *RSF: The Russell Sage Foundation Journal of the Social Sciences* 3(3): 202–21. DOI: 10.7758/RSF.2017.3.3.09.

Donovan, Sarah. A. 2015. "An Overview of the Employment-Population Ratio." Congressional Research Service publication 7-5700. Washington: Congressional Research Service.

Eichengreen, Barry. 2015. *Hall of Mirrors: The Great Depression, the Great Recession, and the Uses— and Misuses—of History*. New York: Oxford University Press.

Farber, Henry S. 1999. "Alternative and Part-Time Employment Arrangements as a Response to Job Loss." *Journal of Labor Economics* 17(4): 142–69.

———. 2011. "Job Loss in the Great Recession: Historical Perspective from the Displaced Workers Survey, 1984–2010." NBER Working Paper No. 17040. Cambridge, Mass.: National Bureau for Economic Research.

Farber, Henry S., Dan Silverman, and Till M. von Wachter. 2017. "Factors Determining Callbacks to Job Applications by the Unemployed: An Audit Study." *RSF: The Russell Sage Foundation Journal of the Social Sciences* 3(3): 168–201. DOI: 10.7758/RSF.2017.3.3.08.

Giuliano, Paola, and Antonio Spilimbergo. 2014. "Growing Up in a Recession." *Review of Economic Studies* 81(2): 787–817.

Glaeser, Ed. 2014. "Secular Joblessness." In *Secular Stagnation: Facts, Causes and Cures*, edited by Coen Teulings and Richard Baldwin. Washington, D.C.: Center for Economic and Policy Research Press.

Greenhouse, Steven. 2011. "Union Membership in U.S. Fell to a 70-Year Low Last Year." *New York Times*, January 21.

Gruber, Jonathan. 1997. "The Consumption Smoothing Benefits of Unemployment Insurance." *American Economic Review* 87(1): 192–205.

Grusky, David B., Bruce Western, and Christopher Wimer, eds. 2011. *The Great Recession*. New York: Russell Sage Foundation.

Hagedorn, Marcus, Fatih Karahan, Iourii Manovskii, and Kurt Mitman. 2013. "Unemployment Benefits and Unemployment in the Great Recession: The Role of Macro Effects." NBER Working Paper No. 19499. Cambridge, Mass.: National Bureau for Economic Research, October.

Hall, Robert E. 2012. "Quantifying the Forces Leading to the Collapse of GDP After the Financial Crisis." Unpublished working paper. Stanford University.

———. 2014. "Quantifying the Lasting Harm to the U.S. Economy from the Financial Crisis." In *NBER Macroeconomics Annual* 2014, vol. 29, edited by Jonathan Parker and Michael Woodford. Cambridge, Mass.: National Bureau for Economic Research.

Hout, Michael, and Erin Cumberworth. 2012. "The Labor Force and the Great Recession." Inequality Research Brief. New York: Russell Sage Foundation and Stanford Center on Poverty, October.

Hout, Michael, and Orestes P. Hastings. 2014. "The Social Recession: Americans' Subjective Reactions to the Great Recession and Lagging Economy Since 2006." Paper presented at annual meeting of the American Sociological Association. San Francisco (August 16–19, 2014).

Hout, Michael, Asaf Levannon, and Erin Cumberworth. 2011. "Job Loss and Unemployment During the Great Recession." In *The Great Recession*, edited by David Grusky, Bruce Western, and Christopher Wimer. New York: Russell Sage Foundation.

Jacobsen, Linda A., and Mark Mather. 2010. "U.S. Economic and Social Trends Since 2000." *Population Bulletin* 65(1): 1–16.

Jacobson, Louis S., Robert LaLonde, and Daniel Sullivan. 1993. "Earnings Losses of Displaced Workers." *American Economic Review* 83(4): 685–709.

Jaimovich, Nir, and Henry E. Siu. 2012. "The Trend Is the Cycle: Job Polarization and Jobless Recoveries." NBER Working Paper No. 18334. Cambridge, Mass.: National Bureau for Economic Research.

Kahn, Lisa B. 2010. "The Long-Term Consequences of Graduating from College in a Bad Economy." *Labour Economics* 17(2): 303–16.

Kahn, Lisa B., and Erika McEntarfer. 2014. "Employment Cyclicality and Firm Quality." NBER Working Paper No. 20698. Cambridge, Mass.: National Bureau for Economic Research.

Kalil, Ariel. 2013. "Effects of the Great Recession on Child Development." *Annals of the American Academy of Political and Social Science* 650(1): 232–50.

Kalleberg, Arne L. 2011. *Good Jobs, Bad Jobs: The Rise of Polarized and Precarious Employment Systems in the United States, 1970s to 2000s*. New York: Russell Sage Foundation.

Kocherlakota, Narayana. 2010. "Inside the FOMC." Speech given by president of Federal Reserve Bank of Minneapolis in Marquette, Michigan, August 17. Available at: www.minneapolisfed .org/news-and-events/presidents-speeches /inside-the-fomc; accessed August 3, 2016.

———. 2012. "Planning for Liftoff." Speech given at Gogebic Community College, Iron Wood, Michigan (September 20). Available at: https:// www.minneapolisfed.org/news-and-events /presidents-speeches/planning-for-liftoff; accessed August 3, 2016.

Kochhar, Rakesh. 2011. "Two Years of Economic Recovery: Women Lost Jobs, Men Found Them." *Pew Research Center* (website), Social & Demographic Trends, July 6. Available at: www.pew socialtrends.org/2011/07/06/two-years-of -economic-recovery-women-lose-jobs-men-find -them; accessed September 5, 2016.

Kochhar, Rakesh, C. Soledad Espinoza, and Rebecca Hinze-Pifer. 2010. "After the Great Recession: Foreign Born Gain Jobs; Native Born Lose Jobs." *Pew Research Center* (website), October 29. Available at: www.pewhispanic.org/2010/10/29 /after-the-great-recession-brforeign-born-gain -jobs-native-born-lose-jobs; accessed June 10, 2015.

Kroft, Kory, Fabian Lange, Matthew J. Notowidigdo, and Lawrence F. Katz. 2016. "Long-Term Unemployment and the Great Recession: The Role of Composition, Duration Dependence, and Nonparticipation." *Journal of Labor Economics* 34 (S1, Part 2): S7–S54.

Kroft, Kory, Matthew J. Notowidigdo, and Fabian Lange. 2013. "Duration Dependence and Labor Market Conditions: Evidence from a Field Experiment." *Quarterly Journal of Economics* 128(3): 1123–67.

Lazear, Edward P., Kathryn L. Shaw, and Christopher Stanton. 2016. "Making Do with Less: Working Harder During Recessions." *Journal of Labor Economics* 34(S1): S333–60.

Lazear, Edward P., and James Spletzer. 2012. "The United States Labor Market: Status Quo or a New Normal?" NBER Working Paper No. 18386. Cambridge, Mass.: National Bureau for Economic Research.

Leamer, Edward. 2007. "Housing Is the Business Cycle." NBER Working Paper No. 13428. Cambridge, Mass.: National Bureau for Economic Research.

Levy, Brian L., Ted Mouw, and Anthony Daniel Perez. 2017. "Why Did People Move During the Great Recession? The Role of Economics in Migration Decisions." *RSF: The Russell Sage Foundation Journal of the Social Sciences* 3(3): 100–25. DOI: 10.7758/RSF.2017.3.3.05.

Lipset, Seymour Martin, and William Schneider. 1987. "The Confidence Gap During the Reagan Years, 1981–1987." *Political Science Quarterly* 101(1): 1–23.

Ljungqvist, Lars, and Thomas Sargent. 1998. "The European Unemployment Dilemma." *Journal of Political Economy* 106(3): 514–50.

Madland, David, and Karla Walter. 2010. "Why Is the Public Suddenly Down on Unions: The Bad Economy Is to Blame—Support Should Recover When the Economy Does." *Center for American Progress Action Fund*, American Worker Project, July. Available at: http://lawprofessors.typepad.com /files/why-is-the-public-suddenly-down-on -unions.pdf; accessed September 30, 2016.

Marinescu, Ioana. 2015. "The General Equilibrium Impacts of Unemployment Insurance: Evidence from a Large Online Job Board." Available at: http://www.marinescu.eu/Marinescu_UI.pdf; accessed August 2, 2016.

Massey, Douglas S. 2012. "The Great Decline in American Immigration?" *Pathways* 2012(Fall): 9–13.

Milkman, Ruth. 2013. "Back to the Future? U.S. Labour in the New Gilded Age." *British Journal of Industrial Relations* 51(4): 645–65.

Milkman, Ruth, and Stephanie Luce. 2017. "Labor Unions and the Great Recession." *RSF: The Russell Sage Foundation Journal of the Social Sci-

ences* 3(3): 145–65. DOI: 10.7758/RSF.2017 .3.3.07.

Moffitt, Robert A. 2012. "The Social Safety Net and the Great Recession." Stanford, CA: Stanford Center on Poverty and Inequality.

Morgan, S. Philip, Erin Cumberworth, and Christopher Wimer. 2011. "The Great Recession's Influence on Fertility, Marriage, Divorce, and Cohabitation." In *The Great Recession*, edited by David B. Grusky, Bruce Western, and Christopher Wimer. New York: Russell Sage Foundation.

Mueller, Andreas, Jesse Rothstein, and Till von Wachter. 2015. "Unemployment Insurance and Disability Insurance." *Journal of Labor Economics* 34(S1): S445–75.

Mulligan, Casey B. 2010. "Aggregate Implications of Labor Market Distortions: The Recession of 2008–9 and Beyond." NBER Working Paper No. 15681. Cambridge, Mass.: National Bureau for Economic Research.

National Bureau of Economic Research. 2010. "The NBER's Business Cycle Dating Committee." Available at: www.nber.org/cycles/recessions .html; accessed August 2, 2016.

Neal, Derek. 1995. "Industry-Specific Human Capital: Evidence from Displaced Workers." *Journal of Labor Economics* 13(4): 653–77.

O'Connor, Kelsey J. 2017. "Who Suffered Most from the Great Recession? Happiness in the United States." *RSF: The Russell Sage Foundation Journal of the Social Sciences* 3(3): 72–99. DOI: 10.7758/RSF.2017.3.3.04.

Ohanian, Lee. 2010. "The Economic Crisis from a Neoclassical Perspective." *Journal of Economic Perspectives* 24(4): 45–66.

Okun, Arthur M. 1973. "Upward Mobility in a High-Pressure Economy." *Brookings Papers on Economic Activity* 4(1): 207–52.

Oreopoulos, Philip, Andrew Heisz, and Till von Wachter. 2012. "Short- and Long-Term Career Effects of Graduating in a Recession." *American Economic Journal: Applied Economics* 4(1): 1–29.

Owens, Lindsay A., and Karen S. Cook. 2013. "The Effects of Local Economic Conditions on Confidence in Key Institutions and Interpersonal Trust After the Great Recession." *Annals of the American Academy of Political and Social Science* 650 (1): 274–98.

Pfeffer, Fabian T., Sheldon Danziger, and Robert F. Schoeni. 2013. "Wealth Disparities Before and

After the Great Recession." *Annals of the American Academy of Political and Social Science* 650(1): 98–123.

Pistaferri, Luigi, Richard Blundell, and Itay Saporta-Eksten. 2016. "Consumption Inequality and Family Labor Supply." *American Economic Review* 106(2): 387–435.

Rampell, Catherine. 2011. "Mancession to He-covery." *Economix* (blog), July 6. Available at: http://economix.blogs.nytimes.com/2011/07/06 /mancession-to-he-covery; accessed August 2, 2016.

Reynolds, Lloyd. 1951. *The Structure of Labor Markets: Wages and Labor Mobility in Theory and Practice.* Westport, CN: Greenwood Press.

Rothstein, Jesse. 2012. "The Labor Market Four Years into the Crisis: Assessing Structural Explanations." *Industrial and Labor Relations Review* 65(3): 437–500.

———. 2017. "The Great Recession and Its Aftermath: What Role for Structural Changes?" *RSF: The Russell Sage Foundation Journal of the Social Sciences* 3(3): 22–49. DOI: 10.7758/RSF.2017.3.3.02.

Rothstein, Jesse, and Robert Valletta. 2014. "Scraping By: Income and Program Participation After the Loss of Extended Unemployment Benefits." Federal Reserve Bank of San Francisco Working Paper No. 2014-06. Available at: http://www .frbsf.org/economic-research/files/wp2014 -06.pdf; accessed September 30, 2016.

Şahin, Ayşegül, Joseph Song, Giorgio Topa, and Giovanni L. Violante. 2014. "Mismatch Unemployment." *American Economic Review* 104(11): 3529–64.

Schmieder, Johannes, Till von Wachter, and Stefan Bender. 2009. "The Long-Term Impact of Job Displacement in Germany During the 1982 Recession on Earnings, Income, and Employment." Columbia University, Department of Economics Discussion Paper Series DP0910-07. New York: Columbia University.

———. 2015a. "The Mechanisms Behind Cyclical and Persistent Costs of Job Loss." Unpublished working paper. University of California, Los Angeles.

———. 2015b. "The Causal Effect of Unemployment Duration on Wages: Evidence from Unemployment Insurance Extensions." NBER Working Paper 19772. Cambridge, Mass.: National Bureau of Economic Research.

Schneider, Daniel. 2017. "Non-marital and Teen Fertility and Contraception During the Great Recession." *RSF: The Russell Sage Foundation Journal of the Social Sciences* 3(3): 126–44. DOI: 10.7758/RSF.2017.3.3.06.

Schwarz, Benjamin. 2009. "Life in (and After) Our Great Recession." *The Atlantic*, October. Available at: www.theatlantic.com/magazine/archive /2009/10/life-in-and-after-our-great-recession /307651/; accessed September 30, 2016.

Song, Jae, and Till von Wachter. 2014. "Long-Term Nonemployment and Job Displacement." Evaluating Labor Market Dynamics, Proceedings from the Jackson Hole Economic Policy Symposium Sponsored by the Federal Reserve Board of Kansas City, Jackson Hole, Wyo. (August 2014). Available at: www.kansascityfed.org/publicat /sympos/2014/2014vonWachter.pdf; accessed September 30, 2016.

Stephens, Melvin, Jr. 2004. "Job Loss Expectations, Realizations, and Household Consumption Behavior." *Review of Economics and Statistics* 86(1): 253–69.

Stevens, Ann Huff. 1997. "Persistent Effects of Job Displacement: The Importance of Multiple Job Losses," part 1. *Journal of Labor Economics* 15(1): 165–88.

Sullivan, Daniel, and Till von Wachter. 2009. "Job Displacement and Mortality: An Analysis Using Administrative Data." *Quarterly Journal of Economics* 124(3): 1265–1306.

Summers, Lawrence H. 2014. "U.S. Economic Prospects: Secular Stagnation, Hysteresis, and the Zero Lower Bound." *Business Economics* 49(2): 65–73.

Surowiecki, James. 2011. "The State of the Unions: Public Support for Labor Unions Hits New Low." *New Yorker*, January 12, 2011.

Taylor, John B. 2010. "Getting Back on Track: Macroeconomic Policy Lessons from the Financial Crisis." *Federal Reserve Bank of St. Louis Review* 92(3): 165–76.

Uggen, Christopher. 2012. "The Crime Wave That Wasn't." *Pathways* 2012(Fall) 14–18.

von Wachter, Till. 2015. "Measuring the Cost of Job Displacement in Terms of Worker and Family Outcomes." Unpublished paper. University of California, Los Angeles.

von Wachter, Till, Jae Song, and Joyce Manchester. 2011. "Long-Term Earnings Losses Due to Mass-

Layoffs During the 1982 Recession: An Analysis Using Longitudinal Administrative Data from 1974 to 2008." Unpublished paper. Columbia University. Available at: http://www.econ .ucla.edu/tvwachter/papers/mass_layoffs_1982 .pdf; accessed September 30, 2016.

Wolff, Edward, Lindsay A. Owens, and Esra Burak. 2011. "Housing and Wealth in the Great Recession." In *The Great Recession*, edited by David Grusky, Bruce Western, and Christopher Wimer. New York: Russell Sage Foundation.

Yagan, Danny. 2014. "Moving to Opportunity? Migratory Insurance over the Great Recession." *Owenzidar* (blog), January 2, 2014. Available at: https://owenzidar.wordpress.com/2014/01/02 /moving-to-opportunity-migratory-insura nce-over-the-great-recession/; accessed September 30, 2016.

PART I

Longer-Term Impact of the Great Recession on Workers and Firms

The Great Recession and Its Aftermath: What Role for Structural Changes?

JESSE ROTHSTEIN

The years since the 2009 end of the Great Recession have been disastrous for many workers, particularly those with low human capital or other disadvantages. One explanation attributes this to deficient aggregate labor demand, to which marginal workers are more sensitive. A second attributes it to structural changes. Cyclical explanations imply that if aggregate labor demand is increased then many of the post-2009 patterns will revert to their pre-recession trends. Structural explanations suggest recent experience is the "new normal." This paper reviews data since 2007 for evidence. I examine wage trends to measure the relative importance of supply and demand. I find little wage pressure before 2015, pointing to demand as the binding constraint. The most recent data show some signs of tightness, but still substantial slack.

Keywords: unemployment, mismatch, wage growth, Great Recession

Between the fourth quarter of 2007 and the second quarter of 2009, real U.S. GDP fell by over 5 percent. The unemployment rate rose from a low of 4.4 percent in May 2007 to a high of 10.0 percent in October 2009, for a twenty-nine-month increase of 5.6 percentage points. This far exceeded the largest previous postwar increase over a similar duration, 3.9 percentage points in 1973–1975.

The National Bureau of Economic Research (NBER) dated the business cycle trough in June 2009. But neither the real economy nor, especially, the labor market recovered quickly after that point. Real output recovered its pre-recession peak in the third quarter of 2011, but remains well below the pre-recession trajectory. Payroll employment took nearly seven years, until May of 2014, to reach its December 2007 level. The unemployment rate remained above 8 percent for forty-three consecutive months (until August of 2012) and above 7 percent for sixty months (until November 2013), each the longest such period since World War II.

As of this writing, the unemployment rate is down to 4.9 percent, only slightly above its level on the eve of the recession. But most of the decline came from reduced labor force participation rather than increased employment:

Jesse Rothstein is professor of public policy and economics and director of the Institute for Research on Labor and Employment at the University of California, Berkeley, and is a research associate of the National Bureau of Economic Research.

© 2017 Russell Sage Foundation. Rothstein, Jesse. 2017. "The Great Recession and Its Aftermath: What Role for Structural Changes?" *RSF: The Russell Sage Foundation Journal of the Social Sciences* 3(3): 22–49. DOI: 10.7758/RSF.2017.3.3.02. This paper extends and expands on the results in Rothstein (2012; 2014). I thank Darian Woods, Peter Jones, and Audrey Tiew for excellent research assistance, and participants in the Russell Sage conference "The U.S. Labor Market During and After the Great Recession" for helpful comments. I am grateful to the Smith-Richardson and Russell Sage foundations for financial support. Copies of the data and computer programs used to generate the results presented in this article are available from the author. Direct correspondence to: Jesse Rothstein at rothstein@berkeley.edu, 2521 Channing Way, Berkeley, CA 94720.

The employment-to-population ratio, which fell by an unprecedented 4.9 percentage points between December 2006 and December 2009, hovered around 58.6 percent for more than four years thereafter and has recovered just one point since then. It remains about 3.5 percentage points below the pre-recession level.

By essentially every measure, low-skilled workers have fared even worse than these already dismal statistics suggest. For workers with high school diplomas but no college (aged twenty-five and up), for example, the employment-to-population ratio fell not by 4.9 but by 6.1 percentage points from the peak to December 2009, fell another 0.5 percentage point over the next year, and has shown no sign of improving since.

Early in the recovery, some observers diagnosed structural problems as impediments to an otherwise quick cyclical recovery. In a 2010 speech, for example, Narayana Kocherlakota, president of the Federal Reserve Bank of Minneapolis, stated, "Firms have jobs, but can't find appropriate workers. The workers want to work, but can't find appropriate jobs. There are many possible sources of mismatch—geography, skills, demography—and they are probably all at work" (Kocherlakota 2010).[1] In this view, poor outcomes for low-skill workers are due to their failure to supply the skills demanded by the market.

The mismatch theory was eventually discredited by the evidence, as it became clear that—at least in 2010—labor market slack was high in nearly all sizable labor markets.[2] But as the weak recovery dragged on, now for the better part of a decade, it has become harder to resist the view that this is the "new normal," and that we are destined for a future of low employment rates and a substantial class of individuals—disproportionately low-skilled—who are more or less permanently detached from the labor market.

This paper reviews data on labor market outcomes over the period since the recession's official end, focusing on the experience of less-skilled workers. I argue that there is no basis for concluding that the recent past represents "the new normal" or that labor demand has tilted more rapidly away from low-skilled workers than at other times in recent decades. Rather, the evidence indicates that labor demand remains very weak for nearly all workers. Policies or events that raise aggregate demand thus promise to do a great deal to return our labor market to one resembling the pre-2007 period.[3]

Less-skilled workers' outcomes have always been disproportionately sensitive to the business cycle, worsening by far more in downturns than do those of more skilled workers and then improving by more when the economy recovers. Thus, if the economy remains in a demand trough, it is not surprising that less-skilled workers have suffered disproportionately, and it is reasonable to expect that this suffering will ease substantially if and when aggregate labor demand recovers.

An important possibility is that cyclical labor demand shortfalls that extend for many years may *create* structural problems, as idle workers' human capital gradually depreciates and they become increasingly disconnected from the labor market such that they are unable or unwilling to return to work when jobs finally become available. This idea has gained currency as an explanation for our current situation. For example, Alan B. Krueger, Judd Cramer, and David Cho (2014) argue that the long-term unemployed exert little or no pressure on the labor market, and conclude that extra-market measures such as expanded social wel-

1. See also Ayşegül Şahin, Joseph Song, Giorgio Topa, and Giovanni L. Violante (2011).

2. See Peter Diamond (2010); Lawrence Mishel, Heidi Shierholz, and Kathryn Edwards (2010); Mishel (2011); Rothstein (2012); and Edward Lazear and James R. Spletzer (2012). The Congressional Budget Office (2012) was more favorable toward structural hypotheses but nevertheless concluded that aggregate demand shortfalls were the primary source of the high unemployment rate.

3. Some have argued that the market, left to its own, will no longer yield sufficient aggregate demand (for example, Summers 2016). Even in these "secular stagnation" models, however, aggressive fiscal and monetary policy can produce full employment. Modeling the determinants of aggregate demand is beyond the scope of this paper, which focuses on diagnosing the current state of the labor market.

fare programs will be needed to support those who remain in this state.

This hypothesis has an important implication: if true, it means that even a labor market that appears to be quite slack from the perspective of workers can be tight from the perspective of employers, who see relatively few qualified, available workers to hire (see, for example, Hall 2014). Employers facing tight labor markets should bid up the wage in order to attract workers. Labor demand shortfalls, by contrast, would have an opposite effect, as unemployed workers bid down equilibrium wages as they compete for the few available jobs.[4] I thus emphasize the examination of wage trends, both in the aggregate and in particular labor markets, for evidence about the appropriate diagnosis of the current situation.

I distinguish between three periods: the recession, ending in mid-2009; the initial recovery, from 2009 through the end of 2014; and the period since the end of 2014. There is more evidence of tightness in the most recent data than in the five preceding recovery years, and the end of 2014 represents a useful dividing point. I focus on the period before that, but discuss how the conclusions are modified by more recent data. Together, the evidence indicates the following:

- The downturn hit less-skilled groups harder than more-skilled groups, and men harder than women.

- The groups that were hit hardest in the downturn rebounded the most in the recovery, so that by 2014 every demographic group had somewhat higher unemployment than before the recession, but much less than at the recession's peak.

- The groups hit hardest were, in general, those that suffer more in every downturn, such as less-skilled men. If anything, non-college-educated men did *better* in this cycle than one would have expected on the basis of past experience.

- Mean real wages stagnated or declined from 2010 through 2014, a conclusion that is not modified by adjusting for changes in the composition of employment or by focusing on new jobs whose wages are presumably more sensitive to prevailing economic conditions. Real wages have risen at an average annual rate of about 2 percent since the beginning of 2015, not enough to make up for years of no increases.

- There is little sign of faster wage growth for any identifiable subgroup of workers, including those in industries with dramatic increases in job openings, those in low-unemployment metropolitan areas, or those with higher skills.

- All education groups saw falling real wages from 2009 to 2014, and have seen increases since then. Mean real wages remain below their 2007 levels for all education groups except those with college degrees, whose wages have risen by a cumulative 2 percent (that is, about 0.2 percent per year) over a nearly ten-year period.

These facts are more consistent with a story of slack labor demand than with one where supply shortfalls are a binding constraint. In a concluding analysis, I explore evidence regarding the implications of prolonged demand shortfalls for future performance. Both reemployment hazards and idleness rates offer some basis for optimism that the overhang will be limited. Although there are some "lost" workers in their late middle ages, the data appear consistent with a labor force ready to take advantage of strong labor demand, if it ever returns.

THE STATE OF THE AGGREGATE LABOR MARKET

In this section I review the main aggregate labor market series over the last decade as a way of framing the later investigation. Figure 1 shows the time paths of aggregate employment, the unemployment rate, and the employment-population ratio from 2004 forward. The figure makes clear that the sharpest downturn was in late 2008 and early 2009, when the economy lost 4.5 million jobs over a six-month period. Job losses continued until February 2010, but

---

4. Of course, the failure of wages to fall quickly in response to labor demand shortfalls is a longstanding and still unresolved puzzle; see, for example, Truman Bewley (1999).

Figure 1. Employment, Employment-Population Ratio, and Unemployment Rate, 2004–2016

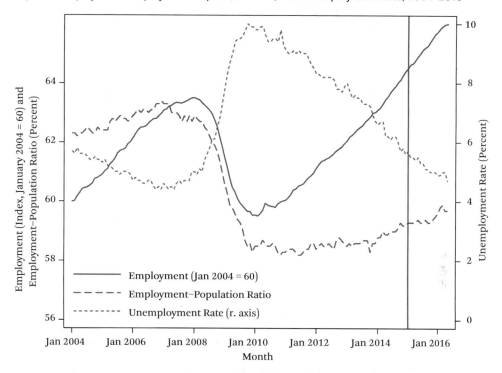

Source: Bureau of Labor Statistics, Current Population Survey and Current Employment Statistics.
Notes: Series are seasonally adjusted. Vertical line marks the end of 2014.

employment has grown consistently since then at an average rate of about 191,000 new jobs per month. This is only a bit faster than is needed to keep up with population growth, however, and as a result the employment-population ratio, which fell from 62.9 percent in January 2008 to 58.2 percent in December 2009, remains well below its pre-recession level. There was no sign of improvement in this series for the first four years after the recession ended. It has trended slowly upward since the end of 2013, gaining one percentage point, or less than one-quarter of the recession-period loss. Thus, although the unemployment rate has fallen from its peak of 10.0 percent in October 2009 to 4.9 percent in June 2016, the bulk of this decline has been due to falling labor force participation among the non-employed.

Figure 2 shows hires, involuntary displacements, layoffs, and quits, as measured in the Job Openings and Labor Turnover Survey (JOLTS). Layoffs rose by nearly 50 percent dur-

ing the 2008–2009 crisis. At the same time, the usually more volatile hires and quits series fell by about 25 percent and 40 percent, respectively.[5] Layoffs peaked in early 2009 and returned to their pre-recession levels by early 2010. Hires and quits bottomed out somewhat later, in the middle months of 2009, and recovered very slowly thereafter, not approaching their pre-recession peaks until 2016. By contrast, job openings, which fell by fully 50 percent during the crisis, recovered more quickly and exceeded their pre-recession peak in June 2014. They have continued to grow since, and in April 2015 they passed their historical record, set in the second ever JOLTS survey in January 2001.

Figure 3 shows the Beveridge Curve, relating job openings, expressed as a share of employment, to the unemployment rate. One expects these measures to be inversely related: in tight labor markets with low unemployment, jobs are filled slowly and the job openings rate is

5. These are counted from December 2007 to the respective series trough in 2009.

Figure 2. Layoffs, Quits, Job Openings, and Hires, 2001–2016

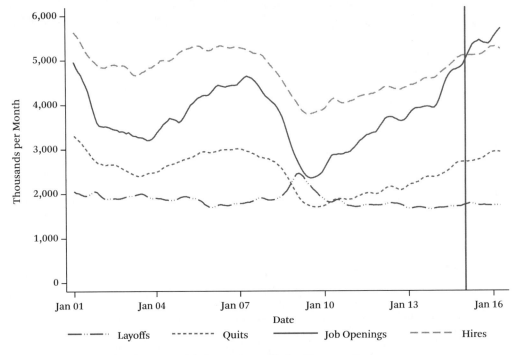

Source: Bureau of Labor Statistics, Job Openings and Labor Turnover Survey.
Notes: Seasonally adjusted data, smoothed using a three-month triangle smoother. Vertical line marks the end of 2014.

therefore high, whereas when unemployment is high vacancies are filled quickly and there are few jobs open at any given time. In search models of the labor market, shifts in the relationship between the two series can indicate changes in the efficiency of the labor market matching process (Blanchard and Diamond 1989).

As figure 3 illustrates, in 2008 and early 2009 the job openings rate fell steadily as unemployment rose, tracing out a curve consistent with—though well beyond the support of—that seen in the prior business cycle. In later 2009 and the first quarter of 2010, however, job openings rose substantially, with no change in unemployment; then, when unemployment began falling in mid-2010, the job openings rate continued to rise, tracing out a curve parallel to the pre-2009 curve but shifted substantially upward: a given unemployment rate now supports a job openings rate about 0.75 points higher than it would have before the crisis.

A number of commentators have interpreted

this apparent shift in the Beveridge Curve as diagnostic of increases in structural unemployment. In this view, an increase in labor demand can be inferred from rising job openings, and the failure of the unemployment rate to fall faster than it has indicates that the currently unemployed are unable or unwilling to fill the newly created positions. This inference is supported by Krueger and his colleagues' (2014) analysis of the duration of unemployment, which argues that a Beveridge Curve that uses the short-term unemployment rate—the share of the labor force that has been unemployed for six months or less—does not appear to have shifted in the same way (see also Ghayad and Dickens 2012).

Although the shift in the Beveridge Curve is certainly consistent with a structural change, it is important to be cautious. There is at least some reason to think that part or all of the shift reflects changes in the meaning of a job opening rather than increases in the difficulty of finding qualified workers.

Figure 3. Beveridge Curve

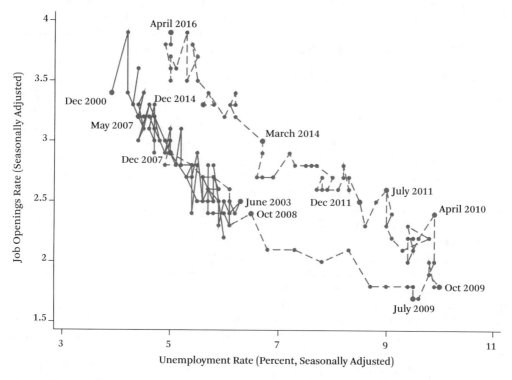

Source: Bureau of Labor Statistics, Job Openings and Labor Turnover Survey and Current Population Survey.

Note: The December 2007 to April 2016 segment is indicated by a dashed line.

Job openings are well defined if hiring is a binary firm decision, as in many search models: once a decision is made to hire another worker, a job opening is posted and the first applicant who arrives (perhaps subject to some well-defined, fixed minimum qualifications) is hired. This, of course, is an extreme oversimplification. In reality, both the wage and the qualifications are choice variables that can influence the rate at which openings are filled.[6]

Consider a firm with labor demand curve $L^D = f(w)$, with $f' < 0$. So long as wages are set exogenously, job openings are well defined as the difference between $f(w^*)$—where w^* is the externally determined wage—and the firm's current employment. But if wages are not fixed there is no unique number of openings.[7] A firm might decide to offer wage $w_{low} < w^*$ for an additional $f(w_{low}) - f(w^*)$ positions, knowing that these jobs are likely to remain open for longer than would a position offering w*. Similarly, the firm might hold out for better-qualified workers, extending its search, or might be less choosy in order to hire more quickly (Diamond

6. Even when the offered wage is not posted with the job advertisement the employer must decide on a bargaining stance once an otherwise suitable candidate is identified. Similarly, the employer sets both minimum qualifications to list with the position and its choosiness among workers meeting those minimum qualifications. Finally, a firm planning to hire may do so without ever posting an official opening (Diamond 2010).

7. This is of course the exact analogue to the somewhat more common claim that unemployment is always voluntary: unemployment simply means that one's reservation wage has been set above the market price. In search models, there can be frictional unemployment and frictional job openings. But even in these models one might observe a range of reservation wages and wage offers, with frictional unemployment rising in the former and frictional vacancies declining in the latter.

2010). Either decision affects the number of measured job openings and the job-filling rate, but neither reflects changes in labor market matching efficiency.

These definitional issues may have become more important since the Great Recession. In previous business cycles, employers seem to have been unwilling to take advantage of labor market weakness by offering lower wages to new hires than they had in the past, or by substantially increasing their required qualifications. The reasons for this are not well understood, but may include concerns about the morale of newly hired and incumbent workers and worries that workers who accept low wages when conditions are weak are unlikely to remain with the firm once business improves (Bewley 1999). These concerns appear to be less salient today. There is anecdotal evidence that two-tier wage structures that distinguish between incumbent and new workers have become increasingly common (Vlasic 2011). Moreover, at least some employers seem to have taken advantage of their strong bargaining positions to be much choosier among job applicants, raising qualifications and drawing out the hiring process with multiple rounds of interviews (Davis, Faberman, and Haltiwanger 2010). All of this could be raising the measured rate of job openings relative to the strength of underlying labor demand. This would be consistent with the divergent behavior of job openings and quits since mid-2009—where the former appears to indicate the tightest market since the JOLTS survey began in 2000, the latter has recovered much more slowly and until quite recently remained well below its 2006 peak. It is thus important to look beyond the Beveridge Curve for evidence that could confirm or disprove the indication that there have been structural changes in the labor market.

HETEROGENEITY ACROSS INDUSTRY, GEOGRAPHY, AND DEMOGRAPHY

Where the unemployment rate and the job openings rate appear to indicate a tight labor market, other measures, particularly quits and the employment-population ratio, indicate rather more weakness. In this section I move beyond the aggregates by examining heterogeneity across different groups of workers. I focus on unemployment as it is the primary measure pointing toward near-full recovery. If demand has recovered in some labor markets but not in others, employers in the former markets will experience the market as tight even as workers in the latter experience it as slack, and worker shortages can coexist with substantial slack. For example, skill-biased technical change might lead to increased demand for high-skill workers, creating simultaneous tightness in the high-skill market and underutilization in the low-skill market. This could rationalize low quit rates with high job openings, as the former reflect the tightness of the markets where existing workers are located and the latter, the tightness of markets where employers would like to expand.

To test this mismatch hypothesis, we need a theory of the boundaries of labor markets. Unfortunately, the available data do not permit precise characterizations. I consider three dimensions that represent important labor market divisions: industry, geography, and demography.

Industry

Everyone knows that the financial services and real estate industries led us into the recession. However, these sectors did not see disproportionate job losses: the employment contractions in these industries in 2007–2009—5.6 percent in finance and 9.1 percent in real estate—were comparable to the economy-wide average.[8] In both absolute numbers and percentage terms, job losses were much larger in construction and durable goods manufacturing, which contracted by one-quarter and one-fifth, respectively.

Since the trough, employment has grown in every major private sector industrial category (though not in federal or state and local government). Mining and logging is a clear outlier. It surpassed its pre-recession peak by mid-2011 and over the longer run saw net growth of 60 percent between early 2003 and the end of 2014

---

8. This of course does not rule out the idea that a shock that began in the financial sector was an important source of the general collapse in demand.

Figure 4. State Unemployment Rates, December 2007 and December 2014

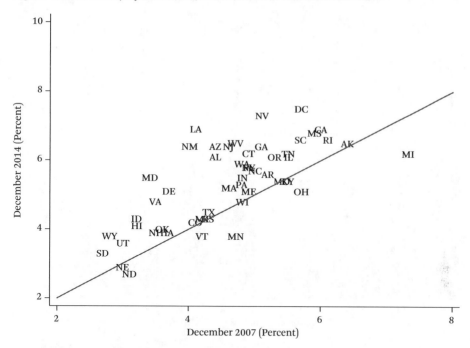

Source: Author's analysis of local area unemployment statistics data.
Note: Seasonally adjusted unemployment rates are used.

(before shrinking by over 8 percent in 2015, likely because of low energy prices). This is clearly a structural change, and there is compelling evidence of important mismatch-based impediments to the growth of this sector (for example, in North Dakota during the extraction boom there). But mining and logging accounts for only about 0.5 percent of national employment. There are only a few other sectors where employment growth between 2007 and 2014 kept up with the growth of the working-age population: professional and business services, education, health and social assistance, arts and recreation, and food and lodging. Notably, one sector where anecdotal stories about labor supply shortages have been common—information—has recovered only one-third of the jobs lost in the downturn.

Thus, insofar as there is mismatch across industrial groups, the tight markets would need to be made up mostly of low- and middle-skill sectors such as lodging and food services and arts and recreation. (There has also been job growth in professional and business services, education, and health, each of which has sub-

stantial numbers of higher-skill jobs.) This is unlikely to account for the poor outcomes of low- and middle-skill workers.

Geography

A second important source of heterogeneity is geographic. The recession hit some areas—most famously, Sun Belt cities such as Las Vegas where the housing boom was most pronounced—harder than others, and the recovery has also been uneven. Mobility rates have fallen in recent decades (Kaplan and Schulhofer-Wohl 2015), so geographically uneven labor demand growth might lead to mismatch. But while the evidence suggests that demand growth has been somewhat uneven, it also indicates that there are few places where demand has been robust enough to make up for the recessionary collapse. Figure 4 shows unemployment rates by state in December 2007 and December 2014. Across the fifty-one states plus Washington, D.C., only seven had an unemployment rate in 2014 that was below its 2007 level. Moreover, these seven include Michigan and Ohio, where the unemployment rates remain reasonably

Figure 5. Unemployment Rates in 2007, 2009, and 2014, by Gender and Education

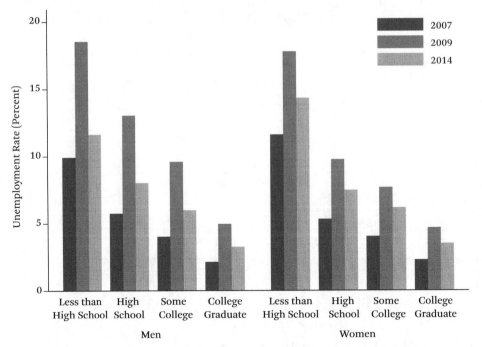

Source: Author's analysis of 2007, 2009, and 2014 Current Population Survey data.
Note: Annual unemployment rates are computed as equally weighted averages of non-seasonally adjusted monthly estimates.

high. Only Minnesota, Nebraska, North Dakota, and Vermont (which total only 3 percent of national employment) also had 2014 unemployment rates lower than 5 percent. At a finer geographic level, unemployment at the end of 2014 remained higher than it was before the recession in 361 of 394 metropolitan statistical areas (MSAs); even today, less than one-third of areas have fully recovered. There is not enough scope for geographic mismatch to have made a meaningful contribution to current woes.

Demography

A third dimension of heterogeneity is demographic, based on gender and education. Construction and manufacturing employment is heavily male and largely non-college-educated, so one might expect that low-skill men would have suffered disproportionately in the recession. Figure 5 shows the unemployment rate by gender and education in 2007, 2009, and 2014.[9] Consistent with the industrial composi-

tion of the cyclical collapse, we see that unemployment rates of less-educated men rose more from 2007 to 2009 than did those of more-educated men or of women of any education level. However, it is notable that low-skill workers had much higher unemployment rates than high-skill workers even in 2007, and that unemployment rates rose by similar proportions for college graduates as for other groups.

In all eight groups, unemployment in 2014 was lower than in 2009 but notably higher than in 2007. The relative recovery was somewhat stronger for men than for women at each education level, and stronger for non-college-educated workers than for those who are more educated, but the general pattern is one of declines proportional to the recessionary increase. This appears more consistent with broad-based swings down and then part of the way back up than with tilts favoring some workers; insofar as there have been tilts, they evidently are *toward* low-skill men.

9. Patterns across groups and over time are similar for employment rates.

ACCOUNTING FOR HETEROGENEITY IN CYCLICAL SENSITIVITY

As noted, the construction and manufacturing industries suffered dramatic employment declines in the downturn. This is not surprising; these sectors have always been more cyclically sensitive than the economy as a whole. Because they disproportionately employ less-skilled men, such workers suffer more than others in every downturn and see better improvements in every recovery. Similarly, youth unemployment has always been highly sensitive to economic conditions (Clark and Summers 1982). This differential sensitivity can account for most of the heterogeneity in outcomes across groups seen in figure 5.

Figures 6 through 8 illustrate this for several different labor market groupings. For each demographic group, I compute the change in unemployment that would have been predicted between 2007 and 2014 given the past cyclical sensitivity of that group's unemployment and the magnitude of the cycle. To form this prediction, for each group g I estimate a time series regression of the form:

$$u_{gt} = \alpha_g + u_{(-g)t}\beta_g + e_{gt}, \qquad (1)$$

where u_{gt} is the unemployment rate for group g in month t and $u_{(-g)t}$ is the average unemployment rate in that month across all groups other than g.[10] The β_g coefficient is analogous to an equity price's beta, and measures the extent to which group g moves with the market: A value of β_g greater than 1 indicates that group g is more cyclically sensitive than others; less than 1 indicates relative insensitivity. I estimate α_g and β_g using monthly observations from 1978 through 2007, then use these coefficients and the observed path of $u_{(-g)t}$ to forecast u_{gt} through 2014.

Figure 6 shows the actual change in unemployment and the change in average forecast values from 2007 to 2014, by gender and education.[11] The figure shows that most of the across-group differences in unemployment growth between 2007 and 2014 are attributable to differences in cyclical sensitivity rather than to unique features of this business cycle. In particular, more-educated workers are always less sensitive than less-educated workers, and that has been true in this period as well. However, the cyclical predictions are not perfect. The most important deviation from the prediction is men without high school diplomas: on the basis of past performance, we would expect their unemployment rate to have been nearly two percentage points higher in 2014 than was actually observed. By contrast, men with college degrees have an unemployment rate a full percentage point higher than before the recession, roughly double the increase that would have been expected based on past patterns. Women of all skill groups have also seen larger increases than past patterns would suggest. These comparisons again suggest that any shifts in demand have been toward low-skill men, away from men with college degrees and from women.

Figure 7 provides another look at the experience of male high school graduates. Here I show the time series of the actual unemployment rate along with predictions from equation (1). (Both series are smoothed; the dashed segment of the latter indicates the out-of-sample portion.) The predicted and actual rates track each other extremely closely, through past business cycles and the current one. The actual experience for this group was worse than the prediction in the depths of the Great Recession, and even for about a year preceding the collapse, but the discrepancy was small relative to the predictable component and closed quickly during the recovery. (An even smaller gap has reopened since 2014.) While other work has documented long-run declines in demand

---

10. I compute $u_{(-g)t}$ using fixed weights for each group $h \neq g$ over time, proportional to the group's average labor force share over the 1978 to 2015 period. I focus on unemployment rather than employment here because the prediction model for employment would need to accommodate secular trends in labor force participation; unemployment has been closer to stationary.

11. Results are similar if I instead predict the change as the difference between the predicted 2014 rate and the actual 2007 rate. In either case I focus on annual averages to avoid seasonality concerns, although the prediction is conducted at the monthly level.

Figure 6. Actual and Predicted Change in Unemployment Rate, 2007–2014, by Gender and Education

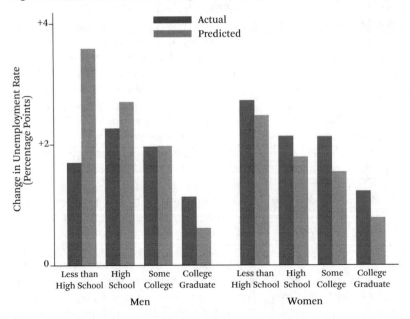

Source: Author's analysis of Current Population Survey data.
Notes: Dark bars show the change between the 2007 and 2014 annual averages of non-seasonally adjusted monthly unemployment rates. Lighter bars show differences in similar averages of predicted unemployment rates, obtained as the fitted values of a regression of the monthly unemployment rate in the gender-education group on calendar month dummies and the unemployment rate across the rest of the labor force, using data from 1978 to 2007.

Figure 7. Actual and Predicted Unemployment Rate of Male High School Graduates, 1978–May 2016

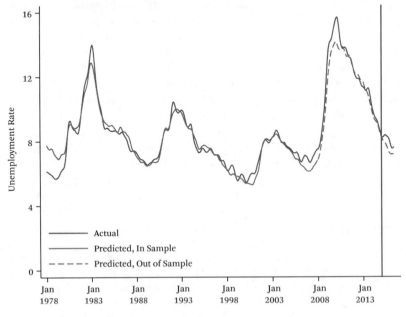

Source: Author's analysis of Current Population Survey data.
Notes: Both series are seasonally adjusted, and smoothed using a three-month triangle smoother. See notes to figure 6 for explanation of predicted unemployment rate series.

Figure 8. Actual and Predicted Change in Unemployment Rate, 2007–2014, by Age

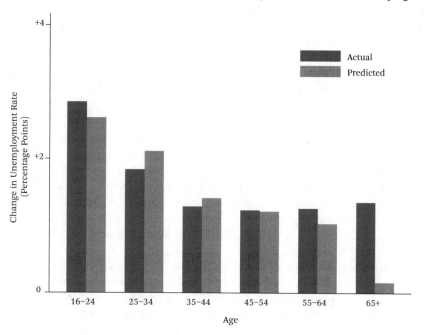

Source: Author's analysis of Current Population Survey data.
Note: See notes to figure 6.

for this group of low-skilled workers, this has evidently not shown up in the unemployment rate, which has been dominated by cyclical factors.

Figure 8 repeats the exercise from figure 6, this time looking at age groups. Unemployment rates rose much more for young people between 2007 and 2014 than for those aged thirty-five and over. But this is always the case in weak labor markets; the unemployment rate for those twenty-five to thirty-four actually rose slightly less than one would have expected, and in any case the difference is small. The only meaningful deviation from predictions is for those aged sixty-five and over: this group's unemployment rate is ordinarily not very cyclically sensitive, but between 2007 and 2014 it rose as much as those for prime-age workers.

One sees similar patterns when looking across industries (not shown). Insofar as there have been structural shifts, they have apparently been toward the goods-producing industries and away from the high-skill services. Unemployment rates remained higher in 2014 than in 2007 for essentially all ages, education levels, genders, and industries. Sectors that

have been more cyclically sensitive in the past saw larger increases, but there is remarkably little heterogeneity beyond this. This pattern appears consistent with a shortfall in aggregate labor demand, and less so with a gradual adjustment to a technological or demand-driven shock that changed the composition of labor demand.

EVIDENCE FROM WAGES

The evidence presented thus far suggests that differential unemployment outcomes over the last several years across education, gender, and age have been largely consistent with what past cyclical patterns would have implied, given the overall state of the labor market. But the unemployment rate is at last now reasonably low, whereas other indicators—the employment-to-population ratio in particular—remain quite depressed. We thus face the important question of whether the economy has fully recovered, with recent outcomes being "the new normal," or whether there remains substantial slack, either in the aggregate or in particular labor markets. There is some disagreement among indicators here, with the job openings rate indicating that (at least some) labor markets are tight and with other indicators—the employment-population ratio or the quits series, for example—indicating that (possibly other) markets are slack.

To adjudicate this issue, we need to look beyond quantities data to prices. If employers are facing shortages of suitable, interested workers—either throughout the economy or in particular labor markets—they should be responding by bidding up the wages of those workers who can be found, presumably above where they were at the last cyclical peak. By contrast, if the large number of people who have moved out of the labor force in the last few years are still relevant to the labor market, then there are in fact a great many workers per job opening, and there is no reason for employers to increase wages. Thus, in this section I examine wage trends for evidence of tightness. I examine the aggregate labor market first, then turn to distinctions across sub-markets.

Aggregate Wages

The solid line in figure 9 graphs the twelve-month change in real mean log hourly wages from 1999 through May 2016. These wages are calculated from the Current Population Survey Outgoing Rotation Groups (CPS ORG), with imputed wages excluded; see the appendix for further details.[12] The figure shows that the last sustained period of mean real wage growth ended in 2002. Average wages were largely stable between 2003 and late 2014, except for a period in late 2008 and 2009 when they rose at an annual rate of about 3 percent and a shorter

period in 2011 when they fell at a −2 percent annual rate.[13] Outside of these periods there was little movement. The most recent data, however, show some signs of strength, with growth at around a 3 percent annual rate in 2015, falling to a 2 percent rate in the first part of 2016.

One concern about aggregate wage trends is composition changes: if the least-skilled workers are the most likely to have lost their jobs in the Great Recession, changes in average wages will overstate what was experienced by individual workers. To address this concern, I use the longitudinal structure of the CPS to match observations on the same individual from month m and month $m+12$, excluding observations that cannot be matched or where the wage is unavailable in either.[14] The dashed line in figure 9, labeled "composition-adjusted," shows the mean year-on-year change in mean wages for those who were employed in both periods. Note that this overstates the growth for workers with constant characteristics, as in this sample the year-on-year change incorporates the effect of aging by one year. In part for this reason, this series is consistently about two points higher than the "all workers" series, and shows average growth of about 3 percent per year between 1999 and 2009. The anomaly in 2008–2009 is reduced here and is plausibly consistent with sampling error. Average growth fell to near zero in 2009, not to reappear until late 2011; it remained around 2 percent for the next several years, only rising above that in 2015.

Workers rarely accept—or perhaps employers rarely demand—reductions in their nominal

12. The CPS is not the only source for information on wage trends, and measures based on employer surveys offer larger samples. But the CPS is the best option for adjusting wages for worker observables or for focusing on newly hired workers. Other series show similar patterns for the "all workers" series depicted by the solid line in figure 9.

13. The price level was falling during much of the 2008–2009 period of real wage growth; nominal wage growth actually slowed in the second half of 2008 and early 2009, from around 4 percent per year to under 2 percent. Similarly, the slowdown in real wage growth in late 2009 and early 2010 reflects stable nominal growth (at an annual rate of about 1.5 percent) and the return of mild inflation.

14. Roughly 40 percent of initial observations lack one-year-ahead wages, about two-thirds of the time because the individual cannot be matched to a year-ahead observation (due to having moved from the original home, to survey nonresponse, or to errors in the CPS identifiers) and the remainder because the person is surveyed in the follow-up but is no longer employed or lacks a valid wage. Attrition among the continuously employed may be correlated with wage growth. The reweighting exercise described in the text partially addresses this possibility.

Figure 9. Twelve-Month Change in Mean Wages (Percent)

Source: Author's analysis of Current Population Survey data.
Notes: Composition-adjusted series compares wages within individuals across surveys twelve months apart. New Jobs are those within the previous three months. All series are weighted by weekly hours and smoothed using a three-month (nine-month for the new jobs series) triangle smoother.

wages within existing jobs. This rigidity may have masked trends in the wages offered to new hires. To zero in on the latter, I take advantage of the fact that the CPS makes it possible to identify workers in the ORG sample who have started new jobs within the previous three months. The dotted line in figure 9 shows the trend in mean wages for such workers. This series closely resembles the "all workers" series, with a similar pattern of rising real wages in 2008–2009, falling real wages starting in early 2010, and moderate growth in the most recent data.

Thus, aggregate data suggest that the labor market remained weak, with too little demand to generate even modest wage growth, at least until late 2014. Wages have begun growing since then. This is perhaps consistent with the long-delayed arrival of labor market tightness that is forcing employers to offer higher wages in order to attract and retain workers. Even in the recent data, however, the growth rate is modest, and the recent trend would need to

continue for some time to make up for the roughly zero average growth over the previous decade.

Individual Labor Markets

As discussed earlier, aggregate data can mask differences across individual labor markets. It is possible that particular labor markets are tighter and showing more dramatic wage growth than is apparent in figure 9, or that some markets tightened earlier than 2015 even while others remained slack. To examine this, I examine changes in employment, hours, and wages of newly hired workers by education, gender, age, and industry between 2007–2008 and 2013–2014. Note that this window ends before the most recent run-up.

Columns 1 and 2 of table 1 show estimated changes (and standard errors) in mean wages of newly hired workers in different submarkets. Note that these are cumulative changes over six years, not annual rates of increase. To limit confounding due to changes in the composition of workers—as would occur, say, if manufacturing hires shifted from unskilled laborers to skilled machine operators—I use a regression to adjust for changes in workers' observed characteristics. Specifically, I regress log real hourly wages for new hires in the period 2004–2006 on a quadratic in age; indicators for education-by-gender, state, and industry-by-education; and separate linear age terms for each gender-education group. I then use the coefficients to form predicted log wages for new hires in 2007 and later, and compare these to the observed wages. Table 1 shows the change in the mean log wage residual in each cell and the standard error for this change.

Across education-by-gender and age cells, only over-sixty-five workers (and, to a much lesser extent, those aged fifty-five to sixty-four) saw nontrivial real wage increases over this period, amounting to a bit over 1 percent per year. Across industries, nontrivial wage changes are seen in mining and logging and in finance and insurance, though only the second is statistically significant and each is less than 1 percent per year over the period. There is thus no sign of mean wages being bid up at the level of education groups, age, or broad industrial sectors.

Columns 3 to 6 of table 1 present other indicators of labor market tightness: the change in total employment and the change in the average number of hours worked. (Employment changes are measured in percentage points on the employment-population ratio for education-by-gender and age groups, and as percentages for industry groups. Neither is adjusted for observables as in columns 1 and 2.) A few industries did see substantial employment growth over this period, but this is not in general matched by substantial wage growth. The mining and logging sector, as noted earlier, is the exception that proves the rule; among other industries, only education and lodging and food services saw increases in both employment and wages, and in each case the wage increases were trivial. Across demographic

groups, only the 65-plus age category saw an increase in the employment rate.[15] The story is similar for hours. Two sectors—finance and insurance and education—show small increases in average hours, but of these only finance shows any tightness on other margins. Taken as a whole there is little sign of tightness.

This analysis thus suggests that essentially none of the identified markets have tightened to the point where demand began to outstrip supply, at least by the end of 2014. It nevertheless remains possible that these market definitions are too coarse and that employers in more tightly defined submarkets have had trouble finding workers with suitable skills. Falling demand in other submarkets might make it impossible to detect rising wages for workers in short supply via examinations of highly aggregated averages.

One way to assess this is to examine points in the wage distribution other than the mean. If some markets are tight, it might be possible to see this manifested as a rightward shift in the relevant portion of the wage distribution. I compared the 2007–2008 and 2013–2014 distributions of starting wages, adjusted for observable characteristics as in columns 1 and 2 of table 1. The solid line in figure 10 shows the change in wages at different percentiles in the new-hires adjusted wage distribution between the two periods.[16] Thus, for example, it indicates that the 75th percentile of this distribution was roughly unchanged; that the upper quartile of the distribution shifted right by as much as three percentage points, and that everywhere below the 75th percentile the distribution shifted left by a similar magnitude. This figure thus shows that any wage increases were concentrated in the upper quartile of workers, and that even here real wages increased by less than half a percentage point per year.

For comparison, figure 10 also shows comparable measures of the changes in real wage distributions between 2000–2001 and 2005–2006 and between 1994–1995 and 1999–2000. The former closely resembles the pattern in the

15. Recall from figure 8 that the older workers' unemployment rate also rose. As figure 16 shows, labor force participation rose substantially for those sixty-five and over.

16. To eliminate spurious changes due to changes in the real value of the CPS topcodes, I censor weekly earnings at the real value of the 2015 topcode.

Table 1. Change in Employment Rates, Working Hours, and Mean Real Wages Adjusted for Observables of New Hires, 2007–2008 to 2013–2014

	Δ Mean Real Wages Adjusted for Observables (Percent)		Δ Employment Rate (Percentage Points)		Δ Weekly Hours	
		SE		SE		SE
	(1)	(2)	(3)	(4)	(5)	(6)
Overall	−1.7	(0.3)	−3.8	(0.0)	−0.42	(0.02)
By education and gender						
Male, less than high school	−2.1	(1.1)	−5.3	(0.2)	−0.03	(0.07)
Male, high school diploma	−1.8	(0.9)	−6.1	(0.1)	−0.71	(0.04)
Male, some college	−3.4	(0.9)	−5.9	(0.1)	−0.96	(0.04)
Male, college graduate (B.A.+)	−1.3	(1.0)	−3.7	(0.1)	−0.82	(0.04)
Female, less than high school	−1.6	(1.2)	−3.7	(0.2)	−0.39	(0.09)
Female, high school diploma	−0.7	(0.9)	−5.1	(0.1)	−0.71	(0.04)
Female, some college	−1.3	(0.8)	−5.3	(0.1)	−0.62	(0.04)
Female, college graduate (B.A.+)	−1.7	(0.9)	−2.9	(0.1)	0.10	(0.04)
By age						
16–24	−3.8	(0.6)	−5.1	(0.1)	−0.69	(0.05)
25–34	−2.2	(0.7)	−3.4	(0.1)	−0.56	(0.03)
35–44	−1.9	(0.8)	−2.7	(0.1)	−0.38	(0.03)
45–54	−2.6	(0.8)	−3.3	(0.1)	−0.36	(0.03)
55–64	1.4	(1.1)	−0.8	(0.1)	−0.05	(0.04)
65+	4.6	(2.1)	1.9	(0.1)	0.88	(0.08)
By industry						
Agriculture	0.0	(3.0)	percent Δ		−0.61	(0.37)
Mining and logging	4.8	(3.7)	23.1		−0.39	(0.22)
Construction	−3.8	(1.4)	−19.4		−0.02	(0.06)
Durable goods mfg.	−1.0	(1.4)	−12.9		−0.03	(0.05)
Nondurable goods mfg.	−0.8	(1.8)	−11.0		−0.40	(0.06)
Wholesale trade	−4.5	(2.3)	−3.4		−0.10	(0.08)
Retail trade	−4.1	(0.9)	−1.0		−0.86	(0.05)
Transport and utilities	−1.3	(1.8)	2.2		−0.38	(0.08)
Information	−0.6	(2.7)	−10.1		−0.06	(0.10)
Finance and insurance	3.4	(1.7)	−4.0		0.35	(0.05)
Real estate	−5.3	(3.1)	−5.7		−0.11	(0.12)
Professional and business services	−2.9	(1.1)	6.2		−0.41	(0.05)
Education (private)	0.4	(2.0)	16.1		0.06	(0.10)
Health and social assistance	−2.3	(1.0)	14.5		−0.18	(0.04)
Arts and recreation	−2.2	(2.4)	6.7		−0.84	(0.13)
Lodging and food services	0.6	(1.0)	9.9		−0.97	(0.06)
Other services	0.0	(1.8)	1.3		−0.78	(0.08)
Federal government	−1.6	(2.1)	−0.1		−0.18	(0.07)
State and local government	−2.2	(1.0)	−1.7		−0.08	(0.04)

Source: Author's analysis of Current Population Survey data.

Notes: Adjusted estimates in columns 1 and 2 are the changes in mean residuals from a log wage regression, estimated on 2004 to 2006 data, with controls for education-by-gender, state, and industry-by-education indicators, an age quadratic, and interactions of a linear age term with education-gender indicators. Regression is estimated only on new hires, defined as those who began their jobs within the previous three months. Standard errors in column 2 do not account for sampling error in the regression coefficients. Industry employment changes are based on Current Employment Survey data.

recent data, consistent with the widespread view that the labor market was never very tight during the post-2001 expansion. The latter series is quite different, with real growth of about 9 percent (nearly 2 percent per year) throughout the distribution. Evidently, in a truly tight labor market, such as was seen during the late 1990s, real wages can grow substantially throughout the distribution.

Figures 11, 12, and 13 explore potential heterogeneity in the 2007–2008 to 2013–2014 distributional change. I do not track individual workers over time, so the analysis here can only examine changes in the (conditional) distribution, not changes for workers at particular points in the distribution. This could lead me to miss tightness in particular markets. For example, increases in wages in a low-wage submarket combined with decreases in a second, slightly higher-wage submarket could offset each other with little effect on the overall distribution. (Note, however, that this is more plausible for unconditional wages; because I examine wages after adjusting for observables, heterogeneous shifts across different submarkets are unlikely to balance out in this way.)

The Current Population Survey sample is not large enough to permit detailed analysis of wage distribution changes within individual industries or geographic groups. As an alternative, I divide the sample into subgroups based on proxies for potential labor market tightness. In figure 11, I divide industrial sectors based on the increase in job openings between 2009 and 2014. The solid line shows the sectors with below-average increases in openings and the dashed line those with above-average increases. Wage declines at the bottom of the distribution are smaller in the latter sectors, consistent with their labor markets' being relatively tight. But even in these industries there is no sign of meaningful wage growth through the bulk of the distribution. Moreover, what growth there is at the top of the conditional wage distribution is coming from industries that have not seen large increases in job openings.

Figure 12 focuses on geography. Here, I divide MSAs into two groups by their 2014 unem-

ployment rates; the solid line shows the change in the distribution of starting wages for areas with unemployment rates above 6.1 percent, the median in 2014, while the dashed line shows areas with rates at or below that point. There is no sign that wage growth was stronger in MSAs with lower unemployment rates.

Figure 13 examines skill levels. Using the same flexible wage regression used to predict wages for table 1, I predict a wage level for each newly hired worker in the CPS. I divide workers in half based on this predicted wage, plotting the change in the distribution of starting wages for the less-skilled group with a solid line and the more-skilled group with a dashed line. Insofar as the market for more-skilled workers has tightened more than that for less-skilled workers, we should see the dashed line systematically above the solid line. This is not at all apparent in the figure. Through the middle of the distribution the dashed line is somewhat above the solid line, though not by much, and through most of this range is still negative. In the tails, lower-skill workers seem to have done a bit better than have higher-skill workers.[17]

Figure 14 takes another approach to examining skill differences. Here I compute the cumulative change in mean log real wages from January 2007 forward, separately for four education groups. Wages for the three sub-baccalaureate groups move together throughout the period, with falling wages in early 2007; stagnation in late 2007 and early 2008; recovery in 2008–2009; sustained declines, cumulating to roughly 6 percent, from mid-2009 through 2013; and recovery beginning in late 2014. Mean wages in each group in early 2016 remained 2 to 4 percent below their level nine years before. The college graduates series is the only divergence from this pattern: this group did not see declines in 2007–2008, and although wages did decline between 2009 and 2014, the change was much shallower. College graduates have seen the same growth since 2014 as other groups, but because they began in a better position their wages are now 2 percent above their 2007 level. This is, to be mild, an anemic performance, only 0.2 percent per year.

17. At the lower end of the distribution, the increase for below-average predicted wage workers may reflect increases in the real value of the minimum wage.

Figure 10. Change in Distribution of Starting Wages, by Period

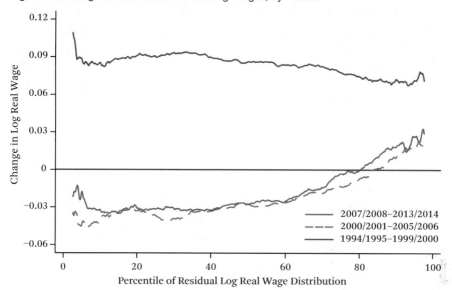

Source: Author's analysis of Current Population Survey data.
Notes: Starting wages are those on jobs that started within the previous three months. Wage distributions are weighted by weekly hours. Percentile changes are computed for each 0.1 percentage point, then smoothed across three adjacent points using a triangle smoother.

Figure 11. Change in Distribution of Starting Wages Between 2007–2008 and 2013–2014, by 2009–2014 Growth in Job Openings in Industry

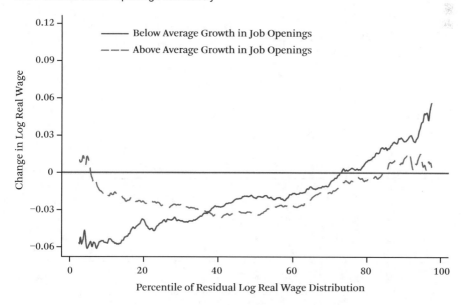

Source: Author's analysis of Current Population Survey data.
Notes: Starting wages are those on jobs that started within the previous three months. Wage distributions are weighted by weekly hours. Percentile changes are computed for each 0.1 percentage point, then smoothed across three adjacent points using a triangle smoother.

Figure 12. Change in Distribution of Starting Wages Between 2007–2008 and 2013–2014, by 2014 Unemployment Rate in Metropolitan Statistical Area

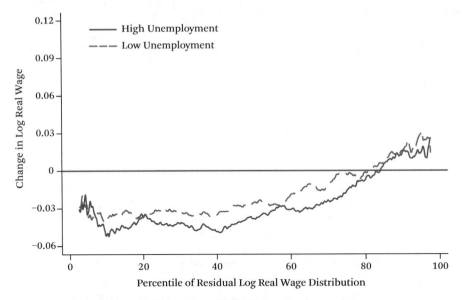

Source: Author's analysis of Current Population Survey data.
Notes: Starting wages are those on jobs that started within the previous three months. Wage distributions are weighted by weekly hours. Percentile changes are computed for each 0.1 percentage point, then smoothed across three adjacent points using a triangle smoother.

Figure 13. Change in Distribution of Starting Wages Between 2007–2008 and 2013–2014, by Predicted Wage

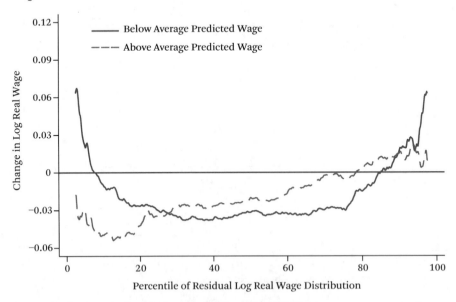

Source: Author's analysis of Current Population Survey data.
Notes: Starting wages are those on jobs that started within the previous three months. Wage distributions are weighted by weekly hours. Percentile changes are computed for each 0.1 percentage point, then smoothed across three adjacent points using a triangle smoother.

Figure 14. Change in Mean Log Real Wages by Education Group Since January 2007

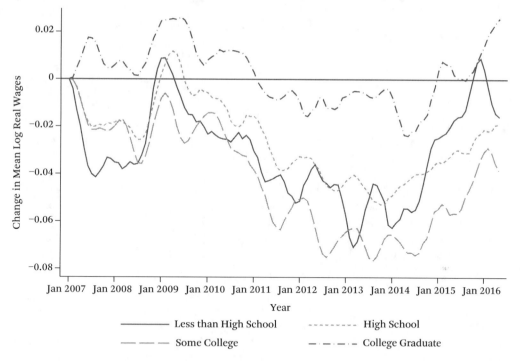

Source: Author's analysis of Current Population Survey data.

Note: Wages are weighted by weekly hours and smoothed using a seven-month triangle smoother.

Across all of the breakdowns in figures 10 through 14 there is no sign of any quantitatively important segment of the labor market where demand has meaningfully outstripped supply in recent years. Wage increases are modest throughout the distribution and are no stronger in submarkets that might plausibly be tight (such as industries with large increases in job openings, or MSAs with low unemployment rates) than in those that clearly are not. Wage pressures appear to have been modest, at least through the end of 2014, throughout the economy. Since then there is some sign of modest growth, but this has a long way to go to catch up to any plausible estimate of productivity growth since 2007.

IMPLICATIONS FOR THE FUTURE

The results thus far demonstrate that supply-side explanations cannot account for the anemic performance of the labor market since the Great Recession, and that demand remained quite slack through at least the end of 2014 and, by most indications, beyond. An important question is whether this sustained demand shortfall will leave an overhang when demand eventually recovers, due to atrophied job skills or other sources of hysteresis.

Forecasting the future is of course hazardous—we have no direct measures of the employability of those out of work. In this section, I investigate two indicators that may be informative about this: transitions out of long-term unemployment, and trends in labor force participation and school enrollment by age.

Reemployment Flows

Much commentary about the labor market during and after the Great Recession has focused on the long-term unemployed. The share of the unemployed who have been out of work for twenty-six weeks or more rose from approximately 17 or 18 percent on the eve of the Great Recession to 45 percent in mid-2010, far higher than had ever been seen before. It has fallen slowly since then, but remains only slightly below the pre-2007 series record, set in 1983.

Hysteresis effects would likely be concen-

Table 2. Unemployment Rates and Long-Term Unemployment Shares by Demographic Group, 2006 and 2014

	Unemployment Rate (Percent)		Long–Term Unemployment Share	
	2006 (1)	2014 (2)	2006 (3)	2014 (4)
Overall	4.6	6.2	21.2	37.3
By education and gender				
Male, less than high school	9.3	11.6	19.5	33.3
Male, high school diploma	5.7	8	22.9	39.4
Male, some college	3.9	6	21.6	37.3
Male, college graduate (B.A.+)	2.1	3.3	26.4	40.5
Female, less than high school	11.5	14.3	17.5	32.4
Female, high school diploma	5.4	7.5	21.1	38.5
Female, some college	4.2	6.2	20.1	35.8
Female, college graduate (B.A.+)	2.3	3.5	20.8	38.1
By age				
16–24	10.5	13.4	15.1	26.4
25–34	4.7	6.5	19.6	37.5
35–44	3.6	4.7	24.1	39.9
45–54	3.1	4.4	27	44.3
55–64	3	4.4	31.4	48.7
65+	2.9	4.6	24.4	47.4

Source: Author's analysis of Current Population Survey data.

Note: The long-term unemployment share is the fraction of the unemployed who have been out of work twenty-seven weeks or more.

trated among the long-term unemployed. Indeed, Kory Kroft, Fabian Lange, and Matthew J. Notowidigdo (2013) find that employers discriminate against the long-term unemployed in hiring (but see Farber, Silverman, and von Wachter, this volume), and Krueger, Cramer, and Cho (2014; see also Hall 2014) conclude that these workers are largely disconnected from the labor market, exerting little supply pressure.

Table 2 shows unemployment rates and long-term unemployment shares across various demographic categories in 2006 and 2014. The long-term unemployment share does not vary nearly as much across gender and education as does the unemployment rate. More-educated workers, whose unemployment rates are very low, tend to have somewhat higher long-term unemployment shares than do those with less education. Across ages, long-term unemployment is somewhat more prevalent among older workers, but the differences are relatively small except in the sixteen-to-twenty-four-year-old group (many of whom have not been in the labor force for long enough to reach long-term unemployment). The general pattern of differences is similar in 2014 as in 2006, again suggesting that there has not been some new technological change in recent years that has left particular groups of workers permanently out of the workforce.

Figure 15 shows the probability that a worker who is unemployed in one month is reemployed in the following month.[18] I show esti-

18. I compute reemployment rates following the procedure used by Rothstein (2011) and Henry Farber and Robert G. Valletta (2013), counting individuals who transit from unemployment to employment, then immediately back to unemployment in the following month, as having remained unemployed throughout. As discussed in

Figure 15. Reemployment Hazards for Unemployed Works, by Duration Group

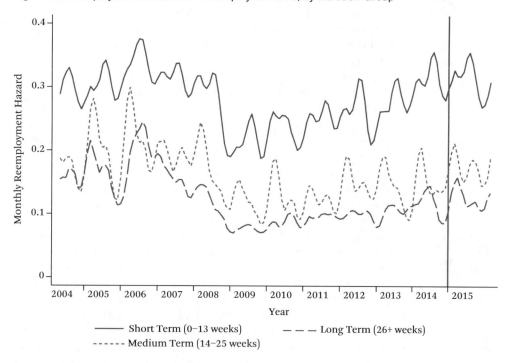

Source: Author's analysis of Current Population Survey data.
Notes: A worker who is unemployed in one month is counted as having been reemployed if he or she is employed in the next month and does not return to unemployment in the month after that. Series are smoothed using a five-month triangle smoother.

mates for three categories of unemployed workers: those who have been unemployed thirteen weeks or less in the initial month; those who have been out of work for fourteen to twenty-five weeks; and the long-term unemployed whose durations of unemployment exceed twenty-six weeks. The figure shows that reemployment rates decline with unemployment duration, primarily when comparing short-term to medium-term unemployed. This might reflect hysteresis, employer discrimination among the unemployed, declines in search effort with unemployment duration (Krueger and Mueller 2011), or heterogeneity in reemployment probabilities. Interestingly, however, the gap in exit rates between the short- and long-term unemployed did not widen dramatically even as the level of the exit rate fell during the recession—all three groups' exit rates fell sharply in 2008, and have recovered slowly since then.[19] The recovery has been perhaps a bit faster for the short-term unemployed; the medium- and long-term unemployed groups have tracked each other quite closely on a slightly shallower trajectory.

Even the depressed reemployment rate seen in recent years, around 10 percent per month, means that half of the long-term unemployed will find new jobs within six months. (The half-life would be three months if the reemployment

---

the two papers cited, many of these repeated transitions appear to derive from misclassification of labor force status in the middle month (see also Poterba and Summers 1986).

19. Krueger et al. (2014) find that the long-term unemployed who transition into jobs are much less likely to remain employed a year later than their short-term unemployed peers. But these rates, too, seem to move in parallel, indicating that little has changed relative to the pre-recession period other than a downward shift in all job searchers' job-finding and job-keeping rates.

rate were 20 percent, as it was before the downturn.) This is not consistent with a long overhang from the stock of long-term unemployed.

One might worry nevertheless that this average rate masks important heterogeneity, and that a subgroup of the long-term unemployed are essentially unemployable. But the similarity of the exit rates for the medium- and long-term unemployed counsels against this view, as with plausible heterogeneity these groups would have quite different compositions (Heckman and Singer 1984). For example, suppose that four-fifths of the newly jobless were highly employable, with monthly reemployment rates of 40 percent, while the remaining fifth were hard to employ, with exit rates of only 5 percent. In this case, the average exit rate for the short-term unemployed would be around 30 percent and that for the medium-term group would be around 16 percent, both consistent with the recent data. But very few of the first group would wind up in long-term unemployment, so the reemployment rate for those who do last that long would be well under 10 percent. That we do not see this divergence does not appear consistent with a heterogeneity model.

Together, then, the evidence on flows from long-term employment into jobs does not seem to be consistent with the existence of a large group of unemployed workers who will remain hard to employ even when the labor market recovers. Although there is no guarantee that the pattern of generally parallel movements seen in figure 15 will persist in the future, it appears likely in light of recent history. If so, then we might expect that a robust labor market—if one ever arrives—will pull the long-term unemployed back from the margins of the market and into higher levels of attachment. Note, moreover, that there is no inconsistency between this optimistic view and the evidence (see, for example, Kroft et al. 2013 and Krueger et al. 2014) that the long-term unemployed do not compete effectively with the short-term unemployed for work; under this story, those who have been out of work for many months are at the margins of the labor market, but if employer demand is robust enough to exhaust other sources of labor, firms will figure out ways to employ even them (Bernstein and Baker 2003).

Labor Market Participation and School Enrollment

The evidence just discussed concerns the long-term unemployed. The other group of great concern going forward is those who have left the labor force entirely. If they have become harder to employ because of extended periods of idleness, this does not bode well for their likelihood of returning to work in the future. On the other hand, insofar as the nonparticipants have taken advantage of their time out of the labor force to build skills, one might expect them to be even stronger candidates for new job openings than they would have been had they remained in unemployment.

The solid line in figure 16 shows how the employment rate has changed for workers of different ages. To avoid spurious changes coming from vagaries of the academic calendar, I use only data from the academic year, the January–April and September–December surveys, in this figure. Note also that the figure does not compare the same worker over time—the employment rate of, say, twenty-five-year-olds in 2005 is compared to that of twenty-five-year-olds in 2013, born eight years later, not to that of the original cohort of workers, who would be thirty-three in 2013.

Overall, the figure shows increases in participation for those in their sixties and seventies, declines of about four percentage points in the employment rates of prime-age workers, and much sharper declines for the youngest workers (those below thirty). The increase among older workers is almost certainly a labor supply effect, perhaps reflecting declining retirement balances that force people to work longer or generational differences in labor force attachment as baby boomers replace earlier cohorts among those in their sixties. Recall from earlier that this group's unemployment rate has gone up as well. (One plausible explanation turns out not to hold up, however: the increase does not reflect rising female labor force attachment in later-born cohorts, as it is similar for men as for women.)

The dramatic decline in the employment rate of the youngest cohorts is a big cause for concern: if young people never get a toehold in the formal economy early in their careers it may be difficult to integrate them later. Past

Figure 16. Change in Employment Rate and Non-idleness Rate by Age, 2005–2006 to 2013–2014

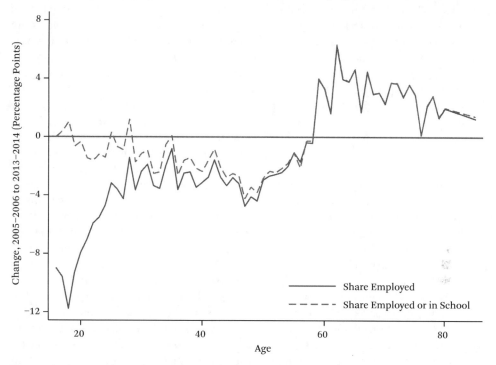

Source: Author's analysis of Current Population Survey data.
Note: Computed from monthly CPS files from January to April and September to December of each year.

evidence indicates that people who enter the labor market in bad economic times see reduced earnings for many years thereafter (Kahn 2010; Oreopoulos, von Wachter, and Heisz 2012). Moreover, changes in labor force participation (not shown) are similar to those in employment—the share of the youngest age groups who are out of the labor force has grown dramatically.

But the dashed line in the figure suggests a much more optimistic story. This line shows the change in an expanded concept of "non-idleness" that includes employment or enrollment in school but not unemployment or nonparticipation among nonstudents. There is no decline here for young workers. Evidently, *all* of the young people who would have been employed in 2005–2006 but were not in 2013–2014 were instead enrolled in school. Pooling all ages, the non-idleness rate fell by only 2.5 percentage points between 2005–2006 and 2013–2014, much less than the 3.9 percentage-point decline in the employment rate.

It is not clear whether this is a labor supply effect (as would arise if it is taking longer for students to finish school or if full-time students are less interested in working while in school than in the past) or a demand effect, reflecting young people remaining in school as a way of waiting out the weak labor market. But concerning the question of whether the lower employment rate reflects a permanent, structural decline in our economy's capacity, the evidence in figure 16 is quite encouraging. It suggests, first, that the supply side of the market is responding to labor market weakness in a way likely to ameliorate any mismatch between changing skill demands and the fixed stock of skills supplied by existing workers and, second, that scarring effects from prolonged weakness are likely to be smaller than they would be if young people were truly remaining idle for years on end.

Additional analyses, not reported here, show that the educational attainment of recent cohorts has risen dramatically, as the additional school enrollment is translating to additional college degrees. This is likely to translate into improved earnings capacity and prosperity in the years to come, although the question remains unresolved whether the additional human capital earned in school will be enough to offset the reduced experience and increased difficulty in getting a toehold on the job ladder experienced by cohorts coming of age in recent years.

DISCUSSION

The performance of the U.S. labor market since 2006 can fairly be described as catastrophic: the unemployment rate was above 8 percent for over three straight years; although it has since come down, the employment-population ratio, which fell by nearly four percentage points after 2007, remains extremely depressed. As in past downturns, this has hit traditionally disadvantaged groups—the less-educated, the young, and members of racial and ethnic minorities—particularly hard.

Many models that economists have used to understand business cycles have difficulty accounting for demand shortfalls that last for many years. In such models, sustained high unemployment can arise only if there are structural impediments to labor market clearing— the unemployed are not looking very hard for work, have raised their reservation wages (the wage level they demand in order to take a job) due to increased implicit taxes on work (including actual taxes as well as benefits foregone), or are in some sense unsuitable for the jobs that are available, perhaps because they lack the appropriate skills or are unwilling to move to where the jobs are.

Drawing in part on these models, many observers have concluded that structural impediments to recovery must have been an important component of the situation from 2010 to 2014. My review of the evidence offers no support for this diagnosis, however. The poor labor market outcomes for low-skill workers are en-

tirely consistent with cyclical explanations, as these workers have always been more sensitive to the business cycle. The most plausible sources of structural problems—labor supply disincentives caused by conditional transfers such as unemployment insurance or geographic immobility caused by housing market frictions—do not appear to be quantitatively important.[20] Moreover, the Beveridge Curve provides at best weakly suggestive evidence regarding the state of the matching function.

Indirect evidence also fails to support the claim. Structural explanations for inadequate recovery, whether due to supply reductions or to mismatch, imply that the labor market has actually been much tighter than it has appeared, at least as viewed from the perspective of potential employers. There is no sign in the data that employers with jobs to fill have had trouble filling them, except perhaps in a few isolated and small submarkets such as resource extraction. Wages have fallen or been stagnant nearly across the board; in the few subgroups where wages have increased (for example, for college graduates), the increase has been anemic and much slower than even the slow rate of recent productivity growth.

We can thus conclude that labor demand shortfalls continued to be an important feature of the labor market and the primary determinant of labor market performance, at least through the end of 2014. While there is some sign of wage growth in 2015 and 2016, it remains modest and has only begun to make up the shortfalls from previous years. There is no support for the view that the anemic recovery to date has been driven by supply shortfalls due to changes in labor supply behavior or mismatch between employer needs and the available pool of labor.

With that said, several caveats are in order. First, although my results point to the importance of aggregate labor demand in understanding recent trends, this is not the place to address the question of how policy might stim-

---

20. Unemployment insurance extensions can explain only about 0.3 percentage points of the 2011 unemployment rate (Rothstein 2011). With regard to geographic mobility, declines are concentrated among renters who should not have been directly affected by the decline in home values (Farber 2012), and any "house lock" effect is quantitatively small (Schmitt and Warner 2011). The most likely explanations for the mobility decline are not consistent with mismatch stories (Kaplan and Schulhofer-Wohl 2015).

ulate additional demand. The results here speak to the importance of accomplishing that goal, but not to the best way to do so.

Second, I have not discussed longer-run structural changes, such as deindustrialization or skill-biased technical change, which may have proceeded smoothly previous to, during, and after the recession. Rather, I have focused exclusively on the very short run, looking for signs of structural explanations for changes between 2007 and the present. My analysis speaks to the question of whether increases in aggregate demand might return our labor market to something resembling its 2007 state, but not to whether further increases could reverse longer-run trends toward reduced male employment-population ratios and higher inequality. Some policy responses—education and training programs and increased income support for low earners in particular—may make sense as a response to long-term trends, even if they cannot be expected to contribute meaningfully in the short run so long as the market is demand constrained.

Third, it is possible that structural changes did occur on the supply side of the market but that these were masked for many years by low aggregate demand. This could help to explain the real wage increases that we have seen at long last in 2015 and 2016. To date, these have not proceeded far enough to signify serious tightness—most workers' wages remain lower than in 2007. But if they persist, there will likely be room for policies aimed at improving job matching, such as search and mobility assistance, and thereby at expanding effective supply.

Finally, and most important: an extremely long downturn is likely to cast a long shadow over our future prosperity, even if this shadow falls more on wages than on employment rates. Productivity has been low in recent years, so even if wages had kept up with productivity the growth would have been unimpressive. Workers displaced in the recession of the early 1980s faced large declines in future earnings, amounting to 20 percent losses even fifteen to twenty years after their initial displacement (von Wachter, Song, and Manchester 2011), and also saw substantial declines in their life expectancy (Sullivan and von Wachter 2009). Other research indicates that young people who enter the labor market during recessions see long-run negative earnings effects (Oreopoulos, von Wachter, and Heisz 2012; Kahn 2010) and that parental job loss hurts children's schooling and labor market outcomes (Oreopoulos, Page and Stevens 2008; Stevens and Schaller 2011; Ananat, Gassman-Pines, and Gibson-Davis 2011). This evidence implies that the extended period of weakness and slow recovery following the Great Recession has produced negative repercussions that will last for decades to come.

DATA APPENDIX

This appendix describes the data used for the wage analyses in the "Evidence from Wages" section. The basis for these analyses is a sample constructed by pooling CPS ORGs from May 2004 through May 2016.

For hourly workers who do not report that they usually receive overtime pay or who report that their weekly hours vary, I use the self-reported hourly wage. For other workers I use weekly earnings divided by weekly hours. Hours are constructed as usual hours on the primary job if that is available. If not, I use actual hours in the previous week if the individual had only one job and if these hours are consistent with the self-reported part-time or full-time status. Otherwise, hours are set to missing (as are wages if the hourly wage is not reported directly).

To protect respondents' confidentiality, those whose weekly earnings are above $2,884 are reported at that level (known as the "topcode") in the CPS data. I inflate topcoded earnings by 40 percent. For the distributional analyses in figures 10 through 13, I impose a new topcode equal to the lowest real value of the topcode over the relevant period—2007 to 2014 for most analyses, but 1994 to 2000 or 2000 to 2006 for others—but do not inflate this to avoid creating holes in the wage distribution. I adjust for inflation using the monthly CPI-U (Consumer Price Index for Urban Consumers) series, and trim at $1 and $200 (in January 2001 dollars). Observations with allocated hourly wages (or weekly earnings, if those are used) are excluded.

Many of the analyses focus on newly started jobs. These are identified by merging the ORG observation to the regular CPS observations in each of the three previous months. This produces a panel of up to four months. An individual is coded as starting a new job if he or she reported in any but the first of these months that she was in a different job than the month before or that her duties or occupation had changed, or if she moved from non-employed (and not on layoff) to employed during the panel.

REFERENCES

Ananat, Elizabeth O., Anna Gassman-Pines, and Christina M. Gibson-Davis. 2011. "The Effects of Local Employment Losses on Children's Educational Achievement." In *Whither Opportunity? Rising Inequality and the Uncertain Life Chances of Low-Income Children*, edited by Greg J. Duncan and Richard Murnane. New York: Russell Sage Foundation.

Bernstein, Jared, and Dean Baker. 2003. *The Benefits of Full Employment: When Markets Work for People*. Washington, D.C.: Economic Policy Institute.

Bewley, Truman F. 1999. *Why Wages Don't Fall During a Recession*. Cambridge, Mass.: Harvard University Press.

Blanchard, Olivier J., and Peter Diamond. 1989. "The Beveridge Curve." *Brookings Papers on Economic Activity* 1989(1): 1–76.

Clark, Kim B., and Lawrence H. Summers. 1982. "The Dynamics of Youth Unemployment." In *The Youth Labor Market Problem: Its Nature, Causes, and Consequences*, edited by Richard B. Freeman and David S. Wise. Chicago: University of Chicago Press.

Congressional Budget Office. 2012. *Understanding and Responding to Persistently High Unemployment*. Washington: Congressional Budget Office. Available at: https://www.cbo.gov/publication/42989; accessed October 6, 2016.

Davis, Steven J., R. Jason Faberman, and John C. Haltiwanger. 2010. "The Establishment-Level Behavior of Vacancies and Hiring." NBER Working Paper No. W16265. Cambridge, Mass.: National Bureau of Economic Research.

Diamond, Peter. 2010. "Unemployment, Vacancies, Wages." Nobel Prize Lecture (December 8). Available at: http://www.nobelprize.org/nobel_prizes/economic-sciences/laureates/2010/diamond-lecture.pdf; accessed October 6, 2016.

Farber, Henry. 2012. "Unemployment in the Great Recession: Did the Housing Market Crisis Prevent the Unemployed from Moving to Take Jobs?" *American Economic Review* 102(3): 520–25.

Farber, Henry S., Dan Silverman, and Till M. von Wachter. 2017. "Factors Determining Callbacks to Job Applications by the Unemployed: An Audit Study." *RSF: The Russell Sage Foundation Journal of the Social Sciences* 3(3): 168–201. DOI: 10.7758/RSF.2017.3.3.08.

Farber, Henry S., and Robert G. Valletta. 2013. "Do Extended Unemployment Benefits Lengthen Unemployment Spells? Evidence from Recent Cycles in the US Labor Market." NBER Working Paper No. W19048. Cambridge, Mass.: National Bureau of Economic Research.

Ghayad, Rand, and William Dickens. 2012. "What Can We Learn by Disaggregating the Unemployment-Vacancy Relationship?" Public Policy Brief No. 12-3. Boston: Federal Reserve Bank of Boston.

Hall, Robert E. 2014. "Quantifying the Lasting Harm to the U.S. Economy from the Financial Crisis." NBER Working Paper No. W20183. Cambridge, Mass.: National Bureau of Economic Research.

Heckman, James, and Burton Singer. 1984. "A Method for Minimizing the Impact of Distributional Assumptions in Econometric Models for Duration Data." *Econometrica* 52(2): 271–320.

Kahn, Lisa B. 2010. "The Long-Term Labor Market Consequences of Graduating from College in a Bad Economy." *Labour Economics* 17(2): 303–16.

Kaplan, Greg, and Sam Schulhofer-Wohl. 2015. "Understanding the Long-Run Decline in Interstate Migration." Working Paper 697. Minneapolis: Federal Reserve Bank of Minneapolis.

Kocherlakota, Narayana. 2010. "Inside the FOMC." Speech in Marquette, Michigan, August 17.

Kroft, Kory, Fabian Lange, and Matthew J. Notowidigdo. 2013. "Duration Dependence and Labor Market Conditions: Evidence from a Field Experiment." *Quarterly Journal of Economics* 128(3): 1123–67.

Krueger, Alan B., Judd Cramer, and David Cho. 2014. "Are the Long-Term Unemployed on the Margins of the Labor Market?" *Brookings Papers on Economic Activity* 2014 (Spring): 229–80.

Krueger, Alan B., and Andreas Mueller. 2011. "Job Search, Emotional Well-Being, and Job Finding in a Period of Mass Unemployment: Evidence from High Frequency Longitudinal Data." *Brookings Papers on Economic Activity* 2011 (Spring): 1–81.

Lazear, Edward P., and James R. Spletzer. 2012. "The United States Labor Market: Status Quo or a New Normal?" NBER Working Paper No. W18386. Cambridge, Mass.: National Bureau of Economic Research.

Mishel, Lawrence. 2011. "Education Is Not the Cure for High Unemployment or Income Inequality." EPI Briefing Paper No. 286. Washington, D.C.: Economic Policy Institute.

Mishel, Lawrence, Heidi Shierholz, and Kathryn Edwards. 2010. "Reasons for Skepticism About Structural Unemployment: Examining the Demand-Side Evidence." EPI Briefing Paper No. 279. Washington, D.C.: Economic Policy Institute.

Oreopoulos, Philip, Marianne Page, and Ann Huff Stevens. 2008. "Intergenerational Effects of Job Displacement." *Journal of Labor Economics* 26(3): 455–83.

Oreopoulos, Philip, Till von Wachter, and Andrew Heisz. 2012. "The Short- and Long-Term Career Effects of Graduating in a Recession." *American Economic Journal: Applied Economics* 4(1): 1–29.

Poterba, James M., and Lawrence H. Summers. 1986. "Reporting Errors and Labor Market Dynamics." *Econometrica*: 1319–38.

Rothstein, Jesse. 2011. "Unemployment Insurance and Job Search in the Great Recession." *Brookings Papers on Economic Activity* 2011 (Fall): 143–213.

———. 2012. "The Labor Market Four Years into the Crisis: Assessing Structural Explanations." *Industrial and Labor Relations Review* 65(3): 437–500.

———. 2014. "The Great Recession and Its Aftermath: What Role for Structural Changes?" Paper presented to the Building Human Capital and Economic Potential conference. University of Wisconsin (July 2014).

Şahin, Ayşegül, Joseph Song, Giorgio Topa, and Giovanni L. Violante. 2011. "Measuring Mismatch in the U.S. Labor Market." Working paper. New York: Federal Reserve Bank of New York.

Schmitt, John, and Kris Warner. 2011. "Deconstructing Structural Unemployment." Research Report No. 2011-6. Washington, D.C.: Center for Economic Policy Research.

Stevens, Ann Huff, and Jessamyn Schaller. 2011. "Short-Run Effects of Parental Job Loss on Children's Academic Achievement." *Economics of Education Review* 30(2): 289–99.

Sullivan, Daniel, and Till von Wachter. 2009. "Job Displacement and Mortality: An Analysis Using Administrative Data." *Quarterly Journal of Economics* 124(3): 1265–1306.

Summers, Lawrence H. 2016. "The Age of Secular Stagnation: What It Is and What to Do About It." *Foreign Affairs*, February. Available at: https://www.foreignaffairs.com/articles/united-states/2016-02-15/age-secular-stagnation; accessed October 13, 2016.

Vlasic, Bill. 2011. "Detroit Sets Its Future on a Foundation of Two-Tier Wages." *New York Times*, September 12.

von Wachter, Till, Jae Song, and Joyce Manchester. 2011. "Trends in Employment and Earnings of Allowed and Rejected Applicants to the Social Security Disability Insurance Program." *American Economic Review* 101(7): 3308–29.

Weathering the Great Recession: Variation in Employment Responses, by Establishments and Countries

ERLING BARTH, JAMES DAVIS, RICHARD FREEMAN, AND SARI PEKKALA KERR

This paper finds that U.S. employment changed differently relative to output in the Great Recession and recovery than in most other advanced countries or in the United States in earlier recessions. Instead of hoarding labor, U.S. firms reduced employment proportionately more than output in the Great Recession, with establishments that survived the downturn contracting jobs massively. Diverging from the aggregate pattern, U.S. manufacturers reduced employment less than output while the elasticity of employment to gross output varied widely among establishments. In the recovery, growth of employment was dominated by job creation in new establishments. The variegated responses of employment to output challenges extant models of how enterprises adjust employment over the business cycle.

Keywords: Great Recesion, job loss, employment, labor hoarding, cyclical employment patterns

How did the U.S. labor market, widely viewed as the most market-driven and flexible among advanced countries, weather the Great Recession and ensuing recovery? The preceding decades' ballyhoo about the great American jobs machine notwithstanding, employment fell sharply in the Great Recession and increased slowly in the recovery so that in 2015, six years into the recovery, the employment-population ratio was 3.6 points lower than in 2007.[1]

Erling Barth is research professor at the Institute for Social Research, Oslo; professor II at the Center for the Study of Equality and Social Organization at the Department of Economics, University of Oslo; and research economist at the National Bureau of Economic Research. **James Davis** is economist and RDC administrator and team lead at the U.S. Census Bureau. **Richard Freeman** is Ascherman Professor of Economics at Harvard University and director of the Sloan Science Engineering Workforce Project at the National Bureau of Economic Research. **Sari Pekkala Kerr** is senior research scientist at Wellesley College.

© 2017 Russell Sage Foundation. Barth, Erling, James Davis, Richard Freeman, and Sari Pekkala Kerr. 2017. "Weathering the Great Recession: Variation in Employment Responses, by Establishments and Countries." *RSF: The Russell Sage Foundation Journal of the Social Sciences* 3(3): 50–69. DOI: 10.7758/RSF.2017.3.3.03. Any opinions and conclusions expressed in this article are those of the authors and do not necessarily represent the views of the U.S. Census Bureau. All results have been reviewed to ensure that no confidential information is disclosed. This work has received support from the Russell Sage Foundation and the Norwegian Research Council (grant no. 227072). Direct correspondence to: Erling Barth at erling.barth@socialresearch.no, ISF, Munthesgate 31, 0208 Oslo, Norway; James Davis at james.c.davis@census.gov, Boston Census Research Data Center, NBER, 1050 Massachusetts Ave, Cambridge, MA 02138; Richard Freeman at freeman@nber.org, NBER, 1050 Massachusetts Ave, Cambridge, MA 02138; and Sari Pekkala Kerr at skerr3@wellesley.edu, WCW, Wellesley College, 106 Central Street, Wellesley, MA 02481.

1. Based on seasonally adjusted May data from Bureau of Labor Statistics Data, "Series ID: LNS12300000: Employment-Population Ratio, 16 Years and Over," http://data.bls.gov/timeseries/LNS12300000 (accessed August 4, 2016).

This paper combines establishment datasets from Census Research Centers—the Longitudinal Business Data Base (LBD) and the Census and Survey of Manufacturers—with decennial census long-form data on the characteristics of employees in establishments and National Science Foundation data on the research spending of firms to analyze the establishment level underpinnings of employment changes in the Great Recession and during recovery.[2] Appendix A summarizes the characteristics of the LBD and of the other datasets that we combined with the LBD establishment data for our analysis.

The paper finds the following:

1. In the Great Recession U.S. firms reduced labor usage proportionately more than GDP, producing countercyclic changes in productivity, in contrast to labor hoarding in past U.S. recessions and labor hoarding in other advanced countries in the Great Recession.

2. Recession job loss was driven by contraction of jobs in establishments that survived the downturn, whereas recovery job gains came largely from new establishments entering the economy.

3. U.S. manufacturing diverged from the bulk of the economy by hoarding labor in the Great Recession.

4. Manufacturing establishments with observably similar characteristics had widely varying responses of employment to output in the downturn and recovery.[3]

The findings show a substantial gap between models of employment in a flexible labor market and actual employment determination in the aftermath of the Great Recession.

EMPLOYMENT CHANGES DIFFERED THIS TIME

Figures 1 and 2 compare GDP and employment in the Great Recession/recovery and in the three preceding cycles relative to their pre-recession values.

Figure 1 displays the ratio of GDP to pre-recession peak GDP by the number of quarters in each of the recessions. The decline in GDP relative to pre-recession GDP shows that the Great Recession was deeper and longer than the previous three recessions. Befitting its name, the Great Recession's loss of output was the largest since the Great Depression.

Figure 2 displays the ratio of the number of jobs before the recession to the number afterward by number of quarters in each recession, where we calculated the quarterly averages from monthly payroll employment data. Given the big decline in output in the Great Recession, it is no surprise that quarterly employment fell more than in the earlier recessions: an over 6 percent loss of jobs from pre-recession quarterly employment to the quarter when employment bottomed out compared to an average loss of below 3 percent in the other recessions depicted in the figure. The finer grained monthly data shows a drop in employment of 5.3 percent from December 2007, when the NBER (National Bureau of Economic Research) dated the beginning of the recession, to June 2009, when it dated the end of the recession. But employment fell for the first eight months of the recovery, bottoming out in February 2010 at 6.3 percent below its pre-recession peak. Employment in the Great Recession was below its previous peak for 26 quarters, substantially exceeding that for the other recessions.

Comparing the two panels, the link between changes in employment and changes in output as employment weakened, indicating that employment had moved from being a coincident indicator of the cycle to a laggard indicator. In the 1981 recession, employment recovery tracked GDP recovery closely. In the 2001 recession, the GDP decline was short but employment kept shrinking after GDP recovered. In the Great Recession, employment fell proportionately more than output and did not begin

---

2. Census Bureau Center for Economic Studies restricted-use data available in the Federal Statistical Research Data Centers, including the Longitudinal Business Data Base, Quinquennial Economic Censuses, Annual Capital Expenditure Survey, Standard Statistical Establishment List, Annual Survey of Manufacturers, and Annual Survey of Services, www.census.gov/ces (accessed October 20, 2016).

3. Output as measured by gross revenues, which is sales.

Figure 1. Ratio of GDP to GDP Before Recession, Quarterly for Last Four Recessions

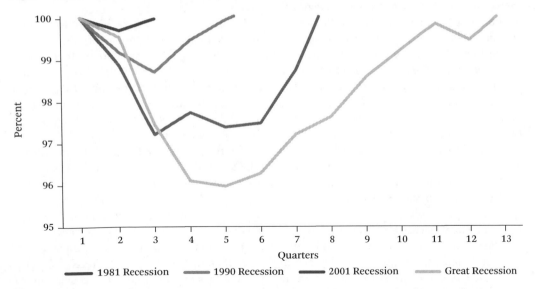

Source: Authors' compilation based on Federal Reserve Bank of St. Louis, Federal Reserve Economic Data.
Note: GDP is GDPC1. We adjusted the monthly employment data to quarterly basis for comparison with quarterly GDP data.

Figure 2. Ratio of Employment to Employment Before Recession, Quarterly for Last Four Recessions

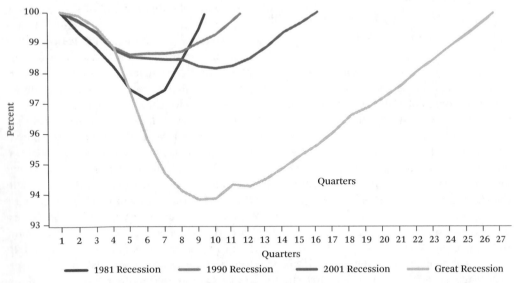

Source: Authors' compilation based on Federal Reserve Bank of St. Louis, Federal Reserve Economic Data.
Note: GDP is GDPC1. We adjusted the monthly employment data to quarterly basis for comparison with quarterly GDP data.

to recover until three quarters after output increased. The 4.2 percent drop in real GDP from peak to trough and the 5.3 percent fall in employment over the same period produces an implicit employment-to-GDP elasticity of 1.26 (− 5.3/4.2). In the recovery, by contrast, GDP's 7.8 percent increase through Q1 of 2015 exceeded employment's 4.8 percent increase, with an implicit employment-to-GDP elasticity of 0.62 (= 4.8/7.8). The rapid drop in labor usage and the slow recovery produced countercyclic labor productivity, contrary to the pro-cyclic labor productivity in earlier recessions (Okun 1970; Solow 1964; Biddle 2014) that led economists to develop labor hoarding models of firms' employment decisions.[4]

LABOR PRODUCTIVITY AND HOARDING

Studies of employment adjustments in the business cycle began with the premise that productivity should vary countercyclically (Biddle (2014). The reason is clear. Recession reductions in employment should raise labor productivity due to the increase in the marginal productivity of variable labor relative to fixed capital. In a recession, workers who remain employed have more capital with which to work and thus should have higher productivity. Recovery increases in employment, by contrast, ought to reduce labor productivity as additional employees lower the capital-to-employee ratio. In addition, selectivity in hiring or firing (which macro models generally ignore) also suggests a countercyclical movement of labor productivity, as firms lay off the least productive workers in a recession and hire them back in recovery. To explain the surprising pro-cyclic movement of labor productivity in the business cycles from the 1960s to the 1990s, analysts developed "labor hoarding" models in which the costs of adjusting employment made workers a quasi-fixed rather than variable factor of production.[5]

In the Great Recession, however, U.S. productivity did not show the drop predicted by labor hoarding. This contrasted with the situation in almost all other advanced countries, where productivity fell in the recession. Table 1 documents the Great Recession pattern of changes in GDP per hour with data on GDP per hour worked for major countries from the Conference Board's International Labor Comparisons (ILC) program. Columns 1 to 3 give the estimated GDP per hour worked in 2007, 2009, and 2012. Column 4 shows the annualized rate of change of productivity in the recession (2007 to 2009), and column 5 gives the annualized rate in the recovery (2009 to 2012). The last column records the difference between annualized productivity growth in the recovery and the recession. Positive differences imply pro-cyclic productivity. Negative differences imply the opposite.

All of the countries save the United States and Japan, which was mired in its lost decade of economic stagnation, had positive recovery-recession differences, implying pro-cyclic movements of productivity. The decline in productivity in most countries came, however, not only from the "normal" costs of adjustments at the heart of hoarding models but also from explicit collective bargaining or government policies to save jobs in the Great Recession. In Sweden, unions and employers negotiated agreements that maintained many jobs during the recession. In Germany, the government introduced a short-term work program and work allowance that subsidized part of labor cost in firms whose receipts had decreased by 10 percent. The Netherlands paid 70 percent of the wages for the nonwork hours of employees whom firms kept "on the job." And so on (Freeman 2013). Absent agreements and policies, European firms would likely have terminated more workers in the recession and hired more in the recovery, attenuating if not reversing the pro-cyclic movement of labor productivity.

Employment adjustments relative to output in U.S. manufacturing, however, looked more like adjustments in non-U.S. OECD (Organization for Economic Cooperation and Development) countries than those in the aggregate United States. Bureau of Labor Statistics data

4. For the impact of pro-cyclic labor productivity in Robert R. Solow's thinking, see Michaël Assous (2013) and Jeff Biddle (2014).

5. Biddle (2014) stresses the important contributions of Charles C. Holt et al. (1960). See Basu and Fernald (2001) for an empirical assessment.

Table 1. Level and Percentage Changes of Real GDP per Hour Worked in the Great Recession (2007–2009) and Recovery (2009–2012)

Country	GDP per Hour in U.S. $ PPP			Annual Percent Change		Recovery-Recession
	2007	2009	2012	2007–2009	2009–2012	
United States	**59.54**	**61.73**	**64.12**	**1.8**	**1.3**	**-0.5**
Canada	46.52	46.6	47.6	0	0.7	0.7
Australia	48.37	50.1	52.85	1.8	1.8	0
Japan	37.45	37.09	35.73	-0.5	-1.2	-0.7
Korea	23.18	24.34	26.83	2.5	3.4	0.9
Singapore	41.93	37.48	41.17	-5.3	3.3	8.6
Austria	51.84	51.96	53.69	0.1	1.1	0.9
Belgium	63.51	61.79	61.87	-1.4	0	1.4
Czech Republic	30.27	29.82	30.69	-0.7	1	1.7
Denmark	58.96	56.35	59.52	-2.2	1.9	4.1
Finland	50.57	47.37	48.97	-3.1	1.1	4.2
France	58.59	57.95	59.49	-0.5	0.9	1.4
Germany	57.43	55.94	58.26	-1.3	1.4	2.7
Ireland	61.78	62.52	71.31	0.6	4.7	4.1
Italy	45.82	44.46	45.36	-1.5	0.7	2.2
Netherlands	60.94	59.52	60.16	-1.2	0.4	1.6
Norway	88.43	85.78	86.61	-1.5	0.3	1.8
Spain	45.25	46.68	49.99	1.6	2.4	0.8
Sweden	53.73	51.58	54.69	-2	2	4
United Kingdom	50	48.26	48.27	-1.7	0	1.7

Source: Conference Board, International Labor Comparisons of GDP per capita per hour worked, 2012, https://www.conference-board.org/ilcprogram/#Productivity (accessed October 25, 2016).

show manufacturing employment declining proportionately less than output in the downturn—a sign of labor hoarding absent substantial bargaining or government policies pressuring or rewarding firms to maintain employment. As a result, from Q1 2008 to Q4 2009 real value added per hour in manufacturing fell by 24 percent while in the recovery real value added per hour increased by 27 percent through Q4 2012.[6] However, Conference Board data tell a different story for real gross output

per hour worked, where gross output includes intermediate goods and materials as well as value added. The data for gross output per hour show increased manufacturing productivity in the Great Recession.[7] The difference between the ILC and BLS measures reflects a divergent movement of the price deflator for real gross output and the price deflator for real value added, whose resolution lies beyond this study.[8]

To better identify the role of the Great Recession and recovery on changes in employ-

6. Federal Reserve Bank of St. Louis FRED Economic Data "FRED - Manufacturing Sector: Real Output Per Hour of All Persons (series OPHMFG)," https://fred.stlouisfed.org/series/OPHMFG (accessed July 20, 2016); Bureau of Labor Statistics, "Major Sector Productivity and Costs Original Data Value, Series ID: PRS30006032, Sector: Manufacturing," http://data.bls.gov/timeseries/PRS30006032 (accessed July 20, 2016).

7. The Conference Board, International Labor Comparisons, International Comparisons of Manufacturing Productivity & Unit Labor Costs Trends, 2014, time series tables downloadable from https://www.conference-board.org/ilcprogram/index.cfm?id=30136 (accessed June 20, 2016).

8. Bureau of Economic Analysis BEA, U.S. Department of Commerce, Gross-Domestic-Product-(GDP)-by-Industry Data, Spreadsheet, www.bea.gov/industry/gdpbyind_data.htm (accessed May 27, 2015). Bureau of Economics

ment from the long-term effects of technological change and capital-labor substitution on employment[9] requires a micro-level analysis of employment, to which we turn next.

CHANGES IN CONTINUING, EXITING, AND ENTERING ESTABLISHMENTS

To probe the micro-underpinnings of the United States' Great Recession employment experience, we decomposed changes in employment into the changes that occur in continuing establishments—those that operated before the downturn and kept operating through the recession—and changes that result from the exit and entry of establishments. Let $E(t)$ be employment in year t; $Ec(t)$ be employment in t in establishments operating in t and $t-1$; $Eb(t)$ be employment in establishments that entered the market in year t (operated in t but not in $t-1$); and $Ed(t-1)$ be employment in establishments that exited the market in year t (operated in $t-1$ but not in t). Then the change in employment from $t-1$ to t is:

$$E(t) - E(t-1) = [Ec(t) - Ec(t-1)]$$
$$+ [Eb(t) - Ed(t-1)], \qquad (1)$$

where $[Ec(t) - Ec(t-1)]$ is the change among continuers and $[Eb(t) - Ed(t-1)]$ is the change due to job creation in entering establishments minus job destruction in exiting establishments.

Dividing both sides of the equation by $E(t) - E(t-1)$ gives the relative contribution of changes in continuers and of exit and entry to each part to the total change from $(t -1$ to $t)$.

Table 2 presents this decomposition for one-digit-sector private sector industries and the entire private sector in the recession and ensuing recovery.[10] Accepting the NBER dating whereby the end of the recession occurred in June 2009, we treat 2009 as the year when the recession ended and the recovery began in the BDS (Business Dynamics Statistics of the U.S. Census Bureau) annual data. The recession-period "All" line in table 1 shows a net loss of jobs of 5.007 million and a larger loss of 5.748 million among establishments that continued operating. The 0.741-million-job difference implies that in the Great Recession, entering establishments hired more employees than exiting establishments terminated. The one-digit-industry data locate one third of the recession job loss in manufacturing and almost 1/4th in construction for 58 percent of all job losses. In two other sectors with large declines in employment, retail trade and services, the decline occurred despite large net employment gains

---

Commerce Department GDP by Industry spreadsheet GDP by Ind_VA_NAICS_1997-2014 shows that manufacturing gross output fell by 17 percent from 2007 to 2009 and increased by 12 percent for a 29 point swing while manufacturing value added fell by 10 percent and then increased by 6 percent for a sixteen-point swing. The price index for gross output increased by 1 percent from 2007 to 2009 and by 16 percent while the price index for value added increased by 4 percent in the recession and 8 percent in the recovery. Martin Bailey and Barry Bosworth (2014, table 2) show different growth of gross output and value added in the computer and electronic products manufacturing industry due in part to differences in value added and gross output price deflators. Susan Houseman et al. (2011) analyze the problems that price indexes create in measuring economic activity in manufacturing.

9. See Acemoglu et al. (2014) for a recent discussion.

10. Aggregate data on employment, job creation, and job destruction are from the Center for Economic Studies (CES), www.census.gov/ces/dataproducts/bds/data_firm.html (accessed June 25, 2015). We use the "Firm Characteristics Data Tables: Economy Wide" table for total counts and the "Firm Characteristics Data Tables: Sector" table for counts by one-digit SIC sectors. The BDS reports yearly employment based on March data, along with the total number of jobs created and destroyed each year based on the last twelve months. Job destruction and creation are jobs lost via establishment deaths or gained via establishment births. The "Establishment Age by Sector" table splits the data by establishment age. The BDS does not define birth in a unique way: an establishment is born when it begins with age zero, but if employment goes to zero and later back to a positive number the establishment is "born again," even if its age is greater than zero. BDS suppresses job counts in cells that fall under a certain firm count.

from exit and entry as continuing establishments contracted jobs massively.

The recovery line labeled "All" in table 2 shows a different pattern. Changes in employment are dominated by exit and entry rather than by continuing establishments. Of the 2.187 million net gain of jobs, 1.385 million (63 percent) was due to new entrants creating more jobs than exiting establishments destroyed. Manufacturing and construction shed jobs through the recovery, with exit and entry accounting for 36 percent of the recovery job loss in manufacturing and 59 percent of the recovery job loss in construction. The importance of exit-entry in the recovery does not contravene the finding that the continuing establishments who make up the majority of establishments dominate changes in employment at all phases of the cycle. Appendix B shows that changes among continuers are the major component of job creation and destruction in the recovery and recession in the LBD data. What is distinct about our exit-and-entry analysis is that it organizes data around net changes in jobs, which depend on differences in job gain and loss among continuers relative to differences in job creation in entering establishments and job destruction in exiting establishments, rather than on the contributions of changes among these types of establishments to total job creation or destruction.

To illuminate further the dominance of continuers in recession job changes compared to exit and entry in recovery job changes, we decomposed employment changes into the changed number of establishments in the continuer, entrant, and exiting groups, and the average number of jobs gained or lost per establishment for each group. The "All" figures for the *recession* in table 3 show that continuing establishments dominated recession job loss because continuing establishments made up about 80 percent of all establishments.[11] In the recession more establishments exited than entered, but an entering establishment created on average 1.2 jobs per job than the exiting establishments eliminated, so that exit and entry produced a modest net gain in employment. In manufacturing, by contrast, nearly 40 percent more establishments exited than entered the market and there was little difference in the average size of entering and exiting establishments, so that exit and entry contributed net to job loss. Still, continuers dominated job loss in manufacturing because of their large 6.4 decline in average employment.

The "All" changes in the recovery section of table 3 tell a different story. The dominance of entry-exit in the recovery is due primarily to the difference between the average gain in employment in entering establishments and the average loss in employment among exiting establishments.[12] Again, however, manufacturing is different. Even in the recovery, more establishments exited than entered in manufacturing (and construction), and the average employment in exiting establishments exceeded the average employment of entrants.

To the extent that establishments that enter the market better fit existing economic

---

11. Using the 2007-to-2009 recession data, continuers made up 79 percent of establishments in 2007 (= 5.121 million continuers / [5.121 + 1.398 establishments in 2007 but gone by 2009]) and 80 percent of establishments in 2009 (= 5.121 / [5.121 + 1.291 establishments in 2009 but not in 2007]). Using the 2009-to-2012 recovery data, continuers made up 73 percent of establishments in 2009 (= 5.148 / [5.148 + 1.916]) and 73 percent in 2012 (= 5.148 / ([5.148 + 1.922]).

12. Let Ne = number of entering establishments, Ae = average employment in those establishments, Nd = number of exiting establishments, and Ad = average employment in those establishments. Then job change from exit and entry is $NeAe - Nd Ad$, which decomposes algebraically into $(Ne - Nd) Ad + (Ae - Ad) Nd + (Ne - Nd)(Ae - Ad)$, where the first term is the different number of entering and exiting establishments, weighted by average employment in exiting establishments; the second term is the difference in average employment in entering and exiting establishments, weighted by the number of exiting establishments; and the last term is the interaction of the two differences. The difference in average sizes times the exiting number of firms accounts for 97 percent of the contribution of exit and entry to growth of jobs.

Table 2. Decomposition of Changes in Employment Among Continuing, Entering, and Exiting Establishments in the Great Recession (2007–2009) and the Recovery (2009–2012)

	Net Change in Employment	Net Job Change, Continuers	Continuers' Percentage of Net Change	Total Jobs Change		Entrants- Exits
				Exits	Entrants	
2007 to 2009						
Agriculture	−10,430	−17,741	170%	−160,293	167,604	7,311
Mining	−64,030	−91,153	142	−61,111	88,234	27,123
Construction	−1,205,115	−947,717	79	−594,760	337,362	−257,398
Manufacturing	−1,679,584	−1,431,927	85	−899,511	651,854	−247,657
Transportation and public utilities	−272,942	−322,193	118	−541,372	590,623	49,251
Wholesale trade	−362,068	−302,771	84	−595,210	535,913	−59,297
Retail trade	−618,246	−1,444,660	234	−2,166,500	2,992,914	826,414
Finance and real estate	−428,766	−444,030	104	−983,565	998,829	15,264
Services	−365,422	−745,614	204	−4,077,073	4,457,265	380,192
All	−5,006,603	−5,747,806	115	−10,079,395	10,820,598	741,203
2009 to 2012						
Agriculture	21,432	−4,483	−21	−207,901	233,816	25,915
Mining	115,599	81,111	70	−87,685	122,173	34,488
Construction	−736,530	−432,529	59	−734,523	430,522	−304,001
Manufacturing	−537,135	−192,563	36	−1,081,277	736,705	−344,572
Transportation and public utilities	38,855	−28,010	−72	−770,913	837,778	66,865
Wholesale trade	−129,494	−54,070	42	−759,643	684,219	−75,424
Retail trade	954,567	−203,979	−21	−2,865,585	4,024,131	1,158,546
Finance and real estate	−163,323	−204,687	125	−1,212,511	1,253,875	41,364
Services	2,623,343	1,841,378	70	−5,675,107	6,457,072	781,965
All	2,187,314	802,168	37	−13,395,145	14,780,291	1,385,146

Source: U.S. Census Bureau, Business Dynamics Statistics, 2012 Release, Firm Characteristics Data Tables: Sector, http://www.census.gov/ces/dataproducts/bds/data_firm.html (accessed October 26, 2016).

Notes: "Total Jobs Change" is the difference between job creation and job destruction that in each year reflects the twelve-month counts of created and destroyed jobs. This number is different than the change in establishment employment in March of each year.

conditions than establishments that exit, differences in their characteristics provide insight into the selectivity of technological and market forces. Figures 3 and 4 display the mean 2007 physical and human capital characteristics of manufacturing establishments that entered or exited in the recession or recovery.[13] A characteristic that is more (less) frequent among entering than exiting establishments suggests that the characteristic's economic value has increased (decreased) over time. The figure shows that entering establishments had larger capital-to-employee ratios, college shares of the work force, and

13. The characteristics are for 2007 to avoid reverse causality from the recession and recovery on the characteristics.

Table 3. Number and Average Employment Size of Exiting and Entering Establishments and Number of Continuing Establishments and Average Change in Employment of Continuers, Great Recession (2007–2009) and the Recovery (2009–2012)

	Exits		Entrants		Continuers	
	Number of Establishments	Average Size at Exit	Number of Establishments	Average Size at Entry	Number of Establishments	Average Δ in Employment
2007 to 2009						
Agriculture	31,448	5.1	31,000	5.4	97,078	−0.2
Mining	4,493	4.8	5,825	15.1	18,747	−4.9
Construction	145,482	4.1	72,722	4.6	370,271	−2.6
Manufacturing	54,477	16.5	39,175	16.6	223,601	−6.4
Transportation and public utilities	71,922	7.5	67,106	8.8	222,527	−1.4
Wholesale trade	77,751	7.7	68,477	7.8	346,446	−0.9
Retail trade	284,831	7.6	289,566	10.3	1,164,850	−1.2
Finance and real estate	171,980	5.7	146,390	6.8	550,140	−0.8
Services	555,527	7.3	570,724	7.8	2,127,064	−0.4
All	1,397,911	7.2	1,290,985	8.4	5,120,724	−1.1
2009 to 2012						
Agriculture	43,142	4.8	46,974	5.0	102,952	0.0
Mining	7,179	12.2	8,535	14.3	20,019	4.1
Construction	175,402	4.2	111,927	3.8	320,593	−1.3
Manufacturing	71,615	15.1	54,017	13.6	212,567	−0.9
Transportation and public utilities	94,270	8.2	99,259	8.4	222,337	−0.1
Wholesale trade	110,191	6.9	100,390	6.8	340,701	−0.2
Retail trade	396,555	7.2	427,479	9.4	1,185,351	−0.2
Finance and real estate	206,686	5.9	207,231	6.1	552,567	−0.4
Services	811,251	7.0	866,066	7.5	2,191,745	0.4
All	1,916,291	7.0	1,921,878	7.7	5,148,832	0.2

Source: U.S. Census Bureau, Business Dynamics Statistics, 2012 Release, Firm Characteristics Data Tables: Sector, http://www.census.gov/ces/dataproducts/bds/data_firm.html (accessed October 26, 2016).

Notes: Total change in employment is calculated as the difference between job creation and job destruction that in each year reflects the twelve-month counts of created and destroyed jobs. Continuing establishments for 2007–2009 (2009–2012) are those that are aged at least two to three years old in 2009 (2012).

made greater investment in computer per employee than exiting establishments but had similar ratios of non-production employees. These differences are consistent with technological upgrading and capital-human capital complementarity in the technology that affects employment.

HETEROGENEITY IN RESPONSES TO OUTPUT SHOCKS

Behind average changes in employment lie distributions in which some establishments change employment more than the average and others less than the average because the market conditions they face differ from the average

Figure 3. In Differential in Characteristic of New Entering Establishments to Exiting Establishments in Manufacturing in Great Recession

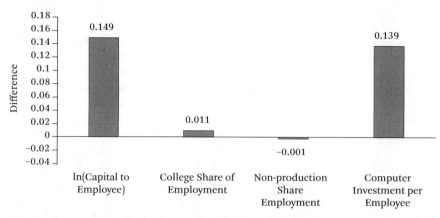

Source: Source: Authors' calculations from the Census Bureau restricted-use Annual Survey of Manufacturers data available in the Federal Statistical Research Data Centers (www.census.gov/ces).
Notes: Entering establishments are those that first appear in the data-set. Exiting establishments are those that disappear from data-set.

Figure 4. In Differential in Characteristic of New Entering Establishments to Exiting Establishments in Manufacturing in Recovery

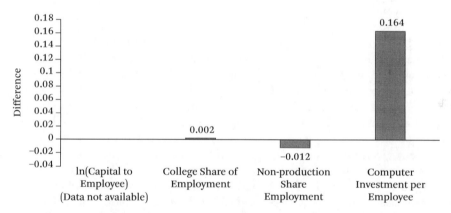

Source: Authors' calculations based on Foster, Grim, and Haltiwanger (2016).
Notes: Entering establishments are those that first appear in the data-set. Exiting establishments are those that disappear from data-set. Data on capital to employment not available in recovery, as capital data are from Foster, Grim, and Haltiwanger (2016), based on calculations that do not extend to 2012.

or their technologies differ, or because they respond differently than other establishments to the same conditions. Regardless of the cause, heterogeneity of responses among establishments is potentially important in the micro-underpinnings of aggregate employment changes in the business cycle.

Next we examine changes in employment relative to output among continuing establishments in manufacturing.[14] We limit our analy-

14. Establishments are included in the calculations if they exist in the beginning and end of each period. Focusing on continuing establishments sidesteps the discontinuity in changes related to exit and entry and potential differences between exit and entry decisions and expansion and contraction decisions.

sis to manufacturing because the yearly production data in the Census Bureau's Annual Survey of Manufacturers allows us to differentiate recession from recovery, whereas production data in the quinquennial Censuses of Production for other sectors lacks the time detail to distinguish the two parts of the cycle. We follow Census Bureau procedures and measure changes in employment relative to average establishment employment in the starting and ending period, in order to reduce the risk that large relative changes in employment for small establishments unduly affects the estimates.[15]

Table 4 shows the average annual changes in employment and output for all establishments and those in the 0–20th, 40th–60th, and the 80th–100th quintiles of changes ranked by rate of increase from lowest to highest. The natural measure of variation in these statistics is the inter-quintile range, defined as the difference between the top quintile's mean change in employment and the bottom quintile's mean change in employment. In the Great Recession, manufacturing employment declined on average by 13 percent while output declined by 18.6 percent, for an implicit employment-to-output elasticity of 0.70, per labor-hoarding behavior. The quintile changes reveal large increases in employment and output at the upper end of the distributions and large decreases at the lower end: a top-quintile employment increase of 42.1 percent compared to a bottom-quintile decrease of 90 percent, giving an inter-quintile range of 132 points; a top-quintile average increase in output of 33.8 percent and a bottom-quintile average decrease in output by 93 percent, giving an inter-quintile range of 127 points.

In the recovery, manufacturing employment fell by 3.8 percent while output increased by 13.1 percent, producing a 16.9 percent increase in productivity. But, as in the recession, the averages masque huge variation: a 78 percent employment drop in the bottom quintile compared to a 57.7 percent increase in the top quintile; a 63.2 percent output drop in the lowest quintile compared to a 72.1 percent increase in the top quintile. The large recession gain in employment and output in the highest quintile of establishments as compared to the large recovery loss of employment and output for the lowest quintile highlights the heterogeneous experience of establishments. Some establishments expand even in a huge recession and some contract even in a recovery.

To see whether the heterogeneity was exceptional to the Great Recession or normal for recent recessions, we computed inter-quintile ranges of change in employment and output in the 2000-to-2002, 1989-to-1991, and 1979-to-1981 recessions. The bottom panel of table 4 shows smaller inter-quintile ranges of changes in those recessions than in the Great Recession and smaller inter-quintile ranges in changes in the recovery phases than in the recovery from the Great Recession. But, the ranges still give evidence of huge heterogeneity.[16]

TECHNOLOGICAL CHANGE AND CAPITAL-LABOR SUBSTITUTION

Like comparisons of the characteristics of entering and exiting establishments, changes in employment or output associated with the characteristics of continuing establishments offer insight into the direction of economic and technological forces. A characteristic that raises growth of output or employment in a regression indicates that market forces favor that characteristic. To see how the attributes of establishments affect employment and output, we regressed changes in employment and output in the Great Recession and in the recovery separately, on a range of factors, including the share of college graduates; capital per employee; computer investment per employee; and whether the firm that owns the establishment did R&D, among others.[17] The regressions

---

15. This problem can also be addressed by weighting observations by the number of employees.

16. Steve Davis, John Haltiwanger, and Scott Schuh (1996) and Haltiwanger (2012), among others, also note the heterogeneity in changes in employment among enterprises.

17. The R&D status for the firm that owned an establishment is from National Science Foundation, Business R&D and Innovation Survey. Another factor in the regressions was the export status of the establishment measured in the share of output sold overseas, which we treat as a covariate control.

Table 4. Changes in the Distribution of Employment and Output (Measured by Sales) of Continuing Manufacturing Establishments in the Great Recession (2007–2009) and Recovery (2009–2012), Compared to Three Earlier Recession and Recoveries

| | Panel A: Great Recession | | | |
| | Employment | | Output | |
	Recession 2007–2009	Recovery 2009–2012	Recession 2007–2009	Recovery 2009–2012
Mean	−0.130	−0.038	−0.186	0.131
Mean of				
First quintile	−0.899	−0.780	−0.929	−0.632
Third quintile	−0.124	−0.004	−0.231	0.146
Fifth quintile	0.421	0.577	0.338	0.721
Range, fifth to first	1.32	1.37	1.27	1.35
	Panel B: Three Previous Recessions			
	Employment		Output	
	Recession 2000–2002	Recovery 2002–2004	Recession 2000–2002	Recovery 2002–2004
Mean	−0.083	−0.063	−0.05	0.025
Range, fifth to first	1.09	1.08	1.21	0.95
	1989–1991	1991–1993	1989–1991	1991–1993
Mean	−0.047	−0.042	−0.024	0.037
Range, fifth to first	1.06	0.97	1.14	1.04
	1979–1981	1981–1984	1979–1981	1981–1984
Mean	−0.087	−0.011	−0.068	0.096
Range, fifth to first	1.08	1.08	1.15	1.04

Source: Authors' calculations from the Census Bureau restricted-use Annual Survey of Manufacturers data available in the Federal Statistical Research Data Centers (www.census.gov/ces).
Note: Table shows relative changes: $\Delta Y/Y$, where Y is the average of the first and the last years. Continuing establishments only.

include a vector of three-digit NACE level industry dummies interacted with the state location of the establishment, so the estimates come from variation within industry-state cells. To ease interpretation of the regressions, we normalized the variables to their average 2007 value so that the constants measure change for an establishment with average characteristics.

Column 1 of table 5 shows the estimated coefficients from OLS (ordinary least squares) regressions of changes in output in the Great Recession on the characteristics. The estimated constant shows that revenue in the average establishment declined 19.2 percent from 2007 to 2009. Column 2 records the estimated coefficients for regressions of changes in employ-

ment in the recession on the characteristics. The estimated constant shows that employment declined by 14.7 percent. The smaller change of employment than of output to the recession reflects "labor hoarding" for establishments with similar characteristics. The characteristics that differentiated entering from exiting establishments in figures 3 and 4 affect output and employment in table 5 in a similar manner: establishments with relatively more college graduates, capital per employee, and computer investment per employee had higher growth than other establishments in the same industry and state during the recession. By contrast, establishments in firms that do R&D averaged a 3.9 point greater increase in output than establishments in non-R&D firms and had a 0.8 point smaller change in employment. This likely reflects the fact that R&D-based technology creates process as well as product innovation. New and improved products add to output and employment whereas new production processes are often labor-saving and can reduce employment.

Columns 3 and 4 examine the relation between establishment characteristics and changes in output and employment in the recovery. An establishment with average characteristics had output growth of 16.9 percent but employment growth of just 3.4 percent reflecting the "jobless recovery." The estimated impacts of establishment characteristics on output and employment in the recovery differ markedly from columns 1 and 2, estimated impacts of characteristics in the recession. The coefficients for the share of college employees and computer investment per employee change from positive in the recession to negative in the recovery. The estimated coefficients on R&D-performing firms shift from positive to negative on output and become more negative on employment. Only the estimated coefficients on capital-to-labor ratios show similar patterns in both phases of the cycle, with capital-intensive firms expanding more in output and employment.[18]

A plausible explanation for the general pattern of sign reversal is labor-hoarding behavior, with establishments that were more negatively impacted by the recession being commensurately less positively impacted by the upturn; and conversely for those less impacted by the recession. Since firms hoard labor in recessions to avoid recruiting labor in recoveries, the hoarding firm will reduce employment less in the recession and increase employment less in the recovery than the firm that does not hoard

labor. Technological change and capital-labor substitution aside, a firm that hoarded completely would lay off no one in a recession and would not have to hire anyone in a recovery to bring output to its pre-recession level. By contrast a firm that treated labor as completely variable would lay off 10 percent of its work force when output fell by 10 percent and rehire all those workers when output regained the pre-recession level.

To assess the extent of job hoarding behavior at the establishment level, we estimate equations linking ln changes in establishment employment to ln changes in establishment output in the recession and recovery periods. Hoarding at the establishment level would show up in an estimated coefficient of the change in employment on the change in output below 1.0. Column 1 of table 6 gives an estimated coefficient on output of 0.389 in the recession period, indicative of considerable hoarding. Column 2 of table 6 gives an estimated coefficient on output of 0.473 in the recovery period, far below the 1.0 that one would get if labor was a completely variable input.

Taking the analysis a step further, the establishment data allow us to make a direct test of the proposition that labor hoarding in recession reduces growth of employment in the recovery. Using the information on the changes in establishment employment and output in the recession, we estimate a "recession hoarding" variable for each establishment and add that measure to the regression of employment changes on output changes in the recovery. Our recession hoarding measure is the residual from the column 1 estimate of the change in employment on output in the recession. The larger the change in employment relative to its predicted level from the regression, the larger is the estimated amount of hoarding.[19] Column

---

18. To see if the Great Recession downturn and recovery differed from downturns and recoveries in earlier recessions, we estimated variants of the table 5 equations for the entire 2007-to-2012 period and for the downturn and recovery in the three previous recessions. We found only modest differences in the relation between the physical and human capital of establishments and the R&D attribute of the owning firm on output and employment.

19. The measure of hoarding can be improved in various ways, such as comparing changes in employment with changes in materials, which the firm is unlikely to hoard, or differentiating production from nonproduction workers, or distinguishing establishments with increases in sales in the recession and decreases in sales in the recovery, but the table 6 analysis suffices to establish the establishment basis of hoarding.

Table 5. Regression Coefficients and Standard Errors for the Relation of Establishment Characteristics on Change in Output (Measured by Sales) and Change in Employment in the Recession (2007–2009) and the Recovery (2009–2012)

	Recession (2007–2009)		Recovery (2009–2012)	
	Output	Employment	Output	Employment
Constant (average pre-recession characteristics)	−0.192*** (0.004)	−0.147*** (0.003)	0.169*** (0.005)	0.034*** (0.004)
College share	0.140*** (0.014)	0.082*** (0.011)	−0.101*** (0.016)	−0.082*** (0.013)
R&D firm	0.039*** (0.005)	−0.008* (0.004)	−0.018** (0.006)	−0.049*** −(0.001)
Computer investment per employee	0.014*** (0.001)	0.005*** (0.001)	−0.007*** (0.001)	−0.001 (0.012)
ln(capital/employee)	0.026*** (0.003)	0.016*** (0.002)	0.036*** (0.003)	0.020*** (0.002)
Industry X state dummies	Y	Y	Y	Y
Adjusted R^2	0.182	0.165	0.138	0.143
N	40,400	40,400	36,500	36,500

Source: Authors' calculations from the Census Bureau restricted-use Annual Survey of Manufacturers data available in the Federal Statistical Research Data Centers (www.census.gov/ces).

Notes: Left-side variables measured as dY/Y, where Y is defined as the average of the last and the first year. Right-side variables measured as levels in pre-recession year (2007). All models include ln(employment/output) in 2007 as well as industry X state dummies. The unit of observation is establishments. The right-side variables are normalized as deviations from the 2007 level, and the constant term may thus be interpreted as the relative change in output and employment for establishments with average characteristics in 2007. The models also include ln(E/S) and ln ratio of exports to output as well as fixed effects for each industry state cell so statistics are generated by variation among establishments in the same state and industry.

***$p ≤ .01$

3 shows that this measure obtains a large significant negative effect in the regression for the change in employment in the recovery. Hoarding evinces itself in the adjustments of employment throughout the distribution of employment and output changes as well as in the different average changes in employment and output in recession and recovery.

Finally, we examine the hoarding notion by contrasting the actual pattern of changes in employment and output to a well-specified counterfactual that abstracts from the business cycle. Assume that absent the recession output, employment would have changed smoothly from 2007 to 2012. This identifies the impact of the cycle as the difference between the actual changes and the counterfactual smooth change. Columns 1 and 2 in table 7 give the regression coefficients of the growth of output and employment on the characteristics of establishments in the 2007–2012 period smooth growth counterfactual.[20] These regressions show that the college-educated share of the workforce had little relation to growth of output or employment over the entire period; that R&D of the firm is associated with increased output but reduced employment; whereas capital-to-employee ratios and computer investments per

20. As in other tables, the output and employment dependent variables were scaled with 2007 as 1.00 so the constants give the growth rates for establishments with the average characteristics.

Table 6. Regression Coefficients (Standard Errors) for Changes in Employment on Changes in Output in Manufacturing Establishments in the Recession (2007–2009) and Recovery (2009–2012)

Dependent Variable	(1) $\Delta E/E$ 2007–2009	(2) $\Delta E/E$ 2009–2012	(3) $\Delta E/E$ 2009–2012
$\Delta S/S$ 2007–2009	0.389*** (0.003)		
$\Delta S/S$ 2009–2012		0.473*** (0.003)	0.476*** (0.003)
Recession labor hoarding			−0.267*** (0.005)
Constant	−0.024*** (0.001)	−0.056*** (0.002)	−0.057*** (0.002)
Adjusted R^2	0.254	0.352	0.392
N	39,700	39,700	39,700

Source: Authors' calculations from the Census Bureau restricted-use Annual Survey of Manufacturers data available in the Federal Statistical Research Data Centers (www.census.gov/ces).
Note: The recession labor hoarding measure is the residual from equation (1).
***$p \leq .01$

employee are positively associated with output and employment. Column 3 gives the annual change in output per employee associated with each characteristic obtained by dividing the difference between the columns 1 and 2 coefficients by 5 for the five years covered.

Columns 4 and 5 record the deviations of productivity measured by output per employee in the recession and in the recovery from the smooth change. For an establishment with average characteristics, productivity increased by 7.1 ln points more in the recession than in the benchmark smooth adjustment. By contrast, the average establishment fell short of the smooth benchmark by 9.5 points in the recovery. Since changes in recession and recovery are deviations from smooth growth, the estimated effects for independent variables in recession and recovery necessarily alternate in sign. The biggest differences in the coefficients are for the share of college graduates. Establishments with high college-educated shares

stabilized productivity over the cycle more than other establishments.[21]

CONCLUSION

Our analysis of aggregate, sectoral, and establishment-level changes in employment and productivity in the Great Recession and recovery document that employment responses differed greatly to changes in output between the United States and other advanced countries, between U.S. manufacturing and the bulk of the U.S. private sector, and among U.S. manufacturing establishments. Taking the economy as a whole, U.S. firms reduced employment proportionately more than output in the Great Recession, in contrast to the labor hoarding behavior in most advanced economies and in earlier U.S. recessions. The main pathway for the huge reduction in U.S. employment was massive contractions of employment by existing establishments. The pathway for job growth in the recovery, by contrast, was dominated by

21. To check the interrelation between employment adjustments in the recession and recovery, we examined the pattern of change in employment relative to materials as well as to revenues. This compares the two inputs that firms can potentially adjust in the short run to changes in demand for output. Over the entire period the ratio of materials to output increased by 9.3 percent—a change that implies materials augmenting technical change—while the cyclic pattern resembles the table 7 pattern of output to employees with slower growth in the recession and faster growth in the recovery relative to the five year smooth alternative—the signature of input hoarding.

Table 7. Estimated Regression Coefficients (and Standard Errors) for Relation Between Change in Employment and Output and Establishment Characteristics, 2007–2012, Average Annual Changes in Output per Employee and Recession and Recovery Deviations from Average Changes

	Estimated Coefficients, 2007–2012		Annual Change in Output per Employee Due to Pre-recession Characteristic 2007–2012	Deviation from Average In Output per Employee	
	Output	Employee		Recession 2007–2009	Recovery 2009–2012
Constant	0.061***	−0.005	0.013	−0.071	0.095
	(0.005)	(0.004)			
Pre-recession characteristics, 2007					
College share	0.012	−0.011	0.005	0.049	−0.033
	(0.017)	(0.014)			
R&D firm	0.017**	−0.072***	0.018	0.011	−0.022
	(0.006)	(0.005)			
Computer investment per employee	0.003*	0.006***	−0.001	0.010	−0.004
	(0.001)	(0.001)			
In capital per employee	0.060***	0.034***	0.005	0.000	0.000
	(0.003)	(0.003)			
Industry X state dummies	Y	Y			
Adjusted R^2	0.149	0.144	–	–	–
N	36,600	36,600	–	–	–

Source: Authors' calculations from the Census Bureau restricted-use Annual Survey of Manufacturers data available in the Federal Statistical Research Data Centers (www.census.gov/ces). See data section for additional variables.

Note: Dependent variables : ΔY/ average of the first and the last years.

*$p \leq .1$; **$p \leq .05$; ***$p \leq .01$

the exit-and-entry of establishments, with new entrants to the market adding greatly to employment. Manufacturing establishments, however, behaved differently, hoarding labor in the recession while evincing widely varying elasticity of employment to gross output in recession and in recovery.

These differences in employment responses challenge simple models of how enterprises adjust employment in downturns and recoveries. Given that labor institutions are generally stronger in the European Union than in the United States, it is natural to attribute U.S.-EU differences in employment responses to the different institutional settings, in particular to greater employment protection legislation and

higher density of collective bargaining in the EU than in the United States.[22] But, as noted earlier, many EU countries introduced explicit policies to preserve jobs in the Great Recession and unions and employer federations negotiated new collective bargaining agreements, suggesting two different institutional explanations for hoarding behavior in Europe. The first explanation attributes most of the smaller employment response to the "normal costs of adjustment" stressed in hoarding models. The second explanation attributes most of the preservation of jobs to the emergency legislation and agreements. An institutional explanation ought to provide estimates of these two routes of impact. It should also explain the sizable dif-

22. See Sandrine Cazes, Sameer Khatiwada, and Miguel Malo (2012). Figure 2 shows the difference between U.S. and European countries in collective bargaining and employment protection legislation

ferences in employment responses among countries beyond the United States in table 1—for instance, why productivity fell in the recession in Britain, Germany, and Denmark, while increasing in Spain, Ireland, and Austria. Analyses that propose institutional explanations for U.S.-EU differences should be tested on the details of the proposed institutions at country and more micro-levels.

The huge layoffs among continuing establishments and higher elasticity of job loss to output in the United States in the Great Recession than in previous recessions may also be partly attributable to institutional changes within the country, such as the continued decline in collective bargaining coverage and the shift in the United States toward temporary contracts for more and more workers. The growth of the "gig economy," characterized by a large number of temporary subs and contract workers, in many nonmanufacturing sectors invariably makes labor a more variable input, which could explain part of the higher elasticity of employment to output in the Great Recession. But with labor more variable, the elasticity of employment to output in the recovery should also be high, which it was not. The timing of the shift from permanent to more temporary labor contracts also does not fit well with job shedding in the recession. Larry Katz and Alan Kreuger (2016) date the shift toward temporary, on-call, and related jobs as occurring largely from 2005 to 2015, mainly occurring after the Great Recession.[23] Perhaps the employment-at-will doctrine that dominates U.S. labor contracts gives most firms sufficient flexibility to lay off workers in a crisis without temporary contracts, on-call work, and the like.[24] The Great Recession collapse of construction, where almost all jobs are short-term gigs, may also have contributed to the absence of labor hoarding in the broad economy.[25]

Within the United States, the finding of continued hoarding behavior in manufacturing poses the question of why manufacturing responded so differently to the Great Recession than most other sectors. One possibility is that globalization allowed U.S. manufacturers to offshore much of the variable part of production work, so that a larger proportion of remaining workers had skills and knowledge that made the adjustment cost of layoffs more expensive than in the past. Testing this proposition requires evidence on the extent to which firms and their suppliers adjusted output and employment overseas in the recession. If U.S. firms vary in their ability to move employment adjustments downstream along their supply chains, globalization may also help explain some of the heterogeneity of employment responses to output among observationally similar establishments. Evidence on establishment-level changes in other advanced countries could also help determine the extent to which the U.S. manufacturing experience in the Great Recession was driven by the technology and global market in the sector as opposed to institutional differences between the United States and other advanced economies.

In sum, the evidence of heterogeneity in responses of employment to output among countries and among observationally comparable manufacturing establishments and the shift in the United States from hoarding labor to shedding jobs more rapidly than output declined in the Great Recession shows that we know less than we thought about how labor markets operate over the business cycle. Will the next recession, in which a much larger proportion of the workforce will hold irregular jobs, produce greater job losses than in 2007–2009? Could

23. Larry Katz and Alan Krueger (2016) show that most of the increase in alternative work arrangements measured by independent contractors, on-call workers, temporary help agency workers, and those provided by contract firms occurred after 2005. See also Katherine Abraham et al. (2016) and David Weil (2014).

24. See "At-Will Employent," https://en.wikipedia.org/wiki/At-will_employment (accessed October 20, 2016).

25. Construction employment declined proportionately with construction spending in the recession. See FRED (Federal Reserve Economic Data) data series, "Total Construction Spending," https://fred.stlouisfed.org /search?st=TTLCONS (accessed August 4, 2016); and "All Employees: Construction," https://fred.stlouisfed.org /series/USCONS (accessed August 4, 2016).

greater reliance on labor institutions determining wage and employment outcomes dampen job losses, and, if so, what would those institutions be? To answer these and related questions requires new economic analyses of labor demand that focus on the factors behind the variability of employment responses and that seek ways to influence those responses along the entire distribution of responses so that our economies can adjust better to the next recession in the business cycle, which seems to be endemic to market economies.

APPENDIX A

Census Bureau's Longitudinal Business Database (LBD)

The establishment-level data are from the U.S. Census Bureau's Longitudinal Business Database (LBD) covering the period from 1977 to 2009. The data include all private employers for all sectors except agriculture. The data are sourced from the Census Bureau's Business Register, which is continually updated using administrative records, Economic Census returns, and surveys such as the Company Organization Survey. The LBD collects establishment payroll and employment data, which we have used to calculate the average establishment wage per employee for establishments with positive employment and payroll.

Survey respondents are asked to use the definition of salaries and wages used for calculating the federal withholding tax. They report the gross earnings paid in the calendar year to employees at the establishment prior to such deductions as employees' Social Security contributions, withholding taxes, group insurance premiums, union dues, and savings bonds. Included in gross earnings are all forms of compensation such as salaries, wages, commissions, dismissal pay, paid bonuses, vacation and sick leave pay, and the cash equivalent of compensation paid in kind. Salaries of officers of the establishment, if a corporation, are included. In an unincorporated concern, payments to proprietors or partners are excluded. Salaries and wages do not include supplementary labor costs such as employers' Social Security contributions and other legally required expenditures or payments for voluntary pro-

grams. The definition of payrolls is identical to that recommended to all federal statistical agencies by the Office of Management and Budget. We added data on education matching the U.S. 2000 Census long-form data (IPUMS) at the six-digit industry and county level to each establishment by industry, at the most detailed North American Industry Classification System code as available in the IPUMS, and county level, with PUMAs (Public Use Microdata areas) mapped to counties.

The LBD follows establishments over time, where considerable effort was invested by the census to recover longitudinal identifiers through linking records and matching names and addresses (Jarmin and Miranda 2002). We use these identifiers to define establishment births, deaths, and continuers. A birth is an establishment that is observed in the data that did not exist five years earlier. Similarly, a death is an observation that does not survive the five years until the next economic census year. Establishments are either single-unit establishments, where the (generally smaller) firm produces in one location, or multi-unit establishments that are part of a company that operates at multiple locations. The 10 percent, median, and 90 percent deciles are calculated by taking a neighborhood of establishments 1 percent on either side of the decile and using the mean of this sample as a pseudo-decile.

APPENDIX B

Job Destruction and Creation Dominated by Changes Among Continuers

The job destruction graph(figure B1) shows the thousands of jobs that were "destroyed" by plant closing or death of an establishment and by reduction of employment among continuing establishments, and their total. For every year, the job destruction by continuers exceeds job destruction by continuing establishments' reducing employment.

The job creation graph (figure B2) shows the thousands of jobs that were created by new establishments entering the market (through birth) and by expansion of employment among continuing establishments, and their total. For every year the job creation by continuers ex-

Figure B1. Job Destruction, by Source

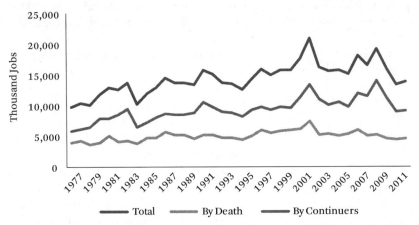

Source: U.S. Census Bureau, Business Dynamics Statistics, 2012 Release, Firm Characteristics Data Tables: Sector, http://www.census.gov/ces/dataproducts/bds/data_firm.html (accessed October 26, 2016).

Figure B2. Job Creation, by Source

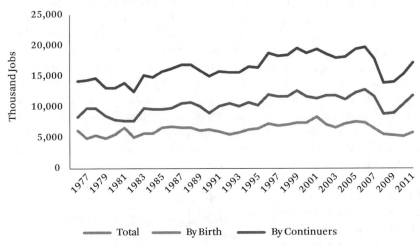

Source: U.S. Census Bureau, Business Dynamics Statistics, 2012 Release, Firm Characteristics Data Tables: Sector, http://www.census.gov/ces/dataproducts/bds/data_firm.html (accessed October 26, 2016).

ceeds job creation by continuing establishments that expand employment.

REFERENCES

Abraham, Katherine, John C. Haltiwanger, Kristin Sandusky, and James R. Spletzer. 2016. "Measuring the Gig Economy." Available at: www.sole-jole.org/16375.pdf; accessed August 4, 2016.

Acemoglu, Daron, David Autor, David Dorn, Gordon H. Hanson, and Brendan Price. 2014. "Return of the Solow Paradox? IT, Productivity, and Employment in U.S. Manufacturing," IZA Discussion Paper No. 7906. January 2014. Available at: http://hdl.handle.net/1721.1/95917; accessed October 20, 2016.

Assous, Michaël. 2013. "Struggle with Medium-Run Macroeconomics: 1956–1995." CHOPE Working Paper No. 2013-17. Available at: https://hope

.econ.duke.edu/sites/hope.econ.duke.edu/files/Assous%20Sept%2013%202013-2.pdf; accessed August 4, 2016.

Bailey, Martin, and Barry Bosworth. 2014. "US Manufacturing: Understanding Its Past and Its Potential Future." *Journal of Economic Perspectives* 28(1): 3–26.

Basu, Susanto, and John Fernald. 2001. "Why Is Productivity Procyclical? Why Do We Care?" In *New Developments in Productivity Analysis*, edited by Charles R. Hultin, Edwin R. Dean, and Michael J. Harper. Cambridge, Mass.: National Bureau of Economic Research.

Biddle, Jeff E. 2014. "Retrospectives: The Cyclical Behavior of Labor Productivity and the Emergence of the Labor Hoarding Concept." *Journal of Economic Perspectives* 28(2): 197–212.

Cazes, Sandrine, Sameer Khatiwada, and Miguel Malo. 2012. "Employment Protection and Collective Bargaining: Beyond the Deregulation Agenda." ILO Employment Working Paper No. 133. Geneva: International Labour Office.

Davis, Steve, John Haltiwanger, Scott Schuh. 1996. *Job Creation and Destruction*. Cambridge, Mass.: MIT Press, 1996.

Foster, Lucia, Cheryl Grim, and John Haltiwanger. 2016. "Reallocation in the Great Recession: Cleansing or Not?" *Journal of Labor Economics* 34(S1): 293–331.

Freeman, Richard B. 2013. Failing the Test? The Flexible U.S. Job Market in the Great Recession." *Annals of the American Academy of Political and Social Science* 65(November): 78–97.

Haltiwanger, John. 2012. "Job Creation and Firm Dynamics in the United States." In *Innovation Policy and the Economy*, vol. 12, edited by Josh Lerner and Scott Stern. Chicago: University of Chicago Press.

Holt, Charles C., Franco Modigliani, John F. Muth, and Herbert A. Simon. 1960. *Planning Production, Inventories, and Work Force*. Englewood Cliffs, N.J.: Prentice-Hall.

Houseman, Susan, Christopher Kurz, Paul Lengermann, and Benjamin Mandel. 2011. "Off Shoring Bias in U.S. Manufacturing." *Journal of Economic Perspectives* 25(2): 61–80.

Jarmin, Ron S., and Javier Miranda. 2002. "The Longitudinal Business Database." CES Working Paper 02–17. Washington: Census Bureau, Center for Economic Studies.

Katz, Larry, and Alan Kreuger. 2016. "The Rise and Nature of Alternative Work Arrangements in the United States, 1995–2015." Cambridge, Mass.: Harvard University and National Bureau for Economic Research, March. Available at: http://scholar.harvard.edu/files/lkatz/files/katz_krueger_cws_v3.pdf; accessed August 4, 2016.

Okun, Arthur. 1970. *The Political Economy of Prosperity*. New York: Norton.

Pugsley, Benjamin, and Ayşegül Şahin. 2014. "Grown-Up Business Cycles." Federal Reserve Bank of New York Staff Report No. 707. New York: Federal Reserve Bank of New York, December. Available at: www.newyorkfed.org/media library/media/research/staff_reports/sr707.pdf; accessed August 4, 2016.

Solow, Robert R. 1964. "Draft of Presidential Address on the Short Run Relation of Employment and Output." Robert Solow papers, Box 70, Folder 1964, David M. Rubenstein Rare Book & Manuscript Library, Duke University, Durham, N.C.

Weil, David. 2014. *The Fissured Workplace*. Cambridge, Mass.: Harvard University Press.

PART II
Social Consequences of the Great Recession

Who Suffered Most from the Great Recession? Happiness in the United States

KELSEY J. O'CONNOR

The lowest level of reported happiness since the 1970s occurred in 2010, which was the result of a negative long-term trend and the Great Recession. However, the Recession's far-reaching consequences were not equally felt. The foreign-born fared the worst, men worse than women, and non-youth worse than youth (eighteen to twenty-four). Declining income and rising unemployment best explain the effects. People reported no change in happiness from the Great Recession when excluding the effects of declining income. This analysis is based on data from the General Social Survey (1972 to 2014). Micro-economic regressions, including macro controls, are used to estimate group-specific trends and deviations from trend occurring in 2008 and 2010. Fixed-effects analysis also supports the main conclusions.

Keywords: Great Recession, happiness, subjective well-being, demographic groups, General Social Survey

The Great Recession was the most severe recession in the United States since the Great Depression. Annual GDP per capita growth was negative during the years 2008 and 2009 (World Bank 2015). The annual unemployment rate reached its highest levels since 1982 and remained above 7.0 percent until 2014 (U.S. Bureau of Labor Statistics 2015a). The median house price declined by 12.6 percent from 2007 to 2009 and had still not recovered by 2012 (U.S. Bureau of the Census 2015). Each measure represents a significant negative shock to the American people, but how were they affected?

Did some population groups fare better than others, and can we explain why? To answer these questions, I provide evidence from nationally representative surveys, from the General Social Survey (GSS), of self-reported evaluations of one's life, commonly referred to as subjective well-being (SWB) or more simply, happiness. Data from the GSS Panel (2006 to 2014), which tracks the same individuals over time, was also used to supplement the main analysis.

In economics, the well-being impacts of past business cycles have been most commonly

Kelsey J. O'Connor is a PhD candidate in economics at the University of Southern California.

© 2017 Russell Sage Foundation. O'Connor, Kelsey J. 2017. "Who Suffered Most from the Great Recession? Happiness in the United States." *RSF: The Russell Sage Foundation Journal of the Social Sciences* 3(3): 72–99. DOI: 10.7758/RSF.2017.3.3.04. I thank Professor Richard Easterlin for his guidance as my research adviser; Robson Morgan for contributing comments and ideas; conference participants for helpful comments; John Ifcher, Arne L. Kalleberg, Rosanna Smart, and Till M. von Wachter for comments on previous drafts; and, for financial assistance, the University of Southern California and the project "Tuscany: A Global Laboratory for Quality of Life," promoted by Tuscany Region, Toscana Promozione and E.di C.s.p.a.-Polo Lionello Bonfanti, Prot. 2014/3014/8.4.1/30, Decreto n.135 del 28/04/2014 and Decreto n. 325 del 15/12/2014. Direct correspondence to: Kelsey J. O'Connor at kelseyoc@usc.edu, University of Southern California, Department of Economics, 3620 S. Vermont Ave., KAP 300, Los Angeles, CA 90089.

measured in terms of economic growth, unemployment, and inflation (for example, the misery index), but in more recent years there has been a growing interest in measures of SWB (Stiglitz, Sen, and Fitoussi 2009). SWB may be better suited than more traditional economic metrics to this purpose. For example, Robert Lucas (1987) argues that business cycles are not very important when considering their effects on aggregate consumption. In response, Justin Wolfers (2003) uses SWB and finds macroeconomic volatility to have "moderate but important" effects on well-being. Justin Wolfers (2003), and others focusing on SWB, contribute to the economics of happiness, which is a relatively new area of research but one that is becoming increasingly important.

This study is the first to document the SWB impacts of the Great Recession, measured as deviations from long-term trends, disaggregated by population group, and to provide statistical evidence for the mechanisms affecting happiness in the United States during this period. To understand the effects of the Great Recession, estimates of group-specific deviations from group-specific trends are necessary for two reasons. First, the happiness trends are generally negative, but not strictly. They vary especially by race and gender (Blanchflower and Oswald 2004; Stevenson and Wolfers 2008b, 2009, 2012; Herbst 2011). Second, different population groups report different average happiness levels, and as different trends suggest, they are subject to different long-term forces that may have persisted through the Great Recession.

In addition to the varying trends in happiness, the results show that each population group reported significant declines during the Great Recession. For the population as a whole, 2010 marks the lowest level of reported happiness in the United States since consistent measurement began in the 1970s. The declines during 2010 vary substantially, however. The foreign-born, who were the greatest impacted, reported a decline more than three times greater than the full population. Men were impacted more than women, young adults less than people older than twenty-four, and Hispanics more than non-Hispanics. Comparison with the 1980s recession shows that the duration of the Great Recession's well-being impacts

was longer, but that the 1980s' impact was deeper. The 1980s' depth is partially explained by a greater decline in women's happiness, however, the overall mechanisms are not yet well understood. In contrast, the declines reported in 2010 can be statistically explained by declining income and rising unemployment. The large decline reported by the foreign-born in 2010 is not surprising when one considers that they reported declines in both income and employment that were each among the largest for the groups studied. The conclusion that declining income best explains the declines in happiness during the Great Recession is further supported by robustness checks, including panel analysis with individual fixed effects.

The results suggest that recessions have a large impact on well-being (contrast with Lucas 1987), and the mechanisms are not surprising. Declining family income affects consumption, the ability to meet financial obligations, and has many indirect effects. Unemployment similarly has many consequences, not only through income but also nonpecuniary factors. Countercyclical income and employment support may be the most effective for mitigating the well-being effects of future recessions, and policymakers may want to target certain populations.

EVIDENCE FROM PAST LITERATURE

A review of the past evidence points to income and unemployment as key variables to account for the Great Recession's impact. Two closely related studies, Carol Graham, Soymya Chattopadhyay, and Mario Picon (2010) and Angus Deaton (2011), each show that unemployment and income measures (including stock prices) are correlated with SWB during the Great Recession in the United States. Unemployment, short-term changes in income, and to a lesser extent inflation have been consistently shown to be related to SWB in a broad context (di Tella, MacCulloch, and Oswald 2001, 2003; Stevenson and Wolfers 2008a; Easterlin et al. 2010; Diener, Tay, and Oishi 2013; Dolan, Peasgood, and White 2008; Winkelmann and Winkelmann 1998), and during economic crises (Wolfers 2003; Bjørnskov 2014; Arampatzi, Burger, and Veenhoven 2015). Thus the expectation is that the Great Recession directly reduced SWB through increased unemployment and reduced income.

What other factors might be important, and were there any that mitigated the income and employment shocks? There is some evidence that welfare-state policies mitigated the effects. Robson Morgan (2015) shows that greater net income replacement rates reduced the SWB declines reported by European nations during the Great Recession, and generous labor market policy helps to reduce the negative association between SWB and unemployment (Carr and Chung 2014; Wulfgramm 2014). However, not all policies are beneficial. Morgan (2015) shows that employment protection legislation exacerbated the well-being effects of the Great Recession in Europe, and Christian Bjørnskov (2014) shows that "wellbeing losses during crises are substantially larger in countries with tighter regulations of credit, labour or product markets" (175). Concerning different population groups, young adults are expected to be affected more by recessions (Bell and Blanchflower 2011). Better-educated people and married people are happier than their counterparts (Dolan, Peasgood, and White 2008) and they may have also fared better through additional support or better coping mechanisms. In contrast, parents are less happy in the United States (Herbst and Ifcher 2014), and this association may have increased during the Great Recession through additional income needs or concern for their children's future.

The most closely related studies, Graham, Chattopadhyay, and Picon (2010) and Angus Deaton (2011), provide some helpful insight, but comparability is limited. As mentioned, they point toward income and unemployment as potential channels, and similar to the present study, each shows SWB declining from early 2008 into 2009. However, they show SWB trending upward beginning in 2009, and recovery by the end of 2009 for Graham, Chattopadhyay, and Picon (2010) and 2010 for Deaton (2011). In contrast, SWB does not recover until 2012 in the present study. This difference can be explained primarily by different benchmarks. They measure recovery to the early 2008 SWB levels, while I measure recovery to long-term trend levels, and 2008 was below trend.

What is more important for comparison, the data used in Graham et al. (2010) and Deaton (2011) have limitations. Both papers use SWB data from the Gallup Healthways Well-Being Index, which is a daily survey beginning in 2008. The first limitation relates to the daily survey, which may be overly sensitive to day-to-day events, some that may be important, and "some that have only dubious implications for well-being" (Deaton 2011, 23). Second, the Gallup SWB data are biased downward by the presence and placement of political questions in the survey that also varies over the study period. Deaton (2011) implements corrections for the political question bias, but the analysis depends on the corrections' validity. Last, their analyses are necessarily limited to focus on short-term relationships because the survey begins in 2008. Free from the limitations associated with Gallup's daily data, the present analysis is better placed to study the effects of the Great Recession on happiness in a long-term context.

HAPPINESS DATA AND METHODS

The General Social Survey (National Opinion Research Center 2015a) is the primary source of happiness data for time-trend analysis in the United States. In thirty waves it covers the forty-two-year period from 1972 to 2014. The survey collects demographic, economic, and attitudinal information for more than fifteen hundred people per wave. Unlike daily surveys, the waves are fielded over a period of several months (typically February to April). It should be noted, however, that there have been changes that could affect time trends (that is, sample composition), but consistent with the past literature, population weights were applied and problematic samples dropped (for example, 1972).[1]

The GSS measures happiness as the response to the question, "Taken all together, how would you say things are these days— would you say that you are very happy, pretty happy, or not too happy?" This happiness question is one of many SWB questions. Similar to life satisfaction, it is more evaluative in nature. As the name implies, evaluative questions focus

---

1. See the appendix for a discussion of the population weights and of which samples have been dropped.

on how the respondent evaluates his or her life. They account for more than how a person feels at given point in time, in contrast to experienced well-being measures (such as "How happy were you yesterday?"). Questions like the GSS happiness question are thought to provide consistent and meaningful measures of well-being (they are reliable and valid). They show a high degree of correlation between subject responses over a short period of time, are well explained by life circumstances, predict future behavior, and correlate well with other subjective and objective measures of well-being. For a further discussion of the types of SWB questions and their reliability and validity see Arie Kapteyn and colleagues (2015) and John F. Helliwell and Shun Wang (2012).

The impacts of the Great Recession were estimated as group-specific deviations from group-specific long-term trends, using individual-level happiness regressions, with repeated cross-sectional data from the GSS. Each regression has two population groups that were selected based on fixed characteristics.[2] Deviations in happiness were estimated for women compared to men, African Americans compared to whites and other races, young adults ages eighteen to twenty-four (also referred to as youth) compared to older people,[3] foreign-born compared to native-born, and nonwhite Hispanics compared to non-Hispanics. The regressions use dummy variables for the years 2008 and 2010 (referred to as Recession dummies), fixed characteristics (for example, birth-cohort), group indicators, a linear trend, a dummy variable for past recession years, and group interactions with trend and the recession

dummies, to obtain group-specific trends and deviations-from-trend. By excluding additional control variables, the recession dummies capture the full short-term impacts of the Great Recession and any additional effects experienced during 2008 and 2010. This model is referred to as the base model and will be built upon in subsequent analysis. The particular estimating equations and control variables are listed in the table footnotes (presented in ordinary least squares form, "OLS" for simplicity).

Consistent with the past literature, the regressions are performed using an ordered probit specification to account for the ordinal nature of the happiness data (similar to Stevenson and Wolfers 2009 and Ifcher and Zarghamee 2014). Unlike OLS, ordered probit regressions do not make the assumption that people treat the difference between "very happy" and "pretty happy" the same as the difference between "pretty happy" and "not too happy."[4] Ordered probit regressions estimate the probability of each response category as a discrete ordered choice. The resulting coefficients, however, do not apply linearly. So to ease interpretation of the results, I also provide the marginal effects for the probabilities of responding "very happy," which are locally linear and can be interpreted like OLS coefficients. A marginal effect also shows the total effect for a group (that is, it includes the main effect and interaction term for the group of interest).

The paper focuses on explaining the declines in reported happiness in 2010. The GSS was not conducted in 2009, and the 2008 survey was fielded prior to much of the Great Recession's

2. Based on fixed characteristics, the group composition should remain the same over time. Selective migration could still affect the group composition, especially for the foreign-born, but if we assume those affected most during the Great Recession were the most likely to move, then the Great Recession's impacts were understated not exaggerated.

3. Identification of the effect of being a youth during the Great Recession depends on the birth-cohort variables. The youngest birth cohort is defined as those born in 1986 or later (1986-cohort), and in 2010, the entire youth group belongs to the 1986-cohort. As a consequence the youth variable interacted with 2010 is directly collinear with this birth-cohort variable in 2010, and identification relies on the 1986-cohort variable's association in alternative years (2004, 2006, 2008, 2012, and 2014). To determine if identification for the effect of being a youth during 2008 and 2010 is a problem (in 2008 youth belong to two cohorts), I estimated the same specification for youth without including the birth-cohort variables, and found similar results. The sample sizes and five alternative years provide sufficient variation for consistent identification.

4. A further discussion of this approach can be found in Ada Ferrer-i-Carbonell and Paul Frijters (2004).

Figure 1. U.S. Happiness 1973–2014; Annual Proportions Reporting "Very Happy," "Pretty Happy," or "Not Too Happy"

Source: Author's calculations based on NORC 2015a.
Notes: How level of happiness is scored: "Very Happy" = 3, "Pretty Happy" = 2, "Not Too Happy = 1."
No controls, sample weights and adjustments applied. See appendix for details.

effects.[5] Although the Great Recession officially began in December of 2007, much of the economic decline occurred later. The collapse of Lehman Brothers, the largest bankruptcy in U.S. history, occurred on September 15, 2008. The largest-percentage decline in GDP occurred from the third quarter 2008 to the fourth quarter 2008 (U.S. Bureau of Economic Analysis 2015a). The official unemployment rate did not exceed 7.0 percent until December 2008, where it remained until December 2013 (U.S. Bureau of Labor Statistics 2015b). For this reason, the happiness figures for 2008 are presented along with 2010, but the discussion focuses on 2010.

It is important to note that self-reported income used throughout the paper is total family income, from all sources, before taxes, not conditional on employment, and adjusted for inflation and household size. Previous researchers using the GSS have also used family income (for example, Stevenson and Wolfers 2009; Ifcher and Zarghamee 2014), because missing values for individual income greatly exceed those for family income (40 percent compared to 10 percent). Analysis using personal income is discussed in the robustness section and shows that the main result does not depend on income measure.

5. The 2008 General Social Survey was fielded between April and September. Although the Great Recession officially began in December of 2007, by the time of fielding, the self-reported economic factors had not changed significantly. The unemployed population share had only increased slightly (2008: 3.4 percent; 2006: 3.3 percent), and self-reported real family income, per household equivalent, had not significantly declined (2008: 33,826; 2006: 33,776). Note the GSS-based unemployment information is for unemployed people as a percentage of the total population, not the labor force.

Table 1. Deviations from Long-Term Trends; Marginal Effects by Group from Ordered Probit Regressions with Happiness as the Choice Variable—Probability of Reporting "Very Happy," 1973–2014

Panel A	Full Sample		Women	Men	Black	White and Other
2008	−0.020***		−0.010*	−0.031***	−0.087***	−0.011***
	[−5.312]		[−1.739]	[−3.181]	[−7.953]	[−3.082]
2010	−0.046***		−0.032***	−0.062***	−0.034***	−0.048***
	[−12.245]		[−5.000]	[−5.799]	[−2.965]	[−13.208]
Trend	−0.002***		−0.003***	−0.002**	0.000	−0.003***
	[−3.310]		[−4.072]	[−2.019]	[0.471]	[−3.707]
Difference in year effects						
2008–2010	0.026***		0.022***	0.031***	−0.053***	0.037***
	[47.215]		[18.374]	[25.309]	[25.970]	[56.150]

Panel B	Youth	25 and Older	Foreign-Born	Native-Born	Hispanic	Non-Hispanic
2008	−0.023**	−0.020***	−0.068***	−0.014***	−0.076***	−0.014***
	[−2.348]	[−5.026]	[−5.271]	[−3.489]	[−4.951]	[−4.008]
2010	−0.021*	−0.049***	−0.151***	−0.031***	−0.089***	−0.036***
	[−1.834]	[−13.177]	[−9.810]	[−7.476]	[−5.113]	[−8.329]
Trend	−0.002**	−0.002***	0.001	−0.003***	0.003	−0.005***
	[−2.346]	[−3.286]	[0.536]	[−3.496]	[1.033]	[−4.335]
Difference in year effects						
2008–2010	−0.002	0.030***	0.083***	0.017***	0.013**	0.023***
	[0.378]	[33.586]	[21.850]	[29.906]	[2.178]	[19.804]

Source: Author's calculations based on table 2.
Notes: Marginal effects, probability of reporting "very happy," are estimated from corresponding regressions in table 2. The two other reporting categories are "pretty happy" and "not too happy." Nativity data are available beginning in 1977. Hispanic data are available beginning in 2000.
t statistics in brackets (clustered by year).
*$p < .10$; **$p < .05$; ***$p < .01$

DESCRIPTION OF WELL-BEING IMPACTS

A smaller share of Americans report being "very happy" today than in the early 1970s, and the lowest recorded share is for the year 2010. Although the Great Recession officially ended in 2009 (National Bureau of Economic Research 2014), happiness did not recover to pre-period trends until 2012. Figure 1 illustrates the negative trend, the low mean score in 2010, and the subsequent recovery.

Statistical Significance of Declines by Population Group

The size of the declines during the Great Recession, and how they compare across groups, is summarized in table 1, based on the results in table 2. Each group was statistically less likely to report being "very happy" during 2008 and 2010, and the declines were usually statistically greater in 2010. The foreign-born were greatest impacted. With a 15.1-percentage-point reduced probability of reporting "very happy" in 2010, they reported a substantially larger decline than the full sample, which reported a corresponding decline of 4.6 percentage points. The next largest decline, 8.9 percentage points, was for Hispanics, which is not surprising because more than one-third are foreign-born. In contrast, youth (ages eighteen to twenty-four) reported the smallest decline, only 2.1 percentage

Table 2. Group-Ordered Probit Regressions; Choice Variable: Happiness, 1973–2014

Group	Full Sample (1)	Women (2)	Black (3)	Youth (4)	Foreign-Born (5)	Hispanic (6)
Women	0.072***	0.150***	0.072***	0.072***	0.060***	0.023
	[4.047]	[4.928]	[4.051]	[4.050]	[3.334]	[0.817]
Black	-0.328***	-0.328***	-0.513***	-0.329***	-0.298***	-0.225***
	[-10.403]	[-10.409]	[-8.520]	[-10.428]	[-10.197]	[-6.580]
Youth	-0.107***	-0.106***	-0.108***	-0.105**	-0.109***	-0.147**
	[-3.856]	[-3.804]	[-3.876]	[-2.413]	[-3.374]	[-2.388]
Group					-0.250***	-0.871***
					[-4.649]	[-2.802]
Past recession	-0.049**	-0.049**	-0.049**	-0.049**	-0.055*	-0.077***
	[-2.130]	[-2.164]	[-2.110]	[-2.125]	[-1.826]	[-5.408]
Trend	-0.007***	-0.005**	-0.007***	-0.007***	-0.008***	-0.014***
	[-3.304]	[-2.014]	[-3.698]	[-3.284]	[-3.493]	[-4.283]
Year 2008	-0.055***	-0.086***	-0.029***	-0.054***	-0.039***	-0.037***
	[-5.358]	[-3.209]	[-3.095]	[-5.062]	[-3.503]	[-4.067]
Year 2010	-0.126***	-0.172***	-0.128***	-0.134***	-0.085***	-0.099***
	[-12.491]	[-5.887]	[-13.432]	[-13.384]	[-7.535]	[-8.594]
Trend X group		-0.004**	0.009***	-0.000	0.010***	0.024***
		[-2.298]	[4.117]	[-0.095]	[4.989]	[2.578]
2008 X group		0.059	-0.256***	-0.012	-0.154***	-0.184***
		[1.544]	[-7.932]	[-0.411]	[-4.451]	[-4.041]
2010 X group		0.086**	0.016	0.074**	-0.344***	-0.160***
		[2.025]	[0.445]	[2.215]	[-8.663]	[-2.911]
Observations	32,945	32,945	32,945	32,945	28,803	11,371
R^2 (pseudo)	0.010	0.010	0.010	0.010	0.009	0.008

Source: Author's calculations based on NORC 2015a; NBER 2014.

Notes: Omitted groups are men, white, and other races, ages twenty-five and older, native-born, and non-Hispanics. Additional control variables include age, age squared, ten-year birth cohort, and mother's and father's education. The estimated regression (specified in OLS) is: $happy_{igt} = \alpha_0 + \beta' x_{it} + \delta preces_t + \lambda_0' time_t + \lambda_1' time \times group_2 + \varepsilon_{igt}$. $happy_{igt}$ is reported happiness for individual i belonging to one of two groups g in year t; x_{it} is a vector of individual characteristics; $preces_t$ is a dummy variable for past recessions; $time_t'$ is the vector (1 $trend_t$, d_{08} d_{10}), where $trend_t = year_t - 1972$ and d_t are dummy variables for the years 2008 and 2010; $group_2$ is a dummy variable for the demographic group of interest. The coefficients of vector λ_0 are the main effects common to all groups, and the marginal effects are obtained from the nonlinear combination of the main effect and the interaction coefficient (that is, λ_0 and λ_1). Nativity data are available beginning in 1977. Hispanic data are available beginning in 2000.

t statistics in brackets (clustered by year).

*$p < .10$; **$p < .05$; ***$p < .01$

points, even though they were expected to be one of most affected groups (Bell and Blanchflower 2011). Compared to their reference groups, men reported a statistically greater decline (in 2010), and so did: blacks (2008), nonyouth (2010), foreign-born (2008 and 2010), and Hispanics (2008 and 2010).

The statistical significance of differences between groups is obtained from the group interactions in the ordered-probit-regression results presented in table 2. For example, the coefficient on "2010 X Group" in column 3 provides an estimate of blacks' experience in 2010 relative to whites' and other races' experience, and in this instance, blacks do not experience a statistically significant difference. The row labels for "Group" refer to the group listed in the column head (that is, in column 2 women are the main group while men are the omitted group). "Year 2008" should be interpreted as the deviation from "Trend" for the omitted group. The 2010 decline for a specified group (reported in table 1) is the nonlinear combination of "Year 2010" and "2010 X Group."

The results for the foreign-born and youth may be surprising, but self-reported declines in income and employment provide plausible explanations. Data from the GSS (reported in appendix table A3) show the foreign-born experienced both a substantial decline in income (21 percent from 2006 to 2010) and increase in unemployment (5.2 percentage points). Youth, in contrast, reported the smallest increase in unemployment from 2006 to 2010 at 1.8 percentage points. Youth also reported a large decline in income, but as mentioned, income is measured as total family income, and it is not clear whom youth are including in "family" income. Moreover, Graham, Chattopadhyay, and Picon (2010) also states young people (nineteen to thirty-five years of age) responded less to events during the Great Recession than older people.

Statistical Significance of Observed Trends in Happiness

Although the focus is on the Great Recession, a few of the long-term trends warrant notice. The first is for women, who report declining levels of happiness in both absolute terms and relative to men. The absolute trend is shown in table 1 by the "Trend" marginal effect. Specifically it means that the probability of women reporting "very happy" declined on average by 0.3 percentage points per year over the period 1973 to 2014.[6] Given the host of improvements in objective indicators for women, it may be surprising that the decline was greater than for men (shown by the negative and statistically significant "Trend X Group" coefficient in table 2, column 2). Comparable results and potential explanations are discussed in Betsey Stevenson

and Justin Wolfers (2009) and Chris Herbst (2011).

During this period, most groups report a negative trend; however, that is not true for blacks, foreign-born, and Hispanics. In the present study blacks report a positive, though statistically insignificant, trend, and past studies have shown a significant-positive trend. The difference is likely because the present study extends the analysis from 2008 to 2014 (contrast with Stevenson and Wolfers 2012), and the trend has flattened out in recent years. Significant or not, a positive trend in the United States is unusual. Blacks' long-term trend has been discussed in the literature (Stevenson and Wolfers 2008b, 2012); the trends for the foreign-born and Hispanics should be the subject of future research.

GREAT RECESSION CHANNELS— EXPLAINING THE IMPACTS

Declines in income and employment provide plausible explanations for the declines in happiness reported during the Great Recession, but were other factors important? Did GDP per capita or the aggregate unemployment rate affect happiness beyond their direct effects on individual income and employment? Were other individual characteristics important? What about housing prices? The following sections identify the plausible channels through which the Great Recession operated, and the statistical methods to obtain the results.

Methods and Variables to Identify Plausible Channels

To identify plausible channels, regional and quarter-of-interview controls, personal characteristics, macro variables, and interactions with certain micro controls are sequentially added to the base model. As mentioned, the base model includes fixed-individual characteristics, a dummy for past recessions, a linear trend, group indicators, Recession dummies (for the Great Recession only), and interactions to obtain group-specific deviations from long-term trends. The additional control variables include traditional micro characteristics that affect hap-

6. On average women are approximately 12.3 percentage points less likely to report being "very happy" in 2014 than they were in 1973.

piness (Dolan, Peasgood, and White 2008) and certain macro-economic variables. In particular the macro pathways include log GDP per capita and lagged log GDP per capita, the unemployment rate, log median house price, the inflation rate, income inequality (Gini coefficient), and government assistance (social expenditures). Lagged log GDP per capita is included because GDP per capita and GDP per capita growth have both been shown to be important variables in the literature, and adding both log GDP per capita and its lag is statistically more flexible than GDP per capita or GDP per capita growth separately. In this context, the unemployment rate could be interpreted as affecting feelings of job security, because controls for individual employment status are also included. Income inequality could be interpreted as affecting trust and feelings of fairness (Oishi, Kesebir, and Diener 2011). GDP and the unemployment rate were measured at the census division level, the median house price at the census region, and the others at the country level. The specific variables and their sources are detailed in the appendix table A4.

When adding control variables, if the statistical significance of a Recession dummy is reduced, then the added variable helps account for the previously unidentified effects associated with the Great Recession years. In the next step, key micro-control variables are interacted with the Recession dummies. Interactions are important because they allow for the relationships of the interacted variables to change during the Great Recession. The relationships could change because people's preferences change, the economic and social context changed, and because the source of variation is likely due to the Great Recession. With interactions, the original Recession dummies (main effects) capture only the remaining variation during that year that is not associated with that channel.

The sample has been restricted to people reporting family income, employment status,

and each of the micro-characteristics of interest. Nativity in particular affects the sample because it was not added to the GSS until 1977. The Gini coefficient also limits the period to 2012 because it was not available for 2014 at time of writing. The analysis based on Hispanic origin is restricted further to the period beginning in 2000, because data on Hispanic origin were not available previously. The base model used to describe the initial declines is an exception. It uses the longest period available, from 1973 to 2014, for each group except those based on nativity and Hispanic origin.[7]

As with the descriptive analysis the regressions are conducted using an ordered probit specification, and the particular estimating equations are listed in the table footnotes (presented in OLS form for simplicity). In what follows the analysis is first performed for the population as a whole, including robustness checks. Then group-specific deviations are estimated as outlined earlier.

Plausible Channels—Average Relationship for Full Population

The primary mechanisms affecting happiness during the Great Recession are income and unemployment. The results are presented in tables 3 and 4. Table 3 presents the first set of results with sequentially added controls, and table 4 further adds micro-control Recession interactions. Adding micro controls, including income, labeled "ln(eqv. inc.)," and employment status, reduces the decline reported by the population as a whole, and is enough to reduce the significance of past recessions, though not of the Great Recession. The interactions with the Recession dummies are necessary to statistically account for the Great Recession's effects, discussed later in connection with table 4. The common trend can be statistically accounted for by adding marital status. This result makes sense as marriage is positively associated with happiness, and the married-population share declined over the

---

7. If sample period is a concern, there are two models that retain the same main conclusions with adjusted sample periods. First, the base model with added location and quarter of interview controls uses the period from 1977 to 2012, and shows similar deviations during 2008 and 2010 (in table 3). Second, the base model with added controls, but excluding nativity and the Gini coefficient, to retain the period from 1973 to 2014, provides similar explanations (discussed in the section on robustness).

Table 3. 2008 and 2010 Deviations from Long-Term Happiness Trends; Ordered Probit Regressions for Full Sample with Added Micro and Macro Controls (2008 and 2010)

	(1)	(2)	(3)	(4)	(5)	(6)	(7)	(8)
Year 2008	-0.055***	-0.114***	-0.109***	-0.126***	-0.123***	-0.125***	-0.170***	-0.148***
	[-5.045]	[-5.913]	[-5.707]	[-6.838]	[-6.562]	[-7.556]	[-5.575]	[-6.138]
Year 2010	-0.126***	-0.150***	-0.143***	-0.147***	-0.145***	-0.116***	-0.076**	-0.066**
	[-11.650]	[-9.098]	[-8.736]	[-8.536]	[-8.350]	[-7.407]	[-2.155]	[-2.322]
Trend	-0.007***	-0.011***	-0.011***	-0.007**	-0.007**	-0.006*	-0.002	-0.000
	[-3.120]	[-3.432]	[-3.365]	[-2.162]	[-2.107]	[-1.867]	[-0.418]	[-0.013]
Past recession	-0.054*	-0.068**	-0.065**	-0.055	-0.055	-0.047	-0.039*	-0.022
	[-1.818]	[-2.100]	[-2.143]	[-1.551]	[-1.548]	[-1.393]	[-1.902]	[-0.956]
Women	0.060***	0.044**	0.050***	0.078***	0.082***	0.094***	0.093***	0.093***
	[3.314]	[2.514]	[2.795]	[3.582]	[3.727]	[4.527]	[4.505]	[4.507]
Black	-0.299***	-0.303***	-0.236***	-0.164***	-0.153***	-0.126***	-0.127***	-0.128***
	[-10.151]	[-8.929]	[-6.403]	[-4.089]	[-3.874]	[-3.243]	[-3.247]	[-3.245]
Youth	-0.110***	-0.084**	-0.043	0.047	0.041	0.048	0.046	0.046
	[-3.409]	[-2.286]	[-1.259]	[1.202]	[1.065]	[1.204]	[1.155]	[1.160]
Foreign	-0.024	-0.025	-0.046	-0.076*	-0.075*	-0.064	-0.063	-0.063
	[-0.647]	[-0.631]	[-1.143]	[-1.872]	[-1.846]	[-1.593]	[-1.579]	[-1.576]
High school and less			-0.086***	-0.094***	-0.090***	-0.065**	-0.064**	-0.065**
			[-2.588]	[-2.872]	[-2.797]	[-2.029]	[-2.018]	[-2.015]
Bachelor's degree or more			0.131***	0.109***	0.104***	0.072**	0.073**	0.073**
			[3.537]	[2.984]	[2.866]	[1.972]	[2.026]	[2.019]
Republican			0.037***	0.031***	0.031***	0.028***	0.028***	0.028***
			[6.686]	[5.554]	[5.643]	[5.160]	[5.150]	[5.149]
Religious			0.205***	0.157***	0.162***	0.156***	0.156***	0.156***
			[5.797]	[4.454]	[4.578]	[4.472]	[4.487]	[4.484]
Never married				-0.424***	-0.475***	-0.416***	-0.418***	-0.417***
				[-7.917]	[-8.776]	[-7.725]	[-7.840]	[-7.807]
Unmarried				-0.592***	-0.597***	-0.554***	-0.557***	-0.556***
				[-27.883]	[-28.218]	[-26.304]	[-26.444]	[-26.456]
Parent					-0.090***	-0.059***	-0.059***	-0.059***
					[-4.480]	[-3.151]	[-3.174]	[-3.141]

(continued)

Table 3. (continued)

	(1)	(2)	(3)	(4)	(5)	(6)	(7)	(8)
Employed part-time						-0.061** [-2.157]	-0.060** [-2.121]	-0.060** [-2.124]
Unemployed						-0.340*** [-5.590]	-0.333*** [-5.374]	-0.334*** [-5.374]
Out of workforce						-0.009 [-0.273]	-0.009 [-0.289]	-0.009 [-0.291]
ln(eqv. inc.)						0.124*** [11.783]	0.122*** [11.524]	0.123*** [11.672]
ln(GDPpc)							-0.277 [-0.680]	
Lag ln(GDPpc)							0.472 [1.464]	
Unemployment rate							-0.018** [-2.115]	-0.021*** [-3.421]
Gini							-2.380** [-2.539]	-2.524*** [-2.691]
ln(house price)							-0.094 [-0.978]	
Inflation							0.003 [0.632]	
Location and quarter controls	No	Yes	Yes	Yes	Yes	Yes	Yes	Yes
Observations	28803	24161	24161	24161	24161	24161	24161	24161
R² (pseudo)	0.008	0.010	0.017	0.039	0.039	0.045	0.045	0.045

Source: Author's calculations based on NORC 2015a; NBER 2014; BEA 2015b; BLS 2015c; Census 2014, 2015; World Bank 2015.

Notes: Additional control variables include age, age squared, ten-year birth cohort, and mother's and father's education. Location and quarter controls are dummies for census division, rural location, and quarter of interview. The estimated regression (specified in OLS) is $happy_{it} = \alpha_0 + \beta' \mathbf{x}_{it} + \gamma' \mathbf{y}_t + \delta preces_t + \lambda_0 trend_t + \lambda_1 d_{08} + \lambda_2 d_{10} + \varepsilon_{it}$; $happy_{it}$ is reported happiness for individual i in year t; $\mathbf{x}_{it}$ is a vector of individual characteristics; $\mathbf{y}_t$ is a vector of macroeconomic variables, $preces_t$ is a dummy variable for past recessions; $trend_t = year_t - 1972$ and d_t are dummy variables for the years 2008 and 2010. For specification 1, the full sample is used (1973–2014). For specifications 2 to 8, the sample is restricted to the years 1977 to 2012, because nativity data are available beginning in 1977, and the Gini coefficient is not available for 2014.

t statistics in brackets (clustered by year).

*$p < .10$; **$p < .05$; ***$p < .01$

period from approximately 70 to 50 percent (shown in appendix table A1).

In general, the coefficients in table 3 are in the expected direction and statistically significant. Women are happier; blacks less happy; higher education is positively associated with happiness; and Republicans, religious people, married couples, and nonparents are all happier. The happiness association with being foreign-born or a young adult depends on other covariates. At the macro-level, income inequality and the unemployment rate play the largest role. Recall that income inequality could be interpreted as affecting trust and feelings of fairness (Oishi, Kesebir, and Diener 2011), and the unemployment rate can be interpreted as affecting feelings of job security when individual employment status is also controlled. In contrast to what one might expect, housing prices at the census division level do not help explain the declines. Social expenditures, GDP per capita, and inflation were also dropped because they are not statistically important. Social expenditures were not presented because they reduced comparability across columns (they are only available beginning in 1980).[8]

Table 4 presents the more important results. The happiness declines from long-term trends are accounted for by the added micro-control interactions, which as explained later, is shown by the "Year 2010" dummy (panel A) being reduced in magnitude and significance. Specifically, full-time-employed people are not statistically less happy than trend in 2010, and people report the trend level of happiness when excluding the effects of income.[9]

Column 1 of table 4 presents the results from the base model with location and quarter-of-interview controls added. The subsequent columns include the macro and micro controls from table 3's column 8, and add interactions with key micro-variables. In column 2, employment status is interacted with the Recession

dummies. Because the omitted category is "employed full-time," the Recession dummies capture the effect of being employed full-time during the years 2008 and 2010. Thus, the insignificant "Year 2010" dummy (column 2) means full-time-employed people did not report a decline from long-term trends in 2010. In column 3, income is interacted with the Recession dummies, and the 2010 dummy indicates that after accounting for income changes, people are not statistically less happy than trend levels. Remember, the income measure is adjusted family income from all sources, and is not conditional on employment.

Column 4 indicates that people with high school or less education are less happy than those with more education (panel C), and education is more important during the Great Recession (see the negative coefficient on the high school–Recession interactions in panel B). Lower educated people may be more vulnerable to the effects of the Great Recession or have inferior support systems. Moving across the columns, married people are happier on average (panel C), and never married people are even worse off during the Great Recession (column 6, panel B). Marriage could mitigate the negative effects of the Great Recession, but unmarried people (separated, divorced, and widowed) people were not differentially affected during the Great Recession. Column 7 shows that parents (married and unmarried) were also not differentially affected during the Great Recession (insignificant parent-Recession interactions), but when controlling for marriage during the Great Recession (column 8), parents do report a larger negative relationship with SWB. As a reminder, the coefficient on 2010 is for the omitted category with continuous controls accounted for separately, which means the positive and significant coefficient on 2010, in column 8, shows that married people who are full-time employed, have no kids, have more

8. Social expenditures may still affect the transmission of the Great Recession's effects, but self-reported income includes government transfers. For this reason we cannot identify the full effects of social expenditures while income is controlled.

9. Like all regression results, this result is conditional on the other controls included in the regression. The section on robustness discusses the effects of employment and income from the base model without additional micro and macro controls.

Table 4. Ordered Probit Regressions for U.S. Sample with Added Controls and Interactions, 1997–2012

Panel A	(1)	(2)	(3)	(4)	(5)	(6)	(7)	(8)
Past recession	-0.068**	-0.022	-0.022	-0.022	-0.021	-0.020	-0.021	-0.021
	[-2.100]	[-0.935]	[-0.957]	[-0.937]	[-0.930]	[-0.880]	[-0.929]	[-0.896]
Trend	-0.011***	-0.000	-0.000	-0.000	-0.000	-0.000	-0.000	-0.000
	[-3.432]	[-0.008]	[-0.015]	[-0.003]	[-0.004]	[-0.074]	[-0.006]	[-0.048]
Year 2008	-0.114***	-0.163***	-0.789***	-0.854***	-0.722***	-0.578***	-0.716***	-0.354**
	[-5.913]	[-5.872]	[-6.385]	[-6.713]	[-5.714]	[-4.335]	[-5.614]	[-2.559]
Year 2010	-0.150***	-0.043	-0.023	0.061	0.155	0.230	0.149	0.273*
	[-9.098]	[-1.228]	[-0.172]	[0.437]	[1.138]	[1.599]	[1.085]	[1.873]
Employed part-time X 2008		0.073**		0.096***	0.096***	0.110***	0.095***	0.113***
		[2.304]		[3.033]	[3.072]	[3.509]	[3.037]	[3.600]
Unemployed X 2008		-0.065		-0.020	-0.021	0.011	-0.021	0.029
		[-1.031]		[-0.311]	[-0.321]	[0.184]	[-0.326]	[0.471]
Out of workforce X 2008		0.027		0.047	0.049	0.043	0.049	0.052
		[0.841]		[1.427]	[1.476]	[1.286]	[1.495]	[1.592]
ln(eqv. inc.) X 2008			0.063***	0.067***	0.057***	0.046***	0.057***	0.038***
			[5.617]	[5.938]	[5.130]	[3.968]	[5.135]	[3.227]
Employed part-time X 2010		-0.027		-0.034	-0.033	-0.035	-0.033	-0.034
		[-0.840]		[-1.096]	[-1.072]	[-1.122]	[-1.083]	[-1.086]
Unemployed X 2010		0.233***		0.227***	0.236***	0.238***	0.237***	0.236***
		[3.622]		[3.466]	[3.578]	[3.662]	[3.600]	[3.619]
Out of workforce X 2010		-0.104***		-0.110***	-0.106***	-0.111***	-0.107***	-0.109***
		[-3.342]		[-3.530]	[-3.351]	[-3.517]	[-3.406]	[-3.494]
ln(eqv. inc.) X 2010			-0.004	-0.010	-0.017	-0.022*	-0.017	-0.023*
			[-0.370]	[-0.851]	[-1.437]	[-1.832]	[-1.491]	[-1.929]

Panel B	(1)	(2)	(3)	(4)	(5)	(6)	(7)	(8)
High school X 2008					-0.057**	-0.053**	-0.057**	-0.045*
					[-2.421]	[-2.326]	[-2.379]	[-1.908]
High school X 2010					-0.053**	-0.055**	-0.053**	-0.052**
					[-2.170]	[-2.314]	[-2.149]	[-2.122]
Never married X 2008						-0.160***		-0.270***
						[-3.654]		[-6.038]
Never married X 2010						-0.092*		-0.114**
						[-1.914]		[-2.333]
Unmarried X 2008						0.013		0.005
						[0.514]		[0.183]
Unmarried X 2010						0.030		0.027
						[1.100]		[0.988]
Parent X 2008							-0.009	-0.163***
							[-0.343]	[-7.752]
Parent X 2010							0.018	-0.038*
							[0.632]	[-1.763]

(continued)

Table 4. (continued)

Panel C	(1)	(2)	(3)	(4)	(5)	(6)	(7)	(8)
High school and less		-0.065**	-0.065**	-0.064**	-0.058*	-0.058*	-0.058*	-0.058*
		[-2.021]	[-2.014]	[-2.014]	[-1.727]	[-1.720]	[-1.719]	[-1.717]
Bachelor's degree or more		0.074**	0.073**	0.074**	0.074**	0.074**	0.074**	0.075**
		[2.035]	[2.003]	[2.019]	[2.033]	[2.027]	[2.035]	[2.056]
Never married		-0.416***	-0.417***	-0.416***	-0.416***	-0.402***	-0.416***	-0.396***
		[-7.804]	[-7.808]	[-7.806]	[-7.803]	[-7.212]	[-7.812]	[-7.053]
Unmarried		-0.556***	-0.556***	-0.555***	-0.555***	-0.558***	-0.555***	-0.558***
		[-26.424]	[-26.378]	[-26.347]	[-26.286]	[-23.976]	[-26.278]	[-23.893]
Parent		-0.058***	-0.058***	-0.058***	-0.058***	-0.057***	-0.059***	-0.047**
		[-3.111]	[-3.143]	[-3.112]	[-3.115]	[-3.089]	[-2.950]	[-2.444]
Employed part-time		-0.063**	-0.061**	-0.064**	-0.064**	-0.065**	-0.064**	-0.065**
		[-2.041]	[-2.146]	[-2.087]	[-2.094]	[-2.120]	[-2.094]	[-2.132]
Unemployed		-0.357***	-0.334***	-0.358***	-0.359***	-0.360***	-0.359***	-0.360***
		[-5.339]	[-5.372]	[-5.362]	[-5.370]	[-5.409]	[-5.372]	[-5.408]
Out of workforce		-0.005	-0.010	-0.006	-0.007	-0.006	-0.007	-0.006
		[-0.141]	[-0.323]	[-0.190]	[-0.202]	[-0.169]	[-0.200]	[-0.182]
ln(eqv. inc.)		0.123***	0.120***	0.120***	0.121***	0.122***	0.121***	0.123***
		[11.705]	[10.504]	[10.477]	[10.506]	[10.525]	[10.491]	[10.530]
Macro controls	No	Yes	Yes	Yes	Yes	Yes	Yes	Yes
Observations	24,161	24,161	24,161	24,161	24,161	24,161	24,161	24,161
R² (pseudo)	0.010	0.045	0.045	0.045	0.045	0.046	0.045	0.046

Source: Author's calculations based on NORC 2015a; NBER 2014; BEA 2015b; Census 2014.

Notes: Additional control variables include age, age squared, ten-year birth cohort, mother's and father's education, census division, rural location, quarter of interview, woman, black, youth, foreign-born, Republican, and religious. Macro controls include the unemployment rate and Gini coefficient. The estimated regression (specified in OLS) is $happy_{it} = \alpha_0 + \beta'\mathbf{x}_{it} + \gamma'\mathbf{y}_t + \delta preces_t + \lambda_0 trend_t + \lambda_1 d_{08} + \lambda_2 d_{10} + \lambda_3'\mathbf{c}_{it} d_{08} + \lambda_4'\mathbf{c}_{it} d_{10} + \varepsilon_{it}$. $happy_{it}$ is reported happiness for individual i in year t; x_{it} is a vector of individual characteristics; $\mathbf{y}_t$ is a vector of macro economic variables; $preces_t$ is a dummy variable for past recessions; $trend_t = year_t - 1972$ and d_t are dummy variables for the years 2008 and 2010. $\mathbf{c}_{it}$ is a vector of individual variables or channels that may explain the Great Recession. They are also included in $\mathbf{x}_{it}$. The sample is restricted to the years 1977 to 2012, because nativity data are available beginning in 1977, and the Gini coefficient is not available for 2014. t statistics in brackets (clustered by year).

*$p < .10$; **$p < .05$; ***$p < .01$

than a high school education, and excluding income effects, showed an increase in happiness during 2010 (at 10 percent significance).

It is interesting to note that the declines in happiness observed in 2008 are not well explained. As discussed earlier, the survey in 2008 preceded much of the economic decline, and it is likely for this reason that the decline in 2008 cannot be explained by economic factors. Note too, however, that education, marital status, and parental status also fail to explain the impacts in 2008. It is possible that Americans perceived uncertainty in anticipation of the economic declines and that reduced their happiness.

Robustness Checks
Additional results emphasize the importance of income during the Great Recession. In the previous analysis, the deviations were measured from a linear trend, and the decline during 2010 was statistically explained with micro, macro, and micro-interaction determinants. However, the models may face problems with endogeneity associated with behaviorally chosen variables, and it is possible that the long-term trends are nonlinear. For these reasons, two robustness checks were used.

The first check uses regressions that separately add the income and employment status interactions to the base model. This reduces endogeneity concerns because the variables resulting from behavioral choice are excluded, and the main effects of income and employment should capture any endogenous relationship that is not specific to 2008 or 2010. As an added benefit, the full period (1973 to 2014) is retained when excluding nativity and the Gini coefficient from the regressions. The second check uses a cubic trend in place of the linear trend.

The 2010 marginal effects, or changes in probability of reporting "very happy," are reported in appendix table A5. Remember the marginal effects are associated with the 2010 dummy or main effect excluding the interaction terms. Without additional controls, the interactions between income and the Recession dummies are sufficient to account for the decline in happiness reported in 2010 (shown in column 3), and this result does not depend on a linear trend (column 5). In contrast, full-time-employed people are statistically less happy in 2010 (column 2). Without controls, they report a smaller decline in 2010 than the average person, but the decline is still statistically significant. Reduced income is the most important channel affecting happiness during the Great Recession, and this result holds under multiple scenarios. However, it is important to remember that income and unemployment are not independent of each other. Changes in adjusted family income may result from changes in personal wages, family member wages, household composition, and government transfers, or may have been caused by unemployment or underemployment.

As mentioned, adjusted family income was relied upon because personal income data were more likely to be missing (40 percent compared to 10 percent). However, it may be expected that the happiness-income relation depends on the source of income. To determine if the income measure drives the key results, an additional robustness test was used. In column 6 of table A5, real personal income and its interactions with the Recession dummies were added to the base model. Results for the comparable analysis using adjusted family income are presented in column 3. Comparing the two estimates, the results are visibly different, but neither is statistically significant. Like adjusted family income, reduced personal income in 2010 can account for the average reported decline in happiness in 2010.

Happiness Changes by Individual
The interpretation of the long-term analysis is limited to comparisons of different people. To measure the effects of variable changes over time for a given person, longitudinal or panel data are necessary. Using the relatively new GSS Panel data (covering the period 2006 to 2014) I further tested the mechanisms affecting happiness during the Great Recession using a fixed-effects logit specification.[10] The main conclu-

10. In 2006 the General Social Survey added a longitudinal component that tracks the same people over time, and there are now three separate overlapping panels, each with three waves, that collectively cover the years

sion is the same. Declining income statistically explains the happiness declines in 2010. However, this result may be considered more robust, because individual fixed effects capture omitted time-invariant factors.

The panel analysis is similar to the long-term but differs in a few important aspects. Year dummies are added for each year in the sample excluding 2010, making it the reference period, not long-term trends. Then similar to the robustness checks, income and employment status are separately added to see if they can explain the year effects. 2010 was used as the reference period because it had the lowest level of happiness and was the only year that each GSS panel was fielded.[11] Fixed-effects logit specifications are used with the binary variable "very happy" because ordered probit models are not possible with fixed effects (Cameron and Trivedi 2005, 796).[12]

Appendix table A6 presents the results. Column 1 includes only the year dummies (fixed effects are also included with the model). Compared with 2010, each year is positively associated with the probability of reporting "very happy." Note the estimates do not have a linear interpretation, but consistent with previous findings they are increasing away from 2010 (that is, people are happiest in 2006 and 2014). Column 2 adds controls for income and employment status. Each year is still statistically significant and positive. Accounting for the period–average income and employment relationships is insufficient to account for the 2010 decline in happiness.

Column 3 excludes the income control, but interacts employment status with each year. The results show that a full-time-employed person (the omitted category) or someone with no change in employment status[13] reports comparable happiness in 2008 and 2010 (2008 is not

statistically different from 2010). However, they are happier in the other years when compared to 2010.

Column 4 presents the main effects for each year when income-year interactions are used. Excluding the effects of income, individuals are not statistically more likely to report "very happy" during 2006, 2008, or 2012. They are equally happy in 2010, which is consistent with the long-term analysis. However, the 2014 main effect is statistically significant, which indicates people are happier in 2014 than in 2010, even when excluding the effects of differences in income.

Channels by Population Group

The explanations of the Great Recession's effects for various population groups are similar to those for the population as a whole. Declining income statistically accounts for the declines in happiness reported by each group in 2010, with one exception. Rising unemployment is also important.

A summary of the results can be illustrated with the reported declines before and after accounting for the plausible channels. In figure 2 the darker bars correspond to the 2010 declines in the probability of reporting "very happy." The first estimates are from the base model and are repeated from table 1. Note that as before, the deviations are negative and statistically significant at 5 percent for each population group except youth (eighteen to twenty-four). The lighter gray bars are for the base model, but with additional channels controlled. Specifically, the light gray deviations show the "effects" of 2010, excluding income's association with happiness. Notice that the confidence intervals greatly increase, and for men and blacks, what were statistically significant and negative deviations are now positive and sig-

---

2006 to 2014. The first panel was fielded in 2006, 2008, and 2010, the second panel in 2008, 2010, and 2012, and the last panel (to-date) was fielded in 2010, 2012, and 2014.

11. See the preceding note, regarding the General Social Survey.

12. There are ordered logit estimation techniques that allow fixed effects (Ferrer-i-Carbonell and Frijters 2004), but the binary-response logit model is consistent and simpler to implement.

13. The effect of not changing employment status is treated the same as being in the reference group because fixed-effects models estimate the effects of changes in independent variables. Also, anyone who did not report a change in "very happy" over the period is dropped from the regression.

Figure 2. 2010 Deviation from Long-Term Trend—Change in Probability of Reporting "Very Happy," Two Models by Population Group

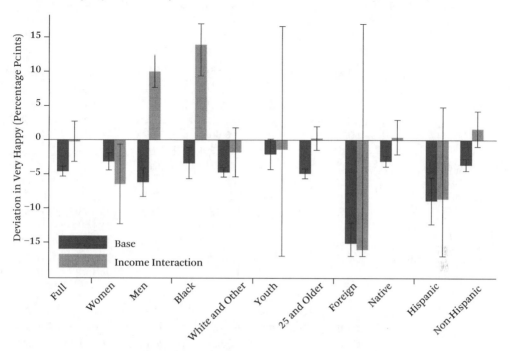

Source: Author's calculations based on tables 1, 2, and 5.

Notes: The value of nearly –5 for "Full" (Base) indicates that the full sample was approximately 5 percentage points less likely to report being "very happy" in the year 2010, when compared to long-term trends. "Base" corresponds to the estimates reported in table 1, based on the regressions in table 2. "Income Interaction" shows the deviations excluding the effects of declining income. The figures correspond to the estimates reported in table 5, Income Interaction row, which for the full sample, are based on table 4, column 3. Error bars represent 95 percent confidence intervals. They have been truncated when extending beyond –17 or 17 to reduce the size of the figure.

nificant. The 2010-reported decline in happiness is accounted for with micro and macro controls, and income–Recession-dummy interactions. Women are, however, an exception when using income interactions. The supporting estimates are presented in table 5, along with alternative models.

Table 5 provides a summary of the 2010 change in the likelihood a population group will report being "very happy." The estimates are marginal effects from ordered probit regressions for the 2010 dummy or main effect. The first row repeats the declines reported in table 1. Subsequent rows show how the declines change as controls are added to the base

model. For the full sample, the rows correspond to the columns in tables 3 and 4 (specific columns are described in the footnotes). Compared to the base model, the model for the row labeled "Micro controls" adds dummies (without interactions) for census division, rural location, quarter of interview, education level, Republican, religious, marital status, parent, employment status, and income. The macro controls include the unemployment rate and the Gini coefficient. The statistically insignificant marginal effect for Hispanics in row 2 means the micro controls are sufficient to account for their 2010 decline in reported happiness.[14]

14. The analysis for Hispanic and non-Hispanic groups only covers the period from 2000 to 2012 based on availability of the Hispanic variable and Gini coefficient. It is likely due to the shorter period that Hispanics only require

Table 5. 2010 Deviation from Long-Term Trend—Change in Probability of Reporting "Very Happy" by Population Group with Specified Controls

Panel A	(1) Full Sample	(2)	(3) Women	(4) Men	(5) Black	(6) White and Other
Base	-0.046***		-0.032***	-0.062***	-0.034***	-0.048***
	[-12.245]		[-5.000]	[-5.799]	[-2.965]	[-13.208]
Micro controls	-0.040***		-0.020***	-0.063***	-0.030**	-0.042***
	[-7.318]		[-3.123]	[-6.931]	[-2.512]	[-6.357]
Macro controls	-0.023**		-0.003	-0.046***	-0.016	-0.024**
	[-2.315]		[-0.280]	[-4.144]	[-1.235]	[-2.205]
Employment interaction	-0.015		0.008	-0.038***	0.016	-0.018
	[-1.224]		[0.556]	[-2.749]	[1.054]	[-1.368]
Income interaction	-0.003		-0.065**	0.100***	0.139***	-0.018
	[-0.167]		[-2.181]	[8.402]	[5.968]	[-0.997]
Employment and income interactions	0.007		-0.059**	0.146***	0.314***	-0.015
	[0.466]		[-2.061]	[8.880]	[6.129]	[-0.834]
High school, employment, and income interactions	0.019		-0.061*	0.150***	0.324***	-0.009
	[1.363]		[-1.865]	[8.775]	[4.128]	[-0.497]

Panel B	(1) Youth (18–24)	(2) Twenty-Five Years and Older	(3) Foreign-Born	(4) Native-Born	(5) Hispanic	(6) Non-Hispanic
Base	-0.021*	-0.049***	-0.151***	-0.031***	-0.089***	-0.036***
	[-1.834]	[-13.177]	[-9.810]	[-7.476]	[-5.113]	[-8.329]
Micro controls	-0.044***	-0.041***	-0.127***	-0.029***	-0.012	-0.035***
	[-2.774]	[-5.706]	[-4.935]	[-4.594]	[-1.448]	[-5.579]
Macro controls	-0.032*	-0.022**	-0.109***	-0.010	-0.028	-0.051
	[-1.652]	[-2.133]	[-4.803]	[-0.861]	[-0.452]	[-0.832]
Employment interaction	-0.029	-0.014	-0.057**	-0.009	0.004	-0.062
	[-1.123]	[-1.160]	[-2.321]	[-0.652]	[0.056]	[-0.916]
Income interaction	-0.014	0.002	-0.161	0.004	-0.021	0.014
	[-0.153]	[0.275]	[-0.893]	[0.317]	[-0.428]	[0.940]
Employment and income interaction	0.022	0.006	-0.017	0.005	-0.022	0.005
	[0.279]	[0.736]	[-0.122]	[0.323]	[-0.392]	[0.159]
High school, employment, and income interaction	n.a.	0.019***	0.143*	0.007	n.a.	0.010
		[2.861]	[1.712]	[0.519]		[0.334]

Source: Author's calculations based on NORC 2015a; NBER 2014; U.S. BEA 2015b; Census 2014.

Notes: The first row of each panel corresponds with table 1. The subsequent rows correspond as follows: row 2 = table 3, column 6; row 3 = table 3, column 8; row 4 = table 4, column 2; row 5 = table 4, column 3; row 6 = table 4, column 4; row 7 = table 4, column 5. Results were omitted if the bin size was too small (for example, there were less than thirty youths in the sample who were full-time employed and also had a high school or less education in 2010). For the same reason specifications including interactions for parents and marital status were excluded.

t statistics in brackets (clustered by year).

*p < .10; **p < .05; ***p < .01

The rows beginning with "Employment interaction" add Recession year interactions with: (1) employment status (employed full-time is omitted); (2) income; (3) employment status and income; and (4) high school education (less than high school omitted), employment status, and income. The row "Income interaction" presents the estimates associated with figure 2. With the interactions, the reported marginal effects represent the deviations for the omitted category or excluding the effects of income. The last row, for example, is based on the model with micro- and macro controls, and interactions with employment status, income, and high school or less education (table 4, column 5), and the marginal effect is for people employed full-time, with more than a high school education, and excluding the association with income.

Moving down the rows in table 5, column 1, the reduced magnitude and significance of the 2010 "effects" show that the unexplained decline in happiness reported in 2010 can be accounted for with micro and macro controls (shown by the reduced magnitude), but requires income or unemployment interactions to completely account for the decline (reduced significance). Similar to the full-sample results, interactions are necessary to account for the average decline reported by several groups, specifically, whites and other races, youth, and those older than twenty-four. For other groups, reduced feelings of job security and increasing income inequality (macro controls) are sufficient (women, blacks, native-born, and non-Hispanics). In stark contrast, women do not report a decline in 2010 with unemployment interactions, but they do when controlling for income interactions, even full-time-employed women. This result is unexpected and should be explored further in future analysis.

Among some of the other interesting results,

recall that the foreign-born showed the largest decline in the likelihood of reporting "very happy" during 2010 (15.1 percentage points). Table 5, panel B, column 3, shows that even the full-time-employed foreign-born reported a 10.9-percentage-point decline, which is substantial because the next-largest decline, excluding for Hispanics, was for men at only 6.2 percentage points (table 1, panel A).[15] The 10.9-point decline for the full-time-employed foreign-born is 75 percent greater than the average for men (employed and unemployed). However, adding the income interaction is sufficient to account for the foreign-born's reported decline in happiness (table 5, panel B, column 3, the decline is large but no longer statistically significant). Income interactions are important for other groups, too, especially men and blacks who become statistically happier in 2010 when excluding the effects of income.

The figures by population group are based on the same analysis that was applied to the full sample, but with added group interactions. Full regression results that form the basis for Table 5 (analogous to tables 3 and 4) are available upon request.

COMPARISON WITH THE 1980S RECESSION

The early 1980s was another period of significant economic decline. Periods of 1980, 1981, and 1982 were officially recognized as recessions (National Bureau of Economic Research 2014), and in some ways this period may have been worse than the Great Recession. The annual unemployment rates, at more than 9.5 percent, were the same or higher in 1982 and 1983 than in 2009 and 2010. However, the annual unemployment rate did decline below 8.0 percent in 1984, but remained above 8.0 percent during the Great Recession until 2013 (U.S. Bureau of Labor Statistics 2015a). Which period

---

controls for the period-average relationship between income and unemployment to statistically account for the declines in 2010.

15. Hispanics were not referenced due to the large overlap between Hispanics and the foreign-born. In the weighted GSS sample, more than one-third of Hispanics are foreign-born; conversely, more than one-third of the foreign-born are Hispanic, although the exact figures depend on the survey year.

had a greater impact on the American people? And did the 1980s recession affect SWB through the same channels, especially unemployment and income?

The 1980s results (available upon request) show that 1983 was in fact associated with a larger decline in happiness than 2010. The population was 6.0 percentage points less likely to report being "very happy" in 1983, and only 4.6 percentage points less likely in 2010. This result is partially explained by women's happiness. Women reported substantially larger declines in 1983 (5.5 percentage points) than in 2010 (3.2 percentage points). This result is unexpected, given that women faced larger decreases in employment and income during the Great Recession than in the earlier recession.[16] The foreign-born again reported greater declines in happiness than the rest of the population, but the difference was not as extreme (1983, 7.2-percentage-point decline; 2010, 15.1-percentage-point decline).[17]

The 1980s recession warrants further analysis. Unlike 2010, the decline in 1983 cannot be explained with declining income and rising unemployment. Even married people who are full-time employed, have no kids, have more than a high school education, and excluding the effects of income, are statistically less happy in 1983 than trend levels. The two recessions also differ in duration. Figure 1 illustrates how long happiness was below trend during the Great Recession, and how short the deviation was during the 1980s. Statistically the Great Recession's impacts started in 2008, at a 2.0-percentage-point decline in happiness from trend, whereas the 1980s happiness decline began in 1982 at only 1.0 percentage point (the decline in 1980 was not statistically significant, and the GSS was not fielded in 1981). To compare the recessions' impacts, future analysis should also account for their duration.

CONCLUSION

Surveys from mid-2010, one year after the official end of the Great Recession, mark the lowest level of happiness in the United States since consistent measurement began in the early 1970s. Declining income and employment from the Great Recession best explain the drop in happiness during 2010. Of the population groups studied, the foreign-born reported declines in both income and employment that were among the largest, and correspondingly, this group reported the largest decline in happiness, which was more than three times as great as that of the full population. Men reported greater declines in happiness, income, and employment than women. Contrary to expectations, young adults (eighteen to twenty-four) reported a smaller decline in happiness than older people, which is likely because they reported one of the smallest increases in unemployment. The most important macro relationships during this period were associated with the rising unemployment rate and income inequality. The other macro variables, GDP, inflation, house prices, and social expenditures, did not statistically affect happiness when individual characteristics were also controlled. To help summarize the results, figure 2 illustrates the initial declines by population group and estimates of the declines excluding the effects of changing income. As a reminder, supporting income and employment data from the GSS are presented in appendix table A3.

The mechanisms are not surprising. As discussed in the literature section, past work on economic crises has pointed to income loss and unemployment as the drivers of declining well-being. In general, income losses have larger negative effects on well-being than the positive effects of gaining an equivalent amount (Kahneman and Tversky 1979), and during the Great

16. Women's 1983 self-reported income was approximately the same as in 1980, and their unemployment share increased by approximately 0.9 percentage points.

17. The analysis for the 1980s mirrors that for the Great Recession. The models employed were the same, except that the Recession dummies were for the years 2008 and 2010, and the 1980s recession dummies were for the years 1980, 1982, and 1983. The past recession dummy was also changed. The 1980s recession years were swapped for the Great Recession years.

Recession this effect was likely amplified. Individuals faced reduced consumption and increased stress associated with meeting financial obligations, especially mortgages. Income loss also affects factors not strictly related. Take spousal job loss as an example; it will reduce family income and possibly affect marital satisfaction. Underemployment is another—it is likely to reduce income and job quality, thus affecting job satisfaction. The effects of unemployment on well-being are also far-reaching. Beyond its effects on income, there are substantial nonpecuniary costs. Liliana Winkelmann and Rainer Winkelmann (1998) show that the nonpecuniary effects of unemployment on life satisfaction are larger than from the loss of income alone. In the introduction to this journal issue, Arne L. Kalleberg and Till M. von Wachter also discuss the effects of job loss during the Great Recession, including the nonpecuniary effects.

The results described here are based on estimates of group-specific deviations from group-specific trends covering a period of approximately forty years, with various micro and macro controls to explain the deviations, and supplemented by panel-data analysis with individual fixed effects. The analysis differs substantively from the two closest studies, by Carol Graham, Soymya Chattopadhyay, and Mario Picon (2010) and Angus Deaton (2011). Without their data limitations, the present analysis is better placed to document the effects of the Great Recession on the SWB of different populations in a long-term context.

APPENDIX

General Social Survey Sample Weights and Restrictions

The following samples were dropped: the African American oversample in 1982 and 1987; surveys that were conducted in Spanish (and could not have been completed in English); the 1972 and 1985 surveys (because the question preceding happiness changed); and observations from split-ballot experiments that were conducted in 1980, 1986, and 1987. The GSS variable WTSSALL was applied to ensure samples approximated the national population. This strategy was employed by Herbst and Ifcher (2014; see 5n4).

Table A1. Population Sample Shares by Demographic, Group General Social Survey, 1977 and 2014

	1977		2014	
Group	No. of Observations	Population Share	No. of Observations	Population Share
Women	1,530	53%	2,446	54%
Black	1,530	11	2,446	15
Youth	1,524	15	2,436	9
Foreign-born	1,529	7	2,446	13
Hispanic	n.a.	n.a.	2,438	14
High school and less	1,526	84	2,446	63
Married	1,530	69	2,443	52
Parent	1,517	74	2,440	71

Source: Author's calculations based on NORC 2015a.

Table A2. Summary Statistics for Key Micro-Variables

	1977			2014		
Variable	Number of Observations	Mean	Std. Dev.	Number of Observations	Mean	Std. Dev.
Happy (scale of 1 to 3)	1,528	2.25	0.64	2,438	2.21	0.63
Age (years)	1,524	43.78	16.86	2,436	47.46	17.39
Female education (years)	1,092	9.05	4.18	1,830	12.05	4.06
Male education (years)	1,249	9.58	3.66	2,198	11.86	3.75
Income (2000$s)[a]	1,372	$25,623	$19,968	2,206	$32,559	$27,965

Source: Author's calculations based on NORC 2015a.

[a]Income is measured as total family income per equivalent household size. Specifically: household income (General Social Survey variable coninc) divided by equivalent household size (GSS household composition and OECD-modified equivalence scale; see Organisation for Economic Co-operation and Development 2015).

Table A3. Self-Reported Income and Unemployment as Percentage of Total Population, by Population Group, 2006–2012

Panel A

	Full Sample		Men		Women	
	Unemployed	Income ($)	Unemployed	Income ($)	Unemployed	Income ($)
2006	3.3%	33,776	3.6%	36,475	3.1%	31,370
2008	3.4	33,826	4.7	36,653	2.3	31,163
2010	7.3	29,501	10.0	31,471	5.1	27,798
2012	5.2	32,474	6.5	35,194	4.1	30,122
Increase in unemployment from 2006 to 2010	4.0	-4,275	6.4	-5,004	2.0	-3,572
Percent change (2010 to 2006)	119.4%	-12.7%	179.9%	-13.7%	62.8%	-11.4%

Panel B

	Black		Nonblack		Youth		Non-Youth	
	Unemployed	Income ($)	Unemployed	Income	Unemployed	Income ($)	Unemployed	Income ($)
2006	5.5%	24,150	3.0%	35,203	6.5%	23,707	2.9%	34,922
2008	8.2	21,495	2.7	35,799	6.5	20,927	3.0	35,430
2010	9.3	21,138	6.9	30,950	8.3	17,653	7.1	30,809
2012	8.6	21,244	4.6	34,487	8.3	22,297	4.8	33,740
Absolute Change (2010 to 2006)	3.8	-3,013	4.0	-4,253	1.8	-6,054	4.3	-4,113
Percent Change (2010 to 2006)	68.7%	-12.5%	133.1%	-12.1%	28.5%	-25.5%	148.9%	-11.8%

Panel C

	Native		Foreign		Hispanic		Non-Hispanic	
	Unemployed	Income ($)	Unemployed	Income ($)	Unemployed	Income ($)	Unemployed	Income ($)
2006	3.5%	34,086	1.3%	33,146	6.5%	26,862	3.0%	34,467
2008	3.6	33,795	1.5	34,118	2.9	25,027	3.5	34,796
2010	7.4	29,981	6.5	26,196	10.5	16,385	6.8	31,378
2012	5.5	32,420	2.8	33,194	6.7	25,289	5.0	33,451
Absolute Change (2010 to 2006)	3.9	-4,105	5.2	-6,950	4.0	-10,477	3.8	-3,089
Percent Change (2010 to 2006)	110.9%	-12.0%	395.5%	-21.0%	62.4%	-39.0%	126.0%	-9.0%

Source: Author's calculations based on NORC 2015a.

Notes: Income is total real family income (from all sources) adjusted for household size.

Table A4. Key Macroeconomic Variables and Their Sources

Variable	Unit	Value 1977	Value 2014	Aggregation	Source
Real GDP per capita[a]	2000$s	24,428	45,873	By census division	U.S. Bureau of Economic Analysis 2015b: Regional Economic Accounts
Unemployment Rate	Percent of labor force	7.03	6.18	By census division	U.S. Bureau of Labor Statistics (2015c): Local Area Unemployment Statistics
Inflation rate	Percentage Change in CPI	6.49	1.62	U.S aggregate	World Bank (2015) World Development Indicators
Social expenditure[b]	Percent of GDP	12.80	18.70	U.S aggregate	Organisation for Economic Co-operation and Development (2014) Social Expenditure Database
Median house price	2000$s	127,765	240,226	By census region	U.S. Census Bureau (2015) New Residential Sales Historical Data: Sales Price by Houses Sold
Gini coefficient[c]	n.a.	0.36	0.45	U.S. aggregate	U.S. Census Bureau (2014) Current Population Survey, Annual Social and Economic Supplements. Table F-4. Gini Indexes for Families, by Race and Hispanic Origin of Householder: 1947 to 2013
Past recession[d]	Dummy	0	0	U.S. aggregate	National Bureau of Economic Research (2014) Recession Dating Committee

Source: Author's compilation from sources listed in table.

[a]The North American Industry Classification System's current GDP per capita by state was extended back using Standard Industrial Classification GDP per capita by state. GDP was then aggregated and adjusted for population by census division, and then inflation.

[b]1977 Social expenditure value is for 1980. Data are available beginning in 1980.

[c]2014 Gini coefficient is for 2013. 2014 is not yet available.

[d]Coded: 1 for the years: 1974, 1975, 1980 to 1983, 1990, 1991, 2001, and 2002.

Table A5. 2010 Deviation from Long-Term Trend: Change in Probability of Reporting "Very Happy," Full Sample, 1973–2014

	(1)	(2)	(3)	(4)	(5)	(6)
Year 2010	-0.046***	-0.029***	-0.001	-0.044***	-0.001	-0.015
	[-12.245]	[-5.401]	[-0.320]	[-14.013]	[-0.323]	[-1.456]
Number of observations	32,945	32,945	30,227	32,945	30,227	21,191

Source: Author's calculations based on NORC 2015a.

Notes: Marginal effects correspond to λ_2 from the ordered probit regressions, detailed below. Column 1 replicates the base model, table 2, column 1. Column 2 includes the main effect for employment status and its interaction with 2008 and 2010 (excludes income). Column 3 includes the main effect for income and its interaction with 2008 and 2010 (excludes employment status). Column 4 uses a cubic trend, but no additional control variables. Column 5 uses the cubic trend with the main effect for income and interaction. Column 6 repeats column 3, but uses real personal income as opposed to adjusted family income.

All models include the control variables: woman, black, youth, age, age squared, ten-year birth cohort, and mother's and father's education. The estimated regression (specified in OLS) is: $happy_{it} = \alpha_0 + \beta'x_{it} + \delta preces_t + \lambda_0 trend_t + \lambda_1 d_{08} + \lambda_2 d_{10} + \lambda_3'c_{it}d_{08} + \lambda_4'c_{it}d_{10} + \varepsilon_{it}$. $happy_{it}$ is reported happiness for individual i in year t; x_{it} is a vector of individual characteristics; $preces_t$ is a dummy variable for past recessions; $trend_t = year_t - 1972$ and d_t are dummy variables for the years 2008 and 2010. c_{it} is a vector of individual variables that may explain the Great Recession's effects.

Table A6. Fixed Effects Logit Regressions, GSS Panel 2006–2014; Dependent Variable "Very Happy" Main Effects by Year (Base = 2010)

	(1)	(2)	(3)	(4)
2006	0.357***	0.339***	0.433***	-0.779
	[2.995]	[2.826]	[2.588]	[-0.619]
2008	0.163*	0.144*	0.132	-0.096
	[1.907]	[1.685]	[1.068]	[-0.107]
2012	0.154*	0.144*	0.317***	0.656
	[1.883]	[1.758]	[2.764]	[0.763]
2014	0.397***	0.396***	0.544***	2.334**
	[3.429]	[3.394]	[3.276]	[2.284]
Employment and income	no	yes	no	no
Employment by year	no	no	yes	no
Income by year	no	no	no	yes

Source: Author's calculations based on NORC 2012, 2013, 2015b.

Notes: Overlapping panel described in note 10. 1,195 individuals observed three times for a total of 3,585 observations. Column 2 adds controls for income (ln[eqv. inc.]) and employment status. Omitted category is full-time employed. Column 3 interacts employment status with year, but excludes income controls. Column 4 interacts income with year, but excludes employment controls.

Reported year main effects correspond to λ_τ in the following specification (in OLS form for simplicity): $Veryhappy_{it} = \alpha_i + \beta'x_{it} + \sum_{\tau=1}^{2}(\lambda_\tau + \gamma_\tau'x_{it})d_\tau + \varepsilon_{it} \sum_{\tau=4}^{5}(\lambda_\tau + \gamma_\tau'x_{it})d_\tau + \varepsilon_{it}$. $Veryhappy_{it}$ takes the value of 1 if individual i reports being "very happy" in year t; x_{it} is a vector of individual characteristics. d_τ are dummy variables for each period (2006 = 1; 2008 = 2; ... 2014 = 5).

t statistics in brackets (clustered by individual).

*$p < .10$; **$p < .05$; ***$p < .01$

REFERENCES

Arampatzi, Efstratia, Martijn J. Burger, and Ruut Veenhoven. 2015. "Financial Distress and Happiness of Employees in Times of Economic Crisis." *Applied Economics Letters* 22(3): 173–79. DOI: 10.1080/13504851.2014.931916.

Bell, David N. F., and David G. Blanchflower. 2011. "Young People and the Great Recession." *Oxford Review of Economic Policy* 27(2): 241–67. DOI: 10.1093/oxrep/grr011.

Bjørnskov, Christian. 2014. "Do Economic Reforms Alleviate Subjective Well-Being Losses of Economic Crises?" *Journal of Happiness Studies* 15(1): 163–82. DOI: 10.1007/s10902-013-9442-y.

Blanchflower, David G., and Andrew J. Oswald. 2004. "Well-Being over Time in Britain and the USA." *Journal of Public Economics* 88(7–8): 1359–86. DOI: 10.1016/S0047-2727(02)00168-8.

Cameron, Adrian Colin, and P. K. Trivedi. 2005. *Microeconometrics: Methods and Applications.* New York: Cambridge University Press.

Carr, Ewan, and Heejung Chung. 2014. "Job Insecurity and Life Satisfaction: The Moderating Influence of Labour Market Policies Across Europe." *Journal of European Social Policy* 24(4): 383–99. DOI: 10.1177/0958928714538219.

Deaton, Angus. 2011. "The Financial Crisis and the Well-Being of Americans." *Oxford Economic Papers* 64(1): 1–26. DOI: 10.1093/oep/gpr051.

di Tella, Rafael, Robert J. MacCulloch, and Andrew J. Oswald. 2001. "Preferences over Inflation and Unemployment: Evidence from Surveys of Happiness." *American Economic Review* 91(1): 335–41.

———. 2003. "The Macroeconomics of Happiness." *Review of Economics and Statistics* 85(4): 809–27. DOI: 10.1162/003465303772815745.

Diener, Ed, Louis Tay, and Shigehiro Oishi. 2013. "Rising Income and the Subjective Well-Being of Nations." *Journal of Personality and Social Psychology* 104(2): 267–76. DOI: 10.1037/a0030487.

Dolan, Paul, Tessa Peasgood, and Mathew White. 2008. "Do We Really Know What Makes Us Happy? A Review of the Economic Literature on the Factors Associated with Subjective Well-Being." *Journal of Economic Psychology* 29(1): 94–122. DOI: 10.1016/j.joep.2007.09.001.

Easterlin, Richard A., Laura Angelescu McVey, Malgorzata Switek, Onnicha Sawangfa, and Jacqueline Smith Zweig. 2010. "The Happiness-Income Paradox Revisited." *Proceedings of the National Academy of Sciences of the United States of America* 107(52): 22463–68. DOI: 10.1073/pnas.1015962107.

Ferrer-i-Carbonell, Ada, and Paul Frijters. 2004. "How Important Is Methodology for the Estimate of the Determinants of Happiness?" *The Economic Journal* 114(497): 641–59.

Graham, Carol, Soymya Chattopadhyay, and Mario Picon. 2010. "Adapting to Adversity: Happiness and the 2009 Economic Crisis in the United States." *Social Research* 77(2): 715–48.

Helliwell, John F., and Shun Wang. 2012. "The State of World Happiness" in *The World Happiness Report,* edited by John F. Helliwell, Richard Layard, and Jeffrey Sachs. Available at: http://issuu.com/earthinstitute/; accessed December 12, 2016.

Herbst, Chris M. 2011. "'Paradoxical' Decline? Another Look at the Relative Reduction in Female Happiness." *Journal of Economic Psychology* 32(5): 773–88. DOI: 10.1016/j.joep.2011.07.001.

Herbst, Chris M., and John Ifcher. 2014. "The Increasing Happiness of Parents." Unpublished Paper. Arizona State University, School of Public Affairs.

Ifcher, John, and Homa Zarghamee. 2014. "The Happiness of Single Mothers: Evidence from the General Social Survey." *Journal of Happiness Studies* 15(3): 1219–38. DOI: 10.1007/s10902-013-9472-5.

Kahneman, Daniel, and Amos Tversky. 1979 "Prospect Theory : An Analysis of Decision under Risk." *Econometrica* 47(2): 263–92.

Kalleberg, Arne L., and Till M. von Wachter. 2017. "The U.S. Labor Market During and After the Great Recession: Continuities and Transformations." *RSF: The Russell Sage Foundation Journal of the Social Sciences* 3(3): 1–19. DOI: 10.7758/RSF.2017.3.3.01.

Kapteyn, Arie, Jinkook Lee, Caroline Tassot, Hana Vonkova, and Gema Zamarro. 2015. "Dimensions of Subjective Well-Being." *Social Indicators Research* 123(3): 625–60. DOI: 10.1007/s11205-014-0753-0.

Lucas, Robert E. 1987. *Models of Business Cycles.* Oxford, UK, and New York: Basil Blackwell.

Morgan, Robson. 2015. "Labor Market Policy and Subjective Well-Being During the Great Recession." Unpublished Paper. University of Southern California.

National Bureau of Economic Research. 2014. "US Business Cycle Expansions and Contractions." Available at: www.nber.org/cycles/cyclesmain.html; accessed December 1, 2014.

National Opinion Research Center. 2012. "GSS 2006 Sample Panel Wave 3, Release 2." Chicago: University of Chicago, National Opinion Research Center.

———. 2013. "GSS 2008 Sample Panel Wave 3, Release 1." Chicago: University of Chicago, National Opinion Research Center.

———. 2015a. "GSS 1972–2014 Cross-Sectional Cumulative Data (Release 2, April 17, 2015)." Chicago: University of Chicago, National Opinion Research Center.

———. 2015b. "GSS 2010 Sample Panel Wave 3, Release 1." Chicago: University of Chicago, National Opinion Research Center.

Oishi, Shigehiro, Selin Kesebir, and Ed Diener. 2011. "Income Inequality and Happiness." *Psychological Science* 22 (9): 1095–1100. DOI: 10.1177 /0956797611417262.

Organisation for Economic Co-operation and Development 2014. "Social Expenditure Aggregated Data." Available at: http://stats.oecd.org/OECD Stat_Metadata/ShowMetadata.ashx?Dataset =SOCX_AGG&ShowOnWeb=true&Lang=en; accessed December 1, 2014.

———. 2015. "What Are Equivalence Scales?" Available at: www.oecd.org/eco/growth/OECD-Note -EquivalenceScales.pdf; accessed August 11, 2016.

Sacks, Daniel W., Betsey Stevenson, and Justin Wolfers. 2012. "The New Stylized Facts About Income and Subjective Well-Being." IZA Discussion Paper Series, no. 7105. Bonn, Germany: Institute for the Study of Labor. Available at: http:// ftp.iza.org/dp7105.pdf; accessed August 5, 2016.

Stevenson, Betsey, and Justin Wolfers. 2008a. "Economic Growth and Subjective Well-Being: Reassessing the Easterlin Paradox." *Brookings Papers on Economic Activity* 2008(1): 1–87. DOI: 10.1353 /eca.0.0001.

———. 2008b. "Happiness Inequality in the United States." *Journal of Legal Studies* 37(S2): S33–79. DOI: 10.1086/592004.

———. 2009. "The Paradox of Declining Female Happiness." *Economic Policy* 1(2): 190–225. DOI: 10.1257/pol.1.2.190.

———. 2012. "Subjective and Objective Indicators of Racial Progress Subjective and Objective Indicators of Racial Progress." *Journal of Legal Studies* 41(2): 459–93. DOI: 10.1007/BF00300445.

Stiglitz, Joseph E. Amartya Sen, and Jean-Paul Fitoussi. 2009. "Report by the Commission on the Measurement of Economic Performance and Social Progress." Report from the Commission on the Measurement of Economic Performance and Social Progress. Available at: www .stiglitz-sen-fitoussi.fr/en/index.htm; accessed September 30, 2016.

U.S. Bureau of Economic Analysis (BEA). 2015a. "Table 1.1.6 Real Gross Domestic Product, Chained

Dollars: Annual and Seasonally Adjusted Quarterly." Available at: http://www.bea.gov/itable /index.cfm?ReqID=9#reqid=9&step=3&isuri=1&9 03=6; accessed August 1, 2015

———. 2015b. "Regional Economic Accounts: Current Gross Domestic Product by State (NAICS and SIC), and Population." Available at: http:// www.bea.gov/regional/downloadzip.cfm; accessed July 1, 2015.

U.S. Bureau of the Census (Census). 2014. Current Population Survey, Annual Social and Economic Supplements, "Table F-4. Gini Indexes for Families, by Race and Hispanic Origin of Householder: 1947 to 2013." Available at: http://www .census.gov/hhes/www/income/data/historical /inequality; accessed January 1, 2015.

———. 2015. New Residential Sales Historical Data, "Median and Average Sales Price of Houses Sold by Region." Available at: www.census.gov /construction/nrs/pdf/pricerega.pdf; accessed May 1, 2015.

U.S. Bureau of Labor Statistics (BLS). 2015a. "Annual Unemployment Rate: Not Seasonally Adjusted for Population 16 Years and Over." Available at: http://data.bls.gov/timeseries/LNU0400 0000?years_option=all_years&periods_option =specific_periods&periods=Annual+Data; accessed July 1, 2015.

———. 2015b. "Monthly Unemployment Rate: Seasonally Adjusted for Population 16 Years and Over." Available at: http://data.bls.gov/timeseries /LNS14000000; accessed August 1, 2015.

———. 2015c. Local Area Unemployment Statistics, "Annual Unemployment Rate: By Census Division." Available at: http://www.bls.gov/lau /#data; accessed July 1, 2015.

Winkelmann, Liliana, and Rainer Winkelmann. 1998. "Why Are the Unemployed So Unhappy? Evidence from Panel Data." *Economica* 65(257): 1–15. DOI: 10.1111/1468-0335.00111.

Wolfers, Justin. 2003. "Is Business Cycle Volatility Costly? Evidence from Surveys of Subjective Well-Being." *International Finance* 6(1): 1–26. DOI: 10.1111/1468-2362.00112.

World Bank. 2015. World Development Indicators. Available at: http://data.worldbank.org /data-catalog/world-development-indicators; accessed July 1, 2015.

Wulfgramm, Melike. 2014. "Life Satisfaction Effects of Unemployment in Europe: The Moderating Influence of Labour Market Policy." *Journal of European Social Policy* 24(3): 258–72. DOI: 10.1177/0958928714525817.

Why Did People Move During the Great Recession? The Role of Economics in Migration Decisions

BRIAN L. LEVY, TED MOUW, AND ANTHONY DANIEL PEREZ

Labor migration offers an important mechanism to reallocate workers when there are regional differences in employment conditions. Whereas conventional wisdom suggests migration rates should increase during recessions as workers move out of areas that are hit hardest, initial evidence suggested that overall migration rates declined during the Great Recession, despite large regional differences in unemployment and growth rates. In this paper we use data from the American Community Survey to analyze internal migration trends before and during the economic downturn. First, we find only a modest decline in the odds of adults leaving distressed labor market areas during the Great Recession, which may result in part from challenges related to the housing price crash. Second, we estimate conditional logit models of destination choice for individuals who migrate across labor market areas; we find a substantial effect of economic factors such as labor demand, unemployment, and housing values. We also estimate latent class conditional logit models that test whether there is heterogeneity in preferences for destination characteristics among migrants. Over all, the latent class models suggest that roughly equal percentages of migrants were motivated by economic factors before and during the Great Recession. We conclude that fears of dramatic declines in labor migration seem to be unsubstantiated.

Keywords: migration, Great Recession, latent class conditional logits

As the Great Recession (from late 2007 to mid-2009) was concluding and the sluggish recovery was beginning, many researchers and federal officials bemoaned the lack of internal migra-tion for jobs (Fletcher 2010; Moretti 2012). Labor migration during a downturn is an important mechanism for local labor markets to cope with employment declines and regional differences

Brian L. Levy is a PhD candidate in the Department of Sociology and predoctoral trainee at the Carolina Population Center at the University of North Carolina at Chapel Hill. **Ted Mouw** is associate professor in the Department of Sociology and faculty fellow at the Carolina Population Center at the University of North Carolina at Chapel Hill. **Anthony Daniel Perez** is assistant professor in the Department of Sociology and faculty fellow at the Carolina Population Center at the University of North Carolina at Chapel Hill.

© 2017 Russell Sage Foundation. Levy, Brian L., Ted Mouw, and Anthony Daniel Perez. 2017. "Why Did People Move During the Great Recession? The Role of Economics in Migration Decisions." *RSF: The Russell Sage Foundation Journal of the Social Sciences* 3(3): 100–25. DOI: 10.7758/RSF.2017.3.3.05. This research received support from the Population Research Training grant (T32 HD007168) and the Population Research Infrastructure Program (R24 HD050924) awarded to the Carolina Population Center at the University of North Carolina at Chapel Hill by the Eunice Kennedy Shriver National Institute of Child Health and Human Development. Direct correspondence to: Brian L. Levy at blevy@unc.edu, 155 Hamilton Hall, CB 3210, University of North Carolina, Chapel Hill, NC 27599; Ted Mouw at tedmouw@email.unc.edu, 155 Hamilton Hall, CB 3210, University of North Carolina, Chapel Hill, NC 27599; and Anthony Daniel Perez at adperez@unc.edu, 155 Hamilton Hall, CB 3210, University of North Carolina, Chapel Hill, NC 27599.

in economic vitality (Blanchard and Katz 1992; Gallin 2004). Moreover, the extent to which individuals are willing to relocate for employment during an economic downturn has important implications for two common policy response strategies: income replacement programs such as unemployment insurance (Rothstein 2011) and employment-incentivizing programs such as public service employment (Ellwood and Welty 2000; Wiseman 1976) and hiring or worker credits (Neumark 2011). Specifically, the relative investment in each strategy, as well as the mix of funding allocated to specific programs, should depend on the manner in which individuals respond to employment shocks.

The widespread concern about declining migration arose as data from the Current Population Survey (CPS) revealed a substantial drop in interstate migration starting in 2006 and holding throughout the recession (Frey 2009). This drop would accord with previous research on recessionary migration that finds a limited response to poor economic conditions (Gordon 1985; Greenwood 1997; Pissarides and McMaster 1990). Since the Great Depression, seven of the nine recessions have seen declines in migration, and migration since 1948 has been strongly pro-cyclical (Saks and Wozniak 2011). During the Great Recession, declining equity in owners' homes had an especially strong impact by locking homeowners into their local areas and potentially preventing interregional migration (Karahan and Rhee 2012; Modestino and Dennett 2012). Recent analyses, however, question the accuracy of fears that migration declined in response to the downturn. The large drop in migration occurred between May 2006 and May 2007, before the Great Recession (Saks and Wozniak 2011). Further, in the context of a steady decline in migration since the 1980s (Molloy et al. 2014), the drop during the Great Recession is unremarkable and consistent with long-term trends (Kaplan and Schulhofer-Wohl 2011). Thus, it remains important to assess whether or not economic migration declined during the Great Recession.

A central challenge for empirical analyses of migration is the heterogeneity in preferences of migrants. On the one hand, the increased migration that federal officials expected in response to the recession evokes a labor migra-tion model. Classic labor economic theory posits that job availability should be a salient factor, with differences in regional economic conditions as drivers of migration (Hicks 1932, as cited in Greenwood 1975). A large body of research highlights the general salience of economic factors for migration (Davies, Greenwood, and Li 2002; Fishback, Horrace, and Kantor 2006; Greenwood 1997; Hornbeck 2012; Kennan and Walker 2011; Mare and Choy 2001; Milne 1993; Treyz et al. 1993). On the other hand, some migrants certainly move for non-economic reasons. In fact, Mark D. Partridge and colleagues (2012) find that although across-county migration for better geographic amenities remained roughly constant from 1990 to 2007, migrants were less responsive to differences in labor demand from 2000 to 2007 than they were from 1990 to 2000.

Extant analyses adopt a choice framework for migration decisions that constrain preferences to be constant across individuals, which might be problematic if there is heterogeneity in the basic types of movers and their preferences for destination locations. In this paper, we estimate choice models that allow for variation in preferences; specifically, we analyze migrants' destination preferences using latent class conditional logit (LCCL) models, which allow coefficient estimates to vary across class categories. Not only does this better align our empirical estimation with current theories of migration, but it also allows us to classify individuals as migrating for economic or other reasons based on an interpretation of the set of coefficients for each latent class and the relative probabilities of class membership.

We use the large scale of the American Community Survey (ACS) to investigate the determinants of migration decisions before (2005 to 2007) and during (2008 to 2011) the economic downturn associated with the Great Recession. The ACS allows us to analyze migration with greater geographic precision, at the labor market level, than previous nationally representative analyses, which examine interstate migration. This is important, as we later demonstrate, because the types of individuals likely to migrate and the destination characteristics attracting migrants vary between state and substate models. We estimate logit and multinomial logit models of the decision to remain in one's labor market or migrate to a new area. These models describe the composition of migrants, whether the types of individuals likely to migrate changed during the recession, and the push factors associated with the decision to leave a labor market. Next, we analyze migrants' destination preferences using latent class conditional logit models. These models make a methodological contribution to the study of migration by relaxing the traditional independence of irrelevant alternatives (IIA) assumption and exploring heterogeneity in destination preferences among migrants. We discuss changes in the composition and preferences of migrants during the Great Recession and conclude by considering whether or not economic migration truly declined.

PREVIOUS LITERATURE

Everett Lee (1966) argues that both origin push and destination pull factors affect migration decisions, although individuals respond to these factors differently. Moreover, as obstacles to out-migration increase—such as housing lock during the Great Recession (Modestino and Dennett 2012)—pull factors become increasingly important. The push-pull theory predicts that out-migrating individuals will be relatively advantaged compared to their non-migrating peers at their origin location, which serves to push them toward migration. Conversely, migrants are relatively disadvantaged when compared with individuals at their destination location, and the advantages of the destination pull them to migrate. Thus, individuals migrate to achieve improved conditions. Although originally applied internationally, this perspective offers a useful lens for examination of American internal migration during the Great Recession. Specifically, when an individual's community experiences a negative economic shock, he or she becomes more likely to migrate and will be attracted to destinations with strong economic conditions.

Economic Conditions and Migration

Previous research generally notes a strong link between economic conditions and migration flows, although this relationship may weaken during recessions as workers become less willing or able to migrate (Greenwood 1997; Gordon 1985; Pissarides and McMaster 1990). A common measure of economic conditions is unemployment. Empirical findings are not always consistent, but most show that personal unemployment and regional unemployment are associated positively with out-migration, and relative regional advantages in economic conditions are associated within in-migration. Departures from this trend are more common in research based on aggregate-level data rather than individual-level studies (Greenwood 1997; Herzog et al. 1993; Mare and Choy 2001). Paul S. Davies, Michael J. Greenwood, and Haizhenz Li (2002) find that the relationship between unemployment and interstate migration is stronger during years with a high mean unemployment that has a large variance; higher levels of unemployment may raise the salience of economic concerns for migration decisions, and larger variance may provide better information to migrants.

Other measures of economic conditions also suggest that migrants are more likely to relocate to economically advantaged locations, whether measured by changes in gross domestic product (Milne 1993) or government spending on public works and relief jobs during the Great Depression (Fishback, Horrace, and Kantor 2006). Although regional differentials in wages and wage growth are correlated with migration (Barro and Sala-I-Martin 1992; Kennan and Walker 2011; Pissarides and McMaster 1990; Treyz et al. 1993), labor migration is three times as responsive to unemployment as it is to wages (Beaudry, Green, and Sand 2014; Blanchard and Katz 1992). In sum, previous research using various measures of economic conditions generally finds a positive relationship between economically advantaged locations and in-migration, and both the most common measure of economic conditions and the measure with one of the strongest relationships to migration is the unemployment rate.

Recent research, however, suggests that this pattern may have changed—or at least become more nuanced. Mark D. Partridge and colleagues (2012) find that although positive labor demand shocks were associated with greater in-migration to a county from 1990 to 2000, this pattern had disappeared and perhaps even turned slightly negative from 2000 to 2007. The authors argue that local labor supply absorbed a greater degree of labor shocks in the recent period, a pattern that would resemble European labor market dynamics. Moreover, long-distance migrations have been declining for several decades (Molloy, Smith, and Wozniak 2011), and recent evidence suggests that relevant job offers have made such transitions less desirable, perhaps due to fewer job openings with high wage premiums (Molloy, Smith, and Wozniak 2014). In fact, those who migrated from a distressed origin to a more advantaged destination during the Great Recession fared no better on economic outcomes than those who stayed behind (Yagan 2014).

If there was little to no benefit to migrating to an economically advantaged destination, this would explain why fewer people might be willing to undertake such a move. Still, it would not explain any increase in migration to economically *distressed* areas. Atif Mian and Amir Sufi (2014) observe that the counties hit hardest during the Great Recession did not experience net out-migration and actually saw their populations rise. If this increase results from growing preferences for distressed locations among migrants, this would indicate movement away from a labor model of migration. Actually, the increase likely resulted from the diminished influence of origin economic conditions on out-migration decisions; that is, fewer people moved away from economically depressed areas. In-migration to areas hit hardest by the crash did not rise during the recession (Mian and Sufi 2014; Monras 2015). Thus, among migrants, a labor migration model may have persisted.

Over all, the evidence, particularly the recent evidence, on the relationship between economic conditions and migration decisions is mixed. Generally, unemployment is positively related to out-migration and negatively related to in-migration, which is consistent with a push-pull model of migration. Still, the direction and magnitude of these relationships in the context of the Great Recession are unclear. With the potential for increased obstacles to migration during a recession, we argue that destination-specific economic characteristics

might be especially important. Thus, we hypothesize:

H1: Better-destination economic (pull) conditions attract more migrants. Theory suggests the relationship will strengthen during the recession as individuals make economically efficient moves informed by greater variance in economic conditions.

H2: Worse-origin economic (push) conditions encourage migration.

Housing and Migration

Although a location's housing stock is generally thought of as an amenity (Ritchey 1976), with affordable housing attracting internal migrants to destinations (Sasser 2010), the housing market played a prominent role in the Great Recession. Two unique economic features of the recent recession were the pronounced role of the housing market collapse in the onset of the recession and the persistence of high and prolonged unemployment. Some research posits a link between these phenomena, indicating that housing values and the housing market may have functioned as an economic factor during the Great Recession. Homeowners experienced much sharper declines in their migration rates than renters from 2005 to 2010; in fact, renter migration during the period is statistically indistinguishable from its long-term trend (Kothari, Saporta-Eksten, and Yu 2012).

Some research proposes negative equity and housing lock as an explanation for this pattern of migration (Karahan and Rhee 2012; Modestino and Dennett 2012). When living in states with greater shares of underwater nonprime mortgages (Modestino and Dennett 2012) or metropolitan areas with declining home prices (Karahan and Rhee 2012), individuals are less likely to out-migrate. At the individual level, findings are mixed. Using the American Housing Survey, Fernando Ferreira, Joseph Gyourko, and Joseph Tracy (2012) find that underwater homeowners are one-third as likely to migrate as similar homeowners who are not underwater on their mortgage. On the other hand, studies using credit report data and the Panel Study of Income Dynamics find a positive relationship between negative equity and migration (Coulson and Grieco 2013; Demyanyk et al. 2014). Ultimately, extant research identifies at most a modest role for housing lock in inhibiting moves that would reduce the unemployment rate (see Modestino and Dennett 2012). Neighborhood or community lock, wherein falling housing values of a labor market area keep individuals from moving (even if they are not underwater), is a possibility, but the extent of its impact remains in question.

Unfortunately for all individuals who live in areas with declining housing values, the declines are strongly correlated with reductions in nontradable employment in a potentially causal manner (Mian and Sufi 2014). Along with fewer jobs, the housing bust accounts for half a point's worth of the rise in unemployment during the Great Recession (Karahan and Rhee 2012). Adam Herkenhoff and Lee E. Ohanian (2011) further argue that half of a point of the persistently high unemployment rate is due to mortgage modification programs and their reduction of economic incentives for migration.

The relationship between housing conditions and migration may be best detected when housing is operationalized at the labor market level rather than the household level. Alicia Sasser (2010) finds that incomes and labor market conditions had larger impacts than the housing market on interstate migration over the past three decades; from 1997 to 2006, however, housing affordability had an impact comparable to that of labor market conditions, indicating growing salience of housing at the labor market level for out-migration decisions.

Given the importance of the housing sector for the economic health of labor market areas (LMAs) immediately before and during the recession (Charles, Hurst, and Notowidigdo 2012), we argue that strong housing markets discourage out-migration and encourage in-migration. In the lead-up to the Great Recession, LMAs with booming housing prices exhibited greater economic vitality. Areas that aggressively built new homes during the housing bubble were left with an oversupply of housing stock following the economic collapse, however, and these same boom LMAs became bust LMAs. The excess supply depressed demand for building new homes, and both home prices and housing-related employment crashed. Thus, we hypothesize:

H3: Growth in housing prices retains and attracted residents prior to the Great Recession, but during the downturn, previously booming housing markets busted and became a push factor encouraging out-migration and discouraging in-migration.

Socioeconomic Differences in Migration

There is very limited evidence on group-level differences in population adjustment to changes in economic conditions (Bound and Holzer 2000). Racial minorities are less responsive to economic differences across metropolitan areas (Martin 2001), but at least part of this relationship is explained by the lower responsiveness of less-educated or lower-skilled individuals (Bound and Holzer 2000) to changes in the labor market. Individuals with greater educational attainment and greater skills are more responsive to economic shocks and regional disparities (Notowidigdo 2011; Wozniak 2010; Yankow 2003). Thus, we hypothesize:

H4: Adults with college degrees will be more responsive economic conditions, particularly during a recession.

DATA

In this paper we use ACS data from 2005 to 2011 to model migration before and during the Great Recession. The ACS is conducted by the Census Bureau and is an annual national random sample of 1 percent of the American population. The survey gathers data on a range of demographic and economic topics and provides annual, representative estimates of populations at the Public Use Microdata Area (PUMA) level. PUMAs are groups of census tracts and counties that contain between 100,000 and 200,000 individuals. Although the Census Bureau has been fielding the ACS every year since 2000, it was expanded to become a full 1 percent national sample starting in 2005, which was the same year that it began reporting migration information and PUMA data on the current residence and, for movers, their PUMA of residence from the prior year. To analyze migration at the labor market area—a unit of analysis bet-

Table 1. Migration and Unemployment Rates, by Year, for Migration Decision Models

	2005–2006	2006–2007	2007–2008	2008–2009	2009–2010	2010–2011
Unemployment rate	4.90	4.90	5.00	8.27	9.15	8.53
Migrants						
New labor market area	4.20%	3.93%	3.82%	3.57%	3.49%	3.64%
New state	2.57%	2.42%	2.31%	2.17%	2.12%	2.21%
Distance						
0–100 miles	1.2%	1.13%	1.12%	1.05%	1.04%	1.07%
100–300 miles	1.08%	1.01%	0.98%	0.9%	0.89%	0.94%
300–1,000 miles	1.21%	1.12%	1.07%	1.02%	0.96%	1.00%
1,000+ miles	0.7%	0.67%	0.64%	0.59%	0.59%	0.62%

Source: Authors' tabulations.

ter suited to capturing meaningful economic differences—we transform PUMAs to LMAs when possible. Specifically, we transform PU-MAs to metropolitan statistical areas (2000 definition) using a crosswalk available from the Missouri Census Data Center;[1] for rural PUMAs that do not correspond to a metropolitan labor market, we define the labor market as the migration PUMA (see *migpuma1* at Ruggles et al. 2010). The ACS is uniquely suited to analyze migration during a period of rapid economic change because it measures annual migration flows and a rich set of economic covariates (for example, employment, industry of occupation, and housing value). Moreover, because the majority of migration occurs within a state, analyzing flows within and across LMAs permits measurement of migration dynamics with much more precision than do interstate models.

In addition to the 2005-to-2011 ACS microdata samples, we also use the 5 percent Census 2000 sample from the Integrated Public Use Microdata Series (IPUMS) database developed by Steven Ruggles et al. (2010). The Census 2000 sample provides controls for base level flows between LMAs. For analyses, we restrict our sample to repeated cross-sections of adults ages twenty-five to sixty-four who did not report living abroad during the past twelve months. We weight all analyses using the relevant person or household weight. We similarly weight and restrict the tabulations of LMA characteristics, but we calculate these on the sample of all individuals residing in an LMA, regardless of age.

Migration

In our analysis, our main dependent variable is a categorical variable measuring whether or not an individual has moved across (LMAs) in the past year (either across or within states), although we also run a parallel analysis for cross-state mobility to make our results compatible with previous research. We further subclassify cross-LMA mobility by the distance of the move (less than one hundred miles, one hundred to three hundred miles, three hundred to one thousand miles, and more than one thousand miles). We do not consider within-LMA moves as migration because such movers' economic prospects are unlikely to change appreciably. Table 1 shows how moves are distributed over our study period. Specifically, we find an appreciable drop in migration throughout most of the study period followed by a small recovery beginning in 2010–2011. The steepest declines for moves of all types correspond tightly with the official timing of the Great Recession (2008 to 2009) and the more protracted rise in unemployment (2008 to 2011). Long-

1. The crosswalk is available at Missouri Census Data Center, http://mcdc2.missouri.edu/websas/geocorr2k.html (accessed August 6, 2016).

distance moves—especially those of three hundred to one thousand miles—experienced the greatest relative declines over time. Although our definition of the recession window (2008 to 2011) is longer than the official federal definition, the protracted effects of the downturn on unemployment lasted long past the end of the decline in gross domestic product (GDP) that officially defines a recession. Moreover, it is precisely these types of high-unemployment conditions under which a standard model would predict labor migration as a response.

Unemployment Rate

As a general measure of the economic vitality of an area, we calculate the unemployment rate as the percentage of individuals in the labor force who are not employed. In our models of destination choice, unemployment is likely to be partly endogenous to migration decisions. Thus, despite the unemployment rate providing a general measure of an area's economy, it is limited by both the potential endogeneity and its inability to isolate sector-specific shocks that may have been especially important during the Great Recession. As a result, we calculate two instrumental variables for sector-specific economic changes.

Labor Demand Shocks

A key challenge in estimating the effect of labor demand on migration is that observed changes in employment are endogenous to labor supply changes such as in-migration. In this paper we use an instrumental variable approach to estimate changes in labor demand for tradable goods using the Timothy Bartik (1991, 2013) shift-share approach. The idea is that in industries that produce tradable goods, local employment responds to national-level changes in the demand for those goods. In other words, whereas changes in labor demand at a factory that produces refrigerators reflect aggregate national changes in the demand for refrigera-

tors, changes in labor demand in nontradable industries such as construction, hotels, or restaurants are a function of local demand for those products because they are not tradable across geographic areas. Consequently, an instrumental variable for labor demand shocks in tradable goods that is not correlated with local labor supply changes can be constructed by using employment trends in specific industrial employment at the national level. Our instrument uses the lagged local manufacturing employment mix combined with the weighted national-level changes in industry-specific employment over the past year. By removing the portion of labor demand endogenous to local factors, the instrument captures labor demand shocks resulting from macroeconomic forces. We calculate manufacturing labor demand as

$$\hat{L}_{it} = \sum_{j=1}^{N} e_{ijt-1} \left(\frac{\tilde{e}_{ijt} - \tilde{e}_{ijt-1}}{\tilde{e}_{ijt-1}} - \frac{e_t - e_{t-1}}{e_{t-1}} \right) \quad (1)$$

where e_{ijt-1} is the share of an LMAs' (i) jobs that are in industry[2] j in time period $t-1$, $\tilde{e}_{ijt}$ is national employment in industry j excluding the LMA, and e_t is the national employment. Removing each LMA's employment from the national employment components of that LMA's instrument avoids correlation between the instrument and the error term.[3] The use of this shift-share instrument based on local industry mix and national employment changes is widespread in the literature (Blanchard and Katz 1992; Wozniak 2010; Notowidigdo 2011; Charles, Hurst, and Notowidigdo 2012).

It is important to note that, by construction, this measure is intended to capture changes in labor demand in the manufacturing sector. At the same time, an increase in local employment in this sector should have spillover effects on local employment in the nontradable sector, as the demand for housing and services increases to fulfill the needs of new manufacturing employees. Enrico Moretti (2010) uses the

---

2. We operationalize industry of employment using three-digit industry codes, which offers substantial precision in measuring changes in industry demand.

3. In addition, because the ACS does not provide representative data at the LMA level for 2004, we estimate 2004 LMA industry composition using the 2005 industry mix for each LMA. The 2004 ACS does provide nationally representative estimates of employment by industry, and we use the change from 2004 to 2005 to calculate 2005 manufacturing labor demand changes by LMA.

Bartik measure of labor demand changes in manufacturing to estimate these spillover effects and finds that for each new job in manufacturing, approximately 1.6 additional jobs are created in the nontradable sector. Nonetheless, although this instrumental variable approach will arguably capture exogenous changes in labor demand for manufacturing industries, a key aspect of the regional variation in the Great Recession's impact was the depth of the bust in construction, which is what we turn to next.

Housing Prices

On a theoretical level, variation in housing prices across metropolitan statistical areas represents a major source of cost-of-living differences and should be included in any model of interregional migration. Moreover, since the collapse of the U.S. housing market catalyzed the Great Recession, LMA housing prices are likely to provide a key indicator of an LMA's economic health, construction sector vitality, and thus its attractiveness to potential movers and stayers. Just like the problem described earlier with respect to changes in employment levels, however, observed changes in housing prices reflect not only the increased cost of housing per se but also the inflows of migrants who are drawn to particular metropolitan areas because of sustained high levels of labor demand or desirable amenities. In other words, variables measuring changes in housing prices will be endogenous to migratory flows and including them as explanatory variables in individual level models of migration may result in a situation of reverse causality.

To circumvent this endogeneity problem, we again employ an instrumental variable approach. Following Albert Saiz (2010) and Charles, Hurst, and Notowidigdo (2012), we use the lagged share of land available for development within an LMA as a proxy for the sensitivity of housing prices to changes in housing demand. Housing prices tend to be higher in LMAs with limited land available for development for two reasons. First, areas with low land availability tend to be more productive, pay higher wages, and have greater amenities, which is what draws people to live in the area, raises housing prices, and reduces the level of land availability.[4] Second, the geographic and topographical features of the land—a sizable share of developable land already built up, large internal water bodies, undevelopable wetlands, and excessively sloped areas—reduce the price elasticity of housing supply. This GIS and satellite-based measure of exogenous land availability relies solely on preexisting characteristics of local housing markets, making it an ideal choice of instrumental variable for housing prices. See Saiz (2010) for an in-depth explanation of the construction of this variable and the motivation for using it as a measure of the price elasticity of housing supply.

In a study of employment trends in the run-up to the Great Recession, Charles, Hurst, and Notowidigdo (2012) find that a lagged measure of land availability strongly predicts changes in MSA-level housing prices and construction employment. We use data on land availability at the county level for 2006 from Guangqing Chi and Hung Chak Ho (2013), which we aggregate up to the LMA level to match the geographic data used in our paper. Chi and Ho use satellite data from the 2006 National Land Cover Database to calculate the percentage of land available for development by excluding area that is already built up or consists of surface water, wetlands, public land, or has a slope greater than 20 percent.[5] Table 2 shows the re-

---

4. In other words, low levels of land availability reflect specific factors that make an urban area attractive for migrants. Otherwise, there would be no reason to live in an area with higher housing prices.

5. To generate a land availability index for 2000, we adjust the 2006 data from Chi and Ho (2013) by subtracting the estimated amount of land used in new construction in each county between 2000 and 2006. We calculate the land use of new construction by first estimating the average lot size of new construction in the 2011 American Housing Survey as a function of county-level land availability using a regression model. Then, we predict the average lot size of new construction for each county using the 2006 land availability levels, and multiply this by the number of new homes constructed in the county between 2000 and 2006. Data on residential construction at the county level is available from the Census state and county data base: https://www.census.gov/support/USACdataInfo.html (accessed October 10, 2016).

Table 2. Relationship Between the 2000 Land Availability Index and the Change in Housing Values

Variables	(1) 2005 ch_valueh	(2) 2006 ch_valueh	(3) 2007 ch_valueh	(4) 2008 ch_valueh	(5) 2009 ch_valueh	(6) 2010 ch_valueh	(7) 2011 ch_valueh
Land availability index	-0.543*** (0.0497)	-0.777*** (0.0591)	-0.816*** (0.0533)	0.0579*** (0.0160)	0.134*** (0.0187)	0.209*** (0.0210)	0.242*** (0.0231)
Constant	1.773*** (0.0353)	2.052*** (0.0420)	2.156*** (0.0379)	0.950*** (0.0114)	0.879*** (0.0133)	0.832*** (0.0149)	0.798*** (0.0164)
Observations	666	666	666	666	666	666	666
R^2	0.152	0.206	0.261	0.019	0.072	0.130	0.142

Source: Authors' calculations.
Notes: For 2005–2007, the change in value is the ratio of the average housing value in the labor market area to the value in 2000. For 2008–2011 it is the ratio of the current value to the value in 2007. Coefficients are log odds. Standard errors in parentheses.
*$p < .05$; **$p < .01$; ***$p < .001$

sults from a preliminary regression of the change in housing prices in LMAs on this land availability index.[6] For the years 2005 to 2007, the dependent variable is the ratio of the current average housing value in the LMA to the value in 2000. For 2008 to 2011 the dependent variable is the ratio of the current value to the value in 2007. During the housing boom years from 2005 to 2007, land availability is negative correlated with housing price changes; LMAs that had preexisting constraints on the amount of land available for development such as San Francisco or New York had the largest increases in prices. During the housing bust from 2008 to 2011 the situation was reversed, and land availability in 2000 is positively correlated with housing price changes.

MODELS OF THE DECISION TO MIGRATE
We begin by modeling the decision to migrate. For comparability to previous state-level analyses, we first estimate a logit of the decision to migrate to a new state based on individual demographics and origin contextual variables. For this state-level model, we tabulate our origin contextual variables at the state level as opposed to the LMA level. Next, we leverage the geographic precision of the ACS data to estimate a logit of the decision to migrate to a new LMA based on individual demographics and

origin LMA contextual variables. Finally, to analyze potential differences in migration correlates by distance, we estimate a multinomial logit of the decision to remain in one's origin LMA, migrate to an LMA within one hundred miles, migrate to an LMA between one hundred and three hundred miles away, migrate three hundred to one thousand miles, and migrate over one thousand miles.

Because the ACS surveys respondents at only one point, we rely on a question asking residence one year prior to survey date to establish origin location in the year prior to the ACS wave and destination location (potentially the same as the origin location) during the ACS wave year. These models pool all years of data, and to assess whether or not the origin and individual characteristics of migrants changed during the recession, we interact a recession dummy variable (survey years 2008 to 2011) with all independent variables. Thus, the logits and multinomial logit shed light on H2 and H3. Further, to explore socioeconomic variation in recessionary migration decisions that we predict in H4, we estimate separate models for adults with and without a bachelor's degree.

Adults do not make these migration decisions in a vacuum based only on their origin locations. The characteristics of potential destinations also play a role. Theoretically, all

6. These data are available for download at Population Research Institute, "Land Developability, www.land developability.org (accessed August 6, 2016).

adults have the same choice set of potential migration destinations; in our models, these choices are all LMAs (or states) in the continental United States. Nevertheless, for many individuals, it is easier to move to a nearby LMA than to one across the country. Thus, we test the sensitivity of our migration decision models to the inclusion of distance-weighted spatial lags that capture the economic characteristics of potential destinations. We take the natural log of distance (in miles) between the centroids of an LMA (or state) and all other areas (or states). We then use the log distances to create inverse distance weights, which we row normalize to sum to 1 for each LMA or state. The spatial lags of economic variables are the weighted means of those variables for all other LMAs or states.

CHOICE MODELS OF DESTINATION LOCATIONS

We estimate conditional logit and latent class conditional logit models of destination choice for individuals who migrate. Both models are motivated by a discrete choice framework with utility maximization, and the difference between the two models revolves around whether or not we allow for individual heterogeneity in the preferences for locational characteristics. In equation 2 we represent the utility of choosing to migrate to destination j as a function of observed characteristics, fixed and random preferences for those characteristics, and a random error term:

$$U_{ij} = (\gamma_j)Z_{ij} + (\beta_j + v_{ij})X, \qquad (2)$$

where U_{ij} is the utility of destination option j for individual i, ε_{ij} is the iid-distributed random error term, and Z_{ij} and X_{ij} are sets of destination-specific variables (or individual-specific variables interacted with destination variables). The Z_{ij} and X_{ij} terms differ in terms of whether their coefficients are fixed or allowed to vary across individuals. The coefficient on Z_{ij}, γ_{ij}, is assumed to be constant across all individuals, while the coefficient on X_{ij} has a fixed component (β_{ij}) and a random component (v_j) that varies across individuals.

In the conditional logit model, we assume that individuals have identical preferences for

these characteristics. In terms of equation 2, this means that all of the explanatory variables are of type Z rather than X, and the choice framework reduces to equation 3:

$$U_{ij} = (\gamma_j)Z_{ij} + \varepsilon_{ij} \qquad (3)$$

The assumption of fixed preferences in equation 3 is another way of saying that the conditional logit model, like the multinomial logit model, makes the independence of irrelevant alternatives (IIA) assumption, which is that the error term ε_{ij} is not correlated across choice categories for the same person (Train 2003, 144). IIA assumes that one's relative preference between two alternatives is independent of what other alternatives are available. This assumption is problematic in a migration context, wherein specific destinations are often comparable to one another. IIA would require, for example, that an aspiring gambler mulling a move from rural Kentucky to Reno would have the same relative preference for Reno regardless of whether other gambling hubs like Las Vegas or Atlantic city were included among the choices.

One of the advantages of the IIA assumption in the conditional logit model is that it allows for the sampling of alternative choices, because the pairwise choice probability is assumed to be unaffected by the inclusion or exclusion of alternative choices (McFadden 1978; Bruch and Mare 2012). For each individual, the researcher can keep the choice that was actually chosen along with a random sample of the alternative choices that were not selected. For models with large numbers of choices, this greatly increases the computational efficiency (Nerella and Bhat 2004).

In the context of our analysis of economic pull factors and migration, an illustration of how the IIA assumption might be violated in migration models is provided by the following example. Imagine that there are two different types of movers: "economic" movers who have strong preferences for regions with high levels of economic growth, and "amenity" movers, who are not motivated by economic considerations. As a result of heterogeneity in mover type, forcing the coefficient on destination growth rates to be the same for these two groups (as in equation 3) means that the effect of mover type on the preference for economic growth enters the model as unobserved heterogeneity in the error term, which will be correlated across high- and low-growth-rate destinations. In other words, economic movers will have positive error terms—that is, $E(\varepsilon_{ij} > 0)$—for high-growth destinations because the coefficient on the variable measuring destination growth rates is constrained to be the same for both mover types and only partially reflects economic movers' preferences for economic growth.

The upshot of this discussion of heterogeneity in preferences for locational characteristics for migration models is that the arbitrary division of cartographic space into a set of mutually exclusive destination choices (such as states or LMAs) may affect the results of the analysis. This is the familiar "red bus, blue bus" problem familiar to discussions of violations of the IIA assumption where a division of the bus category into two choices based on color creates a problem with correlated error terms across choices (McFadden 1974). In terms of our migration example with a conditional logit and heterogeneity in mover types, the estimated effect of economic growth rates will depend on the distribution of growth rates across the destinations. If a change in growth rates over time alters the relative number of high- and low-growth destinations, then this will affect the estimated coefficient on growth rates just as in the example of dividing the "bus" category into additional categories based on a potentially irrelevant characteristic such as color.

The IIA assumption can be relaxed by allowing variation in preferences across individuals as depicted in equation 2, where the coefficients on the X variables are assumed to have fixed and random components. The mixed logit model (Hensher and Greene 2003) is an alternative to the conditional logit model that allows the coefficients to vary across individuals according to some specific parametric distribution. The problem with the mixed logit model for migration, however, is that it does not allow for the sampling of alternative choices (Domanski 2009), which makes it computationally prohibitive to estimate in models with large choice sets.

In this paper we estimate latent class conditional logit models, which are an extension of the basic mixed logit model that allow the coefficients to vary across a finite set of discrete categories (Train 2008). Because the coefficients are constrained to be the same within the latent categories, they allow for the sampling of alternatives while still providing the benefit of relaxing the IIA assumption across the latent classes (Domanski 2009). The LCCL model is estimated in an iterative process where class membership probabilities are calculated indicating the likelihood of each individual belonging to a particular latent class based on the coefficients estimates for each class, and then the coefficients are updated by running separate conditional logit models for each latent class using the class membership probabilities as weights (Train 2008). The process continues back and forth between calculating the membership weights and estimating the coefficients until the combined likelihood of the conditional logit models for each class are maximized. Appendix A provides more details on the estimation procedures. For the purposes of our discussion here the key benefits of the LCCL models is that they allow for variation in the coefficients of destination characteristics across latent classes, and that membership in the latent classes is not determined a priori but by the estimation procedure itself.

For all CL and LCCL models we include several control variables in addition to our focal economic variables. First, we include destination population and the distance between origin and destination as controls for a basic gravity model of migration. Distance also proxies for psychic and informational costs in migration decisions (Greenwood 1975). In addition, we control for baseline flows between LMAs (or states) using Census 2000 by calculating the percentage of migrants in each origin LMA who move to every other LMA. Although these base flows are not origin-destination-pair fixed effects, which are computationally infeasible in most of our preferred models, their logic is similar. Census 2000 flows are a proxy for certain time-invariant characteristics for which migrants have a consistent preference over time. One such characteristic could be cultural ties that encourage migration between two specific LMAs. In the LCCL models, we constrain the coefficients of our control variables to be constant across latent classes to ensure that our latent classes capture variation in preferences on economic variables. This tests the specific improvement in explanatory power of our LCCL models over the CL models for the focal variables. Finally, we test the sensitivity of our LMA-level models to state fixed effects. State effects provide greater control for unobserved, persistent flows to certain destinations that are not attributable to economic shocks.

RESULTS AND DISCUSSION

Table 3 presents the results from our logit models of the decision to migrate. We begin with a state-level logit for comparability to previous research. Model 1 estimates an adult's odds of moving to a new state based on origin-state manufacturing labor demand and unemployment, as well as a host of controls. Surprisingly, adults in states with positive manufacturing shocks were more likely to out-migrate prior to the recession, but they were significantly less likely to out-migrate during the recession. In contrast, state-level unemployment is marginally related to reduced odds of out-migration during the recession, suggesting mixed impacts of origin economic conditions for migration decisions during the recession. Model 2 adds the land availability instrument for the housing market, and the recessionary changes in the relationships of manufacturing labor demand and unemployment with out-migration disappear. Individuals residing in areas with greater land available for development—locations that did not experience a housing boom prior to the recession—were less likely to out-migrate prior to the crash, but they were more likely to out-migrate following the crash. This could provide evidence that housing lock inhibited migration, or it could indicate that adults in states with stronger economies have the resources necessary to move across states.

Model 3 adds controls for distance-weighted characteristics of potential destinations, which play an important role in migration decisions and mask the impact of some origin characteristics. The housing market relationship with migration observed in Model 2 persists, but new patterns for unemployment and manufacturing shocks emerge. Adults living in states with stronger economies, as measured by un-

employment and manufacturing labor demand, were more likely to out-migrate prior to the recession, but these patterns attenuated substantially or even reversed during the Great Recession. This suggests that our second hypothesis, that worse origin economic conditions encourage migration, is realized in the context of the recession. That we continue to observe greater out-migration from states with stronger housing markets suggests that, in contrast to H3, negative equity might actually be inhibiting migration during the crash and driving the observed relationship.

Next, we use the geographic detail of the ACS to estimate comparable logits at the LMA level. Results reveal important differences in the role of origin push factors for the decision to migrate between state- and LMA-level models. Unlike the significant relationship between origin-state manufacturing labor demand and migration to a new state, the association of origin manufacturing shocks with migration to a new LMA is explained entirely by the economic characteristics of potential destinations. Moreover, the negative association between unemployment and out-migration before the recession decreases substantially in magnitude in the LMA-level model, and origin unemployment further discourages out-migration to a new LMA during the recession. The only consistent finding between the state- and LMA-level models is the direction and magnitude of the relationship between housing market vitality and out-migration. In sum, whereas the state models provided qualified support for H2 in the context of the recession, the LMA models provide no support for origin economic conditions directly affecting out-migration decisions before or during the recession.

Why might we observe these differences between the state and LMA models? A potential explanation is that state moves are a different type of migration than within-state, across-LMA moves. State moves are generally greater in distance and may require more resources, which could affect the role of origin push factors. Table 4 presents our multinomial logits of migration distance, which reveal systematic variation in the determinants of migration decisions by the distance of moves. Findings from model 1 (without potential destination spatial lags) and

Table 3. Logit Models of the Decision to Migrate

	Panel 1: State-Level Models			Panel 2: LMA-Level Models[a]		
	Model 1: All Adults	Model 2: All Adults	Model 3: All Adults with Spatial Lags	Model 1: All Adults	Model 2: All Adults	Model 3: All Adults with Spatial Lags
Origin characteristics						
Labor demand	1.779***	2.442***	4.554***	0.415***	0.418***	−0.076
	(0.388)	(0.419)	(0.643)	(0.121)	(0.121)	(0.134)
R*labor demand	−3.079**	−0.666	−6.709***	−0.324[†]	−0.542**	0.108
	(0.962)	(1.147)	(1.393)	(0.182)	(0.185)	(0.194)
Unemployment	0.387	−0.709	−4.78***	−0.101	−0.206	−0.643*
	(0.61)	(0.631)	(0.899)	(0.27)	(0.276)	(0.282)
R*unemployment	−1.052[†]	0.111	3.029**	−1.112***	−1.01***	−0.692*
	(0.635)	(0.657)	(0.961)	(0.291)	(0.296)	(0.322)
Land availability		−0.363***	−0.268***		−0.146***	−0.229***
		(0.054)	(0.057)		(0.024)	(0.028)
R*land availability		0.402***	0.301***		0.238***	0.283***
		(0.067)	(0.07)		(0.03)	(0.035)
Potential destination spatial lags						
Labor demand			112.705***			−12.243***
			(22.767)			(2.512)
R*labor demand			−71.593**			4.429[†]
			(23.344)			(2.623)
Unemployment			−85.346***			106.17***
			(19.621)			(18.633)
R*unemployment			84.406***			−104.022***
			(19.627)			(18.635)
Land availability			8.253***			5.907***
			(2.353)			(1.187)
R*land availability			−2.475			−3.656*
			(2.92)			(1.465)
N	9,543,506	9,479,425	9,479,425	9,538,260	9,474,179	9,466,831

Source: Authors' calculations.

Notes: Base outcome is staying in the same state (models 1 and 2) or LMA (models 3 and 4). Coefficients are log odds. Standard errors in parentheses. All models include controls for the recession (dummy), individual race or ethnicity, gender, age, education, marital status, and disability status, as well as previous year's LMA's population size, racial composition, nativity composition, educational composition, and age composition.

[a] LMA = labor market area.

[†]$p < .1$; *$p < .05$; **$p < .01$; ***$p < .001$

model 2 (including destination lags) are broadly consistent, so we will discuss the results from model 2. Consistent with H2, weak origin economic conditions are positively related to likelihood of short-distance migration. High unemployment, declining manufacturing labor demand, and non-booming housing markets

prior to the recession all are associated with increased odds of migrating to a new LMA that is less than one hundred miles away. None of these associations changed during the Great Recession. Medium- and long-distance moves, however, are negatively related to origin LMA economic vitality. Since short-distance moves

Table 4. Multinomial Logit Models of Migration Distance (N = 9,465,700)

	Model 1: All Adults (No Spatial Lags)				Model 2: All Adults with Potential Destination Spatial Lags			
	Moved <100 Miles	Moved 100–300 Miles	Moved 300–1,000 Miles	Moved 1,000+ Miles	Moved < 100 Miles	Moved 100–300 Miles	Moved 300–1,000 Miles	Moved 1,000+ Miles
Origin characteristics								
Labor demand	-0.271	0.46*	1.157***	1.796***	-0.592**	-0.074	0.577*	1.597***
	(0.194)	(0.222)	(0.243)	(0.357)	(0.215)	(0.246)	(0.266)	(0.406)
R*labor demand	-0.667*	0.523	-0.814*	0.044	-0.172	1.019**	-0.036	-0.031
	(0.292)	(0.346)	(0.372)	(0.565)	(0.308)	(0.363)	(0.388)	(0.6)
Unemployment	3.231***	-2.006***	-1.02†	0.904	3.041***	-2.536***	-1.893***	0.597
	(0.433)	(0.511)	(0.554)	(0.872)	(0.444)	(0.522)	(0.567)	(0.885)
R*unemployment	-1.929***	-0.576	-1.305*	-3.27***	-0.706	-1.086†	-0.853	-3.601***
	(0.472)	(0.551)	(0.592)	(0.919)	(0.509)	(0.603)	(0.648)	(1.005)
Land availability	0.388***	-0.162***	-0.22***	-0.733***	0.483***	-0.199***	-0.558***	-0.569***
	(0.041)	(0.048)	(0.05)	(0.067)	(0.05)	(0.055)	(0.056)	(0.077)
R*land availability	0.099†	0.425***	0.362***	-0.016	0.082	0.47***	0.406***	0.052
	(0.051)	(0.059)	(0.061)	(0.082)	(0.061)	(0.069)	(0.07)	(0.095)
Potential destination spatial lags								
Labor demand					-35.89***	-16.099***	-7.827	38.773***
					(4.444)	(4.687)	(4.862)	(6.736)
R*labor demand					32.134***	3.197	-0.965	-49.779***
					(4.649)	(4.901)	(5.06)	(7.009)
Unemployment					278.514***	137.538***	75.537*	-278.647***
					(33.118)	(34.711)	(36.036)	(49.583)
R*unemployment					-279.961***	-132.166***	-72.535*	282.433***
					(33.122)	(34.715)	(36.04)	(49.59)
Land availability					-7.224***	3.523	27.543***	-11.965***
					(2.127)	(2.293)	(2.197)	(3.12)
R*land availability					1.667	4.257	-4.525†	-6.458†
					(2.595)	(2.851)	(2.728)	(3.888)

Source: Authors' calculations.

Notes: Base outcome is staying in the same labor market area (LMA). Coefficients are log odds. Standard errors in parentheses. All models include controls for the recession (dummy), individual race or ethnicity, gender, age, education, marital status, and disability status, as well as previous year's LMA's population size, racial composition, nativity composition, educational composition, and age composition.

†*p* < .1; **p* < .05; ***p* < .01; ****p* < .001

account for less than a third of all moves, the extent to which weak origin economic conditions spur migration (H2) is quite modest.

Appendices B through D present the results of our re-estimation of the migration decision models from tables 3 to 4, stratified by college-degree status. There is some evidence that adults without college degrees may be less likely than college graduates to move from origin LMAs with high unemployment rates, which aligns with our hypothesis that college graduates would be more responsive to economic conditions (H4). This difference arises because college graduates are more likely to make short-distance moves in response to high origin unemployment, and adults without college degrees are less willing to make medium-distance moves under such conditions. Generally, however, we observe few systematic differences in response to origin economic conditions by education level.

Turning to the destination choices and the pull characteristics that attract migrants, we begin by estimating several CL models of destination selection—the traditional approach to analyzing migration choices. In these models, we estimate separate effects of destination characteristics before and during the recession, which allows for a direct test of whether or not they are statistically different than 0 (and which is mathematically equivalent to estimating a model with main effects for destination characteristics combined with interaction terms for the recession). We do not include a recession dummy variable because it is a constant characteristic of individuals and drops out of the model unless interacted with destination-specific variables. Table 5 presents the results of the CL models.

Panel 1 presents the results of a state-level analysis of migrants' destination choices. Before the Great Recession, migrants generally preferred to move to economically strong destinations. Migrants tended to select states with lower unemployment rates that had housing markets likely to be booming, both of which are indicative of a preference for strong economies (H1). Still, migrants were less likely to select states with increasing manufacturing labor demand, which could indicate mixed preferences or a declining importance of manufacturing as a po-

tential source of employment for movers. Although they may have attenuated slightly, these preferences did not change dramatically during the Great Recession, which is consistent with H1. In addition, there are few systematic differences between college graduates and adults without a college degree. If anything, the former were more sensitive to variations in the unemployment rate, particularly during the downturn, which is consistent with H4 and our findings from the origin push models.

Panel 2 presents the results of our LMA-level analysis of destination selection. Model 1 presents the results without state fixed effects, and most findings are consistent with the state-level models—with the exception of a change in the direction of the relationship between destination labor demand and in-migration. Leveraging the greater geographic detail available in the ACS, we find that migrants prefer destinations with increasing manufacturing labor demand both before and during the recession. This suggests that state-level models may not have the geographic precision necessary to properly estimate destination selection. For all three economic variables, migrants prefer destinations with stable, growing economies prior to the recession, and only our measure of land availability, which identifies booming housing markets that busted during the crash, runs counter to this story during the recession. In general, then, economic characteristics of an LMA play a critical role in destination selection (H1).

Model 2 adds state fixed effects to model 1 to help control for unobserved persistent flows to destinations that are not attributable to our economic variables. The magnitudes of the unemployment and manufacturing demand parameters are substantively unchanged, but the importance of the land availability instrument declines by roughly half during both the pre-recession and recession time periods. This suggests that a meaningful portion of the persistent flows to LMAs with housing booms prior to the recession that subsequently busted are actually due to non-economic factors. These results provide even stronger evidence for a pattern of economic migration that persisted during the Great Recession (H1), at least the pattern of destination selection. Finally, we again find little variation in destination preferences

Table 5. Alternative-Specific Conditional Logits (CLs) of Migrants' Destination Choices—All States and Labor Market Areas with Sampled Destinations

	Panel 1: State-Level CLs of Choice			Panel 2: LMA-Level CLs of Choice (Sampled Choices)			
	Model 1: All Adults	Model 2: College Graduates	Model 3: Non-College Graduates	Model 1: All Adults	Model 2: All Adults	Model 3: College Graduates	Model 4: Non-College Graduates
Census 2000 flows	9.014***	7.417***	10.005***	23.353***	20.28***	17.871***	19.796***
	(0.059)	(0.093)	(0.076)	(0.188)	(0.18)	(0.317)	(0.216)
ln(population)	0.589***	0.696***	0.518***	0.827***	0.852***	1.021***	0.763***
	(0.003)	(0.005)	(0.004)	(0.002)	(0.002)	(0.004)	(0.003)
ln(distance)	-0.589***	-0.547***	-0.625***	-1.242***	-1.312***	-1.127***	-1.407***
	(0.004)	(0.006)	(0.005)	(0.003)	(0.003)	(0.006)	(0.004)
Pre-recession preferences							
Labor demand	-1.824***	-1.272**	-2.078***	0.896***	0.598***	0.541**	0.701***
	(0.273)	(0.459)	(0.34)	(0.1)	(0.102)	(0.197)	(0.12)
Unemployment rate	-4.019***	-6.905***	-2.45***	-4.54***	-3.978***	-9.809***	-1.984***
	(0.345)	(0.561)	(0.438)	(0.193)	(0.195)	(0.372)	(0.231)
Land availability	-0.69***	-0.718***	-0.67***	-0.928***	-0.276***	-0.121***	-0.36***
	(0.019)	(0.03)	(0.024)	(0.016)	(0.016)	(0.028)	(0.019)
Recessionary preferences							
Labor demand	-6.575***	-1.825	-9.325***	0.733***	0.576***	0.573†	0.614**
	(0.832)	(1.346)	(1.057)	(0.159)	(0.16)	(0.304)	(0.189)
Unemployment rate	-2.326***	-5.38***	-0.414	-2.24***	-3.104***	-7.413***	-1.598***
	(0.2)	(0.317)	(0.258)	(0.127)	(0.128)	(0.237)	(0.153)
Land availability	-0.613***	-0.772***	-0.515***	-0.855***	-0.241***	-0.236***	-0.267***
	(0.018)	(0.029)	(0.024)	(0.015)	(0.015)	(0.026)	(0.018)
State fixed effects					x	x	x
N	10,665,931	4,458,591	6,207,340	4,150,666	4,150,666	1,393,468	2,757,198
Log likelihood	-733,993	-295,531	-437,363	-429,073	-419,870	-134,834	-278,812

Source: Authors' calculations.

Notes: Coefficients are log odds. Standard errors are in parentheses.

†$p < .1$; *$p < .05$; **$p < .01$; ***$p < .001$

Table 6. Latent Class Conditional Logits of Labor Market Area Destination Choice with Sampled Destinations

	Pre-recession (2005–2007)		Recession Years (2008–2011)	
	Latent Class 1	Latent Class 2	Latent Class 3	Latent Class 4
Census 2000 flows [constrained]	20.082***			
	(0.181)			
ln(population) [constrained]	0.853***			
	(0.002)			
ln(distance) [constrained]	-1.310***			
	(0.003)			
Labor demand	0.454***	1.147***	-0.058	1.878***
	(0.018)	(0.022)	(0.052)	(0.048)
Unemployment rate	-0.698**	-6.563***	-0.691***	-4.084***
	(0.065)	(0.088)	(0.036)	(0.029)
Land availability	2.138***	-2.831***	-2.652***	2.021***
	(0.001)	(0.001)	(0.000)	(0.000)
Latent class weight	0.2348	0.2072	0.2576	0.3004
Percentage of migrants by period	53.13	46.87	46.16	53.84

Source: Authors' calculations.

Notes: Coefficients are log odds. Standard errors in parentheses. N = 4,150,650. Log likelihood = -394,431. Models include state fixed effects. Census 2000 flows, log population, and log distance are constrained to be constant across latent classes.

$^{†}p < .1$; $^{*}p < .05$; $^{**}p < .01$; $^{***}p < .001$

by college degree status except for the moderately stronger responsiveness of college graduates to the unemployment rate of potential destinations (models 3 and 4).

Although the LMA-level CL model offers an improvement on the state-level CL, we want to test whether the assumption of fixed preferences for economic pull factors may be masking heterogeneity in mover types. As described in the methods section, if there are two types of movers—"economic" movers, who are strongly affected by economic conditions, and "amenity" movers, who are not—then this would violate the IIA assumption and potentially affect the parameter estimates. Thus, we

estimate an LCCL model of LMA destination choice with state fixed effects that relaxes the IIA assumption by allowing destination preferences to vary across latent classes. We include four latent classes in the model—two classes for adults migrating prior to the recession and two classes for adults migrating during the recession.[7] In addition to comparing parameter estimates across the latent classes, we can examine the share of adults in each latent class to assess the change in the distribution of migrants between the periods, conditional on the estimated latent classes. Table 6 presents the results of our LCCL model.[8] These models offer a substantial improvement in explanatory

7. We accomplish this as a pooled model that includes all observations (2005 to 2011) by restricting the latent class weights for adults migrating prior to the recession to be zero for the two recessionary latent classes, and vice versa. Our rationale for including two latent classes for each period is to attempt to isolate migrants motivated by economic considerations from those motivated by other considerations.

8. The results presented in model 5 are those of the best-fitting model based on twenty replications. The log likelihood, coefficients, and weights of the latent classes do not differ substantially across the other models (results available upon request).

power over the traditional CL as evidenced by comparing the log likelihood of model 2 in panel 2 of table 5 (–419,870) with the log likelihood of our LCCL model in table 6 (–394,431).

Examining the pre-recession period (2005 to 2007), adults in latent class 2 (LC2) are clearly more motivated by economic considerations than adults in LC1. Adults in LC2 are significantly more likely to choose destinations with increasing manufacturing labor demand and low levels of unemployment. In addition, these adults chose LMAs with less land available for development, which proxies for areas experiencing a housing boom and strong housing sector prior to the recession. By comparison, adults in LC1 are at most marginal economic migrants, given their modest preferences for lower unemployment and higher manufacturing demand. Moreover, LC1 adults were more likely to choose destinations with comparatively weak housing sectors.

Turning to migrants during the economic downturn (2008 to 2011), we again observe a clear distinction between migrants motivated by economic considerations (LC4) and those motivated by other considerations (LC3). The same differences for unemployment and manufacturing labor demand observed prior to the recession persist during the recession. If anything, the intraperiod difference in preferences by LC for manufacturing demand widens during the recession, but the difference in labor demand preferences shrinks during the recession. Although the coefficient on land availability switches signs for economic migrants between the periods, this is entirely consistent with our expected pattern of economic migration. Economic migrants were more likely to select LMAs with booming housing markets prior to the recession. Once the crash hit and such areas busted, however, economic migrants were more likely to select LMAs that never boomed and thus experienced less of a bust.

Examining the shares of adults in each of the latent classes—the latent class weight—allows us to draw inferences regarding the extent to which motivations for migration changed during the economic downturn. Prior to the Great Recession, roughly 47 percent of migrants were motivated by economic considerations in selecting their destination LMA, whereas during the downturn, 54 percent of migrants exhibited economic preferences in destination selection. This seven-percentage-point increase suggests that, if anything, the share of migrants motivated by economic factors in selecting destinations increased during the Great Recession, which is confirmatory of H1.

CONCLUSION

The past few decades have seen declines in migration as well as a drop in salience of economic characteristics for migration decisions. These declines, coupled with the typical reductions associated with recent recessions (Saks and Wozniak 2011), led to strong concern among policymakers about the lack of migration for jobs during the Great Recession (Fletcher 2010; Moretti 2012). A recessionary drop would negate an important mechanism through which labor markets cope with employment shocks and differentials in economic vitality (Blanchard and Katz 1992; Gallin 2004). Hopes were buoyed somewhat by research suggesting that migration during the Great Recession did not decline at a faster rate than recent trends (Kaplan and Schulhofer-Wohl 2011), but research has yet to disentangle the changes in labor migration during the recession from non-economic migration. Heterogeneity in preferences among migrants poses a severe challenge for traditional empirical models of migration.

We provide new evidence on the extent to which economic migration did or did not decline during the Great Recession. Using the geographic detail and large scale of the American Community Survey, we analyze the push and pull factors (Lee 1966) at play in the migration process before (2005 to 2007) and during (2008 to 2011) the economic downturn. Specifically, we estimate logit and multinomial logit models of the decision to migrate, as well as CL and LCCL models of destination preferences among migrants. These models make several methodological contributions to the migration literature. First, estimating many of our models at both the state and LMA level reveals significant differences in the economics-migration relationship by level of analysis, demonstrating the importance of the precision available with the ACS. Second, incorporating state fixed effects into our LMA-level destination selection models highlights the importance of controlling for unobserved, persistent flows. Third, the heterogeneity in preferences allowed by our LCCL models relaxes the IIA assumption of traditional CL models, and perhaps more importantly it allows us to classify migrants as motivated by economic or non-economic destination characteristics.

Exploring migration push factors, we find that adults living in LMAs with weaker origin economic conditions are less likely to out-migrate. Adults in economically weak LMAs are more likely to make short-distance moves (as opposed to not migrating to a new LMA), but they are less likely to make medium- and long-distance moves. The latter types of moves account for over two-thirds of all moves, so weak economic origin conditions do not generally seem to push adults to migrate (contrary to H2). Some of this effect may be the result of housing lock as adults in labor market areas whose housing markets experienced larger crashes during the recession were less likely to out-migrate, particularly for a medium- or longer-distance move (contrary to H3). We find few systematic differences by college degree status, but college graduates seem to respond to origin unemployment with slightly more out-migration (H4). Over all, our results highlight modest differences with previous research finding increased out-migration from areas with high unemployment (Greenwood 1997; Pissarides and McMaster 1990), but these differences may result from our analysis at the LMA-level. Our state-level estimates provide greater support for a labor migration model during the recession.

Turning to destination pull factors, the CL model demonstrates that migrants are generally responsive to the economic vitality of potential destinations (H1), and this responsiveness was substantively unchanged during the economic downturn. Adults are more likely to choose LMAs with broadly strong economies as measured by unemployment and manufacturing labor demand, but they persist in their likelihood of migrating to LMAs with previously booming housing markets that have busted during the crash (contrary to H3). The positive relationship between labor demand and destination selection that we find suggests a reversal of the decline in importance of potential destination economies over the past two decades found by Mark D. Partridge and colleagues (2012). College graduates may be more responsive to differences in unemployment between potential destinations, but again we find only modest evidence of variation in migration decisions by education level (H4).

Our LCCL models, however, reveal substantial heterogeneity in migration preferences among adults, and the models offer an improvement upon traditional CL estimation for two reasons. First, the models relax the traditional IIA assumption, and second, the models substantially improve our explanatory power for destination selection. On the basis of the results of our LCCL models, we are able to conclude that the number of economic migrants remained stable or even increased during the economic downturn. Roughly 47 percent of adult migrants were economic movers before the recession, and nearly 54 percent of adult migrants were economic movers during the downturn. This aligns with our expected increase in labor migration during the recession (H1).

Ultimately, although adults are generally less likely to out-migrate from an economically distressed LMA, their odds of leaving such labor markets did not decline dramatically during the Great Recession. In addition, more migrants were motivated by economic considerations during the recession than prior to it. Our findings offer suggestive evidence that policymakers' fears during the downturn may not have been warranted. Nevertheless, we did not observe dramatic, large-scale changes in migration behavior that would indicate a widespread shift toward labor migration. Instead, the United States experienced—perhaps even continues to experience—a protracted adjustment to employment equilibrium between labor markets. In a previous downturn in Great Britain, Christopher A. Pissarides and Ian McMaster (1990) found that it can take over twenty years to achieve equilibrium. Thus, during future large-scale recessions, policymakers may consider legislation that incentivizes and supports labor migration of the workforce.

APPENDIX A

Estimation of the Latent Class Conditional Logit Models

As described earlier, the latent class conditional logit (LCCL) model presents a viable alternative to the mixed logit model. Incorporating correlation in migration preferences between some individuals, the LCCL uses discrete latent classes of individuals to allow for variation in the coefficients (β_i) across individuals and yields the following modification to basic equation for the conditional logit model:

$$P_{ic}(j) = \frac{\exp(\beta_c x_{ij})}{\Sigma_k \exp(\beta_c x_{ij})}, \qquad (4)$$

where c represents a number of latent classes. In equation 4, whereas parameter estimates can vary across latent classes, they are forced to be constant within latent class. Equation 4 does circumvent the IIA assumption of constant preferences across individuals, but it accomplishes this in a much more computationally feasible way than the mixed logit. A LCCL model also allows the sampling of choices, which adds to the computational feasibility. Along with these advantages, the LCCL model preserves the multilevel structure of random effects and random coefficients from the mixed logit model by allowing intercepts and parameter estimates to vary across the latent classes.

The LCCL model is estimated using the expectation-maximization (EM) algorithm, and the probability of individual membership in the various latent classes is estimated through an iterative process as part of the model. The probability of a worker (i) choosing destination j is

$$P_i(j) = \Sigma_k[s_c * P_{ic}(j)], \qquad (5)$$

where S_c is the share of individuals in latent class c. The probability of individual i being in latent class c is

$$h_{ic} = \frac{s_c P_{ic}(k)}{P_i(k)}, \qquad (6)$$

where k is the destination that is chosen.

The application of the LCCL technique to the migration literature is novel but demonstrates promise. A recent paper (Liao, Farber, and Ewing 2014) uses LCCL to analyze community preferences within a few counties of Utah. Still, there is yet to be a large-scale application of this method to analyze migration. We offer such an application by estimating LCCL models of migration for individuals migrating to a new LMA from 2005-2011 in the ACS.

APPENDIX B

Table B1. Logit Models of the Decision to Migrate Stratified by College Degree Status

Origin Characteristics	State-Level Models				LMA-Level Models[a]			
	College	College, with SL	No College	No College, with SL	College	College, with SL	No College	No College, with SL
Labor demand	1.477*	3.204***	2.956***	5.224***	0.774***	0.244	0.315*	-0.157
	(0.658)	(0.974)	(0.541)	(0.859)	(0.235)	(0.257)	(0.142)	(0.157)
R*labor demand	-1.66	-8.28***	-0.082	-5.736**	-0.982**	-0.289	-0.438*	0.183
	(1.717)	(2.103)	(1.539)	(1.859)	(0.354)	(0.371)	(0.217)	(0.228)
Unemployment	-1.652†	-5.242***	0.149	-4.011***	0.83	0.264	-0.519	-0.891**
	(0.943)	(1.367)	(0.852)	(1.196)	(0.517)	(0.533)	(0.326)	(0.332)
R*unemployment	1.3	3.787**	-0.917	2.084	-1.711**	-1.051†	-0.867*	-0.655†
	(0.984)	(1.458)	(0.885)	(1.279)	(0.553)	(0.61)	(0.352)	(0.381)
Land availability	-0.479***	-0.403***	-0.271***	-0.163*	-0.256***	-0.315***	-0.116***	-0.208***
	(0.084)	(0.087)	(0.072)	(0.076)	(0.043)	(0.05)	(0.03)	(0.034)
R*land availability	0.359***	0.28**	0.427***	0.308***	0.274***	0.307***	0.221***	0.274***
	(0.103)	(0.107)	(0.087)	(0.092)	(0.053)	(0.063)	(0.036)	(0.042)
Potential destination spatial lags		x		x		x		x
N	2,919,471	2,919,471	6,559,954	6,559,954	2,918,096	2,916,632	6,556,083	6,550,199

Source: Authors' calculations.

Notes: Base outcome is staying in the same state (left models) or labor market areas (right models). Coefficients are log odds. Standard errors in parentheses. All models include controls for the recession (dummy), individual race or ethnicity, gender, age, education, marital status, and disability status, as well as previous year's LMA's population size, racial composition, nativity composition, educational composition, and age composition.

[a] LMA = labor market area.

†*p* < .1; **p* < .05; ***p* < .01; ****p* < .001

APPENDIX C

Table C1. Multinomial Logit Models of Migration Distance for College Graduates (N = 2,916,458)

Origin Characteristics	College Graduates (No Spatial Lags)				College Graduates (with Potential Destination on Spatial Lags)			
	Moved < 100 Miles	Moved 100–300 Miles	Moved 300–1,000 Miles	Moved 1,000+ Miles	Moved < 100 Miles	Moved 100–300 Miles	Moved 300–1,000 Miles	Moved 1,000+ Miles
Labor demand	-0.353	0.657	2.199***	0.615	-1.022*	-0.074	1.925***	0.287
	(0.399)	(0.44)	(0.4)	(0.736)	(0.445)	(0.486)	(0.417)	(0.807)
R*labor demand	-0.592	-0.158	-2.374***	1.223	0.201	0.439	-1.585*	1.116
	(0.62)	(0.686)	(0.618)	(0.995)	(0.655)	(0.719)	(0.628)	(1.054)
Unemployment	4.622***	-0.662	-0.187	2.772*	4.238***	-1.4	-1.072	2.34†
	(0.909)	(0.996)	(0.938)	(1.327)	(0.935)	(1.037)	(0.974)	(1.373)
R*unemployment	-2.872**	-1.188	-1.47	-4.391**	-1.502	-1.392	0.133	-4.58**
	(0.992)	(1.067)	(0.999)	(1.393)	(1.081)	(1.182)	(1.109)	(1.563)
Land availability	-0.016	-0.077	-0.138†	-0.704***	0.222*	-0.069	-0.613***	-0.48***
	(0.079)	(0.085)	(0.08)	(0.103)	(0.095)	(0.102)	(0.092)	(0.12)
R*land availability	0.298**	0.435***	0.317***	-0.004	0.216†	0.492***	0.4***	0.007
	(0.1)	(0.107)	(0.099)	(0.126)	(0.121)	(0.127)	(0.114)	(0.148)
Potential destination spatial lags					x	x	x	x

Source: Authors' calculations.

Notes: Base outcome is staying in the same labor market area. Coefficients are log odds. Standard errors in parentheses. All models include controls for the recession (dummy), individual race or ethnicity, gender, age, education, marital status, and disability status, as well as previous year's LMA's population size, racial composition, nativity composition, educational composition, and age composition.

†*p* < .1; **p* < .05; ***p* < .01; ****p* < .001

APPENDIX D

Table D1. Multinomial Logit Models of Migration Distance for Adults Without a College Degree (N = 6,549,242)

Origin Characteristics	Non-College Graduates (No Spatial Lags)				Non-College Graduates (with Potential Destination Spatial Lags)			
	Moved <100 Miles	Moved 100–300 Miles	Moved 300–1,000 Miles	Moved 1,000+ Miles	Moved <100 Miles	Moved 100–300 Miles	Moved 300–1,000 Miles	Moved 1,000+ Miles
Labor demand	-0.248	0.372	0.725*	2.355***	-0.471†	-0.091	-0.024	2.277***
	(0.221)	(0.261)	(0.308)	(0.373)	(0.243)	(0.346)	(0.346)	(0.43)
R*labor demand	-0.691*	0.669†	-0.199	-0.589	-0.29	1.118**	0.601	-0.693
	(0.33)	(0.403)	(0.467)	(0.68)	(0.347)	(0.421)	(0.493)	(0.718)
Unemployment	2.952***	-2.411***	-1.353*	0.075	2.835***	-2.845***	-2.252**	-0.151
	(0.491)	(0.596)	(0.687)	(1.152)	(0.505)	(0.608)	(0.7)	(1.156)
R*unemployment	-1.758**	-0.504	-1.367†	-2.961*	-0.565	-1.106	-1.528†	-3.302*
	(0.536)	(0.645)	(0.736)	(1.216)	(0.576)	(0.704)	(0.802)	(1.313)
Land availability	0.509***	-0.22***	-0.276***	-0.762***	0.565***	-0.277***	-0.539***	-0.643***
	(0.048)	(0.057)	(0.064)	(0.087)	(0.058)	(0.066)	(0.071)	(0.1)
R*land availability	0.042	0.419***	0.378***	-0.028	0.043	0.459***	0.417***	0.094
	(0.059)	(0.07)	(0.078)	(0.108)	(0.071)	(0.081)	(0.088)	(0.124)
Potential destination spatial lags					x	x	x	x

Source: Authors' calculations.

Notes: Base outcome is staying in the same labor market area. Coefficients are log odds. Standard errors in parentheses. All models include controls for the recession (dummy), individual race or ethnicity, gender, age, education, marital status, and disability status, as well as previous year's LMA's population size, racial composition, nativity composition, educational composition, and age composition.

†$p < .1$; *$p < .05$; **$p < .01$; ***$p < .001$

REFERENCES

Barro, Robert J., and Xavier Sala-I-Martin. 1992. "Regional Growth and Migration: A Japan–United States Comparison." *Journal of the Japanese and International Economies* 6(4): 312–46.

Bartik, Timothy J. 1991. *Who Benefits from State and Local Economic Development Policies?* Kalamazoo, Mich.: W. E. Upjohn Institute for Employment Research.

———. 2013. "Social Costs of Jobs Lost Due to Environmental Regulations." Upjohn Institute Working Paper 13-193. Kalamazoo, Mich.: W. E. Upjohn Institute for Employment Research.

Bartik, Timothy J., and Randall W. Eberts. 2006. "Urban Labor Markets." In *A Companion to Urban Economics*, edited by Richard J. Arnott and Daniel P. McMillen, pp. 389–403. Malden, Mass.: Blackwell.

Beaudry. Paul, David A. Green, and Benjamin M. Sand. 2014. "Spatial Equilibrium with Unemployment and Wage Bargaining: Theory and Estimation." *Journal of Urban Economics* 79(January): 2–19.

Blanchard, Olivier Jean, and Lawrence F. Katz. 1992. "Regional Evolutions." *Brookings Papers on Economic Activity* 1992(1): 1–75.

Bound, John, and Harry J. Holzer. 2000. "Demand Shifts, Population Adjustments, and Labor Market Outcomes during the 1980s." *Journal of Labor Economics* 18(1): 20–54.

Bruch, Elizabeth E., and Robert D. Mare. 2012. "Methodological Issues in the Analysis of Residential Preferences, Residential Mobility, and Neighborhood Change." *Sociological Methodology* 42(1): 103–54.

Charles, Kerwin Kofi, Erik Hurst, and Matthew J. Notowidigdo. 2012. "Manufacturing Busts, Housing Booms, and Declining Employment: A Structural Explanation." NBER Working Paper 18949. Cambridge, Mass.: National Bureau of Economic Research.

Chi, Guangqing, and Hung Chak Ho. 2013. "Land Developability: A Measure of the Proportion of Lands Available for Development and Conversion." Available at http://www.landdevelopability.org.website/index.html; accessed August 6, 2016.

Coulson, N. Edward, and Paul L. E. Grieco. 2013. "Mobility and Mortgages: Evidence from the PSID." *Regional Science and Urban Economics* 43(1): 1–7.

Davies, Paul S., Michael J. Greenwood, and Haizheng Li. 2002. "A Conditional Logit Approach to U.S. State-to-State Migration." *Journal of Regional Science* 41(2): 337–60.

Demyanyk, Yuliya, Dmytro Hryshko, María José Luengo-Prado, and Bent E. Sørensen. 2014. "Moving to a Job: The Role of Home Equity, Debt, and Access to Credit." Federal Reserve Bank of Cleveland Working Paper No. 1305R.

Domanski, Adam. 2009. "Estimating Mixed Logit Recreation Demand Models with Large Choice Sets." Paper presented at the Agricultural and Applied Economics Association Annual Meeting. Milwaukee (July 26–28, 2009).

Ellwood, David T., and Elisabeth D. Welty. 2000. "Public Service Employment and Mandatory Work: A Policy Whose Time Has Come and Gone and Come Again?" In *Finding Jobs: Work and Welfare Reform*, edited by David Card and Rebecca M. Blank. New York: Russell Sage Foundation.

Ferreira, Fernando, Joseph Gyourko, and Joseph Tracy. 2012. "Housing Busts and Household Mobility: An Update." *Economic Policy Review* 18(3): 1–15.

Fishback, Price V., William C. Horrace, and Shawn Kantor. 2006. "The Impact of New Deal Expenditures on Mobility During the Great Depression." *Explorations in Economic History* 43(2): 179–22.

Fletcher, Michael A. 2010. "Few in U.S. Move for New Jobs, Fueling Fear the Economy Might Get Stuck, Too." *Washington Post*, July 30. Available at: www.washingtonpost.com/wp- dyn/content/article/2010/07/29/AR2010072906367.html; accessed September 14, 2012.

Frey, William H. 2009. "The Great American Migration Slowdown: Regional and Metropolitan Dimensions." Washington, D.C.: Brookings Institution. Available at: at: www.brookings.edu/~/media/research/files/opinions/2011/1/12%20 mig ration%20frey/1 209_migration_frey.pdf; accessed September 14, 2012.

Gallin, Joshua Hojvat. 2004. "Net Migration and State Labor Market Dynamics." *Journal of Labor Economics* 22(1): 1–21.

Gordon, Ian. 1985. "The Cyclical Interaction Between Regional Migration, Employment, and Unemployment: A Time Series Analysis for Scotland." *Scottish Journal of Political Economy* 32(2): 135–58.

Greenwood, Michael J. 1975. "Research on Internal

Migration in the United States: A Survey." *Journal of Economic Literature* 13(2): 397–433.

———. 1997. "Internal Migration in Developed Countries." In *Handbook of Population and Family Economics*, Volume 1, Part B, edited by Mark R. Rosenzweig and Oded Stark. Amsterdam, Netherlands: Elsevier.

Hensher, David, and William Greene. 2003. "Mixed Logit Models: State of Practice." *Transportation* 30(2): 133–76.

Herkenhoff, Kyle F., and Lee E. Ohanian. 2011. "Labor Market Dysfunction During the Great Recession." *Cato Papers on Public Policy* 1: 173–217.

Herzog, Henry W., Alan M. Schlottmann, and Thomas P. Boehm. 1993. "Migration as Spatial Job-Search: A Survey of Empirical Findings." *Regional Studies* 27(4): 327–40.

Hornbeck, Richard. 2012. "The Enduring Impact of the American Dust Bowl: Short- and Long-Run Adjustments to Environmental Catastrophe." *American Economic Review* 102(4): 1477–1507.

Kaplan, Greg, and Sam Schulhofer-Wohl. 2011. "Interstate Migration Has Fallen Less Than You Think: Consequences of Hot Deck Imputation in the Current Population Survey." Working Paper 681. Federal Reserve Bank of Minneapolis. Available at: www.minneapolisfed.org/research/wp/wp681.pdf; accessed September 14, 2012.

Karahan, Fatih, and Serena Rhee. 2012. "Geographical Reallocation and Unemployment During the Great Recession: The Role of the Housing Bust." Staff report, no. 605. New York: Federal Reserve Bank of New York. Available at: https://www.newyorkfed.org/research/staff_reports/sr605.html; accessed August 6, 2016.

Kennan, John, and James R. Walker. 2011. "The Effect of Expected Income on Individual Migration Decisions." *Econometrica* 79(1): 211–51.

Kothari, Siddharth, Itay Saporta-Eksten, and Edison Yu. 2012. "The (Un)importance of Mobility in the Great Recession." Available at: http://dosen.narotama.ac.id/wp-content/uploads/2012/03/The-Un-importance-of-Mobility-in-the-Great-Recession.pdf; accessed August 6, 2016.

Lee, Everett S. 1966. "A Theory of Migration." *Demography* 3(1): 47–57.

Liao, Felix Haifeng, Steven Farber, and Reid Ewing. 2014. "Compact Development and Preference Heterogeneity in Residential Location Choice Behaviour: A Latent Class Analysis." *Urban Studies* 52(2): 314–37.

Mare, David C., and Wai Kin Choy. 2001. "Regional Labour Market Adjustment and the Movements of People: A Review." New Zealand Treasury Working Paper 01/08. Wellington, N.Z., December. Available at: http://motu.nz/assets/Documents/our-work/population-and-labour/migration/Regional-Labour-Market-Adjustment-and-the-Movements-of-People-A-Review.pdf; accessed August 6, 2016.

Martin, Richard W. 2001. "The Adjustment of Black Residents to Metropolitan Employment Shifts: How Persistent Is Spatial Mismatch?" *Journal of Urban Economics* 50(1): 52–76.

McFadden, Daniel. 1974. "Conditional Logit Analysis of Qualitative Choice Behavior." In *Frontiers in Econometrics*, edited by Paul Zarembka. New York: Academic Press.

———. 1978. "Modeling the Choice of Residential Location." *Spatial Interaction Theory and Planning Models* 25(1): 75–96.

Mian, Atif, and Amir Sufi. 2014. "What Explains the 2007–2009 Drop in Employment?" *Econometrica* 82(6): 2197–2223.

Milne, William J. 1993. "Macroeconomic Influences on Migration." *Regional Studies* 27(4): 365–73.

Modestino, Alicia Sasser, and Julia Dennett. 2012. "Are American Homeowners Locked into Their Houses? The Impact of Housing Market Conditions on State-to-State Migration." Working Paper No. 12-1. Boston: Federal Reserve Bank of Boston. Available at: www.bos.frb.org/economic/wp/wp2012/wp1201.htm; accessed September 18, 2012.

Molloy, Raven, Christopher L. Smith, and Abigail Wozniak. 2011. "Internal Migration in the United States." *Journal of Economic Perspectives* 25(3): 173–96.

———. 2014. "Declining Migration Within the US: The Role of the Labor Market." Finance and Economics Discussion Series. Staff Working Paper No. 2013-27. Washington: Federal Reserve Board, Divisions of Research & Statistics and Monetary Affairs. Available at: www.federalreserve.gov/pubs/feds/2013/201327/201327pap.pdf; accessed August 6, 2016.

Monras, Joan. 2015. "Economic Shocks and Internal Migration." IZA Discussion Paper No. 8840. Bonn, Germany: Institute for the Study of Labor.

Moretti, Enrico. 2010. "Local Multipliers." *American Economic Review* 100(2): 1–7.

———. 2012. "What Workers Lose by Staying Put."

Wall Street Journal, May 26. Available at: www
.wsj.com/articles/SB1000142405270230361050
4577420701942867414; accessed March 16, 2015.

Nerella, Sriharsha, and Chandra Bhat. 2004. "Nu-
merical Analysis of Effect of Sampling of Alternatives in Discrete Choice Models." *Transportation Research Record*, vol. 1894, pp. 11–19.

Neumark, David. 2011. "Direct Job Creation Policies
in the Aftermath of the Great Recession and Beyond." Available at: http://50.87.169.168/OJS
/ojs-2.4.4-1/index.php/EPRN/article/view/1870
/1868; accessed October 13, 2016.

Notowidigdo, Matthew J. 2011. "The Incidence of Local Labor Demand Shocks." NBER Working Paper No. 17167. Cambridge, Mass.: National Bureau of Economic Research.

Partridge, Mark D., Dan S. Rickman, M. Rose Olfert,
and Kamar Ali. 2012. "Dwindling U.S. Internal Migration: Evidence of Spatial Equilibrium or Structural Shifts in Local Labor Markets?" *Regional
Science and Urban Economics* 42(1–2): 375–88.
DOI: 10.1016/j.regsciurbeco.2011.10.006.

Pissarides, Christopher A., and Ian McMaster. 1990.
"Regional Migration, Wages, and Unemployment:
Empirical Evidence and Implications for Policy."
Oxford Economic Papers 42(4): 812–31.

Ritchey, P. Neal. 1976. "Explanations of Migration."
Annual Review of Sociology 2: 363–404.

Rothstein, Jesse. 2011. "Unemployment Insurance
and Job Search in the Great Recession." *Brookings Papers on Economic Activity* (Fall): 143–213.

Ruggles, Steven, J. Trent Alexander, Katie Genadek,
Ronald Goeken, Matthew B. Schroeder, and
Matthew Sobek. 2010. "Integrated Public Use
Microdata Series: Version 5.0 [Machine-
readable database]." Minneapolis: University of
Minnesota.

Saiz, Albert. 2010. "The Geographic Determinants of
Housing Supply." *Quarterly Journal of Economics*
125(3): 1253–96.

Saks, Raven E., and Abigail Wozniak. 2011. "Labor
Reallocation over the Business Cycle: New Evi-
dence from Internal Migration." *Journal of Labor
Economics* 29(4): 697–739.

Sasser, Alicia C. 2010. "Voting with Their Feet: Relative Economic Conditions and State Migration
Patterns." *Regional Science and Urban Economics*
40(2–3): 122–35.

Train, Kenneth E. 2003. *Discrete Choice Methods
with Simulation*. New York: Cambridge University
Press.

———. 2008. "EM Algorithms for Nonparametric Estimation of Mixing Distributions." *Journal of
Choice Modelling* 1(1): 40–69.

Treyz, George I., Dan S. Rickman, Gary L. Hunt, and
Michael J. Greenwood. 1993. "The Dynamics of
U.S. Internal Migration." *Review of Economics
and Statistics* 75(2): 209–14.

Wiseman, Michael. 1976. "Public Employment as
Fiscal Policy." *Brookings Papers on Economic Activity* 1: 67–114.

Wozniak, Abigail. 2010. "Are College Graduates
More Responsive to Distant Labor Market Opportunities?" *Journal of Human Resources* 45(4):
944–70.

Yagan, Danny. 2014. "Moving to Opportunity? Migratory Insurance over the Great Recession."
Available at: http://eml.berkeley.edu/~yagan
/MigratoryInsurance.pdf; accessed August 6,
2016.

Yankow, Jeffrey J. 2003. "Migration, Job Change, and
Wage Growth: A New Perspective on the Pecuni-
ary Return to Geographic Mobility." *Journal of Regional Science* 43(3): 483–516.

Non-marital and Teen Fertility and Contraception During the Great Recession

DANIEL SCHNEIDER

I examine the effects of the Great Recession on non-marital and teen births. The Recession could have led to reductions in non-marital and teen fertility or the Recession could have had null effects if non-marital and teen fertility are disconnected from economic factors. Using a panel of state-level fertility and economic data, I find that worse macro-economic conditions are associated with lower rates of non-marital and teen fertility. I next analyzed data from the National Survey of Family Growth and find that worsening macro-economic conditions at the national level raise the probability of contraceptive use, of consistent contraceptive use, and of the efficacy of the contraceptive method employed among unmarried women. The results suggest that disadvantaged women moderate fertility in response to severe economic shocks.

Keywords: non-marital fertility, teen fertility, contraception, recession

The economic effects of the Great Recession have been readily apparent in high levels of unemployment and unprecedented levels of mortgage foreclosure. These economic effects have also had important social consequences for American families. Recent research suggests that elevated levels of unemployment and foreclosure led to a substantial reduction, on the order of 5 to 10 percent, in births in the United States (Schneider 2015; Currie and Schwandt 2014; Cherlin et al. 2013; Ananat, Gassman-Pines, and Gibson-Davis 2013).

Reductions in fertility around periods of recession are typically thought of as a rational response to increases in economic hardship and perhaps also to increased uncertainty about the future (Sobotka, Skirbekk, and Philipov 2011). On those grounds, we might expect the Great Recession to have had its largest effects on relatively disadvantaged women—those who are teens, or unmarried, or with limited educational attainment. However, ethnographic and demographic research on non-marital fertility among low-SES (socioeconomic status) women provides good reason to expect that the Great Recession would have relatively limited effects on the fertility of such women. This work finds that economic considerations are relatively disconnected from fertility among low-SES unmarried women and this disconnection may manifest in non-use or inconsistent use

Daniel Schneider is assistant professor of sociology at the University of California, Berkeley.

© 2017 Russell Sage Foundation. Schneider, Daniel. 2017. "Non-marital and Teen Fertility and Contraception During the Great Recession." *RSF: The Russell Sage Foundation Journal of the Social Sciences* 3(3): 126–44. DOI: 10.7758/RSF.2017.3.3.06. I thank the Institute for Research on Labor and Employment at the University of California, Berkeley, and the Robert Wood Johnson Foundation for financial support. I thank Joshua Goldstein, Kristen Harknett, Jennifer Johnson-Hanks, Andrew Kelly, and seminar participants at the University of California, Berkeley and Irvine, and the annual meeting of the Robert Wood Johnson Foundation Scholars in Health Policy Research for their comments on earlier versions of this manuscript. Direct correspondence to: Daniel Schneider at djschneider@berkeley.edu, Department of Sociology, 480 Barrows Hall, Berkeley, CA 94720.

of contraception, or the use of ineffective contraception.

I examine how non-marital and teen fertility responded to the sharp economic shocks of the Great Recession. I first draw on a panel of state-level vital statistics records merged with data on state-level unemployment and foreclosure to estimate how the fertility rates of teen and unmarried women responded to the recession. There is clearly not a direct relationship between economic conditions and births—an important set of proximate determinants of fertility must necessarily have been the mediating processes. To test the pathways by which the recession might have affected fertility, I next draw on data from the 2006-to-2010 cycle of the National Survey of Family Growth (NSFG) to examine whether the recession affected patterns of contraception use among these same groups of women.

I find that at the state-level, non-marital and teen fertility declined significantly with rising unemployment and foreclosure during the years of the Great Recession. I also find that the likelihood of using contraception increased with unemployment and foreclosure over this same time period for unmarried women. There is some evidence that unmarried women exposed to worse economic conditions also used contraception more consistently and used more effective contraceptive methods. However, I find no evidence of a link between national economic conditions and the use of contraception among teenagers during the Great Recession. Together, these findings buttress other recent research finding recessionary reductions in non-marital and teen fertility. The results suggest that some disadvantaged women moderate fertility in response to severe economic shocks, a finding that supports a more nuanced understanding of the relationship between economic factors and fertility in this subpopulation.

FERTILITY IN THE GREAT RECESSION

The Great Recession resulted in substantial economic hardship and uncertainty at the house-hold level. These effects are most broadly captured in the sharp increases in residential mortgage delinquency and foreclosure, the dramatic rise in unemployment, and the pronounced reductions in consumer confidence. Research has also shown that the Great Recession increased household economic hardship and poverty (Bitler and Hoynes 2010; Pilkaus-kas, Currie, and Garfinkel 2012).

Given the substantial investments that many Americans make in their children in the form of basics such as medical care, clothes, food, and shelter as well as other costs such as childcare, schooling, toys, books, and activities (to name just a few), we might well expect that at least in the short term, fertility would decline in the face of these economic shocks. Indeed, this common wisdom is formalized in economic theories of fertility (see Becker 1960) and borne out in a long line of demographic research in the United States that shows a negative effect of aggregate measures of unemployment on fertility (for example, Rindfuss, Morgan, and Swicegood 1988; Macunovich 1996; Schaller 2016; Currie and Schwandt 2014). Such recessionary effects are generally concentrated among younger women and on first births (So-botka, Skirbekk, and Philipov 2011; Adsera 2004). Although recessions may then primarily serve to delay fertility (tempo effects), recent research suggests that exposure to poor economic conditions can also have a permanent effect over the life course, reducing number of children ever born (quantum effects) (Currie and Schwandt 2014).[1]

Recent research in the United States finds evidence of significant negative effects of the Great Recession on fertility using a variety of methodological approaches. One set of analyses simply tracks the time trend in fertility nationally, observing that general fertility rates (GFR) declined nationally with the onset of the Great Recession (Livingston and Cohn 2010; Morgan, Cumberworth, and Wimer 2011). A second set of analyses examines the relationship between area-level measures of fertility and

---

1. Notably, recent empirical research does not seem to bear out William P. Butz and Michael P. Ward's (1979) theory that although raising children is expensive, so is any time that women take off from work for pregnancy, birth, and parenthood—and so a time when the labor market is weak may actually be a very good time to have a child.

area-level economic indicators. Livingston (2011) reports that changes in state economic conditions between 2007 and 2008 were related to declines in fertility between 2008 and 2009 and similarly, S. Phillip Morgan, Erin Cumberworth, and Christopher Wimer (2011) show that the change in unemployment between 2007 and 2009 was negatively related to the change in fertility between 2007 and 2009. Andrew Cherlin and colleagues (2013) extend this series to show a negative relationship between the percentage-point change in unemployment between 2007 and 2009 and the percentage-point change in GFR between 2007 and 2011. More recently, Daniel Schneider (2015) assembles a panel of state-level data on fertility and unemployment and foreclosure for the period 2001 to 2013 and finds that worsening macroeconomic conditions are associated with lower general fertility rates and that these effects were largest for younger women.

Variation by Socioeconomic Status

These negative effects of recessionary conditions may not, however, apply to all women and couples equally. The economic hardship perspective on recessions and fertility would suggest that the fertility of women in already disadvantaged subgroups, such as those with lower levels of educational attainment or at risk of a non-marital or teen birth, might be most affected by the recession. In this scenario, the least-advantaged reduce their fertility the most in response to poor economic conditions.

Conversely, recent ethnographic work focused on young unmarried mothers in the United States suggests that for many young disadvantaged women, fertility is effectively disconnected from economic resources. Scholars such as Kathryn Edin and Maria Kefalas (2005) argue that, with few prospects for economic success, these young women see little reason to delay fertility. In these accounts, fertility is not the result of a careful economic calculus, but rather a natural part of the life course essentially removed from economic considerations (Gibson-Davis 2009). Some prior empirical research supports this idea. Cristina Gibson-Davis (2009) finds that in a sample of disadvantaged unmarried parents, improvements in economic

standing are predictive of marriage but not of having a birth. Other work has even shown a positive relationship between unfavorable economic conditions and non-marital fertility (Billy and Moore 1992) and between state-level income inequality and teen fertility (Kearney and Levine 2014). In essence, this work suggests that for disadvantaged and unmarried and teen women, economic factors may exert a weak influence on fertility. In the context of the economic shocks of the Great Recession, we might then expect to find little relationship between unemployment or foreclosure and the fertility of unmarried, teen, or otherwise disadvantaged women.

This research complements a significant body of demographic work on how class and economic expectations shape how women use contraception. This research suggests that disadvantaged unmarried women and their partners do not so much set out to have children in the face of economic scarcity as "drift into parenthood" (Sawhill 2014, 3). Indeed, it is well established that many non-marital and teen births are unintended (Finer and Henshaw 2006), and such unintended births are much more common among less-educated women than among women with a college degree (Musick et al. 2009). The explanation for this mismatch between intentions and fertility is then inconsistent or ineffective use of contraceptive technology (Edin et al. 2007).

There is less consensus on why disadvantaged, unmarried, and teen women are inconsistent in their use of contraception. One explanation notes that although few pregnancies among low-SES unmarried women are explicitly intended, significant ambivalence exists about pregnancy (Augustine, Nelson, and Edin 2009; Edin and Kefalas 2005; Edin et al. 2007; Yoo, Guzzo, and Hayford 2014; Miller, Barber, and Gatney 2013). In their interviews with unmarried parents, Edin et al. (2007) found roughly 65 percent of pregnancies were neither completely planned nor accidental. Instead, the couples often wanted children, but were unsure if the current circumstances were ideal. This spectrum of ambivalence has also been found in national representative studies (Yoo, Guzzo, and Hayford 2014) and among fathers (Augustine, Nelson, and Edin 2009).

Fertility in the Great Recession:
Disadvantage and Proximate Determinants

Despite these contrasting predictions, relatively little research has been done to investigate whether the effects of the Great Recession vary by women's socioeconomic or marital status. There are, though, some notable and useful exceptions. Cherlin and colleagues (2013) examine the time trend in births reported in the American Community Survey data and find that women living at less than 100 percent of the poverty line have the steepest negative gradient in fertility over the years of the Great Recession, through 2011. Elizabeth Oltmans Ananat, Anna Gassman-Pines, and Cristina Gibson-Davis (2013) draw on detailed county-level data from North Carolina merged with information on mass layoffs to examine the effects of the Great Recession on teen births. While we might expect that teen births would be relatively unresponsive to the Great Recession, or might even increase, Ananat, Gassman-Pines, and Gibson-Davis (2013) find the opposite, that births to black teens declined with communitywide job loss in North Carolina. Further, Melissa Kearney and Phillip Levine (2015) also find that teen births declined during the Great Recession. Finally, Schneider and Orestes Hastings (2015) draw on ACS data merged with state-level economic conditions to examine how the Great Recession affected non-marital fertility among low-SES women. They find that unmarried women with a high school degree or less who were exposed to higher rates of foreclosure and unemployment were significantly less likely to have a birth.

These results are somewhat surprising, both because prior theory suggests that fertility is likely to be disconnected from economic factors for unmarried, disadvantaged, and teen women and because prior empirical research shows that a substantial portion of births to these women are unintended and likely are due to inconsistent use of contraception. There are, however, several pathways by which the Great Recession could have affected fertility among these subgroups of women and not all are inconsistent with this existing theory and empirical work.

One such pathway would be an increase in stress-induced miscarriage. Prior research has found that miscarriage increases in response to maternal stress (Nepomnaschy et al. 2006) and the Great Recession, like prior economic recessions, could reasonably be expected to increase economic stress (see Conger, Reuter, and Elder 1999). If such a mechanism were at work in the case of the Great Recession, that could explain the puzzling discrepancy between the apparent decline in births among teens and unmarried women and the existing literature that suggests a weak connection between economic factors and fertility among disadvantaged women. However, I know of no research that has examined this issue in the context of the Great Recession, and the magnitude of fertility declines would appear to be much larger than would be expected from stress-induced miscarriage.

A possible alternative is that more women elected to terminate their pregnancies during the Great Recession due to economic pressure. Evidence of such behavior would not accord with the idea that fertility is disconnected from economic concerns, but would fit with the finding that unmarried, teen, and low-SES women have trouble adopting consistent and effective patterns of contraceptive use. There is relatively little work on how abortion changed during the recession. In one study, Ananat, Gassman-Pines, and Gibson-Davis (2013) infer an increase in abortion from the fact that economic conditions zero to four months after expected conceptions are related to observed teen births in North Carolina. However, nationally, abortions declined markedly during the years of the Great Recession, and reached a low for the period from 2002 to 2011 in 2011 (Pazol et al. 2014). Further, women under the age of twenty and unmarried women accounted for the large majority of all abortions, and rates of abortion declined markedly for these two groups, although the rate of decline among unmarried women was slower between 2007 and 2011 than between 2002 and 2006 (Pazol et al. 2014).

The Great Recession could also have induced more teen and unmarried women to use effective contraception as a means of avoiding births during a period of acute economic constraint. There is somewhat more evidence to support this idea. The strongest evidence to date is reported by Ananat, Gassman-Pines, and Gibson-Davis (2013). Based on analysis of the Youth Risk Behavior Survey for the period 1995 to 2009, Ananat, Gassman-Pines, and Gibson-Davis find that white and black teens are more likely to report using contraception at last sex following mass layoffs in their state. More broadly, women steadily increased their use of long-acting contraceptives (Finer, Jerman, and Kavanaugh 2012) and men increased their use of vasectomy (Najari, Schlegel, and Goldstein 2014) over the period 2006 through 2009. Additionally, a 2009 survey found that 30 percent of female respondents reported using contraception more consistently as a result of the Great Recession (Gold 2009) and some reports based on market-research data suggest that the number of condoms and over-the-counter female contraceptives sold increased in the first months of 2009 as compared to the same period in 2008 (Gregory 2009).

PLAN OF ANALYSIS

I conduct two related empirical analyses. First, I draw on state-level vital statistics records on births to unmarried women and teen women joined with data from private and governmental sources on unemployment and foreclosure to examine whether the Great Recession really did have the effect of reducing births to these two groups of generally disadvantaged women, as found in North Carolina by Ananat, Gassman-Pines, and Gibson-Davis (2013) and nationally for unmarried women using ACS data by Schneider and Hastings (2015). This analysis advances existing work by considering both teen and non-marital fertility nationally during the period of the Great Recession.

Second, I use individual person-month data from the NSFG to examine if the high rates of unemployment and foreclosure found during the Great Recession changed the use of contraception by unmarried and teen women and, specifically, by unmarried and teen women of lower socioeconomic status. Here, I examine if the probability of contraceptive use, the consistency of contraceptive use, and the type of contraception employed was responsive to economic conditions. While Schneider and Hastings (2015) speculate that the Great Recession likely resulted in increased used of contracep-

tive technology among unmarried women, they do not actually test to see if recessionary economic conditions are associated with contraceptive use. Ananat, Gassman-Pines, and Gibson-Davis (2013) do show a relationship between economic conditions and contraceptive use among teens, but do not examine contraceptive practices by unmarried women or low-SES unmarried women.

DATA AND METHODS

State-Level Fertility Data

I create a panel of state-level general fertility rates (GFR) for the period 2003 to 2013. These data are drawn from the natality vital statistics published by the Centers for Disease Control and Prevention's National Center for Health Statistics. I create two key measures of interest. First, I calculate the non-marital GFR as the number of births to unmarried women within a state in a given calendar year divided by the number of unmarried women aged fifteen to forty-five living in the state in the same calendar year. The data for this denominator come from the single-year files of the American Community Survey. Second, I calculate the teen GFR as the number of births to women aged fifteen to nineteen within a state in a given calendar year divided by the number of women aged fifteen to nineteen living in the state in the same calendar year. The data for this denominator come from the National Cancer Institute's Surveillance, Epidemiology, and End Results Program (SEER).

I adjust the models for several time-varying measures of state demographic composition (each lagged on year): the percentage of women age fifteen to forty-four in the state who are black, non-Hispanic, and the percent who are Hispanic; the percentage of women with less than a high school education, with a high school degree or some college; the percentage of women aged twenty-five to thirty-four and the aged thirty-five to forty-four; and the percentage enrolled in school. Each measure is calculated from microdata form the March supplement to the annual Current Population Survey (CPS), collapsed with person-weights to the state-year level. These controls are designed to adjust for any nonlinear changes in state demographic profiles that could drive both fertility patterns and labor market conditions.

My approach follows much existing work in aggregating fertility at the state-level (Schaller 2016; Schneider 2015; Lovenheim and Mumford 2013). As Kearney and Levine (2009) note, these state-level vital statistics data are well measured. Additionally, using state-level aggregates as the outcome allows me to express the effects in terms of the widely used metric of general fertility rates rather than individual likelihoods of having a birth. Finally, from a practical perspective, many of the most commonly used datasets (for example, the National Longitudinal Survey of Youth 1997, Add Health) that would allow for the estimation of the effect of state-level unemployment on individual-level fertility are cohort-specific and so are less useful for understanding the effects of the Great Recession.

National Survey of Family Growth

I complement the state-level fertility data with individual-level data from the 2006-to-2010 cycle of the National Survey of Family Growth (NSFG). The NSFG is a nationally representative survey of Americans aged fifteen to forty-five with oversamples of African Americans, Hispanics, and teenagers. It is conducted by the Centers for Disease Control and Prevention's (CDC) National Center for Health Statistics (NCHS). The multistage stratified sample is constructed by first drawing 110 geographic entities called primary sampling units and dividing those into four subsets. Each subset is then used in turn in each of the four years of fieldwork (Groves et al. 2009). This strategy ensures that interviews that occur later in the interviewing period (2006 to 2010) are not biased in the direction of hard-to-reach respondents.

Separate surveys are conducted of men and women; following the convention in the demographic literature on fertility, I use data on women's reports. The interviews with women were conducted in person by trained female interviewers and lasted an average of eighty minutes. The survey had a 78 percent response rate for female interviewees.

This cycle of the NSFG was in the field from June 2006 through June 2010, spanning the years of the Great Recession. It contains interviews with 12,279 women aged fifteen to forty-five. Though fielded over four years, the NSFG contains only one interview with each respondent. However, because the NSFG collects detailed retrospective data on key variables, it is possible to construct a monthly time series for each respondent for many of the key measures of interest.

Contraceptive Use

The 2006-to-2010 cycle of the NSFG collects a detailed monthly calendar of contraceptive method use based on respondents' retrospective reports. This calendar is designed to collect information on the use of up to four different contraceptive methods during a given month for up to three years from the January before the interview date. Since interviews were conducted between July 2006 and June 2010, contraceptive method data is available from January of 2003 through June of 2010.

This data provide a comprehensive record of the use of contraception at the monthly level over the period from 2003 through mid-2010. I use this data to construct three key variables for analysis. First, I create a dichotomous measure of any contraceptive use in a given month. Second, I create a measure of consistent contraceptive use, which I define as the use of some kind of contraceptive technology in the current month and in each of the prior two months.

Third, I examine the effectiveness of the methods of contraception that respondents employed. Respondents reported using a large variety of contraceptive methods. Scholars have previously estimated the effectiveness of these different types of contraception at preventing pregnancy. Specifically, James Trussell (2011) provides estimates of the share of women experiencing an unintended pregnancy within the first year of typical use of the method. Table 1 provides a listing of these different methods as well as their associated failure rates. I construct a new variable that contains the failure rate corresponding to the contraceptive method used by the respondent. Since respondents can report up to four methods in a given month, I take the failure rate for the single most effective method used in the month.

Table 1. Contraceptive Methods and Percent of Women Experiencing Unintended Pregnancy Within the First Year of Typical Use

Contraceptive Method	Percentage Pregnant Within One Year Given Typical Use
No method	85
Foam	28
Jelly or cream	28
Rhythm method	24
Symptothermal method	24
Withdrawal	22
Female condom	21
Male condom	18
Sponge	18
Diaphragm	12
Contraceptive patch	9
NuvaRing	9
Birth control pill	9
Depo-Provera	6
Female sterilization	0.5
IUD	0.5
Male sterilization	0.15
Hormonal implant (such as Imlanon)	0.05

Source: Author's compilation based on Trussell 2011.

Notes: Methods are those listed by NSFG 2006–2010 respondents in contraceptive method calendar. Unintended pregnancy rates are taken from Trussell et al. (2011). Respondents in the NSFG reporting "emergency contraception" (0.02 percent of person-years), "Respondent sterile" (0.30 percent of person-years), "Partner sterile" (0.05 percent of person-years), "Lunelle" (0.08 percent of person-years), "Other" (0.06 percent of person-years) are set to missing.

Demographic Controls

To maintain parallelism with the state-level analysis, I stratify the NSFG analyses by marital status and by age. For marital status I use re-spondents' retrospective reports of dates of marriage and divorce or separation to construct a complete marital history, and I map that to marital status in a given person-month. I then construct a dichotomous measure of married or unmarried in each person-month. For age, I use respondents' month and year of birth to construct a dichotomous measure of being fifteen to nineteen years old.

Although the state-level vital statistics data cannot be easily stratified by socioeconomic status in addition to marital status or age, such data are available in the individual-level NSFG file.[2] I construct a measure of the respondent's mother's educational attainment, coding mothers as having less than a high school degree or at least a high school degree. This approach of using mothers' educational attainment as a proxy for respondents' social class is also employed by Paula England, Elizabeth McClintock, and Emily Fitzgibbons Shafer (2011) and Melissa Kearney and Phillip Levine (2014).

I also create a set of time-invariant background characteristics of respondents. These include race (white, black, Hispanic, or other), family structure at age 14 (living with both biological parents or not), foreign-born, and the religion in which respondents were raised (none, Catholic, evangelical Protestant, other Protestant, other non-Christian), educational attainment at interview (less than high school, high school graduate, some college, bachelor's degree or higher), and school enrollment. Finally, use of the information on the year and month of respondent's birth permits the construction a time-varying measure of age (included as age and age-squared) and of whether the respondent was cohabiting.

Macroeconomic Conditions

I merge both the state-year-level vital statistics data and the individual-level person-month NSFG data with exogenous macroeconomic data from government and private sector sources.

2. The vital statistics data do contain a measure of mother's education, which could be crossed with marital status to generate a count of non-marital births to less-educated women. However, beginning in 2003, the states began to change the way in which education was reported, moving from the 1989 U.S. Standard Certificate of Live Birth to the 2003 U.S. Standard Certificate of Live Birth. However, the states undertook this change at different times, making harmonization across years very difficult.

First, I assemble data from the Bureau of Labor Statistics (BLS) Local Area Unemployment Statistics (LAUS) on the unemployment rate. This rate is calculated as the number of people looking for work divided by the number of people in the labor force. The BLS LAUS estimates are model-based and rely on data from the Current Population Survey, the Current Employment Statistics, and the Unemployment Insurance system. I use annual state-level rates of unemployment for my analysis of the state-year level vital statistics data. I use monthly national level unemployment rate data for my analysis of the person-month level NSFG data.

Second, I use quarterly data from the Mortgage Bankers Association (MBA) National Delinquency Survey on the foreclosure start rate. This is a measure of the percentage of residential mortgages starting the foreclosure process during the year. I sum the observed quarters in a given year to create an annual state-level measure of foreclosure starts for my analysis of the state-year-level vital statistics data. For the mortgage foreclosure start rate at the national level on a monthly basis, I use the Denton method for interpolating quarterly flow data into a monthly time series. The method allows for expression of the time trend of the quarterly flows in the imputed monthly time series (Bloem, Dippelsman, and Maehle 2001).

These state- and national-level measures of economic conditions likely capture a number of pathways by which poor macroeconomic conditions might affect individual behavior. Most directly, poor conditions serve as a rough proxy for the probability that an individual experiences unemployment or foreclosure. But state-level conditions also likely capture economic hardship short of unemployment and foreclosure, including reduced earnings and economic stress more generally. Even more generally, area-level economic conditions might capture the strain of recession on personal networks and, perhaps most broadly, feelings of economic uncertainty and insecurity, even among those who have not directly experienced economic hardship (Schneider, Harknett, and McLanahan 2016; Gassman-Pines, Gibson-Davis, and Ananat 2015). Recent scholarship on fertility and recession suggests that these feelings of uncertainty may also be important for

shaping fertility behaviors (Schneider 2015; Sobotka, Skirbekk, and Philipov 2011). I do not attempt to disentangle the effects of realized economic hardship from feelings of uncertainty in these analyses, but I note that recent work that attempts to do so finds evidence that both hardship and uncertainty affected fertility and other demographic behaviors during the Great Recession (Schneider 2015; Schneider, Harknett, and McLanahan 2016). I also do not attempt to map these two different measures, unemployment rate and foreclosure start rate, onto different pathways of fertility influence. Rather, I treat both as incomplete but reasonable proxies for the events of the Great Recession.

Figure 1 charts the time trend in these two rates between 2003 and the end of 2009. The foreclosure start rate is relatively flat at a low level until 2006, when it begins to climb sharply. Notably, this increase begins well in advance of the official start of the Great Recession (shaded area), although the foreclosure start rate does peak right at the end of the official recession. The national unemployment rate falls from 2003 through mid-2007 and then begins an extremely sharp and rapid rise, increasing from about 5 percent to nearly 10 percent by the end of 2009. Were this graph to continue, we would see that although the official period of recession ends in mid-2009, the unemployment rate remained at or above 8 percent through the end of 2012.

Analytic Strategy

I first estimate the relationship between state-level economic conditions and state-level non-marital and teen GFR. I construct a state-year-level file merging the fertility rates from vital statistics, the demographic controls, and the measures of the state economy. I estimate an ordinary least squares (OLS) regression model of the relationship between economic conditions and fertility. The model includes a one-year lagged measure of state economic conditions as well as lagged measures of the time-varying state-level demographic attributes discussed earlier. I also include a set of state and year fixed effects as well as a state-specific linear time trend. The state fixed effects account for unobserved time-invariant character-

Figure 1. National Monthly Foreclosure Start Rate and Unemployment Rate (June 2003–January 2010)

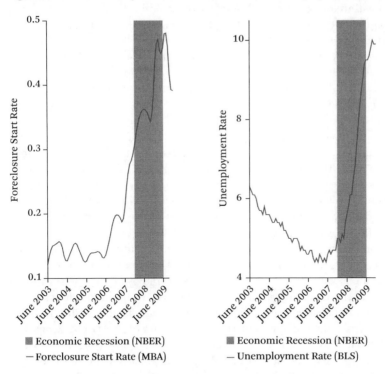

■ Economic Recession (NBER)
— Foreclosure Start Rate (MBA)

■ Economic Recession (NBER)
— Unemployment Rate (BLS)

Source: Mortgage Bankers Association National Delinquency Survey, available at https://www
.mba.org/news-research-and-resources/research-and-economics/single-family-research/national
-delinquency-survey, accessed October 20, 2016; Bureau of Labor Statistics Local Area Unemployment
Statistics.

istics of the state and avoid problems of omitted variable bias arising from the failure to account for such characteristics, such as religiosity, that might be associated with both fertility and the economy. The year fixed effects account for unobserved period characteristics that are stable across states. The inclusion of state-specific linear time trends controls for state-specific time trends in unobserved variables that might bias the relationship between economic conditions and fertility. I also weight the regressions by the average state population over the period 2003 to 2013. The results are robust to omitting the demographic controls and the coefficients are larger without the state-specific linear time trends.

Next, I estimate the relationship between national-level economic conditions and individual-level use of contraceptive technology. I construct a person-month file from the

retrospective questions on contraceptive use in the NSFG. I estimate three sets of regression models; in each I use the national foreclosure start rate and the national unemployment rate six months prior to the reporting month as the key predictors. First, I examine how each measure of economic conditions is related to the use of any contraceptive method in the reporting month. Second, I examine how each measure of economic conditions is related to consistent use (defined as using some kind of contraception in the reporting month and in both of the two months prior) of contraception. Third, I examine the relationship between economic conditions and the specific contraceptive method. For each set of models, I also examine whether the findings hold when only examining native-born women and if there is variation in the effect of national economic conditions by co-

Figure 2. Annual Non-marital and Teen Fertility Rates for Three States with Large Recessionary Increases in Unemployment and Three States with Small Increases (2003–2013)

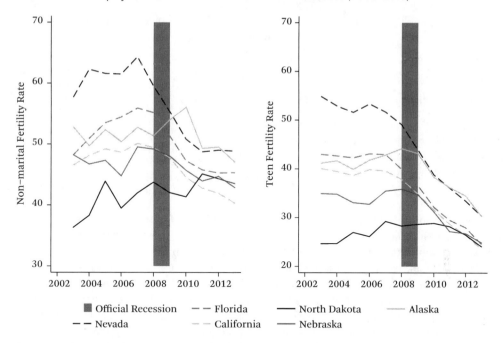

Source: Author's calculations based on data from the vital statistics.

residential status (cohabiting versus single) and by race or ethnicity.

The first two sets of models are estimated using logistic regression. The third set of models, of method effectiveness, is estimated with OLS. In all models I adjust for respondents' age, age-squared, race or ethnicity, family structure at age fourteen, religion raised in, and foreign- or native-born status. I also include year fixed effects and adjust the standard errors for repeated observation of respondents. This strategy reduces the risk of omitted variables bias by using area-level economic conditions, rather than individual-level hardship, to proxy for the effects of the Great Recession. This approach also reduces the risk of reverse causality (wherein a woman might reduce labor force involvement in advance of a birth or pregnancy). I define the "at risk" population to be all female respondents who have ever had sex and are not currently pregnant, according to their retrospectively reported pregnancy and conception calendar data. I then estimate the models separately for unmarried women and for teenage women and then again for unmar-

ried women with less-educated mothers and for teen women with less-educated mothers.

I also conduct several robustness tests. I examine if the results are sensitive to the choice of lag on the measure of macroeconomic conditions. I also estimate a set of person fixed effects models that exploit within person changes in contraceptive behavior to estimate the effects of economic conditions on use of contraceptives. I also run a set of "placebo" regressions, using future macroeconomic conditions to predict past contraceptive use. Here, I expect to find no significant relationship. Finally, I examine if error in respondent's recall of events for the construction of the retrospective contraceptive calendars might affect the results.

RESULTS

Time Trends in Non-marital and Teen Births

Figure 2 charts the fertility rates for unmarried women (left panel) and for teen women (right panel) over the years leading up to and following the official dates of the Great Recession

Table 2. State-Level General Fertility Rate by Subgroup and State Macroeconomic Conditions (2003–2013)

	Marital Fertility Rate	Non-marital Fertility Rate	Teen (15–19) Fertility Rate
State foreclosure start rate	−0.32**	−0.38*	−0.41***
State unemployment rate	−0.48*	−0.57*	−0.23
Number of observations	561	561	561

Source: Author's calculations based on data from the vital statistics.
Notes: All models include state and year fixed effects, a state-specific linear time trend, and a set of demographic controls. Standard errors are adjusted for clustering.
*p < .05; **p < .01; ***p < .001

(December 2007 to June 2009) (shaded bar) in six U.S. states: Nevada, Florida, California, North Dakota, Nebraska, and Alaska. The first three (dashed lines) saw the largest absolute increases in unemployment between 2006 and the peak of unemployment recorded during the recession and postrecession period (an average of 7.8 percentage points). The latter three (solid lines) saw the smallest absolute increases in unemployment (an average of just 1.5 percentage points).

For non-marital fertility, there appear to be some clear contrasts in the trend between the states with the largest increases in unemployment and the states with the smallest. In Nevada, Florida, and California, non-marital fertility had been rising in the years prior to the Great Recession and then declined markedly. It is difficult to date the beginning of the decline precisely, but it does appear to begin before the official beginning of the Great Recession. These declines continued through 2011 in all three states and then leveled out in Nevada and Florida, whereas the decline continued through 2013 in California. In contrast, in Nebraska, North Dakota, and Alaska, the patterns appear much less regular.

The time trend is less revealing for teen fertility (right panel). In the three hardest-hit states, teen fertility appears to have begun a sharp decline in 2006 or 2007, with that decline continuing through the Great Recession and beyond. In the less-affected states, teen fertility remained flat through the Great Recession and then declined in Nebraska and Alaska, while remaining basically flat in North Dakota.

Effects of State Economic Conditions on Non-marital and Teen Births

In table 2, I turn from these descriptive charts of change over time to analysis of the relationship between state-level economic conditions and state-level fertility rates. These models estimate, in six separate regressions, the relationship between the state foreclosure start rate and the unemployment rate in the prior year and marital, non-marital, and teen fertility rates. All of the models include state and year fixed effects, a state-specific linear time trend, and demographic controls.

These results show that higher rates of unemployment and foreclosure translated to lower rates of fertility among unmarried women. The coefficient on the state-level foreclosure start rate is negative and significant (b = −0.38, p < 0.05), as is the coefficient on unemployment (b = −0.57, p < 0.05). Based on these estimates, the non-marital fertility rate would be predicted to decline from approximately 49 per 1,000 when unemployment was 3 percent to 44 per 1,000 when unemployment was 11 percent. To size these effects, consider that the non-marital fertility rate increased from 26 per 1,000 in 1970 to a peak of 52 per 1,000 in 2008, an increase of approximately 0.67 births per 1,000 per year. These effects then are comparable in size to about 7.5 years of change in the historical increase in the non-marital fertility rate.

This evidence supports the hypothesis that recessionary economic shocks served to discourage births among unmarried women. Further, it appears that the effects of the Great Re-

Figure 3. Average Marginal Effect of State-Level Unemployment over Time (1990–2013)

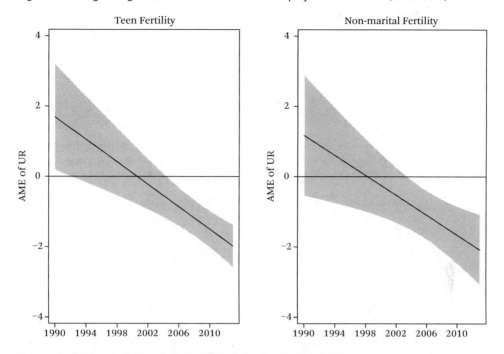

Source: Author's calculations based on data from the vital statistics.
Notes: Plot is based on models that include state and year fixed effects, an interaction between year and unemployment, and a set of demographic controls. Standard errors are adjusted for clustering.

cession were at least as large on unmarried women as on married women (b = –0.32 and b = –0.38, for unemployment on marital and non-marital fertility, respectively, and of –0.48 and –0.57 for foreclosure starts on marital and non-martial fertility, respectively).

The results are similar for teen fertility. The mortgage foreclose start rate (b = –0.41, p < 0.001) is significantly negatively related to the teen fertility rate. The unemployment rate is also negatively related to the teen fertility rate (b = –0.23), but is not significant at conventional levels (p < 0.10).

The non-marital fertility rate includes all births to unmarried women age fifteen to forty-four. Some of these women are teenagers, making it somewhat difficult to distinguish the two measures analyzed above. I re-estimated the models using the non-teen non-marital fertility rate, that is the number of births to unmarried women age twenty to forty-four in each state-year divided by the number of unmarried women age twenty to forty-four in each state-year. The results are entirely consistent with

those above. The coefficient on the state-level foreclosure start rate remains negative and significant (b = –0.36, p < 0.005) and is very similar in magnitude to the models that include non-marital births to women age fifteen to forty-four. The coefficient on the state-level unemployment rate is also little changed (b = –0.55, p < 0.05).

These results support the idea that non-marital and teen fertility are pro-cyclical, declining as economic conditions worsened during the Great Recession. However, this result runs contrary to the idea that economic considerations are disconnected from non-marital and teen fertility or that poor economic conditions might even increase such fertility. One possible explanation for the divergence between these results and prior research is that different periods are being studied. I supplement the main results above with a longer panel of state-level data for the period 1990 to 2013. I re-estimate the models just discussed, but allow the relationship between state-level unemployment and non-marital and teen fertility to vary over time.

Table 3. Relationship between Contraceptive Use by Unmarried and by Teenage Women and National Macroeconomic Conditions (2003–2010)

	Use of Contraception		Consistency of Contraception		Effectiveness of Contraception	
	(1)	(2)	(3)	(4)	(5)	(6)
	All	Low-SES	All	Low-SES	All	Low-SES
Panel A: Unmarried Women						
National foreclosure start rate	0.15**	0.29*	0.13*	0.32*	−0.12*	−0.18*
National unemployment rate	0.01*	0.02	0.01*	0.02	−0.01*	−0.01*
Person-months	239,085	55,668	228,361	53,191	197,103	48,905
	(7)	(8)	(9)	(10)	(11)	(12)
Panel B: Teenage Women						
National foreclosure start rate	0.05	0.33	−0.05	0.07	−0.06	−0.15
National unemployment rate	0.01	0.03	0.02	0.00	−0.01	−0.02
Person-months	41,950	8,102	39,960	7,732	34,851	7,181

Source: Author's calculations from the National Survey of Family Growth 2006–2011 Cycle (CDC).
Notes: All models include year fixed effects, age, age-squared, race or ethnicity, family structure at age fourteen, religion raised in, and being foreign-born. Standard errors are adjusted for clustering. Models 1 to 4 and 7 to 10 are estimated with logistic regression. Average Marginal Effects are reported in the table. Models 5 to 6 and 11 to 12 are estimated with OLS, and coefficients are reported.
*$p < .05$

I find a significant interaction that suggests that the negative effect of unemployment is much more pronounced in the later part of this period. Figure 3 plots the average marginal effect of unemployment on teen fertility (left panel) and on non-marital fertility (right panel). In short, the relationship is essentially null in the 1990s and then grows increasingly negative through the Great Recession.

In sum, it does not appear that fertility and economic considerations are disconnected for these more disadvantaged groups of women. However, these estimates do not reveal the extent to which this relationship between recessionary conditions and birth rates is the result of conscious action. To examine the proximate determinants of these fertility declines, I next turn to analysis of data from the 2006-to-2010 cycle of the NSFG.

Contraceptive Use

Table 3 presents the results from a set of models that examine the association between the national foreclosure start rate and the national unemployment rate and the use of contraception by unmarried women and teen women. Panel A of table 3 presents the results for unmarried women. Models 1 and 2 focus on the use of any contraception, models 3 and 4 on the consistency of contraceptive use (using contraception for three consecutive months), and models 5 and 6 on the efficacy of the contraceptive method employed. For each outcome I present results for all unmarried women and then for unmarried women whose mothers did not graduate from high school.

Contraceptive Practices Among Unmarried Women

Both the foreclosure start rate and the unemployment rate are positively associated with unmarried women using any contraception (model 1), and these results are generally stronger for unmarried low-SES women. As a rough estimate of the size of these effects, I take the predicted probability that an unmarried woman would use any contraception given foreclosure start rates of 0.13 and of 0.45 (corresponding to the 5th and 95th percentiles of the observed values). The model estimates suggest that the probability of use would increase from 66 percent to 70 percent.

Higher rates of foreclosure are also associated with more consistent contraceptive use among unmarried women (model 3). Again, this relationship appears somewhat stronger for low-SES unmarried women (model 4). Here there are no significant relationships between consistency of use and national unemployment rates. Finally, model 5 shows that higher foreclosure rates and higher unemployment rates are associated with using contraceptive methods that are associated with a lower risk of unintended pregnancy (thus the negative coefficient). We again see a slightly larger coefficient on foreclosure for low-SES unmarried women, but no significant relationship for unemployment. In all, it appears that worse economic conditions—particularly higher rates of foreclosure starts—are associated with more contraceptive use, more consistent use, and the use of more effective methods among unmarried women and among low-SES unmarried women.

These models control for cohabitation among unmarried women, but do not allow the effects of the economy to vary by coresidential union status. While cohabitation functions very differently than marriage in the contemporary United States, it is possible that cohabiting women behave differently than women who are not in coresidential unions when it comes to contraceptive behavior. I tested an interaction between cohabitation and macroeconomic conditions and find no evidence of any significant interactions for the unmarried subsample, approximately 30 percent of whom were cohabiting in the average person-month in the analysis.

The control variables generally have the expected relationships with contraception. Taking the model of any contraceptive use for unmarried women, women with less than a high school education are also significantly less likely to use contraceptives than women with more education, with the largest gap being between women with a BA or higher level of edu-

cation. Women who were enrolled in school at the time of interview were also significantly more likely to use contraception than women out of school. Foreign-born women are less likely to use contraception than native-born women, and members of racial and ethnic minorities are less likely to use contraception than non-Hispanic white women.

Prior research on the Great Recession and fertility suggests that changing patterns of immigration, which affected the composition of the immigrant population, can account for some of the apparent recessionary declines in fertility (Cherlin et al. 2013). Schneider and Hastings (2015) find negative effects of state economic conditions on non-marital fertility among low-SES women, even after excluding foreign-born women who migrated to the United States following the Great Recession. I conduct a similar test, excluding foreign-born women from the NSFG analysis sample and re-estimating the models. For the models of contraception use among unmarried women, the results change very little—if anything, the effects are somewhat stronger.

The models described control for race and ethnicity, and the main effects of these variables indicate that compared to their non-Hispanic, white counterparts, non-Hispanic black, non-Hispanic others, and Hispanic women are less likely to use contraceptives and to use them consistently, and are more likely to use less effective methods. It could also be the case that women who are racial and ethnic minorities might be differentially responsive to the Great Recession. In prior related research, Ananat, Gassman-Pines, and Gibson-Davis (2013) find that black teens exhibited the largest reductions in fertility in response to job displacements in North Carolina during the Great Recession, but Schneider and Hastings (2015) find that non-Hispanic, black, non-Hispanic white, native-born Hispanics, and foreign-born Hispanic low-SES unmarried women all exhibit a similar negative fertility response to state-level economic conditions.

I assess whether these relationships between national economic conditions and contraceptive practices hold in four different subgroups of unmarried women: non-Hispanic white native-born women; non-Hispanic black native-born women; Hispanic native-born women; and Hispanic foreign-born women. The effects of national economic conditions on contraceptive behavior are evident among native-born white and Hispanic women and among foreign-born Hispanic women. Of these three groups, the effects appear largest for native-born Hispanic women. There are no significant relationships between national foreclosure rates and contraceptive behavior for native-born unmarried non-Hispanic black women. The national unemployment rate is positively related to any use and to consistent use and is negatively related to efficacy, but only for white, non-Hispanic native-born women.

Robustness

I next test the robustness of the key results in panel A of table 3. In the main models just described, I use a six-month lag on macroeconomic conditions. I first test several alternative lags. For the first outcome variable, any contraceptive use, I tested lags of seven to one months prior to the outcome month. The results were substantively similar to the preferred model. For the second outcome variable, consistent contraceptive use, which uses data from the current and prior two months, I tested lags eight and four months prior to the outcome variable; again, the results were substantively similar to the preferred model. For the third outcome variable, effectiveness of contraceptive method, I tested lags of seven to three months (I did not test lags of one to two months on the basis of the rationale that obtaining a new method takes time). Here, the results were substantively similar when using lags of seven, five, and four months but were not significant when using lags of two or three months.

Second, I conduct a set of "placebo tests," in which I use future economic conditions to predict past contraceptive behavior. Here I do not expect to find any significant relationships between economic conditions and the key outcomes. I tested using a three-month and a six-month lead on the national foreclosure start rate to predict each of the three outcomes for unmarried women. In each case, the coefficient is small and far from conventional levels of statistical significance. (The p-value ranges from 0.619 to 0.959.)

Third, I re-estimate the three key models with individual fixed effects in addition to the year fixed effects that I include in the main models. Because my key predictor, the national foreclosure start rate, is exogenous to unobserved individual-level characteristics, the individual fixed effects are less likely to correct problems of omitted variables bias. However, these models focus squarely on individual respondents who change their use of contraception. In contrast, the main models use between individual comparisons. The advantage of the former is that this process of individual change may be a bit closer to the behavioral model that we have in mind for recessionary effects. I estimate fixed effects logistic regression models to examine the first two outcomes—any contraceptive use and consistent contraceptive use. In both models the coefficients are larger than in the main models and highly significant. However, the relationship between national foreclosure starts and the effectiveness of the contraceptive method is smaller and not significant in the third individual fixed effects model.

Fourth, the NSFG data rely on retrospective reporting of contraceptive use with respondents' being asked to recall practices that took place as long ago as forty-eight months prior to the interview. It is possible that this procedure introduces error into the estimates if respondents recall practices that took place longer ago less accurately. In my main estimates I make use of all available retrospective information on contraceptive practices as well as on marital status. One way to test the sensitivity of these estimates of errors in recall is to restrict the analysis sample to person-month cases that occurred relatively recently prior to the interview month. For instance, we can constrain the analysis sample to include only person-months that occurred up to twelve months before the interview. Here I assess the robustness of the main result to a set of such restrictions, limiting the analysis in turn to person-months that occurred six, twelve, eighteen, and twenty-four months before the interview. Note that this test also serves to limit the period under consideration, since person-months in 2003, 2004, and 2005 are reported at least six months retrospectively and so partially confounds recall with period.

In the models of any contraceptive use, the estimated coefficient on foreclosure is between 1 and 5 percent larger with the shorter recall windows, with the exception of twelve months, where it is 25 percent smaller. The coefficient is significant with the eighteen- and twenty-four-months windows, but not with the six- and twelve-month windows. For consistency of use, the coefficient on foreclosure is between 25 and 35 percent larger with the shorter recall windows, with the exception of eighteen months, where it is only 5 percent larger. The estimate is significant for the twelve-, eighteen-, and twenty-four-month recall windows. For efficacy of use, the coefficient is between 10 percent smaller and 10 percent larger for the windows between twelve and twenty-four months, but it is just two-thirds as large for the six-month window. The estimate is significant of the eighteen- and twenty-four-month windows.

Finally, I use restricted-access geocoded data from the NSFG to re-estimate the main models using state-level economic conditions (and state and year fixed effects) in place of national-level economic conditions. Here I also find consistent evidence of significant positive effects of state-level foreclosure starts and unemployment on contraceptive use and consistency of contraception. Foreclosure and unemployment are also significantly related to the effectiveness of the contraceptive method employed. In general, the effect sizes are larger, likely reflecting that state-level economic conditions more closely proxy for household hardship than national conditions (while still capturing something of the climate of uncertainty).

Contraceptive Practices Among Teens

Panel B of table 3 presents the results of similar main models, but now for teenage women. Here the results are much weaker. There are no significant relationships between macroeconomic conditions and teens' use of contraception, their consistency of use, and their use of more effective methods. Restricting the sample to native-born women does not appreciably change these null effects. However, disaggregating by race and nativity shows modest effects of national foreclosure and unemployment on

the contraceptive practices of white native-born teens who are more likely to use any method, to use the method consistently, and to use effective methods when conditions are worse.

I also tested alternative recall windows, as I did earlier for unmarried women. In general, the effects are null for both foreclosure and unemployment. The only exception is a twelve-month recall window with the use of national unemployment. There, worse economic conditions are significantly associated with the use of more effective contraceptive technology, more consistent use, and the use of any contraception. In general, the results for teenagers are weaker and less consistent than for unmarried women, though present under some model specifications.

DISCUSSION

The Great Recession's effects on Americans did not stop at increased joblessness and foreclosure or lost hours and depressed income. These economic effects reverberated through households to shape fundamental aspects of the life course. A growing body of research makes a convincing case that the Great Recession depressed fertility. In this article I show that these effects extended to unmarried and teenage women. Most narrowly, this analysis of the fertility effects of the Great Recession is useful because it is important to assemble an empirical record of how this economic downturn affected Americans' lives. More broadly, I argue that the events of the Great Recession provide a kind of social laboratory to investigate more general questions of sociological and demographic interest.

I use these events to test the idea that the fertility of unmarried and teen women, and particularly socioeconomically disadvantaged women, is fairly disconnected from economic concerns. This prior research would suggest that the economic shocks of the Great Recession might have had few effects on these women's fertility. However, I find that the Great Recession did have pronounced negative effects on non-marital and teen fertility, a finding in accord with recent prior work by Schneider and Hastings (2015), Ananat, Gassman-Pines, and Gibson-Davis (2013), and Melissa Kearney and Phillip Levine (2015). Existing theory further suggested that one reason for the relative disconnect between economic concerns and fertility is the difficulty that many unmarried, teen, and low-SES women face in effectively using contraception. However, I find that at least some members of these subgroups did increase contraceptive use in response to the Great Recession, with national economic conditions correlated with use of contraception, consistency of use, and efficacy of method.

Notably, I do not find effects of either foreclosure or unemployment on the contraceptive practices of non-Hispanic native-born unmarried black women. This is surprising in part because black women experienced large percentage-point increases in unemployment during the Great Recession. One interpretation is that these results suggest some continued support for the idea that poor economic conditions might not much affect disadvantaged women's fertility.

However, other recent research finds negative effects of the Great Recession on the fertility of unmarried black women (Schneider and Hastings 2015) and on black teens (Ananat, Gassman-Pines, and Gibson-Davis 2013). One possibility is that, as Ananat, Gassman-Pines, and Gibson-Davis (2013) suggest, the Recession's effects on black women's fertility operated through other proximate determinants such as changes in sexual activity, miscarriage, or abortion.

This research is subject to some important limitations. First, in the state-level analysis, I am unable to specifically examine low-SES unmarried and teen women's fertility rates. However, the very large share of births to women in these groups is known to be to socioeconomically disadvantaged women. Second, in the person-level analyses of the NSFG, I reply on national-level variation in economic conditions and examine only the period through 2010. Future work could usefully exploit state-level variation in economic conditions to identify the effects of the Great Recession on contraceptive use and could employ the 2011-to-2013 cycle of the NSFG to extend this work through the period of high unemployment following the official end of the Great Recession. Third, this work documents the relationship between economic conditions and fertility and shows a plausible proximate determinant of this relationship; it does not examine women's thinking about the relationship between recessionary conditions and fertility.

Finally, this work does not tell us whether these reductions in teen and non-marital fertility will be temporary or more permanent. Recent research suggests that cohorts of women exposed to higher levels of unemployment may experience permanent reductions in lifetime fertility (Currie and Schwandt 2014), but much other demographic work finds that effects of recessions are generally temporary. For the cohort of teenagers exposed to the Great Recession, it would seem very likely that their lifetime teen fertility will be depressed, if only because most of their teen years played out during the long Great Recession. A somewhat different but also interesting question is whether the low rates of teen and non-marital fertility caused by the Great Recession will remain or will rise. The recovery from the Great Recession has been quite slow and the economic situation of many less-skilled workers remains quite precarious. These factors suggest that there could indeed be some more lasting and permanent effects of the Great Recession and its aftermath on fertility and perhaps a lasting reduction in non-marital fertility. Further, the Affordable Care Act's requirement that health insurance plans provide contraception at no cost to the insured may also function to maintain these low rates of non-marital and teen fertility.

In all, this research suggests that there is a need for a more nuanced understanding of the relationship between economic constraints and non-marital and teen fertility. One explanation of the discordance between this finding a negative effect of poor economic conditions on non-marital fertility and prior research suggesting a null or positive effect is that the nature of the relationship between economic hardships and non-marital and teen fertility has changed—that a positive or null relationship has become negative in an era of rising inequality, increasingly precarious work, and ongoing substantial macroeconomic shocks. Perhaps it is the case that in normal economic times, a steady diet of economic deprivation really does become disconnected from fertility decision-making but that extraordinary economic shocks, as seen in the Great Recession, can trigger conscious fertility avoidance behavior.

REFERENCES

Adsera, Alicia. 2004. "Changing Fertility Rates in Developed Countries: The Impact of Labor Market Institutions." *Journal of Population Economics* 17(1):17–43.

Ananat, Elizabeth Oltmans, Anna Gassman-Pines, and Cristina Gibson-Davis. 2013. "Community-Wide Job Loss and Teenage Fertility: Evidence from North Carolina." *Demography* 50(6): 2151–71.

Augustine, Jennifer March, Timothy Nelson, and Kathryn Edin. 2009. "Why Do Poor Men Have Children? Fertility Intentions Among Low-Income Unmarried U.S. Fathers." *Annals of the American Academy of Political and Social Science* 624(1): 99–117.

Becker, Gary. 1960. "An Economic Analysis of Fertility." In *Demographic and Economic Change in Developed Countries*, edited by the Universities-National Bureau Committee for Economic Research (George J. Stigler, chairman). New York: Columbia University Press.

Billy, John, and David Moore. 1992. "A Multilevel Analysis of Marital and Nonmarital Fertility in the U.S." *Social Forces* 70(4): 977–1011.

Bitler, Marianne, and Hilary Hoynes. 2010. "The State of the Safety Net in the Post-welfare Reform Era." *Brookings Papers on Economic Activity* 2010(Fall): 71–127.

Bloem, Adriaan, Robert Dippelsman, and Nils Maehle. 2001. *Quarterly National Accounts Manual: Concepts, Data Sources, and Compilation*. Washington, D.C.: International Monetary Fund.

Butz, William P., and Michael P Ward. 1979. "The Emergence of Countercyclical US Fertility." *American Economic Review* 69(3): 318–28.

Cherlin, Andrew, Elizabeth Cumberworth, Stephen Morgan, and Christopher Wimer. 2013. "The Effects of the Great Recession on Family Structure and Fertility." *Annals of the American Academy of Political and Social Science* 650(1): 214–31.

Conger, Rand, Martha Reuter, and Glen Elder. 1999. "Couple Resilience to Economic Pressure." *Journal of Personality and Social Psychology* 76(1): 54–71.

Currie, Janet, and Hillary Schwandt. (2014). "Short- and Long-Term Effects of Unemployment on Fertility." *Proceedings of the National Academy of Sciences* 111(41): 14734–39.

Edin, Kathryn, Paula England, Emily Fitzgibbons Shafer, and Joanna Reed. 2007. "Forming Fragile Families: Was the Baby Planned, Unplanned, or In Between?" In *Unmarried Couples with Children*, edited by Paula England and Kathryn Edin. New York: Russell Sage Foundation.

Edin, Kathryn, and Maria Kefalas. 2005. *Promises I Can Keep: Why Poor Women Put Motherhood Before Marriage*. Berkeley: University of California Press.

England, Paula, Elizabeth McClintock, and Emily Fitzgibbons Shafer. 2011. "Class Differences in Birth Control Use and Unintended Pregnancies." In *Social Class and Changing Families in an Unequal America*, edited by Marcia Carlson and Paula England. Stanford, Calif.: Stanford University Press.

Finer, Lawrence, and Stanley Henshaw. 2006. "Disparities in Rates of Unintended Pregnancy in the United States, 1994 and 2001." *Perspectives on Sexual and Reproductive Health* 38(2): 90–96.

Finer, Lawrence, Jenna Jerman, and Megan L. Kavanaugh. 2012. "Changes in Use of Long-Acting Contraceptive Methods in the United States, 2007–2009." *Fertility and Sterility* 98(4): 893–97.

Gassman-Pines, Anna, Christina Gibson-Davis, and Elizabeth Ananat. 2015. "How Economic Downturns Affect Children's Development: An Interdisciplinary Perspective on Pathways of Influence." *Child Development Perspectives* 9(4): 233–38.

Gibson-Davis, Cristina. 2009. "Money, Marriage, and Children: Testing the Financial Expectations and Family Formation Theory." *Journal of Marriage and Family* 71(1): 146–60.

Gold, Rachel. 2009. *A Real-Time Look at the Impact of the Recession on Women's Family Planning and Pregnancy Decisions*. New York: Guttmacher Institute.

Gregory, Sean. 2009. "What Sells in a Recession? Canned Goods and Condoms." *Time*, March 11, 2009.

Groves, Robert, William Mosher, James Lepwoski, and Nicole Kirgis. 2009. "Planning and Development of the Continuous National Survey of Family Growth." *Vital and Health Statistics* 1(48): 1–64.

Kearney, Melissa, and Phillip Levine. 2009. "Subsidized Contraception, Fertility, and Sexual Behavior." *Review of Economics and Statistics* 91(1): 137–51.

——. 2014. "Income Inequality and Early Nonmarital Childbearing." *Journal of Human Resources* 49(1): 1–31.

——. 2015. "Investigating Recent Trends in the U.S. Teen Birth Rate." *Journal of Health Economics* 41(C): 15–29.

Livingston, Gretchen. 2011. "In a Down Economy, Fewer Births." Technical report. Washington, D.C.: Pew Research Center. Available at: http://www.pewsocialtrends.org/2011/10/12/in-a-down-economy-fewer-births; accessed August 7, 2016.

Livingston, Gretchen, and D'Vera Cohn. 2010. "US Birth Rate Decline Linked to Great Recession." Pew Research Center. Available at: http://www.pewsocialtrends.org/2010/04/06/us-birth-rate-decline-linked-to-recession; accessed October 14, 2016.

Lovenheim, Michael, and Kevin Mumford. 2013. "Do Family Wealth Shocks Affect Fertility Choices? Evidence from the Housing Market." *Review of Economics and Statistics* 95(2): 464–75.

Macunovich, Diane. 1996. "Relative Income and Price of Time: Exploring Their Effects on US Fertility and Female Labor Force Participation." *Population and Development Review* 22(Supp.): 223–57.

Miller, Warren, Jennifer Barber, and Heather Gatny. 2013. "The Effects of Ambivalent Fertility Desires on Pregnancy Risk in Young Women in the USA." *Population Studies* 67(1): 25–38.

Morgan, S. Phillip, Erin Cumberworth, and Christopher Wimer. 2011. "The Great Recession's Influence on Fertility, Marriage, Divorce, and Cohabitation." In *The Great Recession*, edited by David Grusky, Bruce Western, and Christopher Wimer. New York: Russell Sage Foundation.

Musick, Kelly, Paula England, Sarah Edgington, and Nicole Kangas. 2009. "Education Differences in Intended and Unintended Fertility." *Social Forces* 88(2): 543–72.

Najari, Bobby, Peter N. Schlegel, and Marc Goldstein. 2014. "National Vasectomy Rates and Family Planning Attitudes After the Great Recession." *Fertility and Sterility* 102(3): e12.

Nepomnaschy, Pablo, Kathleen Welch, Daniel McConnell, Bobbi Low, Beverly Strassman, and Barry England. 2006. "Cortisol Levels and Very Early Pregnancy Loss in Humans." *Proceedings of the National Academy of Sciences* 103(10): 3938–3942.

Pazol, Karen, Andreea A. Creanga, Kim Burley, and Denise Jamieson. 2014. "Abortion Surveillance—United States, 2011." *Surveillance Summaries* 63(SS11): 1–41.

Pilkauskas, Natasha, Janet Currie, and Irwin Garfinkel. 2012. "The Great Recession, Public Transfers, and Material Hardship." *Social Service Review* 86(3): 401–27.

Rindfuss, Ronald, S. Philip Morgan, and Gray Swicegood. 1988. *First Births in America: Changes in the Timing of Parenthood.* Berkeley: University of California Press.

Sawhill, Isabel. 2014. *Generation Unbound: Drifting into Sex and Parenthood Without Marriage.* Washington, D.C.: Brookings Institution Press.

Schaller, Jessamyn. 2016. "Booms, Busts, and Fertility: Testing the Becker Model of Gender-Specific Labor Demand." *Journal of Human Resources* 51(1): 1–29.

Schneider, Daniel. 2015. "The Great Recession, Fertility, and Uncertainty: Evidence from the States." *Journal of Marriage and Family* 77(5): 1144–56.

Schneider, Daniel, Kristin Harknett, and Sara McLanahan. 2016. "Intimate Partner Violence in the Great Recession." *Demography* 53(2): 471–505.

Schneider, Daniel, and Orestes Hastings. 2015. "Socio-economic Variation in the Demographic Response to Economic Shocks: Evidence from the Great Recession." *Demography* 52(6): 1893–1915.

Sobotka, Tomas, Vegard Skirbekk, and Dimiter Philipov. 2011. "Economic Recession and Fertility in the Developed World." *Population and Development Review* 37(2): 267–306.

Trussell, James. 2011. "Contraceptive Efficacy." In *Contraceptive Technology*, 20th rev. ed., edited by Robert A. Hatcher, James Trussell, Anita L. Nelson, Willard Cates, Jr., Felicia H. Stewart, and Deborah Kowal. New York: Ardent Media.

Yoo, Sam Hyun, Karen Benjamin Guzzo, and Sarah R. Hayford. 2014. "Understanding the Complexity of Ambivalence Toward Pregnancy: Does It Predict Inconsistent Use of Contraception?" *Biodemography and Social Biology* 60(1): 49–66.

Labor Unions and the Great Recession

RUTH MILKMAN AND STEPHANIE LUCE

This article examines the impact of the Great Recession on the U.S. labor movement. After reviewing the classic industrial relations literature on the relationship between unionization rates and business cycles, we analyze historical union density trends. After documenting the relentless downward trend in the private sector from the early 1980s, with no apparent relationship to the business cycle, we analyze the negative impact of the political dynamic that unfolded in the wake of the Great Recession on public-sector unionism in sharp contrast to what took place during the Great Depression. We also explore the new forms of labor organizing that have emerged in the private sector, which have capitalized on the growing public concern about rising inequality sparked by Occupy Wall Street.

Keywords: unions, union density, recession, industrial relations, organizing

"The Great Depression invigorated the modern American labor movement," the *New Yorker* economic columnist, James Surowiecki (2011), declared in January 2011. "The Great Recession has crippled it." Although the economy has gradually climbed out of the crisis precipitated by the 2008 financial debacle, the U.S. labor movement indeed appears crippled. In 2015, only 11.1 percent of the nation's wage and salary workers were union members, and the figure was an even lower 6.7 percent in the private sector—a pale shadow of unionism in the mid-1950s, when overall density (the proportion of workers who are union members) stood at about 35 percent (and higher in the private sector, although comparable figures by sector are not available for that period). Public approval

of unions also fell dramatically with the financial crisis, reaching an all-time low in 2009, when the Gallup Poll found that only 48 percent of Americans approved of labor unions, down from 75 percent in the mid-1950s (Saad 2015). That historic peak in union strength and public support reflected two decades of unprecedented government support for collective bargaining and other policies designed to reduce economic inequality. Forged in the crucible of the Great Depression, the institutions associated with those New Deal policies have been deeply and deliberately eroded over recent decades. And progressive public policy initiatives to restore the strength of those institutions were conspicuously absent in the aftermath of the Great Recession. On the contrary, the po-

Ruth Milkman is distinguished professor of sociology at the City University of New York Graduate Center and research director of CUNY's Murphy Institute. **Stephanie Luce** is professor of sociology at the City University of New York Graduate Center and professor of labor studies at CUNY's Murphy Institute.

© 2017 Russell Sage Foundation. Milkman, Ruth, and Stephanie Luce. 2017. "Labor Unions and the Great Recession." *RSF: The Russell Sage Foundation Journal of the Social Sciences* 3(3): 145–65. DOI: 10.7758/RSF.2017.3.3.07. Direct correspondence to: Ruth Milkman at rmilkman@gc.cuny.edu, Department of Sociology, CUNY Graduate Center, 365 Fifth Ave., New York, NY 10016; and Stephanie Luce at stephanie.luce@mail.cuny.edu, Murphy Institute/CUNY, 25 W. 43rd St., 19th Floor, New York, NY 10036.

litical influence of anti-union forces—already formidable before the 2008 crash—has continued to mushroom ever since, while the inequality gap has continued to widen.

To be sure, the decline in union density long predated the 2008 financial crisis. Since at least the early 1980s, obituaries for the U.S. labor movement like Surowiecki's have appeared regularly in both scholarly and journalistic writings. Private sector deunionization began in the late 1950s, but accelerated rapidly in the 1970s (see figures 1 and 2). Starting in the early 1980s, often seen as a turning point in the fortunes of organized labor, not only union density but also the absolute number of union members went into free fall (see table 1). As previous research has shown, deunionization contributed significantly to the rapid growth of inequality since the 1970s (Western and Rosenfeld 2011), and is also associated with the deregulation and financialization processes that took off in the same period (MacDonald 2014; Milkman 2013). Yet there has been surprisingly little attention to the impact of the Great Recession—the deepest economic downturn since the 1930s—on the labor movement. Was it the final nail in U.S. labor's coffin, or could it presage some sort of reprise of the 1930s labor upsurge and the public policy shifts that accompanied it?

A useful starting point here is the classic industrial relations literature, which from its inception was concerned with the relationship between unionization trends and business cycles. A century ago, John R. Commons, the field's founder, argued that unions tended to grow in times of prosperity and to decline during economic downturns (Commons 1918, 1:10–11). Shortly after World War II, the eminent labor economist John Dunlop (1948, 190–92) put forward an alternative claim, namely, that spurts in union growth—which by all accounts are the only way in which lasting density increases occur—followed major economic depressions as well as wars. In the latter case, Dunlop suggested, union growth was due to "the rapid rise in the cost of living and the shortage of labor supply relative to demand" that typically accompanies major military conflicts. But he noted that unions also grew in periods of "unrest," during severe depressions like those in the 1890s and the 1930s, when labor organizing was tied to broader radical social movements.

Building on Dunlop's theory, the labor historian Irving Bernstein (1954) argued that ordinary business cycles had little or no effect on unionization rates, and that union growth was spurred only by depressions "so severe as to call into question the very foundations of society" (316), such as the crisis of 1893 and the Great Depression. He noted that both those labor upsurges were marked by a lag effect: unionism grew only after the economy had begun to recover (in 1897 and 1933, respectively). Concurring with Dunlop that wars also stimulate union growth, Bernstein concluded that unions "have been the beneficiaries of disaster" (317). Although there is no evidence that Karl Polanyi (1944) influenced the thinking of Dunlop or Bernstein, some of their arguments are echoed in recent Polanyian analyses of the historical dynamics of global labor movements. Particularly influential here is Beverly Silver's (2003) argument that global labor movement upsurges are an integral feature of broader social responses to historical waves of marketization like those that preceded the Great Depression. Laissez-faire deregulation, Polanyi theorized, stimulates countermovements from below that aim to decommodify labor, demanding protective legislation, unemployment insurance, and unionization (Silver 2003, 17; see also Evans 2008; Burawoy 2010).

However, among U.S. industrial relations scholars and labor economists, the Dunlop-Bernstein perspective had fallen out of favor by the 1960s, when a new consensus view emerged resurrecting the original Commons hypothesis that union membership growth tracked business cycles. The literature of that era, anchored by elaborate multivariate analyses, acknowledged the influence of additional exogenous factors (such as political climate, public attitudes toward unions, and labor legislation) on union density, but the central focus was on business cycles. Thus, Orley Ashenfelter and John Pencavel (1969), in a much-cited analysis of the 1900-to-1960 period, concluded, "A period of increasing employment is favorable to successful organizing drives: the organizing funds of unions will be larger, and the

Figure 1. Private Sector Unionization Rates, United States, 1950–1981

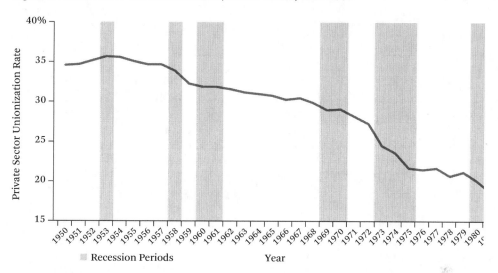

Source: For unionization rates, see www.unionstats.com, "Table I. U.S. Historical Tables: Union Membership, Coverage, Density, and Employment, 1973–2015." For recession dates, see *National Bureau of Economic Research*, "US Business Cycle Expansions and Contractions," www.nber.org/cycles.html. *Note:* See note 2 regarding the absence of data collection in 1982 and the changes in data collection methodology that followed.

Figure 2. Private Sector Unionization Rates, United States, 1983–2014

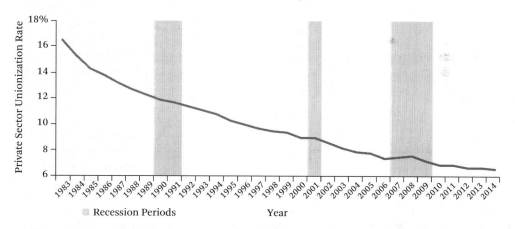

Source: For unionization rates, see www.unionstats.com, "Table I. U.S. Historical Tables: Union Membership, Coverage, Density, and Employment, 1873–2015." For recession dates, see *National Bureau of Economic Research*, "US Business Cycle Expansions and Contractions," www.nber.org/cycles.html. *Note:* See note 2 regarding the absence of data collection in 1982 and the changes in data collection methodology that followed.

potential union member is more receptive," adding, "With the advent of union security agreements . . . increases in employment often lead automatically to upturns in union membership" (437).

A recent review of the literature on union density trends in the United States and other affluent countries similarly concludes that union growth is pro-cyclical: "Employment growth as well as price and/or wage inflation

Table 1. U.S. Union Membership and Density, by Sector, 1983–2014

Year	Private Sector		Public Sector	
	Members	Density	Members	Density
1983	11,980.2	16.5	5,737.2	36.7
1984	11,684.0	15.3	5,655.7	35.7
1985	11,253.0	14.3	5,743.1	35.7
1986	11,084.7	13.8	5,890.5	35.9
1987	10,857.3	13.2	6,055.7	35.9
1988	10,702.4	12.7	6,299.2	36.6
1989	10,536.2	12.3	6,424.2	36.7
1990	10,254.8	11.9	6,485.0	36.5
1991	9,936.5	11.7	6,632.0	36.9
1992	9,737.2	11.4	6,653.1	36.6
1993	9,580.3	11.1	7,017.8	37.7
1994	9,649.4	10.8	7,091.0	38.7
1995	9,432.1	10.3	6,927.4	37.7
1996	9,415.0	10.0	6,854.4	37.6
1997	9,363.3	9.7	6,746.7	37.2
1998	9,306.1	9.5	6,905.3	37.5
1999	9,418.6	9.4	7,058.1	37.3
2000	9,147.7	9.0	7,110.5	37.5
2001	9,141.3	9.0	7,147.5	37.4
2002	8,651.5	8.6	7,327.2	37.8
2003	8,451.8	8.2	7,324.1	37.2
2004	8,204.5	7.9	7,267.1	36.4
2005	8,255.0	7.8	7,430.4	36.5
2006	7,981.3	7.4	7,377.8	36.2
2007	8,113.6	7.5	7,556.7	35.9
2008	8,265.2	7.6	7,832.3	36.8
2009	7,430.8	7.2	7,896.5	37.4
2010	7,091.9	6.9	7,623.1	36.2
2011	7,204.5	6.9	7,550.2	37.0
2012	7,029.9	6.6	7,319.5	35.9
2013	7,312.7	6.7	7,203.0	35.3
2014	7,356.0	6.6	7,218.0	35.7

Source: www.unionstats.com, "Table I. U.S. Historical Tables: Union Membership, Coverage, Density, and Employment, 1973–2015."
Note: Recession periods (shaded rows): July 1990 to March 1991, March 2001 to November 2001, December 2007 to June 2009.

enhances membership growth . . . [but] a rise in unemployment tends to reduce union growth and density" (Schnabel 2013, 258). Our own perspective is closer to Bruce Western's (1997), whose comparative analysis of OECD countries led him to conclude that the institutional context of unionism matters far more than business cycles. "In the right in-stitutional framework, unions grow even through downturns in the business cycle," Western argued. "Without favorable institutional conditions, unions are vulnerable to cyclical changes in the economy and grow only through extra-institutional strategies, such as strike action" (102).

In the United States, scholarly interest in

the relationship of unions to the business cycle receded in the 1980s, as increased attention to union decline eclipsed the earlier preoccupation with explaining patterns of union growth.[1] But in the wake of the Great Recession, the first economic downturn that qualifies as sufficiently "severe" (in Bernstein's terms) to merit comparison to the 1930s, and in the wake of four decades of neoliberal marketization, it seems apposite to revisit the classic questions about the impact of economic crises on union density and on labor movements generally. That is our purpose here.

We begin with an overview of recent density trends in the United States, examining both the private sector, where one would expect the effects of business cycles to be most apparent, and the more highly unionized public sector. The public sector is not explored in the earlier industrial relations literature, simply because when commentators from Commons to Ashenfelter and Pencavel were writing, public sector unionism was extremely limited. In fact, its expansion since the 1960s initially masked the precipitous decline of private sector unionism. However, the shifts in institutional conditions that affected union density after the Great Recession were particularly significant in the public sector.

Our analysis of U.S. union membership trends highlights the relentless decline in both absolute numbers and density since the early 1980s in the private sector, with no apparent relationship to the business cycle. The primary driver of this decline was a wave of concerted employer attacks on labor unions in highly organized sectors; a secondary factor was the limited organizing efforts on the part of unions themselves. Although there is some evidence that organizing efforts may have disproportionately declined in periods of recession, the overall deunionization trajectory for this period does not present a cyclical pattern. On the other hand, the political dynamic that unfolded in the aftermath of the Great Recession negatively affected public sector unions, which had maintained stable levels of density before 2008. And in the private sector, where density is now in the single digits, the center of gravity of the U.S. labor movement shifted toward new forms of organizing. Building on the momentum of the 2011 Occupy Wall Street movement, organized labor has begun to capitalize on growing public concern about inequality in a series of innovative campaigns.

U.S. UNION DENSITY TRENDS AND THE GREAT RECESSION

Union density trends in the U.S. private sector since 1955 do not conform to the conventional wisdom that unionization rates fluctuate in relation to the business cycle (see figures 1 and 2). Instead, the period from 1955 to 2000 was marked by continual and indeed accelerating erosion in private sector union density, during periods of recession and expansion alike. Figure 2 reveals that in the twenty-first century a somewhat different pattern emerged. During the brief 2001 recession, private sector density at first remained flat, but this was soon followed by a resumed decline; similarly, during the Great Recession (2007 to 2009) union density initially increased slightly, and then the downward trend resumed in 2009. In any case, the pro-cyclical unionization pattern suggested in the earlier literature appears to be absent during the entire period shown in figures 1 and 2.

The number of private sector union representation elections held under the auspices of the National Labor Relations Board (NLRB) has also declined sharply since the 1970s (see figure 3). Unlike the density data, these election data do suggest a pro-cyclical pattern, with espe-

---

1. An exception is Lee P. Stepina and Jack Fiorito (1986), who reassessed the earlier literature in the context of their own analysis of data for the period from 1911 to 1982. They argued that the unemployment rate is not a significant predictor of unionization trends, explaining the discrepancy between this finding and those of earlier analysts by reference to the widespread provision of unemployment insurance after the New Deal. This last point parallels the observation by Bruce Western (1997) and Claus Schnabel (2013) that the otherwise pro-cyclical pattern of union growth since the 1960s is absent in countries that have adopted the Ghent system of union-administered unemployment insurance. In the Ghent system, unions, rather than the government, administer social welfare programs and distribute benefits, particularly unemployment insurance.

Figure 3. National Labor Relations Board Representation Elections and Union Win Rates, 1973–2014

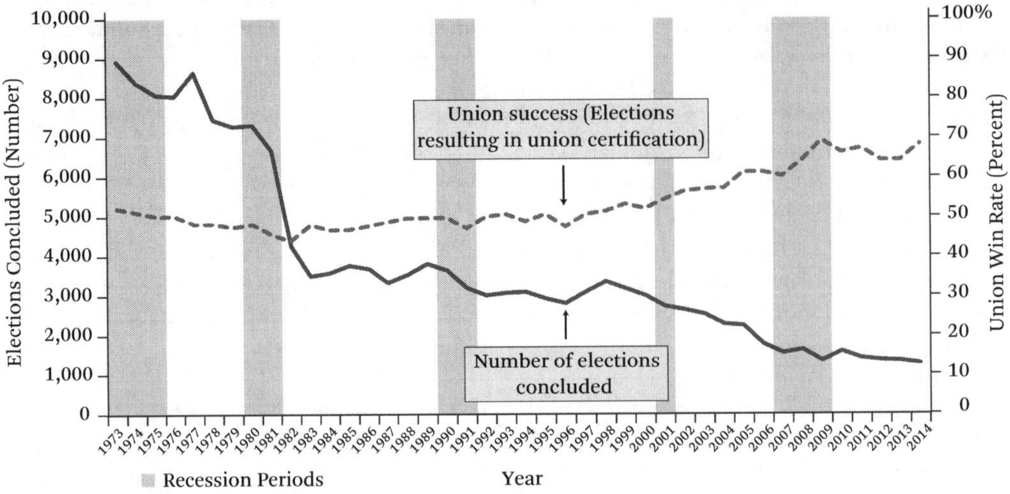

Recession Periods   Year

Source: U.S. National Labor Relations Board, annual reports for fiscal years 1973–2003, available at: https://www.nlrb.gov/reports-guidance/reports/annual-reports (accessed September 16, 2016); U.S. National Relations Board, representation petitions for fiscal years 2004–2014, available at: http://www .nlrb.gov/news-outreach/graphs-data/petitions-and-elections/representation-petitions-rc (accessed September 16, 2016).

cially steep drop-offs in the number of representation elections during periods of recession. But there is no cyclical pattern in regard to the frequency with which unions are successful in winning NLRB representation elections: as figure 3 shows, since the early 1980s the union win rate has increased slowly and steadily, in periods of recession and growth alike.

During the Great Recession the union win rate rose more sharply, although whether or not this is related to the economic downturn is far from clear. In recent years union leaders have become increasingly disenchanted with the NLRB process and have turned instead to alternative paths to union recognition; that is surely one major factor contributing to the long-term decline in the number of NLRB elections. This recent diversification in organizing strategies also means that the pro-cyclical pattern in the number of NLRB elections offers only a partial view of trends in new organizing. And unions have become increasingly strategic in their approach to NLRB representation elections, particularly since the early 2000s, when the Bush administration's NLRB appointments led to a series of decisions that were especially hostile to organized labor (Liebman 2007; Far-

ber 2014). The post-2008 increase in win rates, then, may simply reflect the Obama administration's relatively union-friendly orientation (Scheiber 2015), rather than the impact of the economic crisis. In any case, the recent uptick in NLRB election win rates failed to stem the relentless decline in private sector union density, which has continued without interruption since 2008.

Apart from the effects (or lack thereof) of business cycles, many different factors can affect union density trends. Actively recruiting new members into the ranks of organized labor is the primary way in which unions themselves can act to increase the unionization level. But other forces that affect density are entirely beyond union control. All else being equal, if employment declines in a highly unionized sector of the economy, or expands in a nonunion (or weakly unionized) sector, union density will fall. Conversely, if employment expands in a highly unionized sector or declines in one where unionism is absent or weak, the overall level of union density will rise. In addition, labor market churning is an inherent feature of market economies, with new jobs constantly being created and old ones being destroyed.

This dynamic, along with the effects of population growth and labor turnover, means that simply to maintain union density at a given level requires a great deal of new organizing; to increase density requires even more extensive efforts. In the contemporary United States, where unionization is highly concentrated in "legacy" industries that in most cases are no longer growing, ongoing deunionization is virtually inevitable unless organizers can recruit massive numbers of new members in expanding industries. Although there have been some notable attempts in recent decades at such large-scale recruiting, particularly in the late 1990s, in the face of a hostile institutional environment most U.S. labor unions have concentrated instead on defending their past gains.

These dynamics are particularly salient in the private sector, but economic expansions and contractions also can affect public sector union density. Here, too, institutional factors play a crucial role. In the private sector, the U.S. political and regulatory context became increasingly unfavorable to unionism starting in the 1970s, but that was far less often true in the public sector until very recently. However, in the twenty-first century, and especially since the Great Recession, concerted political attacks on public sector unionism have spread, and anti-unionism has become a cornerstone of conservative ideology. Both reflecting and contributing to this development, public attitudes about unions are sharply polarized politically as well. In a 2015 Gallup poll (Saad 2015), for example, 55 percent of Democrats but only 18 percent of Republicans wanted unions "to have more influence."

Table 1 presents detailed data on U.S. density trends for the years from 1983 to 2014, for both the public and private sectors.[2] It shows that both the absolute number of private sector union members and private sector density declined steadily, in periods of recession and growth alike, over those three decades. By contrast, in the public sector density levels were essentially stable until 2011, regardless of whether the economy was in recession or not. And until 2009, the absolute number of public sector union members increased steadily, apart from minor year-to-year fluctuations. That trend continued into 2009, thanks in part to the American Recovery and Reinvestment Act, signed early that year, which helped to sustain employment levels in many public-sector occupations.

However, in 2010, the absolute number of public sector union members began to decline, reflecting cutbacks in state-level public sector employment tied to austerity measures precipitated by the 2008 financial crisis. More than half the states laid off public employees in fiscal years 2010 or 2011, in efforts to reduce or eliminate budget shortfalls (National Governors' Association and National Association of State Budget Officers 2010). State layoffs of public workers also occurred in some previous economic downturns, but to a far lesser extent than in 2010–2011 (Campbell and Sances 2013, 266–67). In the years just after the Great Recession, public sector job losses disproportionately affected African American and female workers, especially African American women (Laird 2015; Cohen 2015).

Changes in the absolute number of public sector employees do not necessarily presage shifts in union density, however, as they typically affect both the numerator (number of union members) and the denominator (number of workers) of the density ratio. But after the 2010 midterm elections brought Republicans into political power in many key states, austerity measures combined with a wave of direct political attacks on public sector collective bargaining to produce an unprecedented falloff in public sector density (Lafer 2013). Ironically, Wisconsin, where these political attacks were especially prominent, in 1959 had been the first state to pass legislation creating collective bargaining rights for public sector workers. The 2011 attack on public sector bargaining rights led by Governor Scott Walker sparked vigorous resistance and a dramatic political struggle, but ultimately Walker prevailed and the state suf-

2. The federal government briefly stopped collecting data on union membership under the Reagan administration, so no data are available for 1982. Over time, there have been some changes in the data collection methodology as well. For details see Barry T. Hirsch and David A. Macpherson (2015) and Gerald Mayer (2004).

Figure 4. Public Sector Density Declines After Passage of the Restrictive Laws

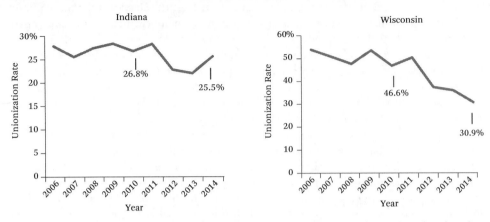

Source: For unionization rates, see www.unionstats.com, "Table II. State: Union Membership, Coverage, Density and Employment by State and Sector, 1983–2015." For list of states with restrictive laws, Lafer 2013.

Figure 5. Public Sector Density Declines Before Passage of the Restrictive Laws

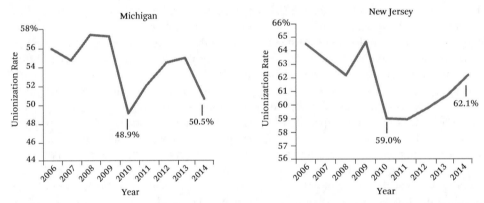

Source: For unionization rates, see www.unionstats.com, "Table II. State: Union Membership, Coverage, Density and Employment by State and Sector, 1983–2015." For list of states with restrictive laws, Lafer 2013.

fered a precipitous loss in public sector union density (see figure 4).

Similarly, Indiana, Michigan, and New Jersey experienced substantial erosion in public sector union density (see figures 4 and 5), although in these states that erosion (and the political attacks on public sector unions that drove it) had actually begun well before the higher-profile wave of attacks that emerged in 2011. On the other hand, in several other states that passed legislation restricting public sector collective bargaining rights in 2011 and 2012, the impact on union density has thus far been minimal or nonexistent (see figure 6). Reflecting these uneven state-by-state patterns, the overall decline in public sector union density nationwide has been relatively modest to date (see table 1).

In the private sector, unionization also varies widely among states; in 2014 density rates ranged from 2.5 percent in North Carolina to 14.9 percent in New York. Unionism in the United States is highly geographically concentrated: in 2014, seven states—California, New

Figure 6. Public Sector Density Fluctuations in Other States with Restrictive Laws

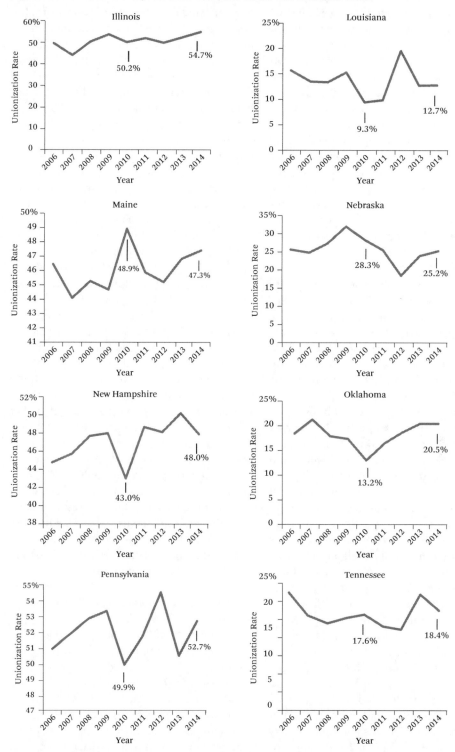

Source: For unionization rates, see www.unionstats.com, "Table II. State: Union Membership, Coverage, Density and Employment by State and Sector, 1983–2015." For list of states with restrictive laws, Lafer 2013.

Note: Does not include states where restrictive laws were passed but later overturned.

York, Illinois, Pennsylvania, Michigan, Ohio, and New Jersey—accounted for over half (53.8 percent) of all private sector U.S. union membership, although for only 36.3 percent of private sector employment (Hirsch and Macpherson 2015). Similarly, 53.5 percent of the absolute loss in private sector density between 2006 and 2014 was absorbed by those seven states. But there was also substantial variation among the seven: the largest private sector union membership losses were in Michigan, Illinois, Ohio, and New Jersey, while California was alone among this group of seven states in experiencing a modest rise in the absolute number of private sector union members. Three of these states—Illinois, Ohio, and especially Michigan—also suffered absolute losses in private sector employment during the 2006-to-2014 period, especially in manufacturing and construction, the industries most affected by the Great Recession. Employment fell in manufacturing in all seven states, with particularly sharp drops in Ohio, Michigan, New York, and New Jersey. Six of these seven highly unionized states also experienced absolute employment declines in construction (New Jersey was the only exception), with particularly steep declines in California and Illinois.

These state-to-state variations have larger implications. Higher unionization rates are associated with lower rates of poverty and inequality, in part because highly unionized states also tend to have politically influential labor movements that seek and often win improved minimum wages and other legislation that benefits union and nonunion workers alike. High unionization levels in particular states can also affect normative expectations for better jobs and more equitable wages (see Western and Rosenfeld 2011; Brady, Baker, and Finnegan 2013). State-level political attacks on private sector unions have been increasing across the nation, along with those focused on the public sector, although thus far Michigan is the only state in this group of seven that has passed right-to-work legislation.

Unionization is unevenly distributed not only geographically but also across industry groups. Moreover, as figures 4 and 5 suggest, as the economy recovered from the Great Recession, nonunion jobs often replaced union jobs. Not only did union membership decline

sharply between 2006 and 2014 in the industries most affected by the economic downturn, but union membership fell faster than employment in all but one of those industries (see figure 7). The lone exception was the construction industry, a unique case both in regard to its central role in the Great Recession and also because building trades workers often retain their union affiliation even while they are unemployed. In manufacturing, wholesale and retail trade, information services, and the finance, insurance, and real estate industry group (FIRE), union membership declined far more than employment in this period. In "other services" and in the highly unionized education and transportation and utilities industries, although employment grew slightly in this period, union membership suffered a decline. Moreover, in those industries where employment did expand over this period, although union membership also grew, in most cases it lagged behind employment growth; the two exceptions were the accommodation and food services industry group and public administration.

Employment growth between 2006 and 2014 was greatest in industries with low union density (in 2006), whereas in industries with higher density, employment growth was weak or negative (see figure 8). In addition, union density declined over the 2006–2014 period in most of these industry groups (see table 2). The only ones where density increased were construction (for the reasons already suggested), accommodation and food services (where the increase was marginal), and public administration. Density was unchanged in professional services and health and social assistance. In the other eight industry groups shown, union density declined, with an especially steep drop in transportation and utilities.

The overall tendency for unionized jobs to be replaced by nonunion ones in the post-2008 recovery is also supported by table 3, which presents data for the nation's twenty most highly unionized occupations. In 2014 those occupations accounted for 43.6 percent of all union members, but only 20.7 percent of total employment. Union density declined in most of these occupations between 2006 and 2014, although it remained stable among construction laborers (for the reasons noted) and rose

Figure 7. Changes in Employment and in Union Membership Between 2006 and 2014, Selected Industry Groups.

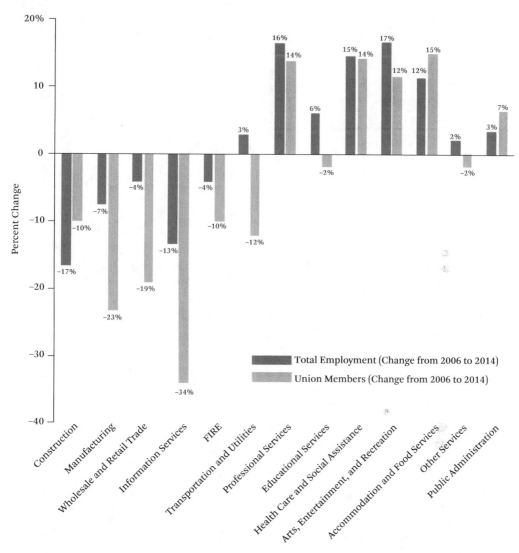

Source: www.unionstats.com, "Table IV. Union Membership, Coverage, Density and Employment by Industry, 1983–2015."

among registered nurses, police officers, secretaries and administrative assistants, and bailiffs, correctional officers, and jailers. Even in states where public sector collective bargaining laws came under attack, police were often exempted; registered nurses and corrections are among the rare fields in which unionization has been strengthened in recent years, a trend that remained intact in the aftermath of the economic crisis.

On the whole, however, unionization continued its relentless long-term decline during the Great Recession. Union density declined in part because new organizing did not keep up with labor force growth, especially in expanding industries and sectors. In addition, employers in many industries actively sought to undermine or eliminate unions in sectors that historically had been highly organized. The result was that growth in nonunion jobs gener-

Figure 8: Change in Total Employment, 2006–2014, and Union Density in 2006, Selected Industry Groups

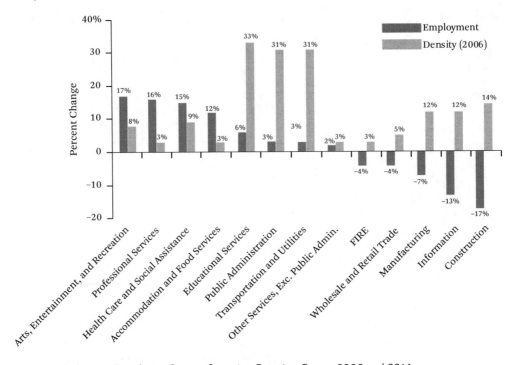

Source: U.S. Current Population Survey, Outgoing Rotation Group, 2006 and 2014.

Table 2. Union Density in Selected Industry Groups, 2006 and 2014

Year	2006	2014
Construction	14.0%	15.1%
Manufacturing	11.8	9.8
Wholesale and retail trade	5.0	4.2
Information services	12.4	9.5
Finance, insurance, and real estate	2.7	2.5
Transportation and utilities	61.0	51.0
Professional services	2.9	2.9
Education services	33.4	30.9
Health care and social assistance	9.0	9.0
Arts, entertainment, and recreation	7.9	7.6
Accommodation and food services	2.5	2.6
Other services	3.3	3.1
Public administration	31.3	32.3
All industries	12.0	11.1

Source: U.S. Current Population Survey, Outgoing Rotation Group, 2006 and 2014.

Table 3. Employment, Union Membership, and Union Density in Selected Occupations, 2006–2014, Ranked by 2014 Union Membership

Occupation	2014 Total Employment	2014 Union Membership	2006 Union Density	2014 Union Density
Elementary and middle school teachers	3,114,449	1,484,906	51.1	47.7
Secondary school teachers	1,085,105	546,239	54.6	50.3
Registered nurses	2,861,760	508,135	16.7	17.8
Police officers	700,292	397,300	56.1	56.7
Driver/sales workers and truck drivers	3,014,250	359,192	14.7	11.9
Janitors and building cleaners	2,206,407	313,402	17.0	14.2
Laborers and freight, stock, and material movers, hand	1,828,120	275,078	17.2	15.0
Teacher assistants	915,093	259,311	30.6	28.3
Postsecondary teachers	1,248,366	235,144	19.0	18.8
Secretaries and administrative assistants	2,878,736	222,880	7.5	7.7
Nursing, psychiatric, and home health aides	1,967,433	217,655	13.4	11.1
Postal service mail carriers	300,945	205,274	74.0	68.2
Fire fighters	301,982	201,229	70.3	66.6
Bus drivers	556,317	199,271	38.4	35.8
Electricians	668,387	189,041	31.0	28.3
Special education teachers	335,695	188,985	57.8	56.3
Bailiffs, correctional officers, and jailers	404,093	178,537	40.7	44.2
Cashiers	3,194,146	170,353	5.4	5.3
Construction laborers	1,369,980	151,945	11.1	11.1
Social workers	765,563	149,093	19.7	19.5

Source: Hirsch and Macpherson 2012, 2015.

ally outpaced that in union jobs, a long-term trend that was also a salient feature of the post-2008 recovery.

AN INSTITUTIONAL PERSPECTIVE

The short-term effects of the Great Recession were far less consequential for unions than the institutional environment, which had been hostile to organized labor for the previous three decades, especially in the private sector, and which continued to deteriorate in the wake of the economic crisis, in sharp contrast to what took place in the Great Depression. Since the late 1970s, employers had become increasingly adept at manipulating the NLRB election process with a variety of tactics that create new obstacles for unions. In the same period, employers also began routinely using "replacement workers" in economic strikes, greatly reducing the effectiveness of what had previously

been a key source of union leverage (Rhomberg 2012). Tactics and strategies vary across industries, but since the late 1970s employers have consistently been on the offensive, acting both to limit the spread of unions into new sectors and to weaken the power and influence of those established unions that have managed to survive (Logan 2006, Bronfenbrenner 2009).

In the aftermath of the 2008 financial crisis, a new wave of political attacks on organized labor emerged. But this was not simply a continuation of employers' previous anti-union efforts: for the first time the public sector became a central battleground. Here the attacks did not come directly from employers—which were government agencies—but rather from political actors. Attempts at undermining public sector unions had appeared periodically before the Great Recession, although they were not related to the business cycle. However, such efforts accelerated enormously in the wake of the 2008 crash and the state and local budget deficits that it helped to create. "Public sector labor law has long been subject to changes," the legal scholar Joseph Slater (2013) concluded after reviewing developments from the 1980s onward. "Nothing, however, prepared those in the field for what was going to happen in 2011" (526).

The attacks on public sector unions that emerged that year were nakedly political in character. The ties between organized labor and the Democratic Party, and unions' longstanding tradition of generously supporting Democratic electoral candidates had for decades made unions anathema for the political right. Now anti-union organizations such as the American Legislative Exchange Council (ALEC) capitalized on the unique opportunity presented by a series of state-level Republican electoral victories in the 2010 midterm elections. In 2011 and 2012 alone, fifteen states passed laws restricting public employees' collective bargaining rights (although three of these were later overturned in popular referenda). ALEC wrote model legislation and disseminated it to sympathetic elected officials in various states, an approach that proved highly effective. Private sector unionism already had declined dramatically; by contrast, in the public sector organized labor's strength remained intact. Thus the unions in that sector were the target.

Although this focus on the public sector was the distinctive feature of the post-2008 period, anti-union efforts continued to escalate in the private sector as well. ALEC and other right-wing groups promoted proposals for "right-to-work" legislation, which prohibits collective bargaining agreements to require that all covered workers pay union dues. Right-to-work laws were introduced in nineteen states in 2011 and 2012, and were soon passed in three former union bastions in the Midwest: Indiana in 2012, followed by Michigan in 2013 and Wisconsin in 2015 (Lafer 2013). ALEC also promoted legislation on a variety of other labor matters, including bills eliminating New Deal–era "prevailing wage" laws. These laws require firms with public contracts to pay the wages and benefits that the majority of workers in a region and occupation receive (typically the wage and benefit level specialized in collective bargain-

ing agreements). Indiana passed legislation eliminating one such law in 2015 (Lafer 2013, Davey 2015). Nine other states already had repealed their prevailing wage laws in the 1980s, but efforts to accomplish this in other states were ramped up in the aftermath of the Great Recession.

By any standard, then, the institutional context in which unions are struggling to survive, which had become increasingly hostile to organized labor over the three decades before the Great Recession, seems even more treacherous in the post-2008 period. This presents a striking contrast to what took place during the 1930s, when the economic crisis was the impetus for a set of major policy breakthroughs in support of collective bargaining and social protection for workers. (Public sector unionism barely existed in that period, so it was simply not part of the equation.) Many of the recent anti-labor legislative proposals put forward by ALEC and other such groups are explicitly designed to undercut or eliminate those New Deal–era protections.

This raises the question: Why are the outcomes after 2008 so different from those in the 1930s? Why did a labor upsurge like the one that developed during the Great Depression not recur in the wake of the Great Recession? Why, instead, does union density continue to stall or decline today? We cannot definitively answer this question, but we can suggest some possible explanations.

Although employer opposition to unions was virulent in the 1930s, just as it is today, there are some differences worth noting. First, President Franklin D. Roosevelt took a bold stand in support of unions and collective bargaining, and he had the political leverage to make that a reality. Obama has taken much weaker positions in defense of unions, and has faced a sharply divided Congress, with one house dominated by elected officials who are notoriously anti-union, all of which greatly constrains his ability to act on even his relatively modest efforts to support organized labor. Second, although employers strongly opposed unions in the 1930s, the depth of the crisis meant that many of them were directly dependent on the federal government to restore stability to the overall economy and to address the problem of cutthroat labor market competition. In this period, a large fraction of the employer community understood the political necessity of agreeing to concessions in regard to collective bargaining in order to save capitalism from itself. By contrast, after the 2008 crash, Congress moved relatively quickly to bail out the banks with no strings attached, and demanded virtually no concessions from employers in return. Once the bailout was accomplished, employers were far less dependent on the administration or on congressional legislation than their counterparts in the 1930s to get the economy running again (although some did benefit from the 2009 American Recovery and Reinvestment Act).

Another possibility is that it is too early to draw definitive conclusions as to the impact of the two crises on labor. The upsurge in union membership occurred several years after the 1929 stock market crash. Although it does not seem likely that anything comparable to the giant upsurge that followed the passage of the National Labor Relations Act of 1935 will recur, that sort of outcome cannot be ruled out entirely. We may just now be seeing the initial fruits of a post-recession organizing upsurge. In 2014 and 2015 union density inched up slightly in a few states and industries (Milkman and Luce 2015; Bureau of Labor Statistics 2016a). The number of large strikes, and the number of workers involved in strikes, also increased slightly in 2015 (Bureau of Labor Statistics 2016b). Moreover, alongside this renewed activity on the part of traditional unions, the labor movement's strategic orientation has begun to pivot, largely in response to the anti-union political climate and employer attacks. Unions and labor movement allies alike are exploring alternative organizational forms that in some respects recapitulate the strategic repertoire of the pre-1930s labor movement (see Milkman 2006, 2013). It is to those developments that we now turn.

NEW DIRECTIONS: "ALT-LABOR" AND TWENTY-FIRST CENTURY U.S. UNIONISM

The besieged organized labor movement began to experiment with a variety of new initiatives in the 1990s and early 2000s. In the late 1990s the AFL-CIO launched an energetic campaign designed to "organize the unorganized," followed a decade later by high-profile efforts to win labor law reform. Several large unions left the AFL-CIO in 2005, forming a rival federation designed to reposition the unions to better cope with the increasingly hostile institutional environment, and again with a professed commitment to expanding new organizing. Although these efforts led to some successful union drives, they were typically modest in scale and thus insufficient to reverse the relentless decline in union density. Other campaigns, such as the effort to pass the Employee Free Choice Act, failed entirely to achieve their goals. Unionism continued to decline, and the situation became increasingly desperate as political attacks on collective bargaining ramped up after the Great Recession.

One response to this dire situation came from a variety of nonunion community-based labor organizations, many of which have come to be known as "worker centers" (Fine 2006) and more recently as "alt-labor" (for "alternative labor") organizations. These groups. which unlike traditional unions were expanding during the 1990s and 2000s, began to experiment with new approaches to worker organizing. Focused especially on immigrants and others concentrated at the very bottom of the labor market, these organizations emerged as highly effective advocates for low-wage workers. They succeeded in calling media and public attention to labor and employment law violations, such as payment below the legal minimum wage (or in some cases outright nonpayment), and won legal remedies for some of the victims. Initially the traditional unions were deeply skeptical of the effectiveness of these approaches, but that gradually changed in the 2000s as more and more individual unions as well as the AFL-CIO began to partner with worker centers.

There were two key turning points in the labor movement's shift in this direction, one before and one soon after the Great Recession. The first came in 2006, when massive immigrant rights marches swept the nation in response to the threat that a draconian immigration bill, "The Border Protection Anti-Terrorism and Illegal Immigration Control Act of 2005" (H.R. 4337), which passed the U.S. House of

Representatives in late 2005, would become the law of the land. Millions of immigrants demonstrated against this legislation in the spring of 2006, mobilized by a coalition of worker centers and immigrant rights groups, with support from some labor unions as well. Immediately afterward, formal partnerships between the AFL-CIO and worker centers began to develop, a process that has continued ever since. These dramatic immigrant rights protests dispelled any lingering doubts in the House of Labor about the "organizability" of low-wage immigrant workers; at the same time the achievements of the worker centers were winning growing respect from traditional unionists.

The second turning point was the Occupy Wall Street uprising, whose meteoric rise in the fall of 2011 transformed the national political debate and raised public awareness about the growing inequality between rich and poor. Organized labor's previous efforts to call attention to rising inequality had failed to gain any traction with the public, but after 2011 unions began to build on the foundation established by the Occupy movement. The most dramatic example is the Service Employees International Union (SEIU)'s organizing campaign in fast-food chains, demanding wages of $15 per hour and the right to unionize. Launched in New York in late 2012, this "Fight for 15" has since spread nationwide, propelled by a series of one-day demonstration strikes that garnered extensive publicity. Although sponsored by a traditional labor union, the SEIU, this campaign essentially has adopted the strategic repertoire of the worker center movement. There is no immediate prospect of union recognition, but the effort has succeeded in shining a bright light on the low wages and other workplace abuses in this industry. The strikes have attracted support from workers in other low-wage sectors: in December 2014, April 2015, and November 2015, airport workers, domestic workers, convenience store employees, and adjuncts joined in the one-day "Fight for 15" strikes (for a fifteen-dollar hourly wage). Another worker-center-like union-sponsored campaign is OUR (Organization United for Respect) Walmart, which launched a series of "Black Friday" strikes as well as other efforts to put pressure on the nation's largest employer to improve its employment practices.

The fifteen-dollar-an-hour demand first floated by the fast-food organizing effort also sparked campaigns to raise the minimum wage in key cities and counties where unions still have a strong presence. Seattle and SeaTac in Washington State, along with others, including San Francisco, Emeryville, and Los Angeles in California, have passed laws that will raise the overall minimum hourly wage to fifteen dollars or higher in the coming years, and advocates have won more modest increases in minimum wages in over a dozen other cities and states across the nation. These highly successful campaigns built directly on the Occupy movement's successes in raising public awareness of inequality. In 2014 alone, fourteen states raised their statewide minimum wage (Luce 2015). Public approval of unions has also increased, climbing back from its low point in 2009 (Saad 2015).

There are no systematic data available on the scale of these alt-labor efforts, but we can sketch the trajectory of their recent growth by drawing on a variety of published accounts. There were 137 worker centers in the United States in 2003 (Fine 2006), and 160 in 2007 (Fine 2007, 57). The number grew substantially in the aftermath of the Great Recession, to over 200 by 2010 (Fine 2011, 615) and, according to one recent estimate, to a total of 230 by 2013 (Narro 2013). In addition, several worker centers that began as local operations have expanded into national operations. These include the Restaurant Opportunities Centers United (ROC-United), with 11 local organizations across the nation; the National Domestic Workers Alliance, with 42 affiliates; and the National Day Laborers Organizing Network, with 43 affiliates (Fine 2015, 17). Other examples include the Food Chain Workers' Alliance (with which ROC-United is also affiliated) and the National Guestworker Alliance. Although there are no reliable estimates of how many workers are affected by these efforts, many of which are modest in size, the Food Chain Workers' Alliance alone claims to represent 300,000 workers. Many of these organizations also have successfully litigated claims of wage theft and won back pay for substantial numbers of workers.

We can be a bit more precise in estimating the numbers of workers who have benefitted from recent increases in the minimum wage. These are summarized in table 4, which suggests that over 2 million workers have been impacted by these new laws at the local level from 2012 to early 2016 alone. Table 4 also includes data on several major employers who have announced wage hikes in response to the "Fight for 15" and related campaigns, which we estimate to have benefitted almost 1 million workers. Table 4 does not include the statewide minimum-wage increases that have been legislated in the aftermath of the Great Recession; an Economic Policy Institute study estimates that those laws had affected 3.1 million workers by 2014 (Cooper 2014).

Table 4. Estimated Number of Workers Impacted by Minimum Wage Increases and Employer-Sponsored Wage Hikes, 2012–2015

A. City/County/Local Minimum Wage Increases	Year Passed	Number of workers impacted
Albuquerque, N.Mex.	2012	40,000
Long Beach, Calif.[a]	2012	NA
San Jose, Calif.	2012	69,000
Bernalillo County, N.Mex.	2013	10,000
Montgomery County, Md.	2013	77,000
Prince George's County, Md.	2013	51,194
Sea-Tac, Wash.	2013	6,300
Berkeley, Calif.[b]	2014	8,400
Chicago, Ill.	2014	400,000
Las Cruces, N.Mex.[b]	2014	6,297
Louisville, Ky.	2014	45,000
Mountain View, Calif.[b]	2014	6,356
Oakland, Calif.	2014	32,500
Richmond, Calif.[b]	2014	3,000
San Diego, Calif.	2014	150,500
San Francisco, Calif.[c]	2014	142,000
Santa Fe County, N.Mex.[b]	2014	6,695
Seattle, Wash.	2014	102,000
Sunnyvale, Calif.[b]	2014	10,895
Washington, D.C.[c]	2014	43,000
Tacoma, Wash.[b]	2014	24,903
Bangor, Maine[b]	2015	10,050
Birmingham, Ala.[b]	2015	12,831
Denver, Colo. school district	2015	1,700
El Cerrito, Calif.[b]	2015	4,022
Emeryville, Calif.[b]	2015	2,227
Johnson County, Iowa[b]	2015	8,920
Lexington, Ky.	2015	31,000
Los Angeles County, Calif.	2015	125,000
Los Angeles, Calif.	2015	600,000
Palo Alto, Calif.[b]	2015	4,643
Portland, Maine[b]	2015	29,850
Santa Clara, Calif.[b]	2015	8,615
Santa Monica, Calif.[b]	2016	34,400
Total		2,187,299

(continued)

Table 4. (*continued*)

B. Large Employers That Announced Minimum Wage Hikes During or After 2012	Number of workers impacted
Aetna	5,700
GAP	65,000
Giant Food Stores	10,000
IKEA	3,360
Indiana University	11,000
McDonalds	90,000
Starbucks	76,400
State University of New York	28,000
Target	138,800
TJX (Target, Marshalls, HomeGoods)	60,320
University of California	3,200
University of Wisconsin–Madison	2,571
Walmart	500,000
Total	994,351

Source: Authors' compilation.

Notes: Estimates of workers impacted come from a variety of sources. Where possible, we used city studies, academic reports, or newspaper articles that estimated the impact, or public company statements announcing wage increases. In cases where these sources provided a range of potential workers covered, we used the midpoint. In a few cases, we calculated our own estimate of potential impact extrapolating from data for cities similar in population size. For further details on this methodology, please contact the authors.

[a]The Long Beach, Calif., ordinance applies only to hotel workers; a citywide minimum wage is under consideration.

[b]Authors' estimate of workers impacted, based on the size of the labor force and coverage data from similar cities.

[c]Washington, D.C., passed an initial citywide minimum wage in 1993 and then raised the wage rate in 2013. San Francisco passed an initial citywide minimum wage in 2003; voters then passed an increase in the wage rate in 2014.

States have set and raised their minimum wages for decades, and increases often come in waves (examples include 2004 and 2006), but local minimum-wage laws are a relatively recent phenomenon. As of 2010, only a handful of cities had passed their own minimum wage ordinances, but between 2012 and early 2016, thirty-two municipalities did so. In September 2015, seven cities in the San Francisco Bay Area announced plans to work together to establish a regional minimum wage, another recent innovation. Organized labor has also promoted a variety of legislative measures at the state and local levels aimed at improving the situation of low-wage workers, mandating benefits such as paid family leave and paid sick days, and improving enforcement of labor standards.

(Milkman and Appelbaum 2013; Reich, Jacobs, and Dietz 2014).

Both these legislative initiatives and the spurt of alt-labor organizing efforts resemble pre–New Deal labor movement strategies, in contrast to the NLRB-based union organizing campaigns that became common in the mid-twentieth century (see Milkman 2013). In the Progressive Era of the last century, labor reform groups and their middle-class allies publicized sweatshops and employer abuses and provided educational and social services for immigrant workers in much the same way that worker centers do today (Flanagan 2002; Stromquist 2006). These reformers also promoted unionization and campaigned for progressive legislation, including the first state minimum-wage laws (although at the time these applied only to women and children). In that era the cities and states were "laboratories of democracy," whose reforms helped to set the stage for the landmark labor and employment legislation of the New Deal.

In the absence of systematic data, we can only sketch the achievements and prospects of the new alt-labor efforts and the flurry of legislative activity that have emerged in a fragmentary way. But they stand out as central components of organized labor's response to the Great Recession. To be sure, these developments have had no apparent effect on the steady decline in union membership and density. But like the parallel efforts a century ago, they could represent the embryo of a Polanyian countermovement in response to the post-1970s wave of neoliberal marketization.

To sum up: Although the Great Recession does not appear to have been a significant factor in the long-term decline in union density, which had been under way for many decades, the 2008 financial crisis nevertheless did impact the labor movement. It opened up political space for right-wing attacks on the rights of unions to exist and bargain collectively in both the private and public sectors, further eroding an already hostile institutional environment. Steep job losses in traditionally unionized industries during and after the Great Recession added to the challenge for the labor movement in maintaining union density. Nevertheless, the surge in successful efforts to increase state and local minimum wages and the growing momentum of innovative organizing efforts like the "Fight for 15" offer some hope that James Surowiecki's (2011) obituary for the labor movement may prove to have been premature.

REFERENCES

Ashenfelter, Orley, and John H. Pencavel. 1969. "American Trade Union Growth: 1900–1960." *Quarterly Journal of Economics* 83(30): 434–48.

Bernstein, Irving. 1954. "The Growth of American Unions." *American Economic Review* 44(3): 301–18.

Brady, David, Regina S. Baker, and Ryan Finnigan. 2013. "When Unionization Disappears: State-Level Unionization and Working Poverty in the United States." *American Sociological Review* 78(5): 872–96.

Bronfenbrenner, Kate. 2009. *No Holds Barred: The Intensification of Employer Opposition to Organizing*. Briefing Paper No. 235. Washington, D.C.: Economic Policy Institute.

Burawoy, Michael. 2010. "From Polanyi to Pollyanna: The False Optimism of Global Labor Studies," *Global Labor Journal* 1(2): 301–13.

Bureau of Labor Statistics. 2016a. "Union Members—2015." Washington: Bureau of Labor Statistics. Available at: http://www.bls.gov /news.release/pdf/union2.pdf; accessed March 5, 2016.

———. 2016b. "Major Work Stoppages in 2015." Washington: Bureau of Labor Statistics. Available at: http://www.bls.gov/news.release /wkstp.nr0.htm; accessed March 5, 2016.

Campbell, Andrea Louise, and Michael W. Sances. 2013. "State Fiscal Policy During the Great Recession: Budgetary Impacts and Policy Responses." *Annals of the American Academy of Political and Social Science* 650(November): 252–72.

Cohen, Patricia. 2015. "Public Sector Jobs Vanish, Hitting Blacks Hard." *New York Times*, May 25, p. A1.

Commons, John R., and associates. 1918. *History of Labor in the United States*. 4 vols. New York: Macmillan.

Cooper, David. 2014. "20 States Raise Their Minimum Wages While the Federal Minimum Continues to Erode." Economic Policy Institute, *Working Economics Blog*, December 18. Available at: http://www.epi.org/blog/20-states-raise-thei r-minimum-wages-while-the-fede ral-minimum-continues-to-erode/; accessed March 1, 2016.

Davey, Monica. 2015. "G.O.P. Expands Labor Battle to Laws Setting Construction Wages." *New York Times*, May 3, p. 17.

Dunlop, John T. 1948. "The Development of Labor Organization: A Theoretical Framework." In *Insights into Labor Issues*, edited by Richard A. Lester and Joseph Shister. New York: Macmillan.

Evans, Peter. 2008. "Is an Alternative Globalization Possible?" *Politics and Society* 36(2): 271–305.

Farber, Henry. 2014. "Union Organizing Decisions in a Deteriorating Environment: The Composition of

Representation Elections and the Decline in Turnout." IZA Discussion Paper No. 7964. Bonn, Germany: Institute for the Study of Labor. Available at: http://www.econstor.eu/bitstream /10419/93364/1/dp7964.pdf; accessed August 31, 2016.

Fine, Janice. 2006. *Worker Centers: Organizing Communities at the Edge of the Dream.* Ithaca, N.Y.: Cornell University Press.

——. 2007. "Worker Centers." *Race, Poverty and the Environment* 14(1): 54–57.

——. 2011. "New Forms to Settle Old Scores: Updating the Worker Centre Story in the United States." *Relations Industrielles/Industrial Relations* 66(4): 604–30.

——. 2015. "Alternative Labour Protection Movements in the United States: Reshaping Industrial Relations?" *International Labour Review* 154(1): 15–26.

Flanagan, Maureen A. 2002. *Seeing with Their Hearts: Chicago Women and the Vision of the Good City, 1871–1933.* Princeton, N.J.: Princeton University Press.

Hirsch, Barry T., and David A. Macpherson. 2012. *Union Membership and Earnings Data Book: Compilations from the Current Population Survey.* Arlington, Va.: Bureau of National Affairs.

——. 2015. *Union Membership and Earnings Data Book: Compilations from the Current Population Survey.* Arlington, Va.: Bureau of National Affairs.

Lafer, Gordon. 2013. *The Legislative Attack on American Wages and Labor Standards, 2011–2012.* EPI Briefing Paper No. 364. Washington, D.C.: Economic Policy Institute.

Laird, Jennifer. 2015. "Still an Equal Opportunity Employer? Public Sector Employment Inequality After the Great Recession." Paper presented at the Population Association of America's 2015 Annual Meeting. San Diego (April 30, 2015).

Liebman, Wilma. 2007. "Decline and Disenchantment: Reflections on the Aging of the National Labor Relations Board." *Berkeley Journal of Employment and Labor Law* 28(2): 569–89.

Logan, John. 2006. "The Union Avoidance Industry in the United States." *British Journal of Industrial Relations* 44(4): 651–72.

Luce, Stephanie. 2015. "$15 per Hour or Bust: An Appraisal of the Higher Wages Movement." *New Labor Forum* 24(2): 73–78.

MacDonald, Ian Thomas. 2014. "Towards Neoliberal Trade Unionism: Decline, Renewal and Transformation in North American Labor Movements." *British Journal of Industrial Relations* 52(4): 725–52.

Mayer, Gerald. 2004. "Union Membership Trends in the United States." Report. Washington: Congressional Research Service, August 31. Available at: http://digitalcommons.ilr.cornell.edu/cgi /viewcontent.cgi?article=1176&context=key _workplace; accessed August 8, 2016.

Milkman, Ruth. 2006. *L.A. Story: Immigrant Workers and the Future of the U.S. Labor Movement.* New York: Russell Sage Foundation.

——. 2013. "Back to the Future? U.S. Labor in the New Gilded Age." *British Journal of Industrial Relations* 51(4): 645–66.

Milkman, Ruth, and Eileen Appelbaum. 2013. *Unfinished Business: Paid Family Leave in California and the Future of U.S. Work-Family Policy.* Ithaca, N.Y.: Cornell University Press.

Milkman, Ruth, and Stephanie Luce. 2015. "State of the Unions 2015: A Profile of Organized Labor in New York City, New York State, and the United States." New York: City University of New York, Murphy Institute. Available at: http://media.wix .com/ugd/90d188_91d7cdc3f75740909eef83a22 cee9cdb.pdf; accessed August 8, 2106.

Narro, Victor. 2013. "Perspectives: Worker Centers and the AFL-CIO National Convention." *Law at the Margins* (blog), September 3. Available at: http://lawatthemargins.com/perspectives-worker -centers-and-the-afl-cio-national-convention/; accessed September 1, 2016.

National Governors' Association and National Association of State Budget Officers. 2010. "The Fiscal Survey of States: An Update of State Fiscal Conditions Spring 2010 and Fall 2010." Available at: http://www.nasbo.org/publications-data /fiscal-survey-of-the-states/archives; accessed September 1, 2016.

Polanyi, Karl. 1944. *The Great Transformation.* Boston: Beacon Press.

Reich, Michael, Ken Jacobs, and Miranda Dietz, eds., 2014. *When Mandates Work: Raising Labor Standards at the Local Level.* Berkeley: University of California Press.

Rhomberg, Chris. 2012. *The Broken Table: The Detroit Newspaper Strike and the State of American Labor.* New York: Russell Sage Foundation.

Saad, Lydia. 2015. "Americans' Support for Labor Unions Continues to Recover." August 17. *Gallup* (website). Available at: http://www.gallup.com

/poll/184622/americans-support-labor-unions
-continues-recover.aspx; accessed September 1,
2016.

Scheiber, Noam. 2015. "Obama Aids U.S. Workers
in Late Push." *New York Times*, September 1, p.
A1.

Schnabel, Claus. 2013. "Union Membership and
Density: Some (Not So) Stylized Facts and Challenges." *European Journal of Industrial Relations*
19(3): 255–72.

Silver, Beverly. 2003. *Forces of Labor: Workers'
Movements and Globalization Since 1870*. New
York: Cambridge University Press.

Slater, Joseph. 2013. "The Strangely Unsettled State
of Public-Sector Labor in the Past 30 Years."
Hofstra Labor and Employment Law Journal
30(2): 504–35.

Stepina, Lee P., and Jack Fiorito. 1986. "Toward a
Comprehensive Theory of Union Growth and Decline." *Industrial Relations* 25(3): 248–64.

Stromquist, Sheldon. 2006. *Reinventing "The People": The Progressive Movement, the Class Problem, and the Origins of Modern Liberalism*. Ur-
bana: University of Illinois Press.

Surowiecki, James. 2011. "State of the Unions," *New
Yorker*, January 17.

Western, Bruce. 1997. *Between Class and Market:
Postwar Unionization in the Capitalist Democ-
racies*. Princeton, N.J.: Princeton University
Press.

Western, Bruce, and Jake Rosenfeld. 2011. "Unions,
Norms and the Rise in American Earnings Inequality." *American Sociological Review* 76(4):
513–37.

PART III

Consequences of Long-Term Unemployment

Factors Determining Callbacks to Job Applications by the Unemployed: An Audit Study

HENRY S. FARBER, DAN SILVERMAN, AND
TILL M. VON WACHTER

We use an audit study approach to investigate how unemployment duration, age, and holding a low-level interim job while applying for a better job affect the likelihood that experienced college-educated females applying for an administrative support job receive a callback from potential employers. First, the results show no relationship between callback rates and unemployment duration. Second, workers age fifty and older are significantly less likely to receive a callback. Third, taking an interim job significantly reduces the likelihood of receiving a callback. Finally, employers who have higher callback rates respond less to observable differences across workers in determining whom to call back.

Keywords: unemployment duration, job finding, interim jobs, age discrimination, audit study

In this project we use an audit study approach (Bertrand and Mullainathan 2004), where we send carefully constructed fictitious job applications to posted job openings, in order to investigate how several characteristics of workers affect the likelihood that they receive a callback after applying for a job. We focus on the recent employment history and age of applicants, paying special attention to the effects of unemployment duration and of taking a low-level interim job. The study is motivated in part by the persistently long duration of unemployment spells experienced by workers in the Great Recession and its aftermath. This pattern is illustrated in figure 1, which plots the mean and median duration of unemployment spells in progress by quarter from 1976 through 2014. Mean unemployment duration peaked in 2011 at almost thirty-seven weeks and has exceeded thirty weeks in all quarters between 2010Q1 and 2014Q2. Both mean and median duration remain well above their levels at any point prior to 2008.

This shift toward longer unemployment spells underscores the importance of understanding whether workers who have been un-

Henry S. Farber is Hughes-Rogers Professor of Economics at Princeton University. **Dan Silverman** is Rondthaler Professor of Economics at Arizona State University. **Till M. von Wachter** is associate professor in the Department of Economics at the University of California, Los Angeles.

© 2017 Russell Sage Foundation. Farber, Henry S., Dan Silverman, and Till M. von Wachter. 2017. "Factors Determining Callbacks to Job Applications by the Unemployed: An Audit Study." *RSF: The Russell Sage Foundation Journal of the Social Sciences* 3(3): 168–201. DOI: 10.7758/RSF.2017.3.3.08. The authors thank the Sloan Foundation for financial support. They also thank Joanna Lahey, Matthew Notowidigdo, and participants in workshops at CREST, Princeton University, the Russell Sage Foundation, the Sloan Foundation, UCSD, and UCLA for helpful comments and discussion. Direct correspondence to: Henry S. Farber at farber@princeton.edu, Industrial Relations Section, Simpson International Building, Princeton University, Princeton, NJ 08544; Dan Silverman at dsilver3@asu.edu, W.P. Carey School of Business, Arizona State University, PO Box 879801, Tempe, AZ 85287; and Till M. von Wachter at tvwachter@econ.ucla.edu, Department of Economics, 8283 Bunche Hall, Mail Stop: 147703, Los Angeles, CA 90095.

Figure 1. Mean and Median Duration of Unemployment Spells in Progress, by Quarter

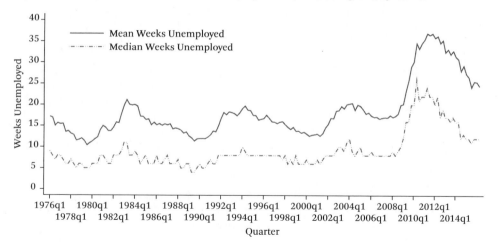

Source: Authors' calculations based on data from the Matched Monthly Files of Current Population Survey.

Figure 2. Monthly Job Finding Rate, by Duration of Unemployment, 2008–2014

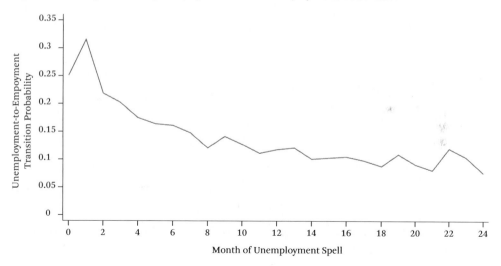

Source: Authors' calculations based on data from the Matched Monthly Files of Current Population Survey.

employed for a long period face more difficulty in finding a job. The labor force transition data suggest that this is the case. Figure 2 contains a plot of the monthly job finding rate (the probability of an U–E, unemployment to employment, transition) by unemployment duration in months based on matched Current Population Survey (CPS) data from 2008 to 2014. This figure shows a sharp decline in the monthly job finding rate from about 25 percent early in

unemployment spells to about 10 percent after one year. In order to study the effect of unemployment duration on the likelihood of callback, we randomly varied the duration of the current unemployment spell across applications in our audit study.

The study is also motivated by an interest in the obstacles that older unemployed workers face in job seeking. Figure 3 highlights the fact that the average duration of unemployment

Figure 3. Average Number of Weeks Spent in Unemployment, by Age

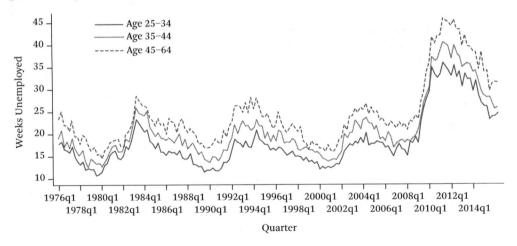

Source: Authors' calculations based on data from the Current Population Survey.

Figure 4. Unemployment Rate of Displaced Workers, by Age

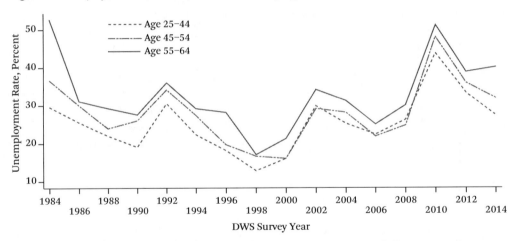

Source: Authors' calculations based on data from the Displaced Workers Supplement of the Current Population Survey.

spells in progress have historically been substantially longer for older workers. For example, from 2014Q1 to 2015Q2, the average duration of an in-progress unemployment spell was twenty-eight weeks for those age twenty-five to thirty-four, thirty-one weeks for those age thirty-five to forty-four, and thirty-six weeks for those age forty-five to sixty-four.

The difficulty that older workers have in finding jobs is further illustrated using data from the Displaced Workers Survey (DWS) from 1984 to 2014. Figure 4 illustrates that older job losers have historically had higher post-

displacement unemployment rates (measured at the DWS survey date). Since the Great Recession period (job loss from 2007 to 2013), job losers twenty-five to forty-four years old had a 26.3 percent unemployment rate, whereas the unemployment rate was 29.9 percent for job losers forty-five to fifty-four years old and 35.1 percent for job losers fifty-five to sixty-four years of age. The difficulties faced by older unemployed individuals lead some to spend long stretches of time out of work, and some never return to employment (Song and von Wachter 2014). Given these patterns, it is important to understand the role of age in hiring and its interaction with work history such as unemployment duration and interim jobs.

Our interest in age affected our study design in two ways. In contrast to several recent audit studies of the effect of employment history on callback rates, our sample consists of mature and older workers, for whom job loss and long-term unemployment may be particularly costly. In addition, to examine the question of how age itself affects the likelihood of callback, we randomly varied applicant's age on a subset of applications, and measured differences in callback rates.

Finally, we were interested in whether ending a recent spell of unemployment with a short-term, lower-level "interim" job, such as in retail sales, is an effective strategy for improving callback rates. It is well documented that in the aftermath of a job loss the degree of mismatch and nonstandard work histories increases, in particular during recessions (Farber 1999; Elsby, Hobijn, and Şahin 2010). How interim jobs can affect callback rates has direct practical relevance for unemployed workers seeking to obtain a good job while making ends meet. Additionally, it is important to understand the extent to which a rise in the incidence in interim employment during recessions affects callback and job finding and, hence, unemployment duration. Yet relatively little is known about the consequences of taking a low-level interim job. Simple theories suggest it could have countervailing effects on callbacks. It might be that holding a low-level interim job signals that the applicant is ambitious and hardworking, increasing the likelihood of callback. Alternatively, it might be that holding a low-level interim job suggests to the employer than the applicant is not suitable for the job for which the application was submitted. This could be a conscious choice of employers or a mechanical reading of the résumé that rules out applicants whose most recent job was not related to the job for which the application was submitted. To investigate the role of a low-level interim job on the likelihood of a callback, we included such an interim job on a random subset of some applications, and then measured differences in callback rates.

In order to focus efficiently on the three variables of interest, we limit the range of variation in other dimensions as is common in studies of this type. Specifically, we limit our applications to administrative support jobs and we restrict the characteristics of applicants: all are female and have a four-year college education. Although this does limit any claims we might make regarding the workforce as a whole, the facts that motivated our analysis regarding the incidence of long-term unemployment and the relationship of age with long-term employment do hold for this subgroup of the labor force. Figure 5 shows average duration of unemployment spells in progress from the CPS since 2003 for college-educated females in administrative support occupations. While the samples are considerably smaller than for those for the entire unemployed sample from the CPS (figure 3), one can clearly see a sharp increase in the average duration of unemployment for these women since the Great Recession, and the average duration of unemployment is significantly longer for older women.[1] Thus, the facts we presented in the introduction to motivate our analysis are important for the particular jobs we study.

Our findings are clear with regard to the three variables of interest. First, we find no relationship between unemployment duration and the callback rate. This is different from the results obtained by Kory Kroft, Fabian Lange, and Matthew J. Notowidigdo (2013)—henceforth this study is referred to as KLN—and Rand Ghayad (2014). Those papers find a negative relationship between callback rates and duration of unemployment that is concentrated in the first six or seven months of an unemployment spell.

For longer spells, those papers estimate that the relationship between unemployment duration and the callback rate is flat. Our findings are closest to those by John M. Nunley and his colleagues (forthcoming), who find no effect

1. Mean unemployment duration for college-educated females in administrative support occupations over the 2008-to-2014 period is 10.2 weeks longer for women aged forty-five to sixty-four than for women aged twenty-five to forty-four (the difference is statistically significant).

Figure 5. Average Weeks Unemployed, by Age, of College-Educated Females in Administrative Support Occupations

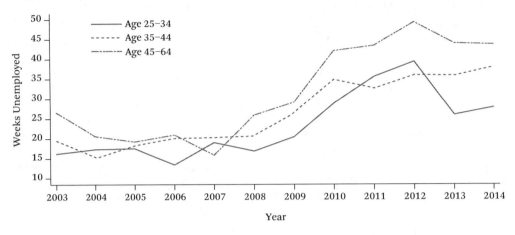

Source: Authors' calculations based on data from the Current Population Survey.

of unemployment duration, either past or present, on callbacks for relatively recent college graduates in the United States.[2] Stefan Eriksson and Dan-Olof Rooth (2014), whose study of the Swedish market also found no effect of unemployment duration on callback rates for jobs that require a university degree, additionally found no effects before six months for lower-skill jobs. As we discuss in detail later in this article, there are many potential reasons for the differences across studies in results with regard to unemployment duration and callbacks. We can explore some of them with existing data, but more data collection is necessary to understand fully what drives the differences.

Second, we find that older workers, those in their fifties, are significantly less likely to receive a callback than workers in their thirties and forties. This is consistent with the results in Joanna Lahey (2008), who finds large negative effects of age on callbacks for women seeking entry-level positions in the United States.

Third, we find that taking a low-level interim job significantly reduces the likelihood of receiving a callback. This last result is similar to that in Nunley et al. (forthcoming). That paper found that relatively recent college graduates in the United States had substantially fewer callbacks if they were currently employed in jobs that did not require a college education

and were not suited to the job for which they were applying.

Our results have some important implications. First, our findings help to underscore that the effect of unemployment duration on callback rates found for younger workers in KLN do not hold universally in the labor market. For the more seasoned female clerical workers we focus on, long-term unemployment has no causal effect on callback rates. Together with the other mixed findings in the literature, our finding calls into question whether the well-known decline in the probability of job finding with unemployment duration is primarily driven by a causal effect of unemployment duration due to employer behavior rather than arising from some other source, such as negative selection or changes in workers' search behavior. Future work should seek to understand better the heterogeneity in treatment effects between studies and demographic groups.

Second, our results strengthen Lahey's (2008) finding and underscore that age discrimination may be a relevant phenomenon in the U.S. labor market. Since we focus on workers with longer labor force histories, our findings suggest that even substantial relevant labor market experience on the résumés we use does not diminish the negative effect of age on callbacks.

2. All of the fictitious applicants in our study had completed a four-year degree.

Third, at a practical level, the fact that interim jobs negatively affect the incidence of callback implies that unemployed workers may be better advised remaining unemployed rather than compromising on job quality—or at least they should not list an interim job on their résumés. Finally, our findings on interim jobs imply that employers do use information on the résumés to make inferences even about mature and older workers. Standard employer learning theory would suggest that the availability of many signals for these workers reduces the effect of any given signal (Farber and Gibbons 1996). This could rationalize our zero result on the effect of unemployment duration, but not the significant effects of interim jobs that we find. It is an open question whether this latter finding implies presence of employer learning in the sense of the theory even for older workers, or whether it is due to mechanical screening of CVs by human resource departments that may, for example, eliminate "bad matches" on the basis of the last entry on the CV.

An additional finding is that, for job listings to which we sent four applications, the negative effect of age and interim job on the incidence of callback is substantially weaker (the effect of unemployment duration remains zero) for those employers with high callback rates (for example, three of four applications received a callback as opposed to one of four applications received a callback). This finding can be interpreted as an indication that employers with a high demand for workers become less selective in deciding whether or not to call back. This is consistent with the idea that particular signals on the résumé may matter less for the incidence of callback in a tighter labor market than in a weaker labor market.

In the remainder of this paper we describe and motivate many details of the experimental design; develop a model of employer learning to guide interpretation of results; present the results of simple, univariate analyses of the experimental treatments on duration of unemployment, age, and interim job; present a multivariate analysis to gain additional precision of the estimates; offer some analysis of the disparate findings in the literature; and present our conclusions.

RESEARCH DESIGN

The design of our audit study reflects several considerations and constraints that have implications for interpreting the results. Since, as with any experiment in the social sciences, our design choices affect the internal and external validity of our results, we describe the design and setting of our study in detail.

An audit study consists in sending fake résumés to actual job postings and measuring the incidence of callback rates. The main estimates consists in differences in callback rates based on randomly assigned differences in résumé characteristics, such as age, characteristics of previously held jobs, or employment dates. It is therefore paramount that the fake résumés and the variation in the informational content be constructed to be as realistic as possible.

To facilitate the tailoring of résumés and reduce idiosyncratic variation in callback rates by job type, we restricted both the type of jobs to which we sent our résumés and the demographic characteristics of the applicants. Applications were limited to white-collar office jobs such as administrative or executive assistants, receptionists, secretaries, office associates, and the like. Because these jobs are disproportionately held by women, and gender differences are not our focus, all applicants had female names. Each applicant had a four-year bachelor's degree from a non-elite public university or college with a current admission rate higher than 65 percent. In contrast to previous studies, our fictitious applicants also had substantial work histories. The work histories consisted of three to six white-collar office jobs, depending on age. Prior to the current spell, these work histories had no spells of unemployment longer than a month in the previous five years. Age or birth year were not listed in the résumés but could be inferred from year of college completion and work experience. No information was included on the résumés regarding race, marital status, or number of children.

The context of our audit study is nationwide in that we submitted job applications to openings in selected cities across the United States. To further be able to tailor our fictitious résumés to jobs and the local labor market, we selected eight cities. Because we also wanted to

Table 1. Unemployment Rates by City and Year

Low Unemployment	2012	2014	High Unemployment	2012	2014
Dallas	6.6	5.0	Charlotte, N.C.	9.2	6.0
Omaha	4.4	3.7	Chicago	9.1	7.0
Pittsburgh	7.2	5.6	Sacramento	10.3	7.2
Portland, Maine	6.1	4.6	Tampa	8.3	6.1
Average	6.1	4.7	Average	9.2	6.6

Source: Bureau of Labor Statistics data.

allow for differences in treatment effects by local unemployment rates, four of the cities we chose had relatively low unemployment rates at the start of our study (Dallas, Omaha, Pittsburgh, and Portland, Maine) and four of which had relatively high unemployment rates in 2012 (Chicago, Sacramento, Tampa, and Charlotte, North Carolina). Table 1 contains city-level unemployment rates for the eight cities in 2012 (early in our study period) and 2014 (late in our study period). The table illustrates the general improvement in the labor market during the extended recovery from the Great Recession. Unemployment rates fell in both the low- and the high-unemployment cities, and the relative ordering of cities by unemployment rate was preserved across groups.

To further enhance the external validity of the experiment, the résumés were crafted to be plausible and tailored to prospective employers in each of the eight cities we studied. Plausibility was created, as in Marianne Bertrand and Sendhil Mullainanthan (2004), by crafting the fictitious résumés from actual résumés posted on a site we did not use for submissions. These actual source résumés were posted for job openings in the occupations we study, but in a city that was not in the experiment. Each element of each source résumé was migrated to each of the eight target cities in which the experiment was conducted. This migration was performed by finding residential addresses,

employers, and institutions of postsecondary education in the target city that are similar to those listed on the source résumé.[3] Names were not migrated but instead were selected to be common, according to the Social Security Administration, among people of the relevant age cohort, but not Hispanic in origin. The names selected are neutral with regard to race and ethnicity—not obviously Asian, African American, or Hispanic. The appendix presents a sample of four résumés that vary with regard to the characteristics of interest: unemployment duration, age, and interim job.

The basic structure of the actual experiment follows now standard methods for "correspondence studies" (see, for example, Bertrand and Mullainathan 2004; Lahey 2008; and KLN). Specifically, we sent our crafted fictitious résumés in matched pairs or quadruples to openings posted on two online job boards. The experiment proceeded in four rounds. Round 1 only randomly assigns unemployment duration to one of two résumés sent to the same job posting. Round 2 differs from round 1 in that both résumés sent to the same job posting receive a random unemployment duration. Round 3 differed from round 2 in that also the presence of an interim job is randomly assigned (independently of unemployment duration). Round 4 differs from round 3 in that also the implied age of the résumé is randomly assigned. Details of each round are as follows:

3. Similarity for the address was defined by the (minimum) Mahalanobis distance between the source address and the target by census tract age, race, education, and income level. Similarity for employers was, for large businesses, achieved by replacing the source employer with its chief competitor in the target city. For small businesses, similarity was achieved by simple search for a target business in the same industry with approximately the same age and number of employees. For government work, the source employer was simply switched to that of the target jurisdiction. Similarity of the postsecondary schools was identified by simple search using national ranking, public or private status, size, and distance to the target city.

Round 1: 2,054 applications for 1,027 jobs. Conducted between March and May 2012, the first round involved submitting two applications (treatment and control) to each of 1,027 job openings spread across the eight cities. In this and all other rounds, the number of applications was roughly proportional to city size. The control applicant to each job had always just entered unemployment, whereas the treatment applicant had been unemployed for a number of weeks drawn at random from the set $\{4, 12, 24, 52\}$. The beginning of the unemployment spell was indicated on the résumé by the end date of the applicant's most recent job. Thus the control applicant's résumé indicated that her most recent job had ended in the month just prior to the month the application was made. The applicant's age varied (thirty-five, forty, fifty-five, or fifty-six) across applications, but age did not vary within the applicant pair for specific job postings. Age was identified by year of graduation from college and reinforced by the employment history. Formatting of résumés was randomly varied to avoid detection of the experiment.

Round 2: 2,430 applications for 1,215 jobs. In the second round, conducted between July and September 2012, the experimental design was identical to the first round with one exception: each applicant had been unemployed for a number of weeks drawn at random, without replacement, from the set $\{0, 4, 12, 24, 52\}$. This change in design allowed us to account for the possibility that the two applicants in a pair were being directly compared by an employer and the control applicant, newly unemployed, was being mistaken for someone currently employed.

Round 3: 1,668 applications for 834 jobs. The third round of the experiment, conducted between November 2013 and April 2014 used the same methods as in round 2 to submit applications in matched pairs.[4]

In this round, however, we introduced the possibility that the applicant held an interim job. Applicants holding an interim job had just started work the month prior to the month of the application, in a relatively low-skilled position at a chain restaurant, a big-box retail store, or a grocery store. These interim jobs involved serving food, stocking shelves, or assisting customers at a register or on a retail floor, and were thus quite different from the career work on the rest of the résumé. The randomization with respect to interim job was conducted at the application level, within matched pair. Thus, both the control and the treatment could be employed in an interim job with some unemployment spell or unemployed with some other unemployment duration. We did not update the start dates of the résumés in this round, with the result that the applicants "aged." Applicant's age varied across job postings from the set $\{36, 37, 41, 42, 56, 57, 58\}$.

Round 4: 6,072 applications for 1,518 jobs. In the fourth and final round, conducted between April and August 2014, we submitted four (rather than two) applications to each of 1,581 openings spread across the eight cities. This increase in the number of applications per job was motivated by two interests. First, we wanted to speed data collection, which experience indicated could be done without risking detection of the experiment by doubling the number of applications per job. Second, we wanted to produce experimental variation in age, within job. Thus, the four applications per job consisted of two each from two different groups. One pair consisted of younger applicants (thirty-seven or forty-two), and the other consisted of older applicants (fifty-seven or fifty-eight). Randomization with respect to holding an interim job and variation in unemployment duration was as in round 3.

4. The delay between rounds 2 and 3 was unintentional—it resulted from two of the authors (Silverman and von Wachter) moving their primary appointments to different universities. Additionally, data were inadvertently collected in Portland, Oregon, rather than Portland, Maine, in round 3. Since the relevant résumés were tailored to Portland, Maine, we do not include the Portland, Oregon, applications in the analysis. Thus, there are only seven cities in round 3.

The fact that the experiment occurred in four stages provided additional sources of variation while not affecting our results. In the empirical work, we begin by analyzing the four rounds separately. We then show that the results that are comparable between the four rounds are sufficiently similar that we can analyze them together.

A MODEL OF LEARNING ABOUT APPLICANT QUALITY

When employers evaluate an applicant for a job, they have incomplete information about the quality of the worker. Employers use observable information available in the worker's application to form an expectation about the worker's quality. This information includes, among other things, worker demographics, education, work history, including characteristics on prior jobs, and unemployment experience. In this section we develop a very simple model of employer learning about applicant quality in order to motivate the analysis and to provide clear predictions and a clear framework for interpreting the results of the audit study.

We assume a profit-maximizing, risk-neutral firm with a single worker. The output (Y) of the firm is equal to the quality of the worker (μ). We assume all potential workers will be paid the same wage so that the firm is interested in hiring the most able worker among applicants for its job opening.[5] Our model captures the employer's process of integrating available information to form an expectation of applicant quality.[6]

Consider applicant i. The firm has incomplete information about μ_i and makes an inference based on a set of k noisy signals. For the purposes of our study, these signals include, among other background information, the applicant's unemployment experience, age, and whether the applicant holds an interim job. Let s_{ij} represent the noisy j^{th} signal of μ_i. We assume this j^{th} signal satisfies

$$s_{ij} = \frac{1}{\alpha_j}\mu_i + \gamma_{ij}, \qquad (1)$$

where γ_{ij} is a normally distributed random variable with zero mean and variance σ_j^2. The parameters α_j are normalizations that account for the fact that some signals are positive and some are negative as well as for differential scaling of the signals. For example, unemployment duration would have $\alpha_j < 0$, but interim job might have $\alpha_j > 0$. The employer's inference problem is to combine the available information on $s_{ij}, j = 1, \ldots, k$ optimally in order to derive an expected value for applicant quality ($E(\mu_i| s_{i1}, \ldots, s_{ik})$).

Think of s_{ij} as prior information on applicant quality so that the posterior beliefs about applicant quality can be derived using a standard Bayesian procedure. Given the distributional assumption regarding the γ_{ij}, each signal s_{ij} about applicant quality is normally distributed with mean $\mu_i|\alpha_j$ and variance σ_j^2. In describing how information about s_{ij} is combined to form the employer's posterior distribution on applicant quality, it is convenient to use the precisions of the random variables rather than the variances. The precision (h) of a random variable is the inverse of the variance, so that s_{ij} with variance σ_j^2 has precision $h_j \equiv 1/\sigma_j^2$. In this normal Bayesian updating model, the posterior distribution of the employer's beliefs about μ_i is normal with a mean that is a precision-weighted average of the k signals. The posterior expectation is

$$E(\mu_i \mid s_{i1}, \ldots, s_{ik}) = \frac{\sum_{j=1}^{k} h_j \alpha_j s_{ij}}{\sum_{j=1}^{k} h_j}. \qquad (2)$$

Consider the implication of the model for the effect of signal m on the likelihood of callback. The marginal effect of a change in s_{im} is

$$\frac{\partial E(\mu_i)}{\partial s_{im}} = \alpha_m \left[\frac{h_m}{\sum_{j=1}^{k} h_j} \right], \qquad (3)$$

---

5. Note that the quality of applicants will likely depend on the offered wage.

6. Although we do not include sequential search in our model, such a model would clearly have the property that the employer will set a reservation worker quality level as part of the search process and call back those applicants whose expected quality exceeds this threshold. Thus, applicants with higher expected quality will be more likely to receive a callback.

which takes the sign of α_m. If signal m is unemployment duration, then, presumably, $\alpha_m \leq 0$, and the marginal effect of unemployment duration is negative. Thus, workers with longer unemployment duration have lower posterior mean worker quality. This makes their posterior expected quality less likely to exceed the necessary threshold and reduces the likelihood of callback. Analogously, if signal m is age and age is a negative signal of worker quality, then $\alpha_m \leq 0$ and older workers have lower posterior mean worker quality. Again, this makes their posterior expected quality less likely to exceed the necessary threshold and reduces the likelihood of callback. Given the opposing predictions regarding the value of holding a low-level interim job, the sign of α_m in this case is unknown, and we have no clear prediction on how the likelihood of callback varies with the holding of a low-level interim job.

There are at least two second-order predictions of the model. First, related to unemployment duration, it is likely that there is more information about applicant quality in the duration of unemployment when the labor market is tighter (lower unemployment rate). In terms of the model, the precision associated with the unemployment duration signal is higher where the local unemployment rate is lower so that there is relatively more updating based on unemployment duration. Formally,

$$\frac{\partial^2 E(\mu_i)}{\partial s_{im} \partial h_m} = \alpha_m \left[\frac{1}{\sum_{j=1}^{k} h_j} \right] \left[1 - \frac{h_m}{\sum_{j=1}^{k} h_j} \right], \quad (4)$$

which has the sign of α_m. Because $\alpha_m \leq 0$ where s_m represents unemployment duration, the negative marginal effect of unemployment duration on the likelihood of callback (equation 3) is larger in absolute value in tighter labor markets (equation 4). In other words, the negative marginal effect of unemployment duration on the callback rate will be more substantial in stronger labor markets.[7]

The other second-order prediction of the model is that where there are more signals of worker quality, the marginal effect of any one signal will be smaller in absolute value. This is

relevant when thinking about the role of applicant age. An older worker has more prior work experience. This comes in the form of more and perhaps longer prior jobs. In the context of the model, longer experience and more information increase the number of signals (k). The marginal effect of a particular signal is given in equation 3. On inspection of this relationship, an increase in k simply increases the denominator in the term in brackets. The result is a reduction in the absolute value of the marginal effect any particular existing signal. This predicts, for example, that the marginal effect of unemployment duration will be smaller for older workers. Intuitively, older workers have a longer employment history that will dilute the effect of recent unemployment on the likelihood of callback.

A final prediction is not based strictly on the updating model. If an employer has a great need for workers as indicated by a higher callback rate for applicants to the particular job, then the employer may not be as selective. The result will be that the threshold posterior mean worker quality necessary for a callback will be lower where demand is high. A clear implication of this is that the marginal effect of particular worker attributes (unemployment duration, age, and the holding of a low-level interim job in case) on the likelihood of callback will be lower for less selective employers.

The foregoing model presents only one way in which employers may use résumé information to draw inferences about applicant suitability for the job. Other approaches may include mechanical screening of résumés to filter out workers that are an obvious mismatch. Another approach would be screening based on tastes for particular worker attributes, such as age. We will not be able to test between alternative approaches, but keep those in mind when interpreting our findings.

DESCRIPTIVE ANALYSIS

We begin by separately analyzing the effect of our three main factors—duration of unemployment, worker age, and presence of interim job—separately. In the next section we analyze the effect of these characteristics jointly. To set

---

7. This is a result found by Kroft, Lange, and Notowidigdo (2013).

Table 2. Average Callback Rate, by Base Unemployment and Round

Weeks of Unemployment	Rounds 1–4	Round 1	Round 2	Round 3	Round 4
Zero	0.101	0.103	0.150	0.085	0.082
	(0.006)	(0.010)	(0.016)	(0.016)	(0.009)
Four	0.099	0.121	0.124	0.081	0.089
	(0.007)	(0.021)	(0.015)	(0.015)	(0.009)
Twelve	0.111	0.122	0.163	0.094	0.096
	(0.007)	(0.021)	(0.017)	(0.016)	(0.010)
Twenty-four	0.108	0.085	0.144	0.105	0.010
	(0.007)	(0.016)	(0.016)	(0.017)	(0.010)
Fifty-two	0.100	0.074	0.141	0.100	0.089
	(0.007)	(0.016)	(0.016)	(0.017)	(0.009)
All	0.104	0.101	0.144	0.093	0.091
	(0.004)	(0.008)	(0.009)	(0.009)	(0.005)
N job postings	4,594	1,027	1,215	834	1,518
N applications	12,224	2,054	2,430	1,668	6,072

Source: Authors' calculations.
Note: Numbers in parentheses are standard errors clustered at the job level.

the stage, note that our mean callback rate across all rounds is 10.4 percent. One plausibility check that our résumés work as intended is that the callback rate was significantly higher (12.2 percent) in our low-unemployment cities than in our high-unemployment cities (8.9 percent), with a p-value of the difference smaller than 0.0005.

Duration of Unemployment
A primary focus of this study is to examine the effect of unemployment duration on the likelihood of an employer callback to a job application. All four rounds incorporated variation in weeks of unemployment including base values of zero weeks, four weeks, twelve weeks, twenty-four weeks, and fifty-two weeks.[8] Table 2 contains mean callback rates overall and by round for each of the five baseline values for unemployment duration. There is no systematic relationship, positive or negative, between the probability of callback and the duration of un-

employment. The hypothesis that the callback rates are equal across unemployment duration treatments cannot be rejected (p-value = 0.53 overall).[9]

The variation in unemployment duration treatment *within* job posting in each round offers the opportunity to examine within-posting variation in callback rates by unemployment treatment. The fixed-effect conditional logit analysis due to Gary Chamberlain (1980) is a natural way to estimate this within-posting effect. Intuitively, the fixed-effect conditional logit conditions on the number of successes (callbacks) within each job posting and asks whether the applicants with longer unemployment durations were less likely to be among those who received the fixed number of callbacks. This approach ignores the job postings for which there was no variation in the outcome. In the 3,076 job postings in rounds 1 to 3, for which there were 2 applications per job posting, 2,591 postings had no callbacks and

8. These are the weeks of unemployment implicit in the applications at fixed dates. Since the applications were submitted over a period of time following that date, the actual durations seen by potential employers are somewhat longer. Actual unemployment duration exceeds each base value by about 4 weeks on average (standard deviation of about 1.1 weeks for each base value).

9. The hypothesis of equality of callback rates across unemployment duration treatments cannot be rejected within any of the four rounds, with p-values ranging from 0.23 in round 1 to 0.71 in round 3.

Table 3. Average Callback Rate, by Unemployment and Number of Callbacks

Weeks of Unemployment	(1) Rounds 1–3 One Callback	(2) Round 4 One to Three Callbacks	(3) Round 4 One Callback	(4) Round 4 Two Callbacks	(5) Round 4 Three Callbacks
Zero	0.493	0.354	0.250	0.397	0.690
	(0.041)	(0.030)	(0.034)	(0.055)	(0.081)
Four	0.457	0.376	0.204	0.493	0.741
	(0.052)	(0.033)	(0.037)	(0.050)	(0.081)
Fourteen	0.548	0.432	0.267	0.524	0.795
	(0.054)	(0.033)	(0.036)	(0.063)	(0.057)
Twenty-four	0.505	0.402	0.271	0.500	0.774
	(0.052)	(0.031)	(0.034)	(0.056)	(0.071)
Fifty-two	0.505	0.421	0.250	0.577	0.731
	(0.053)	(0.032)	(0.036)	(0.054)	(0.081)
N job postings	256	273	150	85	38

Source: Authors' calculations.

Notes: By construction, the average callback rate is 0.5 for postings with one callback in rounds 1 to 3. In round 4, the callback rate is 0.25 for postings with one callback, 0.5 for postings with two callbacks, and 0.75 for postings with three callbacks. Numbers in parentheses are standard errors clustered at the job level.

229 postings had 2 callbacks. This leaves 256 postings with 1 callback. In the 1,518 job postings in round 4, where there were 4 applications per job posting, 1,215 postings had no callbacks and 30 postings had 4 callbacks. This leaves 150 postings with 1 callback, 85 postings with 2 callbacks, and 38 postings with 3 callbacks.

We now present estimates of the average callback rates by unemployment treatment conditional on the number of callbacks received for the job posting (we discuss estimation of the full Chamberlain fixed effects logit model in a later section, "Multivarite Analysis"). Table 3 contains these callback rates conditional on the number of callbacks received. Column 1 of the table contains average callback rates by unemployment treatment for job postings in rounds 1 to 3 with a single callback. There is no obvious relationship between the callback rate and the unemployment treatment, and the hypothesis that callback rates are equal across treatments cannot be rejected (p-value = 0.85). Column 2 shows average callback rates in round 4 for job postings with one to three callbacks for each treatment. These appear to show, counter to expectations, that callback rates are higher where a longer unemployment spell is indicated on the application. However, once again the hypothesis that callback rates are equal across treatments cannot be rejected (p-value = 0.46).

The last three columns of table 3 shows average callback rates in round 4 for job postings with one, two, and three callbacks, respectively, for each treatment. In no case can the hypothesis that callback rates are equal across treatments be rejected (p-values = 0.78, 0.32, and 0.91 respectively).

The theory outlined in "A Model of Learning about Applicant Quality" implied that the marginal effect of unemployment duration will be larger in tighter labor markets. This suggests that there might be a relationship between unemployment duration and the probability of callback in the low-unemployment cities but not in the high-unemployment cities. We do not show the results here, but we repeated our analysis separately in the low- and high-unemployment cities. No perceptible relationship between unemployment duration and the callback rate was found in either group of cities.

Table 4. Average Callback Rate, by Age and Round

	All Rounds	Round 1	Round 2	Round 3	Round 4
Age 35–37	0.110	0.092	0.147	0.092	0.103
	(0.006)	(0.014)	(0.016)	(0.016)	(0.009)
Age 40–42	0.119	0.112	0.150	0.103	0.111
	(0.007)	(0.015)	(0.016)	(0.016)	(0.010)
Age 55–58	0.089	0.099	0.136	0.084	0.076
	(0.005)	(0.014)	(0.016)	(0.014)	(0.006)
All ages	0.104	0.101	0.144	0.093	0.091
	(0.004)	(0.008)	(0.009)	(0.009)	(0.005)
N job postings	4,594	1,027	1,215	834	1,518
N applications	12,224	2,054	2,430	1,668	6,072

Source: Authors' calculations.

Note: Numbers in parentheses are standard errors clustered at the job level.

Age

Figure 4 showed that older job losers are more likely to be unemployed at a fixed date subsequent to a job loss. It has been a long-standing question in labor economics whether the stark differences by age shown in the figure may partly reflect a reluctance by employers to hire older job applicants. More generally, age may be an important factor for employers when selecting new employees. This motivated the random variation of age of applicant in the résumés we submitted as part of our audit study, and, in this section we present our estimates of callback rates as a function of applicant age.

Two applications were submitted to each of 3,076 job postings in rounds 1 to 3, and each job posting was randomly assigned to an age category. Both applications to each job posting listed the same birth date as implied by the year of graduation from college.[10] Approximately one-third of the job postings were randomly assigned in each age category (32.5 percent aged thirty-five to thirty-seven, 33.5 percent aged forty to forty-two, and 34.0 percent aged fifty-five to fifty-eight). Four applications were submitted to each of 1,518 job postings in round 4. Two applications per posting were randomly assigned to be in the oldest age category (fifty-five to fifty-eight) and the remaining two applications were assigned to be in a younger category. The result is that in round 4, roughly one-quarter of the applicants are thirty-five to thirty-seven years of age, one-quarter of the applicants are forty to forty-two years of age, and half of the applicants are fifty-five to fifty-eight years old.

The first column of table 4 contains the callback rates for all four rounds, both overall (last row) and by age group. The overall callback rate is 10.4 percent. There is not a significant difference between the callback rates for applicants aged thirty-five to thirty-seven and applicants aged forty to forty-two (p-value of difference = 0.97). However, the callback rate for applicants aged fifty-five to fifty-eight is substantially and significantly lower (by about two percentage points) than the callback rate for younger workers (p-values of differences < 0.01).

The remaining columns of table 4 contain the callback rates separately by round. While mean callback rates for workers age fifty-five to fifty-eight are lower than the average callback rates for those thirty-five to forty-two, these differences are not statistically significant from zero in the first three rounds. However, there is a substantial difference by age in round 4. In round 4, applicants aged fifty-five to fifty-eight have a 7.6 percent callback rate compared with callback rates in the 10 to 11 percent range

10. In fact, the actual ages of the two applications for a posting could differ by one year, given that age is determined by birth date and the applications were sometimes submitted on different dates.

Table 5. Average Callback Rate, Round 4, by Age and Number of Callbacks

	One to Three Callbacks	One Callback	Two Callbacks	Three Callbacks
Age 35–37	0.457	0.346	0.536	0.737
	(0.029)	(0.026)	(0.067)	(0.058)
Age 40–42	0.511	0.326	0.709	0.763
	(0.029)	(0.028)	(0.050)	(0.058)
Age 55–58	0.311	0.163	0.376	0.750
	(0.022)	(0.019)	(0.043)	(0.041)
N job postings	273	150	85	38

Source: Authors' calculations.

Notes: By construction, the average callback rate is 0.25 for postings with one callback, 0.5 for postings with two callbacks, and 0.75 for postings with three callbacks. Numbers in parentheses are standard errors clustered at the job level.

for younger applicants (*p*-values of differences < 0.005).

The variation in age of applicant within job posting in round 4 offers the opportunity to examine within-posting variation in callback rates by age. As we did earlier with respect to the unemployment treatment, we focus on the job postings for which there was variation in the outcome. We ignore the job postings for which there was no variation in the outcome (the 1,215 of 1,518 postings with no callbacks and the 30 of 1,518 postings with 4 callbacks). This leaves 150 postings with 1 callback, 85 postings with 2 callbacks, and 38 postings with 3 callbacks). We do not estimate Chamberlain fixed effects logit model directly at this point; we do present estimates of the average callback rates by age group conditional on the number of callbacks received for the job posting

Table 5 contains mean callback rates in round 4 for postings that received one to three callbacks. The evidence is clear. Applicants in the oldest age groups received callbacks at a significantly lower rate than applicants in either of the two younger groups. For the 150 postings in which one of four applications received callbacks (for an aggregate callback rate of 25 percent), applicants in their fifties received callbacks at a rate sixteen percentage points less than applicants in their thirties or forties (about a 50 percent lower callback rate). For the 85 postings, postings in which two of

four applications received callbacks (for an aggregate callback rate of 50 percent), applicants in their fifties received callbacks at a rate that is sixteen percentage points less than applicants in their thirties (about a 30 percent lower callback rate) and 30.3 percentage points less than applicants in their forties (about a 47 percent lower callback rate). There is no difference in callback rates by age for the 38 postings in which three of the four applications received callbacks. Applicants in each of the three age groups had callback rates very close to the 75 percent overall rate.

Overall, table 5 confirms the negative effect of age on callback, even holding the job-specific callback rate constant. In addition, the finding of no difference in callback rates by age category for job postings with three callbacks is consistent with our hypothesis that worker characteristics are less important when employers are less selective, as indicated in this case by callbacks to three of four applicants. The high callback rate may reflect a need by the employers to fill a large number of jobs quickly. In this case the employer would accept most of the applicants and be less sensitive to individual characteristics. This implies that these employers should be less sensitive to other worker characteristics as well, and we examine this directly below. However, the overall pattern is clear. Employers are generally substantially less likely to call back older job applicants.

Interim Jobs

An important decision facing an unemployed worker is whether to take an interim job at a lower level than, and not directly relevant to, the job the worker is seeking. The obvious positive aspect of taking such a job is that it provides income to the unemployed worker, particularly if the worker is not receiving unemployment compensation. Another possible advantage is that potential employers may infer from the fact that the worker has taken such a job that he or she is hardworking and strongly motivated to stay employed. However, it is possible that potential employers will infer that the worker is not of appropriate quality precisely because he or she has been working in a lower-level job. In some cases this may be the result of the employer's using some kind of automated or cursory screening of job applications that rejects applications if their most recent job is not relevant to the job for which the applicant is applying.

Which of these potential mechanisms is at work or which dominates is an empirical question that we address. Beginning in round 3, we introduced a treatment to interrupt a spell of unemployment with work at a low-level interim job. We defined an interim job as one with low wages and for which the candidate appeared ill matched in terms of education and previous experience. For example, the interim jobs included sales associate or cashier at a big box or grocery store, and restaurant server. The résumés with such jobs indicate that the job was currently held by the new applicants and started in the month just prior to the application. These jobs interrupted an unemployment spell of varying duration identical to those unemployment spells we investigate directly (zero, four, twelve, twenty-four, or fifty-two weeks). The randomization with respect to interim job was conducted at the application level, within job posting. Interim jobs appeared on an application with probability 0.5. In round 3, with two applications per job posting, there could be zero, one, or two applications with an interim job. In round 4, with four applications per job posting, there could be zero, one, two, three, or four applications with an interim job.

Of the 834 job postings analyzed in round

3, for 219 (26.3 percent) neither of the applications indicated an interim job, for 391 (46.9 percent) one of the two indicated an interim job, and for 224 (26.9 percent) both applications indicated an interim job. Of the 1,518 job postings analyzed in round 4, for 77 (5.1 percent) none of the applications included an interim job, for 438 (28.9 percent) one of the applications included an interim job, for 516 (34.0 percent) two of the applications included an interim job, for 419 (27.6 percent) three of the applications included an interim job, and for 68 (4.5 percent) all four applications included an interim job.

The applications in rounds 3 and 4 varied randomly in unemployment duration and age, and this variation is independent of the variation in interim job. We account for these other dimensions of variation in the multivariate analysis in a later section.

Table 6 contains mean callback rates for rounds 3 and 4 by whether or not an interim job was indicated on the application. The overall callback rate in rounds 3 and 4 was 9.2 percent. The callback rate was 9.8 percent where there was no interim job versus 8.5 percent where there was an interim job. This difference of 1.3 percentage points (15 percent) is statistically significant (p-value = 0.038). When analyzed separately by round, there is no difference in round 3 and a larger statistically significant difference in round 4 (9.9 percent with no interim job versus 8.4 percent with an interim job).

Given the within-job randomization of the existence of an interim job, we once again examine how callbacks vary with an interim job within job posting. Again, this analysis is restricted to applications to job postings for which there was variation in callback. Table 7 contains mean callback rates for postings in round 3 that received one callback and in round 4 for postings that received one to three callbacks. Although the point estimate of the difference in callback rates for single-callback postings in round 3 is negative and substantial in magnitude, this difference is not statistically significant, given the small number of postings (fifty-nine) that meet the sample criteria. The difference in callback rates for postings with one to three callbacks in round 4 is a statistically significant 7.1 percentage points

Table 6. Average Callback Rate, by Interim Job and Round

	All	Round 3	Round 4
All	0.0916	0.0929	0.0912
	(0.0047)	(0.0089)	(0.0055)
No interim job	0.0982	0.0965	0.0986
	(0.0058)	(0.0116)	(0.0067)
Interim job	0.0849	0.0894	0.0837
	(0.0056)	(0.0109)	(0.0064)
Difference	−0.0132	−0.0071	−0.0149
	(0.0063)	(0.0136)	(0.0072)

Source: Authors' calculations.
Note: Numbers in parentheses are standard errors clustered at the job level.

Table 7. Average Callback Rate, Rounds 3 and 4, by Interim Job and Number of Callbacks

	Round 3, One Callback	Round 4, One to Three Callbacks	Round 4, One Callback	Round 4, Two Callbacks	Round 4, Three Callbacks
No interim job	0.556	0.432	0.314	0.515	0.718
	(0.049)	(0.017)	(0.018)	(0.025)	(0.035)
Interim job	0.453	0.361	0.184	0.485	0.784
	(0.042)	(0.020)	(0.018)	(0.025)	(0.037)
Difference	−0.102	−0.071	−0.130	−0.029	0.066
	(0.090)	(0.029)	(0.035)	(0.050)	(0.071)
N postings	59	273	150	85	38

Source: Authors' calculations.
Notes: By construction, the average callback rate in round 3 is 0.5 for postings with one callback. Similarly, the average callback rate in round 4 is 0.25 for postings with one callback, 0.5 for postings with two callbacks, and 0.75 for postings with three callbacks. Numbers in parentheses are standard errors clustered at the job level

(p-value = 0.015). This difference is driven by a large negative difference in callbacks by interim job status (13.0 percentage points) for the 150 postings that received a one call-back (p-value < 0.0005). The differences in callback rates by interim job status for postings with two or three callbacks are not statistically significant.

The overall pattern of results suggests that holding a job that is lower skill and irrelevant to the job for which the individual is applying reduces the likelihood of a callback, at least for selective employers. It appears that an unemployed worker is better off remaining unemployed and searching for work rather than being employed in a low-level job while searching.

Alternatively, if an applicant has taken a low-level interim job, she may be better off not listing this job on her résumé.

In addition, again the finding of a significant difference in callback rates by interim job status in round 4 only for jobs with one callback and not for jobs with more callbacks is (as with age) consistent with our hypothesis that worker characteristics are more important when employers are more selective, as indicated in this case by callbacks to a single applicant.

MULTIVARIATE ANALYSIS

We now turn to a multivariate analysis that models the probability of callback as a function of unemployment duration, age, and interim job. This analysis first uses both within- and between-posting variation in application characteristics. We choose the logit model for several reasons. In principle it should provide a better approximation of the functional form for binary choice probabilities with a relative low incidence.[11] Given the canonical sample design of recent audit studies that provide random variation *within*, a particular advantage of the logit model is that it provides a consistent approach that allows us to obtain estimates that rely on within-posting variation via the Chamberlain fixed effects logit model. Finally, the logit model allow us to contrast the fixed effects estimate with a random effects logit, our preferred specification.

The random effects model accounts for the fact that job postings are randomly drawn from the underlying population and may differ in their mean callback rate. This model is appropriate (yields consistent estimates) where the baseline variation across job postings in their callback rates is uncorrelated with the observed applicant characteristics of interest. Given our approach in sending résumés to job listings with key characteristics varying randomly, we would not expect the job-specific callback rate to be correlated with résumé characteristics so that estimates derived using the random effects model should be consistent. More generally, since the three treatments were assigned independently to résumés, there is no reason to expect that the multivariate analysis in general, and the conditional logit in particular, will affect our main results.

Table 8 presents the main results of our multivariate analysis. We report our findings in terms of odds ratios, which for small probabilities are approximately the ratio of probabilities

of callback given a treatment versus no treatment.[12] Age enters as a dummy variable for whether a worker is fifty-five to fifty-eight years of age (rather than thirty-five to forty-two). The first three columns present results for the logit, random effects logit, and fixed effects logit, respectively, pooling four rounds.

Recall that in all four rounds unemployment durations differ among applications sent to the same job posting; in addition, in rounds 3 and 4 there is also variation in incidence of interim jobs among applications sent to the same job posting; in addition, in round 4 age differs among applications sent to the same job posting as well. The simple logit and random effects logit models (columns 1 and 2) use all available variation for all factors, even if they were not randomly assigned within jobs. The between-job variation yields valid estimates, since the pairing of résumés with jobs was effectively random with respect to job and résumé characteristics. To make sure our results are not affected by the inclusion of variation between jobs, we then implement the fixed effects logit model, which relies only on within-posting variation. The within variation for unemployment duration is coming from all four rounds; it is coming from round 4 for age; it is coming from rounds 3 and 4 for interim job. To examine a specification where all three factors are treated symmetrically, we then restrict the analysis to round 4, where there are four applications per job posting and within-job posting variation in all three factors. The logit, random effects logit, and fixed effects logit for data from round 4 only is shown in columns 4 to 6 of table 8.

Given that we have purposefully chosen to work with a homogeneous groups of workers, the only control variable, other than dummies

---

11. We have reproduced these findings with linear probability and probit models, and the results are not affected by the choice of functional form.

12. Let $p(1) \equiv Pr\{Callback = 1 | X, D = 1\}$ and $p(0) \equiv Pr\{Callback = 1 | X, D = 0\}$, where D represents one of our right hand side dummy variables and X represents the remaining variables in the model. Then the odds ratio R is defined as

$$R \equiv \frac{p(1)/(1-p(1))}{p(0)/(1-p(0))} = exp\{\beta_D\}$$

where β_D is the coefficient on D. Where the probabilities involved are small, the odds ratio is approximately the ratio of probabilities.

Table 8. Logit, Random Effects Logit, and Conditional Logit Estimates: Odds Ratios

Variable	(1) Logit All Rounds	(2) Random Effects Logit All Rounds	(3) Fixed Effects Logit All Rounds	(4) Logit Round 4	(5) Random Effects Logit Round 4	(6) Fixed Effects Logit Round 4
Four weeks	0.973	0.948	0.951	1.092	1.103	1.053
unemployed	(0.084)	(0.139)	(0.151)	(0.152)	(0.235)	(0.235)
Twelve weeks	1.140	1.260	1.278	1.206	1.388	1.413
unemployed	(0.100)	(0.181)	(0.203)	(0.181)	(0.289)	(0.312)
Twenty-four weeks	1.084	1.158	1.170	1.243	1.388	1.350
unemployed	(0.092)	(0.164)	(0.182)	(0.174)	(0.285)	(0.290)
Fifty-two weeks	0.990	1.111	1.178	1.092	1.310	1.353
unemployed	(0.086)	(0.163)	(0.188)	(0.154)	(0.278)	(0.301)
Age 55–58	0.791	0.566	0.531	0.687	0.528	0.529
	(0.055)	(0.059)	(0.063)	(0.056)	(0.063)	(0.063)
Interim job	0.850	0.725	0.715	0.839	0.735	0.728
	(0.065)	(0.088)	(0.092)	(0.073)	(0.095)	(0.100)
Low local	1.430	2.003	–	1.161	1.285	–
unemployment	(0.117)	(0.292)		(0.155)	(0.281)	
$\hat{\rho}$		0.780			0.704	
		(0.011)			(0.024)	
Log L	−4018.4	−3551.2	−569.9	−1840.8	−1515.2	−393.1
χ^2	4.14	4.52	4.42	2.86	4.02	4.20
p-value	0.39	0.34	0.35	0.58	0.40	0.38
Sample size	12,224	12,224	1,604	6,072	6,072	1,092

Source: Authors' calculations.
Notes: The χ^2 and p-value refer to the test statistic for the null hypothesis that the four coefficients on unemployment duration are jointly zero. Columns 1 and 2 include indicators for the round of the experiment. Numbers in parentheses are standard errors. Standard errors in columns 1 and 4 are clustered at the job level.

for rounds in columns 1 and 2, is a dummy for whether the city was initially classified as one of our low-unemployment cities (Dallas, Omaha, Pittsburgh, and Portland, Maine) or as one of our high-unemployment cities (Chicago, Sacramento, Tampa, and Charlotte, North Carolina). This effect is identified only from between- job-opening variation.

Overall and as expected, the results in table 8 confirm our three main findings from the previous section. There is no detectable effect of unemployment duration on callback rates. The χ^2 test statistic and corresponding p-value we present are for the null hypothesis that the four coefficients on the unemployment duration dummies are jointly equal to zero. In none of our models can we reject this null hypothesis. Again, we find there is a precisely estimated negative effect (an estimated odds ratio less than 1) of age on the callback rate. Finally, there is a substantial negative effect of reporting holding an interim job on the callback rate.

The first column of table 8 shows basic logit estimates pooling all four rounds, clustering standard errors at the job level. The second column adds random effects. As expected, controlling for random variation in the callback rates across openings improves the fit of the model substantially, as indicated by the improvement in the log-likelihood value, and reduces standard errors slightly. The odds ratio on age drops from 0.8 to 0.57. We have no economic explanation for this, since the random effects are not correlated with the independent variable. However, their presence changes the interpretation of the coefficient. Whereas the coefficients of the logit model can be interpreted as the average effect in the population, coefficients of the random effects model are the effects holding constant the within-opening callback propensity of a given job posting. The third column contains estimates of the Chamberlain fixed effects logit model, which uses only those job postings for which there was variation in callback rates (one callback in rounds 1 to 3 and one to three callbacks in round 4). As expected, given the random assignment of characteristics to résumés, the fixed effects estimates are virtually identical to the random effects estimates in column 2. In order to formally compare the random and fixed effects models, we performed a standard Hausman test comparing the random and fixed effect specifications. The value of the χ^2-test statistic (six degrees of freedom) is 2.69 with p-value of 0.85, implying we cannot reject the hypothesis that the fixed effects are uncorrelated with the factors included in the model.

Columns 4 to 6 show the results of repeating the analysis using only data from round 4, where there are four applications per opening and within-opening random variation in all three factors. The results are very similar compared to the model pooling all rounds. The only notable difference is that the coefficient on the dummy for a low local unemployment rate in columns 4 and 5 is no longer statistically significant (odds ratio not significantly different from 1). Note, however, that round 4 was fielded substantially later than the earlier rounds, and, while differences in unemployment rates across labor markets persisted, they were smaller in 2014 (when round 4 was fielded) than earlier.

Column 6 then presents findings for the fixed effects logit model for round 4. As we noted, the model is identified only from quadruplets of job applications in which callback varies (one to three callbacks to four applications). Dropping the 1,215 job postings for which we received no callbacks and the 30 job postings for which all four applications received callbacks leaves 1,092 observations for 273 job postings, a reduction of over 80 percent with respect to the full round 4 model in columns 4 and 5 (6,072 observations for 1,518 job postings). Nevertheless, the results in column 6 are very similar to those from the random effects logit in column 5, particularly with regard to the effect of age and interim job. Once again we performed a Hausman test of the hypothesis that the fixed effects are uncorrelated with the factors included in the model. The value of the χ^2-test statistic is 1.63 with p-value of 0.95, implying, as with the estimates for all four rounds, that we cannot reject the hypothesis that the fixed effects are uncorrelated with factors included in the model.

Overall, the results in table 8 confirm our main findings using the full power of the pooled sample. We tried various alternative specifications, none of which yielded additional statistically meaningful findings. In particular, we tried to assess whether the effects of unemployment duration, age, and interim jobs vary with the local unemployment rate. This is particularly interesting, because a key result of KLN's analysis was that the effect of unemployment duration on callback rates is lower in markets with higher unemployment rates. Not surprisingly, our finding, that unemployment duration on the résumé does not affect the callback rate, does not vary with the local unemployment rate. We also do not find that the effect of age or interim jobs varies by the state of the local labor market.

Again mirroring our univariate analysis, in table 9 we replicate the main logit model using observations only from round 4 separately for jobs with different numbers of callbacks. Column 1 from the table simply replicates column 4 from table 8. Column 2 then shows the results when we drop jobs for which either all or none of the résumés we sent received a callback. Our results on age and interim jobs are unchanged, with older applicants and applicants who re-

Table 9. Logit Estimates for Round 4 by Number of Callbacks: Odds Ratios

Variable	(1) Any Callback	(2) 1–3 Callbacks	(3) 1 Callback	(4) 2 Callbacks	(5) 3 Callbacks
Four weeks unemployed	1.092	1.119	0.761	1.470	1.400
	(0.152)	(0.225)	(0.248)	(0.524)	(0.850)
Twelve weeks unemployed	1.206	1.450	1.113	1.702	1.692
	(0.181)	(0.306)	(0.326)	(0.732)	(1.058)
Twenty-four weeks unemployed	1.243	1.287	1.227	1.525	1.564
	(0.174)	(0.253)	(0.363)	(0.561)	(1.004)
Fifty-two weeks unemployed	1.092	1.314	0.925	2.081	1.179
	(0.154)	(0.261)	(0.283)	(0.783)	(0.698)
Age 55–58	0.687	0.481	0.373	0.363	0.965
	(0.056)	(0.076)	(0.086)	(0.132)	(0.447)
Interim job	0.839	0.758	0.476	1.016	1.423
	(0.073)	(0.096)	(0.098)	(0.217)	(0.575)
Low local unemployment	1.161	0.963	1.072	0.991	0.941
	(0.155)	(0.091)	(0.048)	(0.037)	(0.087)
Constant	0.107	0.889	0.686	1.085	1.955
	(0.015)	(0.150)	(0.158)	(0.350)	(0.866)
Log L	−1840.8	−712.1	−326.9	−223.0	−84.5
χ^2	2.86	3.82	2.33	3.83	0.85
p-value	0.58	0.43	0.67	0.43	0.93
Sample size	6,072	1,092	600	340	152

Source: Authors' calculations.

Notes: The χ^2 and p-value refer to the test statistic for the null hypothesis that the four coefficients on unemployment duration are jointly zero. Numbers in parentheses are standard errors clustered at the job level.

port holding an interim job substantially less likely to receive a callback.[13] Columns 3 to 5 in table 9 then show the results for different number of callbacks per application. Consistent with the findings in our univariate analysis, the effect of age is present for only applications to jobs with one or two callbacks. There is no significant difference in callback rates by age for jobs with three callbacks. The effect of reporting the holding of an interim job is present only for applications to jobs with one callback. There is no significant difference in callback rates by interim jobs for jobs with two or three callbacks. Consistent with the earlier results, there is no relationship between the likelihood of callback and unemployment duration for any group we study.

The pattern of results in table 9 confirms our finding from the descriptive analysis presented earlier that employers who are eager to hire—and hence have a higher callback rate for their job posting—are less choosy—in other words, résumé characteristics appear to matter less in determining callback than for employers that have a lower callback rate for their job posting. When employers are "hungry" for workers, they are less selective than when they are not so needy. This supports the view that a strong labor market can play an important role in reducing the disadvantage of particular types of applicants, such as older applicants, who otherwise would be at a disadvantage when searching for jobs.

13. Note that column 2 in table 9 uses the same sample as column 6 in table 8, and the results are very similar.

RECONCILIATION WITH EARLIER WORK

Our finding of no relationship between the duration of unemployment and the likelihood of a callback for mature and older workers is consistent with some prior audit studies and at odds with others. The closest parallel studies that find important effects of unemployment duration is that of Kroft, Lange, and Notowidigdo (2013) and Ghayad (2014). Those studies finds that in the United States in the period 2011–2012 longer unemployment spells reduced callback significantly for younger workers. In contrast, Nunley and his colleagues (forthcoming) find that for relatively recent U.S. college graduates, unemployment duration has no effect on callbacks. The results of a Swedish audit study by Stefan Eriksson and Dan-Olof Rooth (2014) also pertain to younger workers, and imply no effect of shorter ongoing unemployment spells or past unemployment spells on the callback rate, but a negative effect of long current unemployment spells on callback for less-educated workers.

These studies all follow a comparable basic blueprint, but it is important to recognize that there are subtle and not-so-subtle differences in the implementation that could affect the results. In particular, our study is narrowly targeted at one type of worker in one type of job. By focusing on female administrative support workers with a four-year college education, we have a relatively clean design without having to control for confounding variables. But this is at the cost of potentially limited external validity. Additionally, we cover a fairly wide age range and do not include the very young workers who are the focus of some of the earlier studies.[14]

In this section we explore differences among the studies that could account for the difference in results. We focus particularly on the

KLN (Kroft, Lange, and Notowidigdo 2013) analysis because (1) like the study we report here (which we refer to as FSvW), it is U.S. based in the post–Great Recession period and encompasses most of our cities; (2) many of the jobs in their analysis are of the same type as ours, allowing for a direct comparison in callback rates; (3) the data are publicly available, allowing us to comparable models on their data and our data; (4) the paper has already been highly influential. All of this provides strong motivation to carefully assess the extent to which their approach is comparable to ours.[15]

In the following we focus on five key differences in the design and implementation of the KLN and FSvW studies that could account for the difference in results: (1) outcome measure, (2) type of job for which applications are submitted, (3) time period, (4) choice of cities, (5) education level, and (6) age range of the applicants. We consider each of these in turn.

The Outcome Measure

The KLN analysis focuses on callbacks that include a request for an interview while our study and those of Ghayad (2014) and Eriksson and Rooth (2013) focus on all callbacks, regardless of whether or not there was an interview request. This is reflected in a difference in reported callback rates. Our callback rate was 10.4 percent whereas the KLN callback-with-interview rate was 4.7 percent. Using data supplied by KLN, we calculate that the overall callback rate in KLN was 12.1 percent, comparable in magnitude to the callback rate we found.

The key question here is whether the KLN overall callback rate is negatively related to the length of unemployment spell. In order to address this question, we obtained a copy of the data KLN used. Using both these data and the data from our study, we estimate a simple

---

14. For further discussion of the implications of the variation in findings for the external validity of audit studies, see our summary paper (Farber, Silverman, and von Wachter 2016).

15. Ghayad (2014) collected data in the United States in 2012 for three broad occupations (administrative, sales, and professional) in four broad industries. Eriksson and Rooth (2014) collected data in Sweden in 2007 for seven occupations (business sales assistant, cleaner, construction worker, machine operator, motor-vehicle driver, restaurant worker, and sales assistant). In contrast, our data were collected from 2012 to 2014 for a single broad occupation (white-collar office jobs such as administrative or executive assistants, receptionists, secretaries, and office associates).

Table 10. Reanalysis of the Data on Applications from Kroft, Notowidigdo, and Lange (2013) [KLN] Restricted to the Cities Included in Farber, Silverman, and von Wachter (2017) [FSvW]

Sample	N Applications	Callback Rate	Marginal Effect of Months Unemployed
(1) FSvW data	12,224	10.37	0.00001
			(0.00061)
(2) KLN callbacks and interviews	9,236	4.54	-0.00086
			(0.00024)
(3) KLN, all callbacks	9,236	12.05	-0.00141
			(0.00024)
(4) KLN, administrative and clerical jobs	2,690	3.61	-0.00079
			(0.00037)
(5) KLN, four-year college	3,519	12.56	-0.00202
			(0.00053)
(6) KLN, FSvW cities	1,130	12.12	-0.00192
			(0.00094)
(7) KLN, non-FSvW cities	8,106	12.04	-0.00133
			(0.00037)
(8) KLN, 19–22 years old	674	10.68	-0.00515
			(0.00186)
(9) KLN, 23–26 years old	3,840	11.59	-0.00078
			(0.00054)
(10) KLN, 27–30 years old	3,622	12.78	-0.00197
			(0.00055)
(11) KLN, 31–39 years old	1,100	12.09	-0.00268
			(0.00099)

Source: Authors' calculations.

Notes: Marginal effects on the probability of callback calculated from logit model of callback. Robust standard errors clustered by job id in parentheses.

model of the effect of unemployment duration on the probability of callback. The model we use is a simple logit model with only a constant and the duration of unemployment in months. Table 10 contains the results of this analysis. The first row of this table contains the estimate of the marginal effect of unemployment duration on the callback rate for the overall FSvW sample, and it confirms the finding of no significant relationship in our sample. The second and third rows of this table contain estimates of the marginal effect of unemployment duration on the callback rate for the overall KLN sample for the two definitions of callback. The estimate in row 2 uses KLN's preferred callback-with-interview measure and confirms their finding of a significant negative effect of un-

employment duration. Our reanalysis of the KLN overall callback measure in row 3 shows an even stronger negative relationship between the duration of unemployment and the probability of callback. Thus the difference in outcome measure is not a factor that can explain the difference in findings. The point estimate in row 3 of the table implies a reduction in the probability of callback of about 0.8 percentage points per month of unemployment. This is a reduction of about 7 percent at the mean of 12.05 percent, a substantial effect.

In order to maintain comparability with our analysis, our reanalysis of the KLN data continues using the measure of the overall callback rate rather than the callback-with-interview measure.

Variation in Job Type

All jobs applied for in the FSvW analysis were white-collar office support jobs and all applicants were female. The KLN analysis included applications for three types of jobs: administrative support and clerical, customer service, and sales. The first KLN occupational group, administrative support and clerical, is comparable to the office support jobs in the FSvW analysis, and 96.4 percent of the 2,690 applicants for these jobs in the KLN sample were female.

Row 4 of table 10 contains results of the analysis for the KLN administrative support and clerical jobs. The first thing to note is that the overall callback rate for these jobs in the KLN data is extremely low at 3.61 percent. There were only ninety-seven callbacks to 2,690 applications for this type of job. Still, there is a statistically significant negative relationship between unemployment duration and the probability of a callback. However, it is only about 56 percent of the estimated effect in the overall KLN sample. The point estimate in row 4 of the table implies a reduction in the probability of callback of about 0.5 percentage points. This is a reduction of about 13 percent at the mean callback rate of 3.61 percent, comparable to the implied effect for the full sample in row 3. We conclude that variation in the type of job does not account for the qualitative difference between our results and those of KLN.

Education Level

Related to job type is the skill level of the applicants. All applicants in the FSvW analysis were graduates of four-year colleges. In contrast, the KLN analysis included applicants who had completed high school (20 percent), community college (42 percent), and four-year college (38 percent). There is no difference in callback rates by education level in the KLN analysis, but it is worth investigating whether the relationship of the likelihood of callback with unemployment duration holds up for the KLN four-year college graduates.[16]

Row 5 of table 10 contains results of the analysis for the KLN applicants who have a degree from a four-year college. The callback rate for these applicants is very close to the overall callback rate in the KLN data. The marginal effect of unemployment duration on the probability of callback is significantly negative for the KLN four-year-college graduates and larger in magnitude than for the overall sample (compare rows 6 and 3 of table 10). We conclude that variation in the education level of applicants does not account for the qualitative difference between our results and those of KLN.[17]

Time Period

The KLN analysis is based on job applications submitted between June 2011 and July 2012 whereas the FSvW analysis is based on applications submitted between March 2012 and August 2014. Clearly, the KLN analysis is much earlier in the period of recovery from the Great Recession. This may be part of the explanation for the fact that KLN find a much lower callback rate to their applications for comparable jobs (3.61 percent for administrative and clerical jobs) than we find (10.4 percent).[18] However, the information-based theory highlighted by both KLN and FSvW suggests that, to the extent employers infer worker quality partly from unemployment duration, the negative effect of unemployment duration on the callback rate should *grow* as the recovery proceeds and the labor market strengthens. In fact, even for our data from round 1 in 2012 we find a zero

16. The p-value for test of independence of callback and education in a two-way table is 0.497.

17. We also examined the smaller subset of the KLN sample that consisted of four-year college graduates applying for administrative/clerical jobs. The marginal effect of unemployment duration on the probability of callback is negative but not significantly different from zero in this smaller sample (p-value = 0.14). Given the small size of the sample (936 applicants), we do not draw any conclusion from this result.

18. Eriksson and Rooth (2014) find a callback rate of 25 percent in their 2007 Swedish study. Ghayad (2014) finds a callback rate of 8.3 percent in his 2012 (post–Great Recession) U.S. study. Note that these aggregate statistics refer to broader distributions of worker type.

effect, in contrast with the basic updating model.[19]

A potential source of reconciliation between the disparate findings of KLN and FSvW is suggested by our within-posting analysis. The results in table 9 suggest that observable characteristics are more important when callback rates are lower (say, one callback from four applications as opposed to three callbacks from four applications). The generally lower overall callback rates found by KLN are consistent with employers exercising more discretion in callbacks so that unemployment duration could play a more important role in the time period covered by their sample.

Geographic Variation

As explained earlier, in "Research Design," our analysis was designed to cover eight metropolitan areas, four with relatively low unemployment rates (Dallas, Omaha, Pittsburgh, and Portland, Maine) and four with relatively high unemployment rates (Chicago, Sacramento, Tampa, and Charlotte, North Carolina). In contrast, the KLN analysis covers one hundred large American metropolitan areas.[20] Their analysis includes observations on seven of the eight cities used by FSvW, the exception being Portland, Maine. We investigate the extent to which differences in geographic coverage can account for the difference in findings across the two studies by using the seven-city subset of the KLN data to estimate our simple model of the effect of unemployment duration on the probability of callback.

Rows 6 and 7 of table 10 contain the results of this analysis. Row 6 of the table contains estimates of the marginal effect of a month of unemployment on the probability of callback for the KLN subsample for the seven FSvW cities. There are only 1,130 applications in these cities, so it is not surprising that the marginal effect of unemployment is estimated less precisely. However, the estimate is negative and signifi-

cantly different from zero (p-value = 0.042). The estimated marginal effect for the 8,106 applications from the remaining ninety-two cities in the KLN sample, presented in row 7 of the table, is comparable in magnitude and significantly negative at conventional levels. These results imply that differences in the geographic composition of the KLN and FSvW samples are not likely to account for the differences in results.

Variation in Age

The differences in the implied age range of the résumé is the most striking contrast between our and other audit studies of the effect of unemployment duration on callback. The distributions of age of applicants in the KLN and FSvW samples are largely nonoverlapping. Applicants in the KLN sample range in age from nineteen to thirty-nine, with 99 percent between twenty-one and thirty-three, whereas applicants in the FSvW sample range in age from thirty-five to fifty-eight. As explained earlier, in "A Model of Learning About Applicant Quality," this contrast has the potential to account for the different findings with regard to the relationship between unemployment duration and the probability of callback. KLN note themselves in their conclusion that it is important to assess whether their findings hold for older workers.

Rows 8 to 11 of table 10 contain analyses of the callback rate separately for four age groups in the KLN sample. Callback rates are similar across all four age groups, ranging from 10.7 percent to 12.8 percent.[21] The marginal effect of unemployment duration on the callback rate is estimated to be negative for all age groups. There are significant differences in the marginal effect across age groups (p-value of test that all marginal effects equal = 0.047), but the absolute magnitude of the effect does not decline monotonically with age. The effect is largest by far in absolute magnitude for the youngest applicants (nineteen to twenty-two years

19. Indeed, KLN investigate cross-sectional variation in the marginal effect on callback rates of unemployment duration by local unemployment rates (a second-order effect) and find that the marginal effect of unemployment duration on callback becomes more negative as the unemployment rate falls.

20. Ghayad (2014) covers the twenty-five largest metropolitan areas in the United States.

21. A χ^2 test of independence of age and callback fails to reject independence (p-value = 0.28).

old) then declines for applicants aged twenty-three to twenty-six before rising somewhat for applicants twenty-seven to thirty and for applicants thirty-one to thirty-nine (97.5 percent of whom are thirty-one to thirty-four).

Given the substantial difference in the age ranges covered by KLN and our analyses, it is difficult to conclude anything from the age variation in the effect of unemployment duration within KLN's sample. However, age may be an important factor in accounting for the difference in findings. The older applicants used by FSvW have significant longer work histories that may outweigh any recent unemployment experience when résumés are evaluated by potential employers. The younger applicants used by KLN do not have nearly as extensive a history and so recent unemployment experience may get higher weight in the evaluation of applicants. We also note that the applicants in the Eriksson and Rooth (2014) Swedish study and the Ghayad (2014) U.S. study are all in their twenties with no more than about five or six years of experience, which may account for their findings of significant effects of unemployment duration on callback.

To summarize the comparison with KLN regarding the effect of unemployment duration on the callback rate, the differences in the outcome measure and the choice of cities do not appear to be important factors in understanding the difference in findings. The differences in job type and time period have the potential to explain some but not all of difference in findings. The differences between the studies in applicants' age is a strong candidate to explain the difference. However, the lack of overlap in the ages of applicants in the FSvW and KLN studies make it difficult to draw a definitive conclusion in this regard. Without a single study that includes a full range of ages, our conjecture that the importance of unemployment duration in determining callbacks declines with age remains suggestive rather than conclusive.

FINAL COMMENTS

Based on our audit study of the determinants of the likelihood of callbacks to job applications, we find clear evidence that employers are less likely to call back older applicants (those in their fifties) than younger workers (those in their thirties and forties). This is consistent with work based on the Displaced Workers Survey and administrative data showing that older displaced workers are less likely to be employed subsequent to job loss (Farber 2015) and to suffer long-term nonemployment (Song and von Wachter 2014), and it has potentially important implications for the employment prospects of older job losers. We also find clear evidence that holding a relatively low-level interim job at the time of job application significantly reduces the likelihood of a callback. This suggests that employers may, either mechanically or by rule-of-thumb, overweight the most recent employment spell in screening applications and suggests that those individuals who do take a lower-level interim job should not report such jobs on their applications.

Recent work reports contrasting findings between unemployment duration and the likelihood of callback for younger workers. While prominent papers find a negative relationship between short unemployment durations and callback for the United States (Kroft, Lange, and Notowidigdo 2013; Ghayad 2014), another study finds no such relationship (Nunley et al. forthcoming). Again focusing on younger workers, a related paper for Sweden finds no effect of short unemployment spells but negative effects of long unemployment spells on callbacks for less-educated workers (Ericksson and Rooth 2014). In our work we unambiguously find no relationship between unemployment and callback for mature and older workers. We attempt to reconcile our finding in this dimension with the work of KLN using their data and definitions comparable to ours, but cannot completely resolve the issue. Part of the difference may be the time period, since all of the earlier studies were fielded much earlier in the recovery period from the Great Recession when the labor market was weaker. Another difference, and one we think worthy of further exploration, is that all of the earlier studies focus on younger job applications (mostly in their twenties) whereas our study focuses on job applicants from their mid-thirties to mid-fifties. While there are good theoretical reasons to suspect that unemployment duration could be less important for older job applicants, a single study that covers the full age spectrum is needed to draw a definitive conclusion on this issue.

Finally, our analysis of variation in callbacks within job postings suggests that the effect of observable résumés characteristics (age, interim job) is reduced when employers are calling back a higher fraction of their applicants. Our interpretation of this finding is that when employers are hungry for workers, they are less selective in who they call back. This suggests the power of stimulating aggregate demand as a strategy to improve the employment prospects of applicants who otherwise would not "make the cut" of receiving any positive response to a job application.

APPENDIX–SAMPLE RÉSUMÉS

This appendix contains a set of four sample résumés:

1. Linda Carter, Sacramento, zero weeks' unemployment, older worker, no interim job.

2. Jennifer Smith, Pittsburgh, twenty-four weeks' unemployment, medium-age worker, no interim job.

3. Heather Adams, Dallas, fifty-two weeks' unemployment, younger worker, interim job.

4. Linda Carter, Dallas, twelve weeks' unemployment, older worker, interim job.

Linda Carter

WORK EXPERIENCE

Reliable Crane & Rigging
Sacramento, CA
Administrative Assistant/Receptionist
December 2008 – July 2014

- Responsible for all administrative and most accounting tasks
- Answered very busy telephones, handled customer walk-ins, took orders over the telephone
- Handled inventory, filing, invoicing, collections, updating the company website, and correspondence
- Accurately recorded vendor and customer invoices and payments and matched invoices to purchase orders
- Implemented improved billing and invoicing procedures with unprecedented results
- Personally reconciled over $60,000 in previously-uncollected debt within three months
- Developed excellent relationship with customers and vendors alike

Wilke, Fleury, Hoffelt, Gould
Sacramento, CA
Executive Legal Secretary
March 2002 – December 2008

- Acted as client contact both on the telephone and in person
- Operated under a very heavy work load, managing all administrative tasks
- Set up meetings and arranged travel
- Composed letters and court documents
- Tracked and accounted for all expenses
- Ensured that all work was completed in a timely and efficient manner

Jacobson Markham, LLP
Sacramento, CA
Executive Assistant
March 1998 – February 2002

- Responsible for setting up the practice of a formal federal judge
- Made extensive travel arrangements
- Performed extremely intensive calendaring and scheduling for meetings, appointments, etc.
- Drafted correspondence
- Provided all administrative support to members of the press, board members of prestigious organizations, outside counsel, etc.
- Worked without supervision for lengthy periods of time
- Acted as the point-of-contact for all matters relating to the practice
- Quickly became a favorite among the clients as well as others outside of the firm

Stoel Rives, LLP   Sacramento, CA
Receptionist/Administrative Assistant   June 1994 – November 1997
- Scheduled conference meetings and luncheons for various attorneys and legal secretaries
- Oversaw sending and receiving of faxes, packages, and other correspondence
- Typed final drafts of company documents
- Performed various filing tasks
- Answered multi-line telephone system and greeted clients

California Department of Motor Vehicles   Sacramento, CA
Secretary   November 1986 – May 1994
- Received business and personal telephone callers and provided information and guidance as needed
- Reviewed and distributed all incoming mail for the office
- Maintained office files and records for various property holdings
- Typed memos into final form from rough draft
- Maintained a system for tracking correspondence requiring a reply and alerting the staff of pending deadlines
- Prepared training and travel orders
- Maintained Time and Attendance cards and leave balances

California Department of Motor Vehicles   Sacramento, CA
Clerk Typist/Management Assistant   June 1982 – October 1986
- Reviewed and distributed all incoming mail for the office and recorded suspense dates
- Conducted research using various Department Directives and files in order to provide information necessary to develop administrative procedures for office programs
- Maintained the Directorate files and records for personnel programs
- Typed narrative reports, correspondence and complex reports for the office staff from rough draft
- Performed clerical duties in support of analysis and studies conducted on an individual basis

Creekside Pet Resort   Sacramento, CA
Doggie Day Camp Associate   April 1979 – January 1982
- Greeted the "pet parents" while checking in their dogs
- Set up a filing system for each dog to include shot records, assessments and the pet parents' information
- Assessed new dogs to verify they would be suitable for the day camp
- Made sure the dogs stayed safe while playing and interacting with other dogs

EDUCATION

California State University-Sacramento   Sacramento, CA
B.A. Sociology   May 1978

SKILLS

- Proficient in accounting software and all MS Office applications
- Able to multi-task, prioritize, and adapt as business needs evolve
- Very professional and highly dependable
- Can handle personnel issues, training, and travel coordination

Jennifer Smith

Dec 2006 – Jan 2013 **Alliance Real Estate Associates, LLC,** Pittsburgh, PA
Tenant Coordinator/Administrative Assistant
- Assisted two property managers with onsite management of six property portfolios consisting of over 900,000 square feet
- Addressed and answered tenant questions resolving problems and concerns
- Monitored/received and followed up on all tenant requests and/or concerns using (Workspeed) online tenant request service system
- Conducted weekly tenant visits and documented issues
- Coordinated tenant functions
- Composed and typed memos and posted announcements to Workspeed
- Composed and typed correspondence to tenants regarding late rent notices and operating expenses
- Assisted property managers with annual budget preparation, obtained vendor proposals and executed contracts
- Assisted with monthly/weekly building evaluations and report preparations
- Assisted with A/R and AP reconciliations for vendors and tenants
- Prepared/received purchase orders

Jan 2005 – Dec 2006 **Bank of America,** Pittsburgh, PA
Receptionist
- Answered telephones, greeted visitors, maintained the lobby area, ordered office supplies and updated Excel employee database
- Handled the dissemination of all outgoing mail as well as distribution of incoming mail to appropriate staff
- Assisted HR with orientation as well as the interviewing process, making sure that all applications were filled out by interviewees and directing them to appropriate staff members
- Fingerprinted newly-hired employees, took pictures of new hires, and ordered lunch
- Put together credit files for Hub
- Pulled documents using the Imaging System, Research and problem –solving for customers
- Coordinated meetings, travel arrangements, office parties, and ball game events

| Nov 2002 – Dec 2004 | **Berger Real Estate,** Pittsburgh, PA |
| | *Administrative Assistant* |

- Provided backup secretarial support for nine senior Administrative Assistants, Directors, and other staff members
- Typed and designed excel spreadsheets, general correspondence, memos, charts, tables, and graphs
- Coordinated and set up all office and set up all-office and client meeting luncheons
- Managed all general office orders and online accounts for supplies
- Assisted Leasing/Property Management Department in preparing quarterly surveys, researched and updated owner/tenant information
- Assisted Finance Department with expense reports, typed correspondence, and provided administrative support as required
- Assisted Sales Department in coordinating, binding, and putting together offering memos for selling of buildings and provided administrative support as required
- Assisted with mass mailing of materials
- Scanned and fine-tuned pictures and other materials

| Apr 1995 – Jul 2002 | **Custom Cable Corp,** Pittsburgh, PA |
| | *Administrative Assistant* |

- Managed and coordinated daily office functions for major cable and construction companies
- Reported daily on company activities and work flow to the Regional and Project Managers
- Hired, trained, and supervised interns
- Encouraged and motivated staff to maintain contractual billing agreements
- Coded and processed weekly billing and invoices for payroll
- Maintained weekly quality control and work percentage on company field support team
- Researched and solved payroll problems
- Distributed held checks after discrepancies were taken care of to employees and contractors
- Maintained personnel information and files
- Oversaw that forms for employment were properly filled-out for new employees and contractors

Education

Shippensburg University of Pennsylvania

Skills

- Word, Excel, MS Office Suite, PowerPoint, Outlook, Access, 60 wpm
- Accounts payable/receivable
- Team player
- Excellent communication and follow-up skills, organizational skills and business ethics

Heather Adams

Jul 2014– Present   **Target,** Dallas, TX
Cashier Team Member
- Provides fast and friendly checkout service
- Resolves guest concerns in a calm, respectful manner

Mar 2010 – Jul 2013   **Harbour Group, Inc.,** Dallas, TX
Administrative Assistant
- Capably handled filing, faxing and copying tasks on a daily basis
- Wrote, proofread, and made letters signature-ready
- Professionally answered numerous phone calls using multi-line phones
- Copied and filed signed letters before returning to originator
- Handled scheduling and change of appointments for a very busy Executive Director
- Provided monthly printer counts, inventoried printer cartridges and toners, supplied buy list to IT personnel, and packaged and labeled empty printer cartridges/toners for shipping back to manufacturer for recycling

Jun 2006 – Mar 2010   **Drake Agency,** Dallas, TX
Administrative Support
- Printed CD labels and oversaw burning, scanning, and distribution of company CDs
- Created roster sign-in sheets in PDF format and updated roster sheets in Excel
- Updated files and books as needed for classes
- Formatted documents, adding page numbers, watermarks, and using a PDF Converter
- Edited PowerPoint presentations

Mar 2001 – Jun 2006   **Dallas Employment Service, Inc.,** Dallas, TX
Administrative Assistant

- Responsible for day-to-day secretarial needs: took dictation; typed letters, memos, reports; screened telephone calls; attended meetings; scheduled conference calls
- Managed daily administrative needs of Marketing and Operations Departments including maintenance of Microsoft Outlook calendars, coordination of travel arrangements, in-office meeting planning, and out-of-office meeting planning
- Answered multi-line telephone system and directed calls to appropriate staff

- Pre-interviewed visitors and guests as instructed
- Summarized research and prepared informational packets for staff dissemination
- Greeted internal and external clients and opened correspondence
- Maintained conference rooms and scheduled meetings and handled all travel arrangements
- Attended monthly board meetings, prepared minutes, illustrated monthly newsletters, handled in-unit billing and petty cash, and provided front desk coverage
- Disseminated all correspondence and memos
- Supported building manager and other staff with prompt professionalism

Education

University of Texas-Tyler
Bachelor of Arts, English, 1999

Skills

- Proven ability to work in fast-paced environment
- Detail oriented and capable of multi-tasking
- Excellent communication and language skills
- Adept at PowerPoint, Word, Excel and PDF editing

Linda Carter

WORK EXPERIENCE

Target Dallas, TX
Service Desk Team Member July 2014 – Present
- Resolves guest concerns promptly
- Neatly stocks shelves and maintains a clean store

American Rigging, Inc. Dallas, TX
Administrative Assistant/Receptionist December 2008 – April 2014
- Responsible for all administrative and most accounting tasks
- Answered very busy telephones, handled customer walk-ins, took orders over the telephone
- Handled inventory, filing, invoicing, collections, updating the company website, and correspondence
- Accurately recorded vendor and customer invoices and payments and matched invoices to purchase orders
- Implemented improved billing and invoicing procedures with unprecedented results
- Personally reconciled over $60,000 in previously-uncollected debt within three months
- Developed excellent relationship with customers and vendors alike

Turley Law Firm Dallas, TX
Executive Legal Secretary May 2002 – December 2008
- Acted as client contact both on the telephone and in person
- Operated under a very heavy work load, managing all administrative tasks
- Set up meetings and arranged travel
- Composed letters and court documents
- Tracked and accounted for all expenses
- Ensured that all work was completed in a timely and efficient manner

Stephen Malouf Law Offices Dallas, TX
Executive Assistant March 1998 – February 2002
- Responsible for setting up the practice of a formal federal judge
- Made extensive travel arrangements
- Performed extremely intensive calendaring and scheduling for meetings, appointments, etc.
- Drafted correspondence
- Provided all administrative support to members of the press, board members of prestigious organizations, outside counsel, etc.
- Worked without supervision for lengthy periods of time
- Acted as the point-of-contact for all matters relating to the practice
- Quickly became a favorite among the clients as well as others outside of the firm

Anderson Jones Law Office Dallas, TX
Receptionist/Administrative Assistant June 1994 – November 1997
- Scheduled conference meetings and luncheons for various attorneys and legal secretaries
- Oversaw sending and receiving of faxes, packages, and other correspondence
- Typed final drafts of company documents
- Performed various filing tasks
- Answered multi-line telephone system and greeted clients

Texas Department of State Health Services   Austin, TX
Secretary   November 1986 – May 1994

- Received business and personal telephone callers and provided information and guidance as needed
- Reviewed and distributed all incoming mail for the office
- Maintained office files and records for various property holdings
- Typed memos into final form from rough draft
- Maintained a system for tracking correspondence requiring a reply and alerting the staff of pending deadlines
- Prepared training and travel orders
- Maintained Time and Attendance cards and leave balances

Texas Department of State Health Services   Austin, TX
Clerk Typist/Management Assistant   June 1982 – October 1986

- Reviewed and distributed all incoming mail for the office and recorded suspense dates
- Conducted research using various Department Directives and files in order to provide information necessary to develop administrative procedures for office programs
- Maintained the Directorate files and records for personnel programs
- Typed narrative reports, correspondence and complex reports for the office staff from rough draft
- Performed clerical duties in support of analysis and studies conducted on an individual basis

Camp Bow Wow   Dallas, TX
Doggie Day Camp Associate   April 1979 – January 1982

- Greeted the "pet parents" while checking in their dogs
- Set up a filing system for each dog to include shot records, assessments and the pet parents' information
- Assessed new dogs to verify they would be suitable for the day camp
- Made sure the dogs stayed safe while playing and interacting with other dogs

EDUCATION

University of Texas-Tyler   Tyler, TX
B.A. Sociology   May 1978

SKILLS

- Proficient in accounting software and all MS Office applications
- Able to multi-task, prioritize, and adapt as business needs evolve
- Very professional and highly dependable
- Can handle personnel issues, training, and travel coordination

REFERENCES

Bertrand, Marianne, and Sendhil Mullainathan. 2004. "Are Emily and Greg More Employable Than Lakisha and Jamal? A Field Experiment on Labor Market Discrimination." *American Economic Review* 94(4): 991–1013.

Chamberlain, Gary. 1980. "Analysis of Variance with Qualitative Data." *Review of Economic Studies XLVII* 47(1): 22–38.

Elsby, Michael, Bart Hobijn, and Ayşegül Şahin. 2010. "The Labor Market in the Great Recession." *Brookings Papers on Economic Activity* 41(1): 1–69.

Eriksson, Stefan, and Dan-Olof Rooth. 2014. "Do Employers Use Unemployment as a Sorting Criterion When Hiring? Evidence from a Field Experiment." *American Economic Review* 104(3): 1014–39.

Farber, Henry S. 1999. "Alternative and Part-Time Employment Arrangements as a Response to Job Loss." *Journal of Labor Economics* 17(S4): S142–69.

———. 2015. "Job Loss in the Great Recession and Its Aftermath: U.S. Evidence from the Displaced Workers Survey." IRL Working Paper No. 589. Princeton, N.J.: Princeton University, Industrial Relations Section, May.

Farber, Henry S., and Robert Gibbons. 1996. "Learning and Wage Dynamics." *Quarterly Journal of Economics* 111(4): 1007–47.

Farber, Henry S., Dan Silverman, and Till von Wachter. 2016. "Determinants of Callbacks to Job Applications: An Audit Study." *American Economic Review* 106(5): 314–18.

Ghayad, Rand. 2014. "The Jobless Trap." Available at: www.lexissecuritiesmosaic.com/gateway /FEDRES/SPEECHES/ugd_576e9a_f6cf3b6661e 44621ad26547112f66691.pdf; accessed August 10, 2016.

Kroft, Kory, Fabian Lange, and Matthew J. Notowidigdo. 2013. "Duration Dependence and Labor Market Conditions: Evidence from a Field Experiment." *Quarterly Journal of Economics* 129(2): 1123–67.

Lahey, Joanna N. 2008. "Age, Women, and Hiring: An Experimental Study." *Journal of Human Resources* 43(2008): 30–56.

Nunley, John M., Adam Pugh, Nicholas Romero, and Richard Alan Seals, Jr. Forthcoming. "Unemployment, Underemployment, and Employment Opportunities: Results from a Correspondence Audit Study of the Labor Market for College Graduates." *Industrial and Labor Relations Review*.

Song, Jae, and Till von Wachter. 2014. "Long-Term Nonemployment and Job Displacement." Evaluating Labor Market Dynamics, Proceedings from the Jackson Hole Economic Policy Symposium Sponsored by the Federal Reserve Board of Kansas City, Jackson Hole, Wyo. (August 2014). Available at: www.kansascityfed.org/publicat /sympos/2014/2014vonWachter.pdf; accessed September 30, 2016.

The Changing Consequences of Unemployment for Household Finances

WILLIAM T. DICKENS, ROBERT K. TRIEST, AND
RACHEL B. SEDERBERG

In this article we present new evidence that the capacity of households to cover earnings lost during spells of unemployment through a combination of drawing down of wealth and receipt of unemployment insurance and other transfer payments is very limited and has deteriorated since the 1980s. Since 2006, most households have not had nearly enough financial wealth to smooth their consumption over more than a very short spell of unemployment. Individuals experiencing involuntary job loss also tend to experience substantial earnings reductions upon reemployment, resulting in longer-term deterioration in household finances. Wealth inadequacy to cover lost earnings and the earnings reduction upon reemployment are both especially acute in long unemployment spells, such as those that were prevalent in the aftermath of the Great Recession.

Keywords: household finances, unemployment, earnings losses

The Great Recession not only was more severe in magnitude than other post–World War II economic contractions but also differed qualitatively in its impact on the labor market. Arguably the most important distinguishing characteristic of the Great Recession is the very large and persistent increase in long-term unemployment that it ushered in. The peak unemployment rate in the aftermath of the Great Recession was 10.0 percent, which is somewhat lower than the peak unemployment rate of 10.8 percent during the 1981-to-1982 recession. But, long-term unemployment rose much more during the Great Recession than it did in the early 1980s. The percentage of the labor force unemployed twenty-seven weeks or longer reached

William T. Dickens is University Distinguished Professor and chair of economics at Northeastern University. **Robert K. Triest** is vice president and economist at the Federal Reserve Bank of Boston. **Rachel B. Sederberg** is a doctoral candidate in applied economics at Northeastern University.

© 2017 Russell Sage Foundation. Dickens, Williams T., Robert K. Triest, and Rachel B. Sederberg. 2017. "The Changing Consequences of Unemployment for Household Finances." *RSF: The Russell Sage Foundation Journal of the Social Sciences* 3(3): 202–21. DOI: 10.7758/RSF.2017.3.3.09. We wish to thank Sam Richardson for expert research assistance. We are also grateful to participants at the Russell Sage Foundation conference, "The U.S. Labor Market During and After the Great Recession," in particular Arne Kalleberg and Till von Wachter, participants at the Southern Economic Association annual conference, and two anonymous referees for very helpful comments and discussions. The views expressed in this paper are those of the authors and do not necessarily reflect the views of the Federal Reserve Bank of Boston or the Federal Reserve System. All errors are our own. Direct correspondence to: William T. Dickens at w.dickens@neu.edu, Department of Economics, Northeastern University, 360 Huntington Ave., Boston, MA 02115; Robert K. Triest at robert.triest@bos.frb.org, Research Department, Federal Reserve Bank of Boston, 600 Atlantic Ave., Boston, MA 02210; and Rachel B. Sederberg at sederberg.r@husky.neu.edu, Department of Economics, Northeastern University, 360 Huntington Ave., Boston, MA 02115.

4.4 percent, in early 2010, compared with an early 1980s high of 2.6 percent. The 2010 value was the highest since the Current Population Survey was started in 1948. The long spells of unemployment that became common during the Great Recession and its aftermath likely have a much more substantial impact on household finances and economic welfare than the shorter spells commonly experienced in prior recessions.

In this paper we examine the consequences of the Great Recession, and unemployment more generally, on household finances. In doing so we examine the extent to which households were in a position to maintain their consumption in the face of long spells of unemployment through a combination of drawing down their wealth and receipt of unemployment insurance and other social insurance benefits. We also examine the extent to which unemployed workers suffered a drop in earnings relative to their pre-recession level upon reemployment. Our conclusions are relatively pessimistic on both counts. Most workers are able to cover very few weeks of their reduced income during spells of unemployment by drawing down their financial wealth, and most also suffer substantial reductions in their earnings upon reemployment following a layoff or termination.

Our work most closely follows a study by Jonathan Gruber (2001) in which he examines how wealth buffers the effects of unemployment on consumption. Gruber concludes that workers with the median amount of wealth draw on it when unemployed so as to maintain two-thirds of their pre-unemployment consumption for the typical spell of unemployment. This requires them to draw down their wealth rapidly as their spells become longer. Gruber uses data from the U.S. Census Bureau's Survey of Income and Program Participation (SIPP) panels for 1984 to 1992 for his analysis, and so his data contain relatively few spells of long-term unemployment.

Our study draws on SIPP data through the 2008 panel for which we have data up through mid-2013. This allows us to examine the consequences of the Great Recession, a contraction much more severe than the 1990-to-1991 recession that is captured in Gruber's data. Using methodology similar to Gruber's we find quite different results, with households in recent years being in a much worse position to self-insure against earnings disruptions than in the earlier period. We also use the SIPP to examine the distribution of earnings changes following job changes. Job changes that were precipitated by a layoff or termination typically result in substantial reductions in earnings upon reemployment, especially when a long spell of nonemployment follows the initial job loss. Thus, households' loss of earnings during a spell of unemployment is compounded by reduced earnings upon reemployment.

The Great Recession was especially hard for household finances because of the increased incidence of unemployment—especially long-term unemployment. Even before the Great Recession, many households were not in a position to cover more than a relatively minor earnings disruption by drawing down their wealth. Growth in wealth inequality since the 1980s has left those at the bottom of the distribution much less well prepared for unemployment. Further, the financial crisis and the Great Recession were accompanied by deterioration in household wealth. Finally, the Great Recession had a large effect on the household finances of those who became unemployed. The impact was greatly increased as the fraction of households that experienced layoffs and long spells of unemployment was much higher than in the past.

The rest of this paper is organized as follows: The first section is a survey of recent literature related to this topic. Next we present our empirical results on the ability of households to cover earnings disruptions by drawing down financial wealth. This is followed by presentation of our findings on the changes in labor earnings associated with job changes. The final section is a discussion of the implications of our findings.

RELATED LITERATURE

It is now well established that unemployment shocks have substantial and persistent effects on earnings. Bruce Fallick (1996) and Lori Kletzer (2008) survey early research documenting that workers undergoing involuntary separations tend to experience substantial reductions in earnings that extend for several years following displacement.

Following the insight of Robert Gibbons and Lawrence F. Katz (1991), research has focused on workers displaced during a mass layoff, since such displacements are unlikely to be confounded by selection on worker quality or productivity. Building on this literature, recent work by Till von Wachter, Jae Song, and Joyce Manchester (2009) examines the long-term effects of job displacements from mass layoffs during the 1982 recession. Using administrative records, they find that short-term annual earnings losses due to job displacement are approximately 30 percent, and that losses of over 20 percent persist fifteen to twenty years after displacement.

Aaron Flaaen, Matthew D. Shapiro, and Isaac Sorkin (2003) use data from the SIPP spanning 2001 to 2006 matched to administrative data from the Longitudinal Employer-Household Dynamics (LEHD) program to analyze the earnings losses associated with worker displacement. Interestingly, they find that the two data sources often disagree on whether a job separation is a quit, a termination unrelated to economic conditions, or a separation associated with distressed business conditions. In the case of large firms where the administrative data indicates that there is a mass layoff and the worker indicates that the separation is due to economic distress, the worker's earnings tend to completely recover (relative to workers not separating from employment) within four years of the separation. This suggests that, at least during an economic expansion, a layoff that potential employers can readily identify as unrelated to worker quality results in little or no long-term depression of earnings.

It is debatable whether one should expect earnings losses associated with job displacement during a recession to be more or less persistent than those occurring during an expansion. On the one hand, widespread layoffs during recessions may lead to job separation being a weaker signal of low worker quality during a recession than if the job separation had instead occurred during an expansion, and Emi Nakamura (2008) provides some support for this view. However, the dearth of job opportunities during a recession may result in greater disruption of career trajectories when worker displacement occurs during a recession rather than during an expansion. Using unemployment insurance administrative records for Connecticut, Christopher D. Couch, Nicholas A. Jolly, and Dana W. Placzek (2011) find that the long-term earnings losses of workers displaced during a recession are substantially larger than the long-term earnings losses of those displaced during expansions. Steven J. Davis and Till von Wachter (2011) use a long panel of Social Security earnings records to show that the magnitude of lost earnings associated with displacement in a mass layoff when the unemployment rate is above 8 percent is about double the magnitude of lost earnings associated with displacement when the unemployment rate is below 6 percent. Till von Wachter and Elizabeth Weber Handwerker (2009) examine the consequences for workers of being displaced in a mass layoff in California during the strong economic expansion of the 1990s. They find that although earnings are depressed in the short term, the average displaced worker does not suffer a permanent earnings loss. Overall, research points toward displacement during recessions being associated with more persistent consequences for earnings than with job displacement during expansions.

Recent research by Joseph G. Altonji, Anthony A. Smith, and Ivan Vidangos (2013) decomposes earnings losses from a spell of unemployment into a shorter-lived loss of earnings from a decrease in hours worked, and a more persistent loss in earnings attributed to a decreased hourly wage upon reemployment. The latter could be due to loss of tenure, movement to a lower-paying job, or decline in the worker's human capital. Further research has broken down the impact of income shocks by income groups and suggests that positive shocks to high-income individuals are transitory, whereas negative shocks are persistent. For low-income individuals, positive shocks to income are found to be persistent, whereas negative shocks to income for low-income workers are transitory (Guvenen et al. 2015).

Looking at how workers fared after initial spells of unemployment during the Great Recession, it was found that a drop in earnings often follows an unemployment spell (Dickens and Triest 2012). That study was only able to look at data from the SIPP through 2010, so in this article we expand on the idea of job stability and outcomes using a larger dataset that includes longer spells of unemployment.

The persistent drop in earnings associated with worker displacement implies that many households will need to permanently lower their life-cycle consumption. However, the drop in income during an unemployment spell is often especially severe, and people would be expected to prepare to smooth consumption after job loss. One method to do so is through drawing down wealth, as highlighted in our discussion of the article by Jonathan Gruber (2001). Christopher D. Carroll, Karen E. Dynan, and Spencer D. Krane (2003) examine whether savings (and thus wealth) respond to the risk of unemployment. They find that increased unemployment risk does not lead to an increase in household savings for those who have low permanent income, whereas those with middle to high permanent incomes increase their precautionary savings when there is an increased risk for unemployment. These increases in precautionary savings can be seen in broad measures of wealth that include home equity, but not when a narrower measure of wealth excluding home equity is used.

Another possible method of consumption smoothing comes from borrowing and unsecured debt. James X. Sullivan (2008) finds that when unsecured debt is used as a form of insurance against income shocks, it is done by those who have some assets, and not done by those who have few or no assets. That article has a similar motivation to ours, but examines a different mechanism for maintaining consumption in the face of lower income.

Social insurance and transfer programs such as unemployment insurance, food stamps, and disability insurance serve to partially insure against unemployment risk. Hamish Low, Costas Meghir, and Luigi Pistaferri (2010) find that the welfare value of food stamps is greater than that of unemployment insurance in insuring against unemployment risk. Using data similar to the data we use, Richard W. Johnson and Alice G. Feng (2013) examine income losses among workers who were unemployed six or more months during the Great Recession and

its aftermath. They find that although unemployment benefits helped to cushion the impact of job loss, half of job losers were not receiving unemployment benefits six months into their unemployment spells. In addition to receipt of social welfare and insurance benefits, a family's income loss during unemployment may be buffered by other family members increasing their work hours while one family member is unemployed. The relative importance of the various methods to smooth consumption and income varies both across households and across points in time (Blundell 2014).

It is plausible that financial wealth allows individuals to be pickier when evaluating job offers, and may also allow unemployed people to engage in less intensive job searches than they otherwise would. This would generate a negative correlation between pre-unemployment wealth and the probability of reemployment, and a positive correlation between pre-unemployment wealth and the duration of completed unemployment spells. However, research has shown that employers tend to screen out job applicants with spells of non-employment lasting more than six months (Ghayad 2014), which would tend to discourage individuals from using their wealth to extend unemployment spells.

INCOME REPLACEMENT WITH HOUSEHOLD WEALTH AND UNEMPLOYMENT INSURANCE

Gruber (2001) used the SIPP to identify spells of unemployment, wages of those employed prior to a spell of unemployment, the wealth of those employed prior to a spell of unemployment, and the receipt of unemployment benefits, to analyze the extent to which wealth and unemployment insurance (UI) were adequate to replace lost earnings in the 1984-to-1992 period. Using later panels of the SIPP, we extend Gruber's analysis to see how well people were prepared for the unemployment experienced during the Great Recession.

Due to differences between the questions in the SIPP and the Current Population Survey (CPS) it is not possible to exactly replicate the official definition of unemployment that comes from the CPS. Instead, we define someone as unemployed for a week if during that

Figure 1. Gross Financial Wealth of Employed People

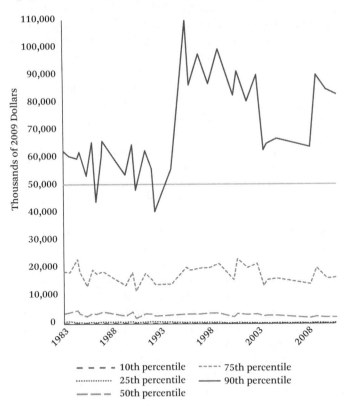

Source: Authors' calculations using data from the Survey of Income and Program Participation.

week the person was not employed and looked for work or if he or she reported being on temporary layoff. The SIPP tells us employment status on a weekly basis. We assume that if someone reports being unemployed during a week, that the person is unemployed for the entire week. We omit unemployment spells that began before the first wave of the panel (left-censored spells), but include spells that are still ongoing when the SIPP panel ends (right-censored spells) and spells that begin or end with missing data. Inclusion of the ongoing spells (and treating them as though they ended as of the end of the SIPP panel) and those that begin and end with missing data will tend to overstate the extent to which individuals could make up for lost earnings by drawing down financial wealth. An exception to treating missing data as ending a spell of unemployment is when there were less than 16 weeks of missing data between weeks of unemployment. In that case we treated the entire period of missing data as part of the spell of unemployment.

Following Gruber, we use three different definitions of wealth. Gross financial wealth is measured at the household level and includes savings and checking accounts, and the value of securities owned. It is a measure of readily accessible funds that can be used to smooth consumption. We chose not to include 401(k)s, 403(b)s, KEOGHs, or IRAs in this category because accessing them typically incurs substantial penalties. Net financial wealth subtracts all debts from gross financial wealth, including both secured (car loans, mortgages) and unsecured (credit cards) debt. Total net worth, as defined by the SIPP, adds the value of real property and the value of retirement accounts to arrive at net financial wealth.

The distribution of real (inflation adjusted, measured in 2009 dollars) gross financial wealth held by employed people is shown in figure 1, for dates when wealth information was

Table 1. Wealth Percentiles for Unemployed Sample

	Start Date of Period	Wealth Percentile				
		10th	25th	50th	75th	90th
Gross financial wealth	October 1984	$0	$0	$641	$6,456	$32,184
	July 1990	0	7	1,077	7,202	33,995
	January 1995	0	0	838	7,134	39,268
	March 2001	0	0	1,021	8,816	48,871
	July 2005	0	0	787	6,793	38,105
	November 2007	0	0	616	6,992	43,427
	September 2011	0	0	581	6,781	43,623
Net financial wealth	October 1984	−8,582	−2,512	0	3,194	27,634
	July 1990	−10,351	−2,813	0	3,964	30,090
	January 1995	−14,701	−3,923	0	3,023	33,953
	March 2001	−18,073	−4,532	0	3,906	42,272
	July 2005	−21,881	−5,609	0	2,412	31,705
	November 2007	−28,503	−7,450	0	2,486	35,206
	September 2011	−24,958	−6,288	0	2,034	33,929
Total net worth	October 1984	−551	1,448	25,361	98,072	211,525
	July 1990	−1,142	1,345	24,474	99,604	230,059
	January 1995	−4,899	619	20,082	100,334	248,627
	March 2001	−8,247	386	27,995	142,778	361,517
	July 2005	−5,933	768	39,368	205,086	495,995
	November 2007	−17,614	0	25,107	173,359	445,314
	September 2011	−13,329	464	31,554	168,954	451,170

Source: Authors' calculations using data from the Survey of Income and Program Participation.

collected in special topical modules of the SIPP. This figure shows that wealth has been very unevenly distributed during the past three decades and that most employed people have very little financial wealth that could be drawn down to use for consumption spending during a spell of unemployment. Gross financial wealth is zero for the bottom 10th percentile for all years, and the 25th percentile of the distribution is either zero or just slightly greater than zero. Median gross financial wealth is small. The 75th percentile of the gross financial wealth distribution has a somewhat erratic pattern. The 90th percentile is also erratic but shows a clear increase between the 1980s and the later period.

The distribution of wealth for those who become unemployed would be expected to differ somewhat from that of all employed people. Table 1 displays the distribution of our three wealth measures for individuals starting a spell

of unemployment subsequent to dates when the SIPP collected information on wealth holdings (again, all dollar amounts are in terms of constant 2009 dollars). We start with the observation that net financial assets and total net worth both declined between the earlier period, analyzed by Gruber, and the start of the Great Recession. In contrast, wealth in the upper part of the total net worth distribution increased over time, as did gross and net financial wealth at the 90th percentile, reflecting a marked increase in wealth inequality over the period covered by our data. Overall, it is striking that individuals in the lower part of the wealth distribution clearly were not in a position to draw down financial wealth to compensate for earnings lost during a spell of unemployment.

Wealth relative to income is more relevant than the dollar amount of wealth in gauging how well equipped people are to smooth over

Table 2. Ratio of Wealth to Earnings on Previous Job for Unemployed at Different Percentiles of the Wealth Earnings Rate

		Wealth-to-Earnings Ratio				
	Spells Starting Between	10th	25th	50th	75th	90th
Gross financial wealth	October 1984–June 1990	0	0	4	36	211
	July 1990–December 1994	0	0	6	39	208
	January 1995–February 2001	0	0	6	56	381
	March 2001–June 2005	0	0	5	44	378
	July 2005–October 2007	0	0	4	37	251
	November 2007–August 2011	0	0	3	31	237
	September 2011–December 2013	0	0	3	32	270
Net financial wealth	October 1984–June 1990	−69	−15	0	15	145
	July 1990–December 1994	−58	−13	0	20	166
	January 1995–February 2001	−115	−21	0	23	292
	March 2001–June 2005	−97	−16	0	22	281
	July 2005–October 2007	−125	−22	0	14	197
	November 2007–August 2011	−137	−24	0	11	164
	September 2011–December 2013	−106	−19	0	11	201
Total net worth	October 1984–June 1990	−3	14	130	537	1,893
	July 1990–December 1994	−6	11	107	443	1,606
	January 1995–February 2001	−30	6	117	650	2,830
	March 2001–June 2005	−33	4	113	642	3,291
	July 2005–October 2007	−22	5	147	992	4,018
	November 2007–August 2011	−60	0	84	600	2,791
	September 2011–December 2013	−41	2	110	729	3,235

Source: Authors' calculations using data from the Survey of Income and Program Participation.

earnings losses during spells of unemployment by drawing down their wealth. This is addressed in table 2, which shows the distribution of wealth relative to weekly earnings. The number of weeks of earnings that could be covered by drawing down gross financial wealth remained quite small for most of the distribution. At the median of the distribution of the ratio of gross financial wealth to weekly earnings, gross financial wealth could cover six weeks of earnings when measured by the SIPP in the early 1990s, but by the start of the Great Recession this had fallen to approximately three weeks. Someone at the 75th percentile of the distribution would have been able to cover approximately thirty-one weeks of earnings by drawing down financial wealth at the start of the Great Recession, with some evidence of a moderate downward trend over time. Looking at net financial wealth, even at the 75th percen-

tile of the distribution individuals would be able to cover only eleven weeks of lost earnings at the start of the Great Recession, down considerably from the 1990s. Analysis of total net worth provides a somewhat more favorable picture, although even by this measure there is little scope for much of the population to draw down wealth to cover lost earnings.

It is debatable whether gross financial wealth, net financial wealth, or total net worth is most relevant to the question of how well equipped people are to compensate for earnings lost while unemployed by drawing down wealth. A case can be made that gross financial wealth is the most relevant measure, because it best reflects the relatively liquid assets that can be readily drawn down and which may have been accumulated partly for precautionary purposes. Total net worth, in contrast, includes the value of illiquid assets that would be diffi-

Table 3. Ratio of Wealth to Earnings Lost Due to Unemployment

			Wealth-to-Loss Ratio			
			Fraction Whose Wealth Covers			
	Spells Starting Between	Median	10 percent of loss	25 percent of loss	50 percent of loss	100 percent of loss
Gross financial wealth	October 1984–June 1990	1.08	67	61	57	51
	July 1990–December 1994	1.38	73	67	61	54
	January 1995–February 2001	1.65	70	66	61	55
	March 2001–June 2005	1.28	67	62	57	52
	July 2005–October 2007	1	67	62	56	50
	November 2007–August 2011	0.57	62	56	51	45
	September 2011–December 2013	0.57	62	56	51	46
Net financial wealth	October 1984–June 1990	0	40	38	35	33
	July 1990–December 1994	0	44	41	38	35
	January 1995–February 2001	0	42	40	38	35
	March 2001–June 2005	0	41	39	37	34
	July 2005–October 2007	0	39	36	34	31
	November 2007–August 2011	0	37	34	32	29
	September 2011–December 2013	0	38	36	33	31
Total net worth	October 1984–June 1990	30.53	85	84	83	81
	July 1990–December 1994	22.04	84	83	81	78
	January 1995–February 2001	29.45	79	78	77	76
	March 2001–June 2005	23.99	78	77	76	74
	July 2005–October 2007	35.91	80	79	78	75
	November 2007–August 2011	16.1	74	73	71	69
	September 2011–December 2013	20.91	76	75	73	71

Source: Authors' calculations using data from the Survey of Income and Program Participation.

cult to tap for purposes of smoothing consumption expenditures while unemployed. If credit lines collateralized by illiquid assets, such as a home equity line of credit, had been established before the start of an unemployment spell, then the illiquid assets might be drawn down through increasing debt. However, once an unemployment spell starts the potential borrower becomes much less credit-worthy and new or increased lines of credit would become difficult or impossible to obtain. If existing loans or lines of credit must be repaid over a fairly short time frame, then a case can be made that net financial wealth is the measure most relevant to our analysis.

Table 3 provides more direct information on the adequacy of wealth to cover earnings losses while unemployed. The "median" column shows the median fraction of lost earnings (calculated as pre-unemployment normal weekly earnings times the length of the completed unemployment spell in weeks) that could be covered by drawing down wealth. The other columns show the percentage of spells where wealth could potentially cover 10, 25, 50, or 100 percent of the earnings lost to unemployment.

There has been a clear deterioration over time in the potential for gross financial wealth to cover the earnings lost during unemployment spells. By the start of the Great Recession, the median amount of lost earnings that could be covered by gross financial wealth was only 57 percent, down from 128 percent in 2001 and 138 percent in 1990. During the Great Recession, gross financial wealth were insufficient to cover even 10 percent of lost earnings for about 40 percent of unemployment spells. Although gross financial wealth covers only a relatively modest proportion of earnings lost in most unemployment spells, during the Great Recession it was sufficient to cover 100 percent of lost earnings for about 45 percent of spells (down from over half in the 1990s). This reflects a combination of there being many short unemployment spells, which can be covered with very modest wealth, and a high degree of inequality in the wealth distribution, with some people capable of covering earnings lost during long spells with their wealth.

As expected, relative to gross financial wealth, a smaller fraction of lost earnings can be covered by net financial wealth and a larger fraction can be covered by total net worth. Strikingly, the fraction of lost earnings that can be covered by wealth decreases over time for all three of the wealth measures that we examine. Clearly, by the time of the Great Recession people were less equipped to cover earnings losses by drawing down wealth than they had been in previous recessions.

In addition to drawing down wealth, individuals may also be able to use social welfare and insurance benefits to cover lost earnings. Tables 4 and 5 shed some light on the quantitative importance of transfer payments to the unemployed. The distribution of benefits from several transfer programs during spells of unemployment is shown in the top panel. Each row in the table shows the benefits received by unemployed individuals at the indicated percentile of the distribution of benefits received for the specified program; rows for the 50th percentile and below are not shown because benefits were zero at these percentiles for all programs in all of the time periods shown. Benefits from any given transfer program are received in only a very small minority of spells. Most unemployed individuals are either not eligible for many of the benefit programs, or do not elect to participate. Consequently, benefit receipt is positive only at the very top of the distribution for most benefit programs.

The relatively small fraction of the unemployed receiving UI benefits in our data is consistent with that found in the Current Popula-

tion Survey (CPS). Examining data from the March 2005 special CPS supplement, Wayne Vroman (2009) finds that 24 percent of unemployed people indicate that they received unemployment insurance benefits; the equivalent calculation for March 2005 in our data yields 26 percent. He notes that the rate of UI benefit application found in the CPS supplement is close to that found in UI program administrative data, suggesting that the CPS estimates are reasonably accurate. The primary reason for the low UI benefit recipiency rate is that most people who meet the official definition of unemployment do not file for benefits (Wandner and Stettner 2000). In the 2005 CPS supplement, over half of the unemployed who do not apply for benefits indicate that they believe that they are not eligible for benefits (Vroman 2009).

The distributions of benefits from transfer programs for unemployed individuals who are recipients of benefits from the program are shown in table 5. Although only a minority of unemployment spells involve receipt of benefits from any given transfer program, transfers play a large role in replacing income—relative to wealth—for those who do receive benefits.

Social welfare and insurance benefits are also quantitatively important as a source of funds for covering earnings lost during spells of unemployment. Table 6 displays for several demographic groups, and by duration of unemployment, the median percentage of earnings lost due to an unemployment spell that could be covered by gross financial wealth or by gross financial wealth plus cumulative benefits from all of the transfer programs shown in table 5. Transfer payments substantially increase the percentage of lost earnings that can be covered, although there is still a clear deterioration over time in the percentage of lost earnings covered, even when transfer payments are included.

There are stark differences over demographic groups in the median percentage of lost earnings covered. Young (less than twenty-five years old) and relatively old (over fifty-five years old) workers have a high median percentage of lost earnings covered (the young because many are living with their parents), although the median percentage decreases going into the great recession. Wealth and transfer pay-

Table 4. Value of Benefits Received by All Unemployed in the 75th and 90th Percentile

				Benefits Received			
	Percentile	October 1984–July 1990	July 1990–January 1995	January 1995–March 2001	March 2001–July 2005	July 2005–November 2007	November 2007–September 2011	September 2011–December 2013
Total UI	75th	0	0	0	0	0	0	0
	90th	393	718	266	487	231	920	574
Total noncash	75th	0	0	0	0	0	0	57
	90th	253	257	142	148	248	360	380
Supplemental Security Income	75th	0	0	0	0	0	0	0
	90th	566	566	665	788	948	1023	1179
Social Security Supplemental Income	75th	0	0	0	0	0	0	0
	90th	0	0	0	0	0	0	0
AFDC/TANF[a]	75th	0	0	0	0	0	0	0
	90th	0	0	0	0	0	0	0
Food stamps/SNAP	75th	0	0	0	0	0	0	15
	90th	233	251	195	138	226	345	356

Source: Authors' calculations using data from the Survey of Income and Program Participation.

[a]Aid to Families with Dependent Children/Temporary Assistance for Needy Families.

Table 5. Value of Benefits Received by Those Receiving Benefits (Dollars)

	Benefits Received Out of Those Receiving Benefits						
Percentile	October 1984–July 1990	July 1990–January 1995	January 1995–March 2001	March 2001–July 2005	July 2005–November 2007	November 2007–September 2011	September 2011–December 2013
Total UI							
10th	198	225	215	256	232	301	270
50th	574	679	626	828	813	924	834
75th	940	1108	1068	1330	1285	1400	1333
90th	1326	1499	1475	1757	1711	1871	1738
Total noncash							
10th	63	40	3	40	40	43	46
50th	254	247	149	172	247	295	290
75th	388	384	323	342	413	496	479
90th	518	515	475	514	558	712	676
Supplemental Security Income							
10th	358	379	383	441	453	479	499
50th	825	846	903	1015	1059	1107	1146
75th	1144	1169	1294	1401	1510	1663	1652
90th	1679	1651	1763	1885	2022	2286	2348
Social Security Supplemental Income							
10th	133	133	129	159	162	178	191
50th	536	570	588	613	631	658	648
75th	587	606	679	728	841	856	864
90th	891	821	1050	1161	1287	1272	1285
AFDC/TANF[a]							
10th	211	195	182	144	121	138	142
50th	501	451	447	365	348	358	315
75th	753	672	639	562	567	531	493
90th	1021	913	830	686	770	686	606
Food stamps/SNAP							
10th	108	116	96	90	105	130	114
50th	264	271	271	265	294	327	315
75th	372	385	392	390	425	512	494
90th	491	500	511	527	558	714	674

Source: Authors' calculations using data from the Survey of Income and Program Participation.

[a] Aid to Families with Dependent Children/Temporary Assistance for Needy Families.

Table 6. Percentage of Loss Covered by Gross Financial Wealth and Wealth Plus Benefit for Median Worker

		Percentage of Loss Covered by Gross Financial Wealth and Wealth Plus Benefit						
		October 1984–July 1990	July 1990–January 1995	January 1995–March 2001	March 2001–July 2005	July 2005–November 2007	November 2007–September 2011	September 2011–December 2013
All unemployed	Wealth	109	138	165	128	100	57	57
	Add cash benefits	146	173	195	153	120	89	76
Ages 25–55	Wealth	67	93	100	60	42	26	25
	Add cash benefits	103	130	123	88	59	48	40
Single adult caring for children	Wealth	0	5	0	0	2	0	0
	Add cash benefits	5	19	4	6	4	1	0
Individuals under 25	Wealth	255	334	283	262	194	133	239
	Add cash benefits	290	357	301	285	216	174	279
Individuals over 55	Wealth	436	471	1091	1046	1339	614	238
	Add cash benefits	471	493	2115	1119	1348	638	242
Prime age non-whites	Wealth	1	12	23	5	8	6	7
	Add cash benefits	36	38	24	17	13	14	14
Unemployed more than 2 weeks	Wealth	44	66	61	39	34	19	20
	Add cash benefits	65	89	75	50	43	31	29
Unemployed more than 25 weeks	Wealth	5	8	5	7	4	3	3
	Add cash benefits	11	13	9	10	8	6	7

Source: Authors' calculations using data from the Survey of Income and Program Participation.

ments make substantial contributions to earnings replacement for both of these groups.

The median percentage of lost earnings covered by wealth is very low for single adult households with children and for prime-working-age (twenty-five to fifty-five years old) nonwhite workers. Transfer payments provide some protection against earnings losses for both of these groups, but the median percentage of lost earnings replaced by transfer payments decreases over time for both groups. The median percentage of lost earnings replaced by transfer payments during spells of unemployment that started early in the Great Recession is just 1 percent for single adults with children and 14 percent for prime-working-age nonwhite individuals. Members of these groups are very vulnerable to economic deprivation during long unemployment spells.

The duration of the unemployment spell has a strong association with the extent to which wealth, or wealth plus benefits, cover lost earnings. Those who are unemployed for very short periods of time are reasonably well prepared to cover their earnings loss, but those who experience a long spell of unemployment tend to be very poorly prepared. This is not surprising—the adequacy of a given amount of wealth decreases as the length of the time without current earnings increases. That said, the contrast between the rows for all unemployed and the rows pertaining to those with unemployment spells exceeding twenty-five weeks is stark.

Further information on the role of transfer payments in covering earnings losses for the demographic and duration groups that we consider is shown in figures 2 through 7. Figures 2, 3, and 4 display the percentage of unemployment spells where at least 10 percent (figure 2), 50 percent (figure 3), and 100 percent (figure 4) of lost earnings could potentially be covered by gross financial wealth. Figures 5, 6, and 7 display the same information, but adds transfer payments to gross financial wealth in calculating the percentage of lost earnings potentially replaced.

Figures 2 through 7 reinforce the findings from table 6 that single adults with children, prime-working-age nonwhite individuals, and those who experience long spells of unemployment are especially disadvantaged in replacing

Figure 2. Percentage of Unemployed with Gross Financial Wealth Exceeding 10 Percent of Loss

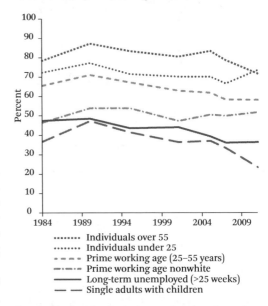

Source: Authors' calculations using data from the Survey of Income and Program Participation.

Figure 3: Percentage of Unemployed with Gross Financial Wealth Exceeding 50 Percent of Loss

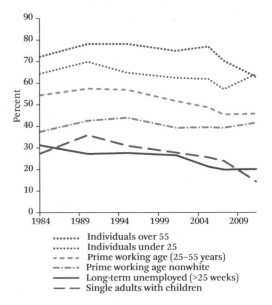

Source: Authors' calculations using data from the Survey of Income and Program Participation.

Figure 4. Percentage of Unemployed with Gross Financial Wealth Exceeding 100 Percent of Loss

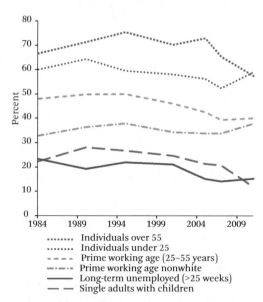

Source: Authors' calculations using data from the Survey of Income and Program Participation.

Figure 5. Percentage of Unemployed with Gross Financial Wealth and Benefits Exceeding 10 Percent of Loss

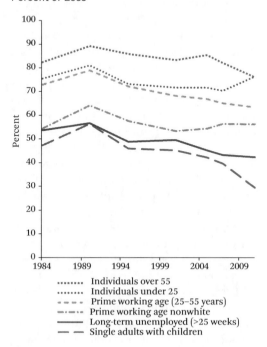

Source: Authors' calculations using data from the Survey of Income and Program Participation.

Figure 6. Percentage of Unemployed with Gross Financial Wealth and Benefits Exceeding 50 Percent of Loss

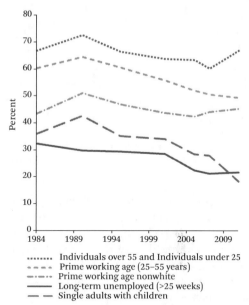

Source: Authors' calculations using data from the Survey of Income and Program Participation.

Figure 7. Percentage of Unemployed with Gross Financial Wealth and Benefits Exceeding 100 Percent of Loss

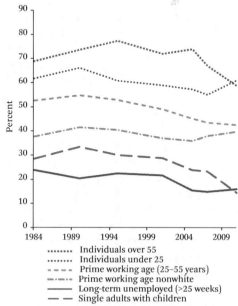

Source: Authors' calculations using data from the Survey of Income and Program Participation.

Table 7. Percentage Change in Earnings from Previous Employment to Initial Earnings in New Employment for Involuntary Job Changers

Panel in Which Job Loss Occurred	Percentile			Percentage of Job Changers Non-employed for Eight or More Months
	25th	50th	75th	
1996 panel	−60	−28	10	17
2001 panel	−31	−28	10	23
2004 panel	−59	−24	12	17
2008 panel	−68	−37	0	39

Source: Authors' calculations using data from the Survey of Income and Program Participation.
Note: Only job losses that occurred in the first two years of the panel are reported here.

earnings lost during spells of unemployment. The figures also reinforce the finding that the percentage of lost earnings potentially replaced either by drawing down gross financial wealth or through the combination of transfer payment receipt and drawing down gross financial wealth has decreased over time.

Comparison of figures 2 and 5 suggests that transfer payments reduce the variance over demographic groups in the percentage of spells where at least 10 percent of lost earnings can potentially be replaced. This phenomenon holds to a much lesser extent for the percentage of spells where at least 50 percent or 100 percent of lost earnings can potentially be replaced, especially for those with long unemployment spells. Social welfare and insurance benefits provide an important safety net, albeit one that provides only a small degree of insurance.

EMPLOYMENT AND EARNINGS INSTABILITY

Unemployment can continue to affect household finances even after an unemployment spell ends with reemployment in a new job. As previously discussed, earlier research has found that individuals often suffer a decrease in earnings relative to their pre-job loss level following an unemployment spell that ends in reemployment. In this section, we present new estimates showing that, on average, those leaving jobs involuntarily (that is, due to layoff or termination) during the Great Recession and its after-

math suffered very large reductions in earnings upon reemployment. The loss of earnings while unemployed is only part of the hit to household finances due to unemployment. The reduction in earnings upon reemployment is also a major source of financial stress, and may be longer-lasting than the spell of unemployment.

Table 7 displays the distribution of the percentage change in real monthly earnings between wave 1 and the first month with positive earnings following reemployment for individuals who were employed in wave 1, subsequently involuntarily lost their wave 1 job within the first two years of the SIPP panel, and were then reemployed before the end of the panel.[1] We include only those losing a job within the first two years of each panel to reduce the problem of not observing the completion of spells of non-employment. The 2008 panel row indicates the consequences for earnings of losing a job during the Great Recession and its aftermath, the 2004 panel row indicates the consequences for earnings of losing a job during more normal labor market conditions, the 2001 panel row reflects the consequences of job loss and reemployment during the slow recovery from the 2001 recession, and the 1996 panel row reflects the experience of workers losing a job and becoming reemployed during the late 1990s economic boom.

The percentage reduction in earnings for job losers is quite large both for those losing jobs during the Great Recession and for those losing jobs during the period of more normal la-

1. In each case, we measure monthly earnings by the mean reported within a wave.

Table 8. Percentage Change from Previous Earnings to Average Earnings Following Reemployment for Involuntary Job Changers

Panel in Which Job Loss Occurred	Percentile			Percentage of Job Changers Non-employed for Eight or More Months
	25th	50th	75th	
1996 panel	−40	−6	32	17
2001 panel	−50	−15	18	23
2004 panel	−45	−12	21	17
2008 panel	−56	−26	9	39

Source: Authors' calculations using data from the Survey of Income and Program Participation.
Note: Only job losses that occurred in the first two years of the panel are reported here.

bor market conditions preceding the Great Recession. The magnitude of the percentage drop in earnings upon reemployment is roughly the same for those losing jobs during the first two years of the 1996, 2001, and 2004 SIPP panels but earnings losses are substantially larger for those losing jobs during the first two years of the 2008 panel. For example, the median reduction in real monthly earnings for those losing jobs during the first two years of the 2004 panel is 24 percent in the first wave following reemployment, while the corresponding earnings reduction for those losing jobs during the first two years of the 2008 panel is 37 percent. This suggests that the Great Recession caused a large increase in the magnitude of job-loss-related earnings reductions relative to the pre-recession era, due to both the large increase in the percentage of workers losing jobs and also the substantial increase in the percentage reduction in earnings for workers who lost jobs. Members of the 2008 panel who involuntarily left jobs were also much more likely to experience a long period of non-employment than those who lost jobs in the pre–Great Recession era, implying that job loss during the Great Recession or its aftermath necessitated a need to stretch available financial resources over a longer period of joblessness than in the earlier era.

Table 8 is identical to table 7 except that it measures the percentage change in monthly earnings between that in the first-wave job and mean monthly earnings in all remaining months of the panel following the start of the first new job rather than just the first month following start of the new job. The percentage

reduction in monthly earnings over the remainder of the panel relative to that immediately upon reemployment depends on the general strength of the labor market. In a tight labor market, such as that of the late 1990s, there are likely to be more favorable opportunities for job hopping and wage growth than in a slack labor market, such as that following the Great Recession. Non-employment spells following loss of an initial reemployment job are also likely to be longer in a slack labor market than in a tight labor market. For these reasons, one would expect earnings upon reemployment over the rest of the panel to be more favorable relative to that immediately upon reemployment in a tight labor market than in a slack labor market.

This prediction is supported by table 8. The distribution of the change in monthly earnings over the rest of the panel is more favorable for most of the distribution relative to the distribution of the change in earnings immediately upon reemployment for job losers in the tight labor market experienced by members of the 1996 panel. This is also true for the members of the 2004 and 2008 panels, who experienced weaker labor market conditions, but to a much lesser extent. A key conclusion that one can draw from the comparison between earnings losses upon reemployment and earnings losses measured over the rest of the panel is that earnings losses tend to be long lived, especially in a slack labor market.

Earnings losses upon reemployment are particularly severe for those who experience long spells of non-employment following their ini-

Table 9. Percentage Change in Earnings from Previous Employment to Initial Earnings in New Employment for Involuntary Job Changers with Long Non-employment Spells

Panel in Which	Percentile		
Job Loss Occurred	25th	50th	75th
1996 panel	−74	−41	0
2001 panel	−74	−38	2
2004 panel	−70	−36	5
2008 panel	−73	−47	−5

Source: Authors' calculations using data from the Survey of Income and Program Participation.
Note: Only job losses that occurred in the first two years of the panel are reported here.

Table 10. Percentage Change in Earnings from Previous Employment to Average Earnings Following Reemployment for Involuntary Job Changers with Long Non-employment Spells

Panel in Which	Percentile		
Job Loss Occurred	25th	50th	75th
1996 panel	−59	−22	25
2001 panel	−65	−37	10
2004 panel	−63	−26	4
2008 panel	−65	−35	6

Source: Authors' calculations using data from the Survey of Income and Program Participation.
Note: Only job losses that occurred in the first two years of the panel are reported here.

tial job loss, as shown in tables 9 and 10. These tables are similar to tables 7 and 8, but show the distribution of percentage earnings change for workers who are non-employed for at least eight full months following their initial job loss. These workers are especially unlikely to have had sufficient assets to maintain their consumption over their spells of non-employment, and one would expect that they would consequently be more likely to accept low-wage jobs than those who had not experienced as large a reduction in consumption expenditures. Overall, these tables strengthen the conclusion in the preceding section that households are not well positioned to insure their consumption spending against job loss. The loss of earnings during spells of unemployment is compounded by the reduction in earnings following reemployment. Both effects are especially severe during the Great Recession due to the increase in long unemployment spells and the elevated risk of further employment instability following initial reemployment.

Many job changes occur for reasons other than layoff or termination. These job changes might result in increased earnings upon reemployment if the change is to a better job or to a better job match, or it may result in reduced earnings if the new job involves fewer hours of work or if the wage reflects the loss of rents or human capital specific to the previous job. In either case, the job change might put the worker at increased risk of future involuntary job loss due to the worker's losing the protective effect of tenure on the previous job. These observations are borne out in tables 11 and 12, which are similar to tables 7 and 8 but pertain to job changes for reasons other than layoff or termination. The median worker experiences little change in earnings when changing jobs, but there is a large spread; some workers experience large percentage increases in earnings and others large decreases. For the 2008 panel, when monthly earnings are averaged over the remainder of the panel following employment in the first new job, the distribution of earnings changes shifts to the left (more negative) compared to when earnings are measured in the wave following employment in the first new job. This leftward shift does not occur in the earlier panels, suggesting that subsequent employment instability was a more important phenomenon for those switching jobs during the Great Recession than for those switching jobs in the pre-recession era.

Finally, for comparison, table 13 shows the change in real monthly earnings over the first two years (through the beginning of the seventh four-month panel wave) of each panel for individuals who stayed in the jobs they held at the start of the panel. Real earnings changes tended to be quite small for the job stayers. By definition, the job stayers did not experience earnings disruptions associated with spells of non-employment. Table 13 shows that they also generally did not experience large reductions in real earnings while employed. It is surprising that even the 25th percentile of earnings

Table 11. Percentage Change in Earnings from Previous Employment to Initial Earnings in New Employment for Other Job Changers

Panel in Which Job Loss Occurred	Percentile			Percentage of Job Changers Non-employed for Eight or More Months
	25th	50th	75th	
1996 panel	−17	0	20	3
2001 panel	−20	0	16	3
2004 panel	−22	0	20	4
2008 panel	−27	0	10	5

Source: Authors' calculations using data from the Survey of Income and Program Participation.
Note: Only job losses that occurred in the first two years of the panel are reported here.

Table 12. Percentage Change in Earnings from Previous Employment to Average Earnings Following Reemployment for Other Job Changers

Panel in Which Job Loss Occurred	Percentile			Percentage of Job Changers Non-employed for Eight or More Months
	25th	50th	75th	
1996 panel	−37	8	52	3
2001 panel	−44	0	40	3
2004 panel	−49	0	38	4
2008 panel	−78	−15	27	5

Source: Authors' calculations using data from the Survey of Income and Program Participation.
Note: Only job losses that occurred in the first two years of the panel are reported here.

Table 13. Percentage Earnings Changes for Job Stayers

Panel in Which Job Loss Occurred	Percentile		
	25th	50th	75th
1996 panel	−9	7	28
2001 panel	−11	8	33
2004 panel	−4	4	23
2008 panel	−8	0	12

Source: Authors' calculations using data from the Survey of Income and Program Participation.
Note: Only job losses that occurred in the first two years of the panel are reported here.

change is only −8 percent (real) in the 2008 panel, which is slightly smaller in magnitude than the approximately 10 percent drop in the 1996 and 2001 panels, although larger than the 4 percent drop in the 2004 panel. This may reflect distressed firms being more likely to terminate workers rather than cut their inflation-adjusted compensation during the time span of the 2004 and 2008 panels. One reason for this may be the very low inflation rates of the later period, and the documented reluctance of firms to cut nominal wages. Table 13 also shows that earnings increases at the 50th and 75th percentiles are somewhat muted during the Great Recession era compared to the pre-recession period.

CONCLUSION

For the last decade, most households have not had nearly enough financial wealth to smooth their consumption over more than a very short spell of unemployment. This situation compares unfavorably to the situation in the late 1980s and early 1990s. The reason for this is not clear, and will be an important topic for future research. Receipt of unemployment insurance benefits reduces the magnitude of this problem modestly, but still leaves most households vulnerable to experiencing a sharp drop in consumption expenditures during spells of unemployment.

This phenomenon has potentially serious consequences for both aggregate economic activity and for household well-being. One of the distinguishing features of economic recessions is a sharp increase in involuntary job loss. Our findings suggest that a period of concentrated job loss would likely result in a drop in aggregate consumption, especially if the rate at which the unemployed find new jobs is relatively low and unemployment durations accordingly increase. Most households do not appear to be in a position to cover a prolonged loss in labor earnings through a combination of drawing down of financial assets and take-up of unemployment insurance benefits or other social welfare transfers. Absent a flow of money from another source, such as increased earnings of other household members, transfers from friends or family members, or increased borrowing, households would have little choice but to decrease their consumption expenditures. In a large economic contraction, such as the Great Recession, this has the potential to cause a substantial reduction in aggregate consumption expenditures.

The decrease in the ability of households to compensate for earnings lost due to unemployment through a combination of drawing down of financial assets and increased receipt of transfer payments since the late 1980s and early 1990s suggests that the consequences of an increase in layoffs and terminations for aggregate consumption has likely become more severe over the same period of time. The diminished ability of households to smooth consumption implies an increase in the amplification of economic shocks, and may make the economy more vulnerable to recessions. This suggests that reforms to the unemployment insurance system may be desirable to counter this effect. The unemployment insurance system is designed both to correct for market failures that leave households vulnerable to economic shocks and to provide an automatic stabilizer to macroeconomic activity. Unfortunately, our findings indicate that there has likely been a decrease over time in the effectiveness of the system in satisfying both of these objectives. Programs to increase the rate at which individuals collect benefits to which they are entitled may be desirable in this regard.

Compounding the problem of insufficient financial wealth to insure against earnings losses while unemployed, individuals are at high risk of earning much less than they did in their previous job upon reemployment following job loss. Even if households had financial assets adequate to cover the earnings lost while unemployed, they would likely still want to decrease their consumption expenditures to reflect their diminished earnings. The clustering of involuntary job separations during recessions amplifies the macroeconomic impact of this effect on aggregate consumption. Regardless of timing, the earnings loss upon reemployment reduces the welfare of affected households. Commercial insurance against this loss is not available because of moral hazard and adverse selection, and in practice households are not financially able to "self-insure" against long-term earnings reductions. Proposals for a new wage insurance program targeted to displaced workers who have suffered earnings reductions, such as that described by Robert J. LaLonde (2007), have the potential to at least partly correct this market failure. Although the primary motivation for wage insurance is to protect the economic welfare of displaced workers, it would also act as an automatic stabilizer of aggregate consumption and facilitate job matching after periods of concentrated layoffs and terminations.

REFERENCES

Altonji, Joseph G., Anthony A. Smith, and Ivan Vidangos. 2013. "Modeling Earnings Dynamics." *Econometrica* 81(4): 1395–1454.

Blundell, Richard. 2014. "Income Dynamics and Life-

Cycle Inequality: Mechanisms and Controversies." *Economic Journal* 124(576): 289–18.

Carroll, Christopher D., Karen E. Dynan, and Spencer D. Krane. 2003. "Unemployment Risk and Precautionary Wealth: Evidence from Households' Balance Sheets." *Review of Economics and Statistics* 85(3): 586–604.

Couch, Kenneth A., Nicholas A. Jolly, and Dana W. Placzek. 2011. "Earnings Losses of Displaced Workers and the Business Cycle: An Analysis with Administrative Data." *Economics Letters* 111(1): 16–19.

Davis, Steven J., and Till von Wachter. 2011. "Recessions and the Cost of Job Loss." *Brookings Papers on Economic Activity.* 43(Fall): 1–72

Dickens, William T., and Robert K. Triest. 2012. "Potential Effects of the Great Recession on US Labor Markets." *B.E. Journal of Macroeconomics* 12(3): 1–40.

Fallick, Bruce. 1996. "A Review of the Recent Empirical Literature on Displaced Workers." *Industrial and Labor Relations Review* 50(1): 5–16.

Flaaen, Aaron, Matthew D. Shapiro, and Isaac Sorkin. 2003. "Reconsidering the Consequences of Worker Displacements: Survey Versus Administrative Measurements." Unpublished paper. University of Michigan.

Ghayad, Rand. 2014. "The Jobless Trap." Unpublished paper. Northeastern University.

Gibbons, Robert, and Lawrence F. Katz. 1991. "Layoffs and Lemons." *Journal of Labor Economics* 9(4): 351–80.

Gruber, Jonathan. 2001. "The Wealth of the Unemployed." *Industrial and Labor Relations Review* 55(October): 79–94.

Guvenen, Fatih, Fatih Karahan, Serdar Ozkan, and Jae Song. 2015. "What Do Data on Millions of US Workers Reveal About Life-Cycle Earnings Risk?" NBER Working Paper No. w20913. Cambridge, Mass.: National Bureau of Economic Research.

Johnson, Richard W., and Alice G. Feng. 2013. "Financial Consequences of Long-Term Unemployment During the Great Recession and Recovery." Unemployment and Recovery Project, Brief 13. Washington, D.C.: Urban Institute.

Kletzer, Lori. 2008. "Job Displacement." *Journal of Economic Perspectives* 12(1): 115–36.

LaLonde, Robert J. 2007. "The Case for Wage Insurance." CSR No. 30. New York: Council on Foreign Relations.

Low, Hamish, Costas Meghir, and Luigi Pistaferri. 2010. "Wage Risk and Employment Risk over the Life Cycle." *American Economic Review* 100(4): 1432–67.

Nakamura, Emi. 2008. "Layoff and Lemons over the Business Cycle." *Economics Letters* 99(1): 55–58.

Sullivan, James X. 2008. "Borrowing During Unemployment Unsecured Debt as a Safety Net." *Journal of Human Resources* 43(2): 383–412.

von Wachter, Till, and Elizabeth Weber Handwerker. 2009. "Variation in the Cost of Job Loss by Worker Skill: Evidence Using Matched Data from California, 1991–2000." Unpublished Paper. University of California, Los Angeles.

von Wachter, Till, Jae Song, and Joyce Manchester. 2009. "Long-Term Earnings Losses Due to Mass Layoffs During the 1982 Recession: An Analysis Using U.S. Administrative Data from 1974 to 2004. Unpublished paper. University of California, Los Angeles.

Vroman, Wayne. 2009. "Unemployment Insurance Recipients and Nonrecipients in the CPS." *Monthly Labor Review,* October, pp. 44–53.

Wandner, Stephen A., and Andrew Stettner. 2000. "Why Are Many Jobless Workers Not Applying for Benefits?" *Monthly Labor Review,* June, pp. 21–33.

The Emotional Toll of Long-Term Unemployment: Examining the Interaction Effects of Gender and Marital Status

GOKCE BASBUG AND OFER SHARONE

Prior research shows that long-term unemployment (LTU) generates a negative emotional toll but leaves unexplored how such toll varies by gender and marital status. Using a mixed-methods approach we examine how the negative emotional toll of LTU is shaped by the interaction of gender and marital status. Our qualitative findings suggest that more unemployed married men than women experience marital tensions that exacerbate the emotional toll of unemployment. Our analysis of survey data show that while marriages improve the well-being of both unemployed men and women, for married men but not women such benefits disappear once we control for household income. These findings contribute to the existing literature by deepening our understanding of how gender and marital status mediate the emotional toll of LTU.

Keywords: long-term unemployment, gender, marital status, well-being

Among the most pernicious and enduring effects of the Great Recession is the rise of long-term unemployment. Although the rate of long-term unemployment has declined from its Great Recession peak, as of 2015 the percent of the unemployed who are long-term unemployed remains at levels unseen prior to the Great Recession going back to at least the 1940s. A well-established literature associates long-term unemployment with a variety of social ills, including poverty, increased risk of physical and mental health problems, deteriorating emotional well-being, high suicide and mortality rates, domestic violence, divorce, and aca-

Gokce Basbug is a PhD candidate at the MIT Sloan School of Management. **Ofer Sharone** is assistant professor at the University of Massachusetts Amherst.

© 2017 Russell Sage Foundation. Basbug, Gokce, and Ofer Sharone. 2017. "The Emotional Toll of Long-Term Unemployment: Examining the Interaction Effects of Gender and Marital Status." *RSF: The Russell Sage Foundation Journal of the Social Sciences* 3(3): 222–44. DOI: 10.7758/RSF.2017.3.3.10. The coauthors' names are listed in alphabetical order. We are grateful for helpful feedback from Arne Kalleberg, Till von Wachter, Susan Silbey, Andrew Weaver, and the anonymous reviewers as well as participants of the Russell Sage Foundation conference, "The U.S. Labor Market During and After the Great Recession," and the MIT Institute for Work and Employment Research Workshop. The gathering of the qualitative data analyzed in this paper would not have been possible without the financial support of the AARP-Foundation and the volunteer efforts and expert support of numerous career coaches and counselors, including Amy Mazur, Deborah Burkholder, Rachelle Lappinen, Deb Elbaum, Arnold Clickstein, Maggie French, Allyn Gardner, Tammy Gooler Loeb, Clare Harlow, Patricia Wakefield, Kit Hayes, Cindy Key, Pam Lassiter, Ed Lawrence, Debbie Lipton, Tom McDonough, Sara Pacelle, Bonnie Petrovich, Martha Plotkin, Ilene Rudman, Lisa Shapiro, Gail Liebhaber, Robin Slavin, Mo Chanmugham, Deborah Federico, Melinda Fabiano, Arleen Bradley, Leigh Doherty, Suzy Drapkin, Patricia Weitzman, Melanie Hamon, Richard Johnson, Karen Samuelson, and Lou Yelgin. Direct correspondence to: Gokce Basbug at gbasbug@mit.edu, 100 Main Street, MIT Building E62-381, Cambridge, MA 02142; and Ofer Sharone at osharone@soc.umass.edu, University of Massachusetts Amherst, Department of Sociology, 528 Thompson Hall, Amherst, MA 01002.

demic underperformance of kids (Sullivan and von Wachter 2009; Van Horn 2013). In light of the historically high rate of long-term unemployment and its associated negative consequences it is important for researchers to develop nuanced understandings of how such effects vary and the extent to which these effects are mediated by other institutions.

In this paper we draw on mixed methods to consider how the negative emotional toll that typically accompanies spells of long-term unemployment differs for men and women, and, more specifically, whether and how marital status interacts with gender in shaping this emotional toll. Our qualitative data show that marriages are often helpful in buffering the emotional toll of long-term unemployment for both men and women, but for approximately half of our interviewees a range of marital tensions arose as a result of their being unemployed. Looking more closely at such tensions reveals a strikingly gendered pattern in which marital tensions related to the provider role were reported only by married men and not by married women. Our analysis of survey data also shows that, overall, marriages are helpful to the well-being of both unemployed men and women. For married men but not for married women, however, the analysis reveals that the significance of the benefits derived from marriage disappears once we control for household income. Taken together these findings make an important contribution to the existing literature by deepening our understanding of how gender and marital status shape and mediate the emotional toll of long-term unemployment. Since this emotional toll is strongly associated with negative effects on physical and mental health, as well as job search discouragement, the findings in this paper have important implications for policymakers and practitioners working to address the fallout from the ongoing crisis of long-term unemployment.

THE GREAT RECESSION AND LONG-TERM UNEMPLOYMENT

The Great Recession is the longest and most devastating economic downturn since the Great Depression (Elsby, Hobijin, and Sahin 2010; Sum et al. 2009). From May 2007 to October 2009 the labor force lost over 7.5 million jobs and the unemployment rate climbed from 4.8 percent to 10.1 percent (Grusky, Western, and Wimer 2011; Katz 2010). Compared to previous recessions, during and after the Great Recession job loss was much higher, reemployment rates were lower, spells of unemployment were longer, the rate of underemployment was higher, and the increase in the number of discouraged workers was substantial (Farber 2011).

The level of economic dislocation and financial devastation brought on by the Great Recession was accompanied by an enormous toll on emotional well-being. Among the most salient indicators of this negative emotional toll are the effects on families, leading to rising divorce rates (Morgan, Cumberworth, and Wimer 2011), increased domestic violence (Schneider, Harknett, and McLanahan 2014), reduced fertility rates (Schneider and Hastings 2014), and diminished child development (McLanahan, Tach, and Schneider 2013).

One of the distinguishing characteristics of the Great Recession was the rise of long-term unemployment, defined by the U.S. Bureau of Labor Statistics as unemployment lasting twenty-seven weeks or longer. May 2015 Bureau of Labor Statistics data showed that 29 percent of the unemployed were long-term unemployed, compared to 18 percent in 2007.[1] In March 2010, the number of long-term unemployed individuals reached over 6.5 million, representing 44.1 percent of the unemployed population, and the long-term unemployment rate increased to 4.3 percent, much higher than the prior postwar era peak of 2.6 percent in 1983 (Katz 2010).

The picture is even more distressing if we additionally consider the estimated number of long-term unemployed workers who became discouraged and have dropped out of the labor force since the Great Recession. In March 2015 the Economic Policy Institute estimated that the U.S. has 3 million "missing workers," defined as potential workers who are neither working nor looking for work due to weak labor

1. Bureau of Labor Statistics, "Unemployment Data," available at http://www.bls.gov/news.release/empsit.nr0 .htlm (accessed May 9, 2015).

market conditions (Gould 2015). Qualitative data suggest that a sizable proportion of missing workers withdrew from the labor market after a prolonged and unsuccessful search for work (Sharone 2013). The ongoing crisis of long-term unemployment can also be seen by examining patterns in unemployment duration. Whereas the mean unemployment duration in past recessions was twenty weeks, in the Great Recession mean duration increased to thirty-five weeks (Farber 2011).

Long-term unemployment affects men and women across varied segments of American society. It is widespread across different education levels, gender and race groups, and occupations and industries (Gould 2015). Recent studies show that long-term unemployment is not limited to individuals who are inflexible and therefore closed to opportunities in other occupations or industries, or to individuals who lack advanced education (Sharone et. al 2015). Although for college-educated individuals the rate of long-term unemployment is lower than for individuals without a college degree, the college-educated long-term unemployment rate is twice as high as it was before the Great Recession. Among the few predictors of long-term unemployment is age. More than half of all unemployed workers over the age of fifty-five are long-term unemployed across all levels of education (Evangelist and Christman 2013).

The severe and negative emotional toll of long-term unemployment is well established, and has been shown to be as harmful to well-being as the loss of income itself (Winkelmann and Winkelmann 1998; Sharone 2013). A line of qualitative studies dating back to the Great Depression (for example, Bakke 1933) consistently show that prolonged unemployment in the United States frequently leads to diminished self-esteem and increased self-blame, which is particularly intense among white-collar workers (Newman 1999; Smith 2001; Wanberg et al. 2012; Sharone 2013; Chen 2015). For example, Katherine Newman's (1999) study of unemployed managers found that most managers perceived their unemployment as a personal failing. Sharone (2013) likewise describes the emotional toll on long-term unemployed white-collar workers, who come to feel that they are "flawed" or "defective."

Meta-analytic reviews of quantitative studies also consistently show that unemployed individuals suffer from significantly lower levels of mental health compared to employed individuals (McKee-Ryan et al. 2005). Longitudinal studies show that when individuals become unemployed their psychological health deteriorates, and upon reemployment their well-being recovers. In addition, meta-analytic findings show that as unemployment duration increases, so does the negative emotional toll and the risk for mental and physical health issues (Paul and Moser 2009). For example, according to a Gallup poll (Crabtree 2014), the depression rate among long-term unemployed workers is 18 percent, compared to 12.4 and 5.6 percent for all unemployed and employed workers, respectively. Underlying the negative emotional toll of unemployment is not only stress induced by the loss of income and savings and the exhaustion of unemployment benefits but also the loss of self-esteem and self-confidence due to the experience of repeated rejections by employers. The longer individuals remain unemployed the more they experience deprivation (Brief et al. 1995), exhaustion of coping resources (Kinicki, Prussia, and McKee-Ryan 2000), and even personality changes (Boyce et al. 2015). Alan B. Krueger and Andreas Mueller (2011) found that unemployed workers' unhappiness increases the longer they stay unemployed, and such unhappiness is particularly salient when they are engaged in job-searching activities.

The association between unemployment and negative physical health outcomes is also established by a long line of research and meta-analyses (for example, Sullivan and von Wachter 2009; McKee-Ryan et al. 2005; Paul and Moser 2009; Brand 2015). A number of studies link the emotional toll of unemployment just described—especially the experience of self-blame and the internalization of stigma among unemployed workers—with negative health outcomes (Rantakeisu, Starrin, and Hagquist 1999; Eales 1989; Creed and Bartrum 2007). Over the past decade a rapidly growing literature on the connection between stigma and health shows that the internalization of stigma is linked, among other mechanisms, to increased diastolic blood pressure (Harrell, Hall, and

Taliaferro 2003; Guyll, Matthews, and Bromberger 2001) and increased cortisol output (Townsend et al. 2011; Dettenborn et al. 2010). These physical responses to internalized stigma are described in this literature as connected to experiences that threaten people's identity and status in social hierarchies, and specifically to experiences involving conditions of uncertainty about outcomes, and in which a successful outcome involves a process of "social evaluation" of the individual by others (Keating 2009, 75; Major and O'Brien 2005). The core experience of unemployment and searching for work is precisely one of repeatedly subjecting oneself to social evaluation under conditions of great uncertainty, which upon repeated employer rejections frequently leads unemployed workers to perceive themselves as "flawed" (Sharone 2013; Newman 1999). A further mechanism linking unemployment and negative physical health is social isolation (Keating 2009; Umberson, Crosnoe, and Reczek 2010; Kawachi and Berkman 2001).

GENDER, MARITAL STATUS, AND THE EMOTIONAL TOLL OF UNEMPLOYMENT

An important but under-studied question is how the negative emotional toll of long-term unemployment varies by gender and marital status. The qualitative literature on this issue yields mixed results. Older studies dating back to the 1930s suggest that unemployment is particularly undermining of married men, due to the effects of the traditional male breadwinner role. For example, Mirra Komarovsky's (1940, 74) classic study of long-term unemployment in the Great Depression, using in-depth interviews, finds that "man experiences a deep frustration because in his own eyes he fails to fulfill what is the central duty of his life, the very touchstone of his manhood—the role of family provider." According to Komarovsky, this emotional toll was more acute for men whose exclusive identity was as providers than for men who also identified as fathers and husbands. A similar finding about the particular vulnerability of married men was reported by Newman's (1999) study of unemployed managers in the 1980s. She explains: "Unemployment strikes at the heart of the masculine ideal. . . . [Having] failed at the task that most clearly de-

fines his role, he suffers a loss of identity as a man" (139). Like Komarovsky (1940), Newman (1999) also found that not all men were equally vulnerable to this emotional toll; specifically, gay men who were not married were much less likely to report the anxiety and anguish expressed by married men.

A more recent qualitative study examining the emotional toll of long-term unemployment challenges the applicability of Komarovsky and Newman's studies in the current era and claims that with changing gender roles it is now married women, more than married men, who are vulnerable to self-blame and the emotional toll of identity loss. According to Carrie Lane (2011), men in the twenty-first century "have an alternative standard of masculinity" where relying on a partner's income is *evidence* of progressive manhood" (121). According to Lane, the unemployed men she interviewed took it as a badge of honor that they were "secure enough in [their] manhood to comfortably rely on [their] wife's income" (117). For women, on the other hand, their increasingly career-based identities mean that relying on their husbands' income is devastating to their self-worth, evoking uncomfortable feelings of being needy and dependent. Thus, in comparing the experiences of unemployed married men and women, Lane (2011) concludes that "women's feelings of dwindling self-worth mirror those of male managers in [Newman's] study far more so than did the comments of their male peers" (126). Lane's claims are interesting, but more research is needed to determine whether a historical reversal has indeed occurred. One limitation of Lane's study is that none of the men who "took pride" in letting their wives support them were part of a dual-earner couple with children. This is significant because other contemporary studies show that the traditional male breadwinner role expectations surface most clearly when married couples have children (Gerson 2011).

Turning to survey studies that compare the unemployment experiences of men and women, we also find mixed results there. Some studies find that men experience more distress associated with unemployment than women, whereas others find no difference (Broman et al. 1995; Leana and Feldman 1991). Meta-analytic findings suggest that men are more negatively affected by unemployment than women (Paul and Moser 2009). Yet several other prior studies show that it takes more time for women to find a job after a period of unemployment, and that long-term-unemployed women's reemployment opportunities come with a greater loss of prior salary than is the case for long-term-unemployed men (Snyder and Nowak 1984).

A different line of studies explores how marital status mediates the negative emotional toll of unemployment. The dominant perspective in the psychology literature is that marriage provides critical social support and acts as a shield in difficult times such as unemployment. Prior studies that examine the effect of being married on unemployment typically focus on the social support aspect of the marriage relationship. For example, cross-sectional studies consistently find that married unemployed individuals are in a better psychological state than single unemployed individuals (Cooke and Rousseau 1984; Leana and Feldman 1991). These findings are consistent with sociological studies suggesting that marriage benefits both men and women and enhances mental health (Simon 2002). In their meta-analytic study, Frances McKee-Ryan and her colleagues (2005) found that married unemployed individuals are more satisfied with their lives than single unemployed ones. Similarly, using British panel data, Andrew E. Clark and Andrew J. Oswald (1994) found that married unemployed individuals experience less mental health distress than single unemployed individuals.

Alongside these studies showing the supportive effects of marriages, the literature also reveals that some unemployed individuals experience negative social support from their spouses, including findings of social undermining, which refers to negative evaluation of the person in terms of his or her attributes or actions (Vinokur and Van Ryn 1993). One of the reasons for such negative social support in marriages is the economic strain experienced in times of unemployment. Economic hardship changes the quality of the relationship and creates conflict in married couples (Conger, Rueter, and Elder 1999). For example, Saul D. Hoffman and Greg J. Duncan (1995) found that a husband's low income significantly increases the risk of marital dissolution. Similarly, Peter Jensen and Nina Smith (1990) found that if the husband is unemployed, divorce is more likely to occur, but this is not the case when the wife is unemployed. However, more recent studies find that either a husband's or wife's unemployment leads to increased likelihood of marital dissolution (Jalovaara 2003; Hansen 2005). Another complicating factor in the current era of stagnating wages is that increased economic interdependence between married men and women prevents both husbands and wives from contemplating separation (McManus and DiPrete 2001).

Although the studies described analyze the effects of gender and marital status on the emotional toll of unemployment, prior quantitative studies have not considered how marital status interacts with gender in mediating this emotional toll. The interaction of gender and marital status is likely important, given the well-documented significant effects of marriage on well-being and given the persistence of gender differences in the experiences of men and women in contemporary society. In light of the existing literature on the effects of marriage, we expect that for both long-term-unemployed men and women, marriage offers some protective benefits and buffers against the emotional toll of unemployment. Marriage is a ready-made support system. In addition to emotional support, marriages also play a social and economic insurance role. However, based on prior qualitative studies such as Komarovsky (1940) and Newman (1999), discussed earlier, for long-term-unemployed men, we hypothesize that marriage is a double-edged sword. On the one hand it provides varied forms of support, but on the other hand—to the extent that stereotypical gendered expectations persist, which focus the male role in the family on breadwinning—long-term unemployment is likely to create tensions. Specifically, we expect that the inability of long-term unemployed men to fulfill the breadwinner role will generate marital distress that will offset the supportive benefits of marriages for men. Given that this tension is premised on the persistence of stereotypical male gender roles, we expect that this particular interaction of gender and marital status will affect men more than women. With respect to women, given the well-documented research on the labor market obstacles facing long-term-unemployed women, we expect that the emotional toll of long-term unemployment will be as difficult for women as for men, and perhaps more so, but that in the case of women, marriage will follow the general pattern of having a salubrious effect on their well-being.

QUALITATIVE DATA AND ANALYSIS

To begin our exploration of how the emotional toll of long-term unemployment varies by gender, and whether and how it is mediated by marital status, we turn to our qualitative data. The qualitative data discussed in this paper are derived from fifty in-depth interviews conducted with long-term-unemployed job seekers in 2013 and 2014. To recruit interview subjects we contacted job seekers through Boston-area career centers, networking groups, and libraries, and invited job seekers to sign up for the opportunity to participate in research in exchange for receiving free support to be provided by volunteer career coaches and counselors. Interested job seekers were asked to complete a short survey so that we could see whether they met the following criteria:

1. Unemployed six months or longer

2. Between the ages of forty and sixty-five

3. Working in white-collar occupations and college-educated

4. Looking for work in the Boston area

Over 800 job seekers signed up for the opportunity to participate, but only 125 met the criteria for participation. Our sample of 125 unemployed job seekers was 55 percent male and 45 percent female, with 70 percent of the sample being married and with a mean age of fifty-four. Our recruiting focused on unemployed workers over the age of forty because, as previously discussed, older workers are more likely than younger workers to get trapped in long-term unemployment. We expect that due to self-selection our sample consists of unemployed job seekers with higher-than-average levels of motivation to continue with their job search and to receive job search support, but we do not expect this particular selection bias

to affect our findings regarding how gender and marital status mediate the emotional toll of long-term unemployment. Our focus on white-collar workers who are college educated may bias our qualitative findings, but such bias likely cuts against our hypothesis regarding how gender and marital status mediate the emotional toll of long-term unemployment. Prior research (for example, Lane 2011) suggests that male breadwinner expectations are less salient for married college-educated men than for married men without a college education. So our qualitative findings regarding college-educated white-collar workers may understate the extent of marital tensions stemming from male breadwinner expectations.

In-depth interviews with a randomly selected subset of fifty long-term unemployed job seekers were conducted prior to any of the job seekers' receiving support. These semistructured, in-depth interviews were conducted either in person or by telephone and lasted one to two hours. We asked participants questions regarding their experience looking for work and the effect of unemployment on their well-being and personal relationships.

The in-depth interviews revealed the intense negative emotions that long-term-unemployed job seekers experience. Consistent with prior research, both male and female job seekers discussed the emotional toll of financial stress and diminishing self-esteem. For example, Deborah, a fifty-two-year-old marketing executive, discussed how job loss has entailed a "profound loss of self-esteem and confidence." She explained: "My job was a huge part of my identity. Huge part of how people saw me. It's hard not to feel like a throw-away." Steven, a fifty-six-year-old computer engineer, succinctly described similar feelings: "I'm embarrassed. I'm humiliated. I feel like a loser."

A vast literature, as previously described, finds that marriages are generally supportive of individuals' emotional well-being. Consistent with this literature, our unmarried interviewees described painful feelings of intense isolation and the absence of support more frequently than the married unemployed workers. For example, Abby, a single woman, told us, "I have no one supporting me. I'm on my own." Even though Abby has friends and extended family, she explains that, "It's not like I'm talking to them every day. I really feel the weight of this is on myself. It's really emotionally devastating to feel that sort of isolation." Gene, a widower, described unemployment as being the "darkest period in my life," and isolation as the most difficult aspect of this period, since his social life had been fully centered around his former work. Being home alone, "I do not talk to anyone on a daily basis." He describes the temporary reprieve from isolation when he goes to a networking support group: "These meetings are helpful sometimes for the camaraderie for a couple hours." But, he adds, "I find myself as the meeting is closing . . . I sit there and go, 'This isn't gonna last much longer. Maybe another twenty minutes. Then I'm going to get in my car and go home. It's going to be dark."

Both unmarried men and women described how as a result of their unemployment their friendships have become more fragile, and thus friends are less available as a source of support. Frank described how his friends have withdrawn: "People that I thought I knew, some have just dropped off the radar and have literally told me not to contact them. It's like they are saying, 'There is something wrong with you. You're not working and we don't want to talk to you.'" Tammy's friends have not cut off contact, but they are "all married, so a lot of times they're tied up with other obligations," and even when they do get together, Tammy feels like "people don't really want to know all the gory details about how depressing it is. They will say, 'Oh, that's awful, it's depressing, let's talk about something else.'" In addition to the discomforts and stigmas that lead friends to withdraw from unemployed workers, other factors lead unemployed workers to withdraw from friends. In part, such withdrawal is due to financial constraints, since being with friends usually involves spending money. Rob put it this way: "I don't have the money to go out and do what my friends are doing." But withdrawing from friends is also the result of social unease rooted in the loss of status. Jack put it this way: "You feel uncomfortable about where you are in your life versus where your friends are. Some of these folks have jobs, ranging from vice presidents to directors, doctors.

So you tend to maybe not socialize as much as you would like to or as you did in the past."

Some single unemployed workers also mentioned that although they would like to find a romantic partner, dating was simply not feasible during unemployment. Denise, with a laugh, rhetorically asked, "I'm already facing rejection right and left on the job front. Who needs more rejection?" But then she added, with a more serious note, "What's the first question anybody asks you when they meet you: 'What do you do for a living?' Well, I don't do anything because I'm one of these people who had the misfortune to be laid off. I can't even see any gentleman taking me seriously." David likewise reported wishing to be in a relationship but then added, "A part of me feels too unworthy to be. . . . I feel 'less than.'"

By contrast to these unmarried job seekers' descriptions of isolation and lack of social support, approximately half of the married job seekers we interviewed described varied forms of positive supports from their spouses. For example, Ryan shared: "I would not have been able to make it through this period without my wife. My wife could not be more supportive." Ryan explained that in the moments when he felt most discouraged his wife would remain "really positive and hopeful" and "she'd say, 'Oh, this is going to be your week, I can see it.'" Jen described her supportive relationship with her husband of thirty years. Despite the fact that at the time of the interview Jen and her husband were about to lose their home to foreclosure, she found much solace in the marriage, explaining: "We have been able to face the terror together and in so doing, we have built a bond that is amazingly durable. Nobody should have to go through what we've been through, but [the marriage] is a tremendous balm."

While unmarried unemployed workers were more likely to describe painful isolation than married workers, marriage does not always alleviate the isolation felt by unemployed workers. In fact, about half our married interviewees also reported experiencing the emotional toll of unemployment in isolation. Steven, who said he felt "embarrassed" and "humiliated," added that despite the fact that he is married, he feels "very much alone," and reflected on how "it's very hard to talk to my wife about it because she's never been through anything like it." Albert shared a similar experience: "My wife has no clue what it's like." The experience of emotional isolation within marriages is not limited to men. Linda, a fifty-eight-year-old woman who has worked for over twenty years in software sales, put it this way: "My husband doesn't understand what I'm going through." Because Linda's husband's salary is sufficient to financially support the both of them, he has difficulties relating to Linda's negative emotions of identity loss and her growing sense of financial vulnerability.

Although our qualitative data suggest that both men and women may experience emotional isolation within marriages, when we look more closely at the narratives of married unemployed workers, a strikingly gendered pattern emerges: about a third of the men, but no women, describe marital tensions due to disagreements over job search intensity and what kind of job the unemployed spouse should seek. Tensions over job search intensity frequently took the form of men reporting that their wives did not think they were exerting sufficient effort to find work. For example, Larry is a software engineering manager specializing in speech recognition. Larry and his wife are under significant financial pressure because they have two school-age children and a large mortgage. Larry describes the strain this has put on his marriage: "[My wife] says, 'You're not doing enough.' What the hell? I can only do so much. She doesn't understand it. She hasn't been through that herself. There is a lot of pressure if you're in a family."

A different but related kind of tension was discussed by Richard, a fifty-year-old public relations professional. Richard and his wife also have young children and feel intense financial stress due to Richard's unemployment. Richard explained, "I've never really been in a position where I wasn't sure whether I could pay the mortgage or buy my food or keep my car repaired." His family is dependent on his income since his wife "doesn't make much money. She's mostly volunteering." Unlike Larry's case, the source of the marital tension, as Richard described it, is not that he is not doing enough on his job search but that he is doing too much job searching and not enough to contribute his

share to the "second shift," child care (Hochschild 1989). Richard put it this way: "My wife feels neglected because I'm wrapped up in job search related things and not spending enough time just doing other things which are a part of daily life. She might think I'm not doing anything but looking for a job is more than forty hours. You always have to be 'on.' That's a stress."

The marital tensions described by Richard and Larry are partly rooted in the difficulties spouses have of understanding the experience of unemployment. The feeling that spouses "don't understand" is frequently reported by both men and women. The distinctly gendered pattern is the lack of understanding coupled with the suggestion that the job seeker is not doing enough on his search, or is not doing enough at home, a complaint that was only reported by male job seekers. Given the abundant research showing that married women do a disproportionate amount of house and care work in families (for example, Gerson 2011) it is perhaps not surprising that women with unemployed husbands may expect more support on the home front. At the same time, for men like Richard who struggle to do the "work" of job searching (Sharone 2013) under the stress of unemployment, this spousal expectation may signal that his wife "might think I'm not doing anything." Interestingly, some unemployed women we interviewed did report the kind of tension described by Richard but not in the context of their marriages. Instead these tensions arose with mothers, sisters, or close friends who were disappointed at not receiving support from unemployed women who, they had presumed, had time on their hands. For example, Nadine, an unemployed unmarried woman, described changes in her relationship with her mother and sister: "They both expect me to pick up a lot more of the pieces. My mom will now ask would you mind stopping at the post office and mailing this package? The subtext is that since 'you're not doing anything why don't you help me?' They don't understand the pressures of looking for work."

Another kind of marital tension that was generally only reported by men focuses on the kind of job the unemployed spouse should seek. A good example is Warren, a sixty-two-year-old environmental scientist, with a seven-year-old child. Despite the fact that Warren's wife works full-time, his family is under considerable financial stress in the absence of his income. Warren reported that his wife has pressured him to seek *any* available job, whether or not in his field, including a low-paying retail position. Warren explained: "It's a huge stress on our marriage. My relationship with my wife is really fraught with difficulty because I didn't realize how much she really wanted a breadwinner in the mix. . . . My wife has been pressuring me to get a job in retail sales, selling camping gear or something."

In his long career as an environmental scientist Warren has taught at Ivy League universities and conducted research funded by multimillion-dollar grants. Although Warren has expanded the breadth of his search beyond teaching and research to include university administration, he has maintained a focus on positions that would allow him to continue making a contribution in his field of expertise. Yet the unexpected toll on his marriage from his hesitation to consider jobs such as in retail sales weighs heavily on Warren as he confides, "I don't want to let my loved ones down. That's a huge thing."

In Warren's case marital tensions arose from his spouse feeling that his search was too narrow; other men report marital tensions arising from spouses thinking their husbands' searches are too broad. James, a fifty-three-year-old former corporate manager, has expanded his search to include finance-related positions in nonprofit companies. James believes that his corporate finance experience can be a valuable asset to a nonprofit company, and that down the road such a position will provide more security and meaning than his former work, even if this would involve an initial pay cut. Yet, James is experiencing tensions in his marriage because his wife does not support his inclusion of nonprofit companies in his search:

I feel I should take a lower-paying job and she's like, "Oh, my god, that's so low." She doesn't want me to take it. She's thinking we're going nowhere with me taking a lower-paying job. I feel like I have a longer-range view of things than her. . . . She's just looking

for how much they are going to pay me right now. And I'm looking at how much I'm going to end up getting after five to ten years.

The kinds of marital tensions described by Warren and James that were common among long-term unemployed men were strikingly absent from the accounts of marital tensions described by women. In both of these cases the marital tensions arising from unemployment are implicitly linked to the extent to which the unemployed male is perceived to be fulfilling the breadwinner role. For Tom, a fifty-five-year-old unemployed sales agent, the link of breadwinning and the state of his marriage was made explicit. Tom noted that the strain in his marriage has been somewhat mitigated due to savings that he had accumulated when he had a job, which means "I've still been able to provide." But, after a pause, he added, "Absolutely, if I wasn't able to provide, I probably would not be married today."

To summarize, as we review the qualitative data, we find that consistent with the existing literature on the positive effect of marriage on wellbeing, about half of our married unemployed workers benefitted from forms of positive support that were less frequently available to unmarried unemployed workers. Yet our qualitative data also reveal two kinds of marital tensions that exacerbate the emotional toll of long-term unemployment. First, both men and women report that marital tensions may arise because of spouses' inability to understand and relate to the difficult experiences of unemployment. Second, unemployed married men but not women describe marital tensions arising from spouses' feeling that the unemployed spouse is not doing enough on his search or is not looking for the right kind of job. It is important to note that the second kind of marital tension, which was only reported by men, was in almost every case accompanied by descriptions of the family's severe economic stress. This is perhaps not surprising, given that tensions surrounding issues like the appropriate level of job search intensity and appropriate job targets are more likely to arise under conditions of economic duress. Although the qualitative data are derived from a relatively small sample, this striking pattern does support our hypothesis that while both men and women generally benefit from being married, in the context of unemployment, lingering male breadwinner expectations for men mean that the benefits of marriage are counterweighed by marital tensions that intensify the emotional toll of long-term unemployment. In the remainder of this paper we explore this hypothesis, using a larger dataset and quantitative analysis.

QUANTITATIVE DATA AND ANALYSIS

To further examine the effects and interactions of gender and marital status in mediating the emotional toll of long-term unemployment, and specifically to explore the hypothesis generated by our qualitative data and the literature discussed in the previous section, we exploit a set of data collected right after the end of Great Recession from a sample of unemployed workers in New Jersey. The Survey of Unemployed Workers in New Jersey was conducted by the Princeton University Survey Research Center from October 2009 to April 2010. The sample consists of 6,025 unemployed individuals who were recipients of unemployment insurance in New Jersey.[2] The unemployed individuals in this study were surveyed for twelve consecutive weeks, with a subset of respondents who were long-term unemployed at the time of the study surveyed for an additional twelve weeks for a total of twenty-four weeks. In total, 39,201 surveys were completed. Table 1 provides information on the sample characteristics.

The survey had two parts: an initial survey, which was administered in the first week and collected information on demographics and income, and a weekly survey, administered in the first week and in each subsequent week, that gathered a wide range of information about respondents' ongoing job search activities, time use, reservation wages, job offers, and emotional states (for a detailed description of the Survey of Unemployed Workers in New Jersey, see Krueger and Mueller 2011). Although at the time of the survey New Jersey's overall unemployment rate was similar to the national unemployment rate, it is important to note that

Table 1. Characteristics of New Jersey Sample

Demographic Group	Percentage of Total Sample
Female	52.1
Male	47.9
Marital status	
Married	48.9
Single	28.0
Separated	3.3
Divorced	12.1
Widowed	1.9
Domestic partnership	5.7
Years of age	
24 or less	6.8
25–34	21.3
35–44	21.1
45–54	26.8
55 or over	24.0
Race	
White	68.0
Black	15.3
Other	5.4
Ethnicity	
Hispanic	9.1
Non-Hispanic	80.8
Education	
Less than high school	7.0
High school	26.0
Some college	26.4
College	40.7
Unemployment duration (weeks of UI paid)	
0–9	11.2
10–19	11.2
20–29	11.9
30–39	10.8
40–49	11.3
50–59	10.1
60 or more	33.6
N	6,025

Source: Authors' compilation based on the Survey of Unemployed Workers in New Jersey.

2. Because the New Jersey data are limited to unemployment insurance recipients it excludes long-term-unemployed workers whose benefits eligibility have expired, as well as unemployed workers who do not qualify for unemployment benefits. This selection bias may exclude unemployed workers experiencing particularly in-

New Jersey's long-term unemployment rate, with 40 percent of its unemployed workers being long-term unemployed, was among the highest in the United States.

The New Jersey dataset is well suited for addressing our theoretical and empirical questions regarding the effects of gender and marital status in shaping the experience of unemployment because it includes information on the emotional state of unemployed respondents as measured by life satisfaction, as well as time spent in a negative mood on a weekly basis. Life satisfaction was measured with the question "Taking all things together, how satisfied are you with your life as a whole these days?" Respondents were asked to pick a level of life satisfaction from a four-point scale ranging from very satisfied to not at all satisfied. The survey also measured respondents' mood with the question "Now we would like to know how you feel and what mood you are in when you are at home. When you are at home, what percentage of the time are you: 'in a bad mood', 'a little low or irritable mood', 'in a mildly pleasant mood', 'in a very good mood?'" Respondents were asked to indicate the percentage of time that they experienced each mood category.

DESCRIPTIVE RESULTS

We begin our analysis by examining descriptive statistics about the reported level of life satisfaction among the unemployed respondents. Table 2 breaks down these responses by gender and marital status. To provide some context for interpreting the responses of the unemployed individuals in the New Jersey survey we also present the responses of employed individuals to the same life satisfaction question from the Princeton Affect and Time Use Survey (PATS). PATS is a national telephone survey that was conducted in the spring of 2006 by the Gallup Organization. Although the whole PATS sample consists of nearly four thousand respondents, for purposes of our comparison with the New Jersey data we limit our analysis to the responses of employed individuals in the PATS data. As seen in table 2, the differences

in the life satisfaction of employed and unemployed individuals are dramatic. Only 5.5 percent of unemployed single females are very satisfied with their lives, compared to 37 percent for employed single females. Overall, married females are more satisfied than single females, regardless of employment status, but again the effect of unemployment is enormous, with the percentage of unemployed married women who are very satisfied with their lives at 8.7 percent, compared to 55 percent for employed married females. Table 2 shows a similar pattern for men, with immense differences in life satisfaction between employed and unemployed men, and as is the case with women, married men report higher levels of life satisfaction than single men. While the comparison between the PATS and New Jersey data is limited by the fact that PATS data were collected three years earlier and are national in scope (as opposed to focusing only on New Jersey), the dramatic differences in the answers to the identical questions about life satisfaction provide a useful baseline for contextualizing the emotional state of unemployed individuals in the New Jersey survey.

For additional descriptive statistics on how the emotional toll of unemployment varies by gender and marital status, we draw on the New Jersey survey data to compare the means of the responses given to the life satisfaction question and the percentage of time respondents reported spending in a bad mood for each group (single female, married female, single male, and married male). In table 3 ANOVA (analysis of variance) statistics show that there is a significant difference between groups. Both unemployed men and unemployed women who are married report more life satisfaction and less time spent in a bad mood than single unemployed individuals.

Our descriptive results are not surprising. We see, first, that consistent with the literature on the emotional toll of unemployment, employed individuals are indeed far more satisfied with their lives than unemployed individuals, and, second, consistent with the literature on the salubrious effects of marriage, married un-

---

tense financial and emotional duress, but in this study such bias is partially mitigated by the fact that the New Jersey data were collected at a time when the federal government extended the maximum unemployment benefit duration to ninety-nine weeks.

Table 2. Levels of Life Satisfaction Expressed by Unemployed and Employed (Figures in Parentheses) Individuals, by Marital Status (Percents)

Level of Satisfaction	Single Female	Married Female	Single Male	Married Male
Very satisfied	5.5 (37)	8.7 (55)	5.9 (34)	9.0 (48)
Satisfied	35.8 (52)	49.9 (38)	31.0 (54)	40.6 (43)
Not satisfied	46.5 (9)	35.8 (6)	51.7 (10)	41.8 (8)
Not at all satisfied	12.2 (2)	5.7 (1)	11.4 (3)	8.7 (1)

Source: Authors' compilation based on the Survey of Unemployed Workers in New Jersey and Princeton Affect and Time Use Survey.

Notes: Percentages in parentheses are nationwide employed individuals' responses from Princeton Affect and Time Use Survey. Sample size for the PATS is 2,048 and 6,025 for the Survey of Unemployed Workers in New Jersey.

Table 3. Means and ANOVA Results for Life Satisfaction Score and Percentage of Time Spent in Bad Mood

	Life Satisfaction Score (1 = not at all satisfied; 4 = very satisfied)	Percentage of Time Spent in a Bad Mood at Home
Single female	2.34	12.98
	(0.76)	(16.33)
Married female	2.61	10.69
	(0.72)	(14.93)
Single male	2.31	14.49
	(0.74)	(17.78)
Married male	2.49	12.36
	(0.77)	(16.57)
F score	49.013**	12.151**
Total N	6,011	5,939

Source: Authors' compilation based on the Survey of Unemployed Workers in New Jersey.

Note: Standard deviations are in parentheses.

**$p < .001$

employed and employed individuals are more satisfied with their lives than single employed and unemployed individuals.

CROSS-SECTIONAL ANALYSES

We next analyze whether the interaction of gender and marital status significantly predicts individuals' life satisfaction and mood. Using data from the initial survey of unemployed New Jersey workers, as seen in table 4, we first regressed life satisfaction on gender, marital status, and a host of control variables such as education, number of children, household income, race, age, and unemployment duration.

In this model, levels of life satisfaction are higher for unemployed women than for unemployed men, and higher for married than single individuals of both genders. When we added the interaction of gender and marital status we see that the interaction term is significantly and negatively related to life satisfaction. This result shows that single males experience the lowest levels of life satisfaction, followed by single females. Married women reported higher levels of satisfaction than married men. The interaction term is also significantly and negatively related to time spent in a good mood. Again, single males, as a group, spend

Table 4. OLS Results with Entry Survey Data

	Life Satisfaction		Time in Bad Mood		Time in Good Mood	
Education	0.018*	0.020*	−0.358*	−0.374*	−0.289	−0.241
	(0.008)	(0.008)	(0.179)	(0.180)	(0.293)	(0.294)
Number of children	0.014ʲ	0.015ʲ	0.197	0.181	−0.000	0.045
	(0.008)	(0.008)	(0.173)	(0.173)	(0.282)	(0.283)
Household income	0.022**	0.022**	−0.393**	−0.386**	0.289*	0.268*
	(0.003)	(0.003)	(0.076)	(0.076)	(0.125)	(0.125)
Unemployment duration	−0.001**	−0.001**	0.023*	0.023*	−0.048*	−0.049**
	(0.000)	(0.000)	(0.008)	(0.008)	(0.140)	(0.014)
Female	0.094**	0.133**	−2.125**	−2.669**	2.063*	3.635**
	(0.020)	(0.027)	(0.432)	(0.581)	(0.706)	(0.949)
Black	−0.061*	−0.057*	0.161	0.109	5.597**	5.749**
	(0.029)	(0.029)	(0.634)	(0.635)	(1.035)	(1.037)
Asian	−0.086ʲ	−0.086ʲ	−3.12*	3.124*	−1.898	−1.910
	(0.047)	(0.047)	(1.018)	(1.018)	(1.663)	(1.662)
American Indian	−0.046	−0.054	1.612	1.728	5.102	4.767
	(0.181)	(0.181)	(3.88)	(3.883)	(6.340)	(6.339)
Pacific islander	−0.191	−0.183	−3.823	−3.924	7.762	8.053
	(0.179)	(0.179)	(3.96)	(3.964)	(6.474)	(6.472)
Hispanic	0.061ʲ	0.062ʲ	0.443	0.420	4.969**	5.036**
	(0.035)	(0.025)	(0.775)	(0.775)	(1.266)	(1.266)
Age groups	0.003	0.004	−1.012**	−1.03**	−0.086	−0.032
	(0.004)	(0.004)	(0.096)	(0.097)	(0.158)	(0.159)
Single	−0.124**	−0.077*	−0.279	−0.952	−1.319	0.624
	(0.023)	(0.032)	(0.510)	(0.701)	(0.833)	(1.144)
Female X single		−0.086*		1.233		−3.564*
		(0.040)		(0.881)		(1.438)
Constant	2.266**	2.237**	22.694**	23.101**	25.822**	24.645**
	(0.051)	(0.053)	(1.107)	(1.144)	(1.808)	(1.869)
R²	0.0411	0.0419	0.0432	0.0436	0.0138	0.0148

Source: Authors' compilation based on the Survey of Unemployed Workers in New Jersey.
Note: Standard errors are in parentheses.
*p < .05; **p < .01

the least amount of time in a good mood, followed by single females. Married women report spending the most time in a good mood, followed by married men. The cross-sectional analyses of the data support our descriptive findings.

PANEL DATA ANALYSIS
One of the distinguishing characteristics of the Great Recession is the crisis of long-term unemployment that came in its wake. For this reason we are particularly interested in explor-

ing how the experience of unemployment changes over time as unemployment duration increases. Because the New Jersey survey of unemployed individuals provides data on the emotional state of respondents on a weekly basis, we are able to run individual fixed effects models to see how the emotional toll of unemployment unfolds over time for married and single men and women. Using panel data also helps reduce the likelihood that our findings are driven by omitted variables, which have the potential to be in relationship with the inde-

Table 5. Fixed Effects Models for Dependent Variable: Life Satisfaction

	Single Female	Married Female	Single Male	Married Male
Unemployment duration	0.0086***	0.0015*	0.002	0.0014*
Constant	1.945***	2.622***	2.292***	2.541***
N of observations	5,159	9,891	3,708	11,398
N of groups	921	1363	757	1573
R²	0.0126	0.0005	0.0007	0.0004

Source: Authors' compilation based on the Survey of Unemployed Workers in New Jersey.
*p < .05; ***p < .001

Table 6. Fixed Effects Models for Dependent Variable: Time Spent in Bad Mood

	Single Female	Married Female	Single Male	Married Male
Unemployment duration	0.222***	0.185***	0.322***	0.141***
Constant	4.090***	1.895	0.1534	5.398***
N of observations	5,131	9,846	3,695	11,366
N of groups	914	1,353	752	1,570
R²	0.0099	0.0101	0.0225	0.0053

Source: Authors' compilation based on the Survey of Unemployed Workers in New Jersey.
***p < .001

pendent variable. By using fixed effects models we can eliminate unobserved heterogeneity across individuals, which might introduce spurious results.

In tables 5 and 6 we present fixed effects models for single females, married females, single males, and married males with the dependent variables of life satisfaction and time spent in a bad mood, respectively. Table 5 shows that as unemployment duration increases, life satisfaction increases for all groups except single males, but the effect sizes are extremely small and therefore not very meaningful.[3] Much more striking are the findings with regard to time spent in a bad mood. As seen in the table 6, as the duration of unemployment increases, time spent in a bad mood significantly increases for all groups.

In short, our findings consistently show that for married and single men and women time spent in a bad mood dramatically increases with longer periods of unemployment, and because we use fixed effects models to look at the same individuals over time we can eliminate the possibility that these findings are driven by observed and unobserved time-invariant differences among individuals. Looking more closely at these findings to explore whether the extent of the increase in time spent in a bad mood significantly differs across groups, we use our panel data to run random effects models, which include the interaction of unemployment duration with married and single men and women. As seen in table 7, the interaction of unemployment duration with gender and marital status reveals a significant difference between single men and married men. The increase in time spent in a bad mood as unem-

3. This finding is unexpected, given that other indicators of negative well-being intensify with increased unemployment; however, it is consistent with Krueger and Mueller (2011), who analyzed the same data and found that self-reported mood worsens as unemployment duration increases but life satisfaction does not. This finding is also consistent with other prior studies that find some evidence of habituation to unemployment as individuals remain unemployed (Clark 2006; Winkelmann and Winkelmann 1998).

Table 7. Random Effects Generalized Least Squares Regression Results

	DV: Time Spent in Bad Mood
Unemployment duration	0.06**
Gender_marital status	
Single female	1.132
Married female	–2.56*
Single male	0.85
Gender_marital status*unemployment duration	
Single female	0.03
Married female	0.02
Single male	0.07**
Constant	10.59**
N of observations	29,806
N of groups	4,554
R^2 within	0.0100
R^2 between	0.0196

Source: Authors' compilation based on the Survey of Unemployed Workers in New Jersey.
Note: Married men is the omitted category.
*$p < .05$; **$p < .01$

ployment continues is significantly higher for single men than for married men. However, it is important to note that although the increase in time spent in a bad mood as unemployment continues is likewise higher for single females than for married females, this difference is not significant.

Taken as a whole, the findings described suggest that marriage mediates and diminishes the negative emotional toll of unemployment for both men and women. In the final step of our analysis we attempt to dig deeper to understand what it is about marriage that is helpful. Our analysis here is guided by our qualitative findings, which suggest that marriages may be less supportive when married couples feel acute financial stress. Moreover, the pattern in the qualitative findings suggest that marital tensions as a result of financial stress are more likely to arise in couples with an unemployed man as compared to an unemployed woman.

To explore whether the salubrious effects of marriage vary by gender under conditions of financial stress, we separated our analysis for married and single men and women. For this analysis, following Daniel Kahneman and his colleagues (2006), we created a new dependent variable called "negative mood" by combining time spent in a bad mood and time spent in a low/irritable mood. We first examine the relationship among marital status, economic strain, and negative mood for men. As can be seen in table 8, model 1, when we regress marital status on negative mood, and control for unemployment duration, we find that, as expected, single men spend significantly more time in negative moods than married men. However, in model 2, when we add household income to the regression we find that after controlling for household income marital status became insignificant. In other words, once we control for the extra household income that typically comes from being married, there is no significant difference between the time spent in a negative mood for single men and married men. To see the effects of other variables in model 3 we included all other control variables, except household income, and still found the significant difference between single men and married men with regard to time in a negative mood. In model 4, when we added household income along with the other control variables, the marital status variable once again became insignificant. One interpretation of this striking finding is that for unemployed men, the benefits of marriage derive more from added income than from other forms of intangible or emotional supports.

We next ran the same models for women, and as can be seen in table 9, the results are strikingly different. In model 1, when we regress marital status on negative mood, and control for unemployment duration, we find that single women, just like single men, spend significantly more time in a bad mood than their married counterparts. The difference between men and women arises when we control for household income in model 2. Unlike men, women benefitted from being married even after controlling for household income, as well as after controlling for all other variables (models 3 and 4). The differences in the effects of marriage

Table 8. Random Effects with Longitudinal Data for Time Men Spent in a Negative Mood

	Model 1	Model 2	Model 3	Model 4
Unemployment duration	0.081***	0.079***	0.128***	0.115***
Single	3.94**	1.104	4.318*	2.646
Household income		-0.780***		-0.670*
Ethnic or racial background				
Black			1.722	-2.825
Asian			6.513*	6.311*
American Indian			-9.455	-9.300
Pacific Islander			-15.202	-14.589
Hispanic			-2.201	-3.450
Age				
20–24			11.098*	10.365*
25–29			12.108**	11.217*
30–34			12.184*	11.166**
35–39			13.835***	13.367***
40–44			11.895*	11.117**
45–49			13.761***	13.643***
50–54			12.775***	12.283***
55–59			10.992**	10.891**
60–64			3.464	3.337
College			-5.821**	-4.869**
Number of children			-0.070	-0.0616
Monthly rent or mortgage payments			0.001*	0.001**
Extended study			-0.701	-0.618
Constant	31.898	39.119	21.955***	27.866***
R^2	0.0069	0.0158	0.0412	0.0471
N of observations	14,945	14,708	12,244	12,041
N of groups	2,302	2,270	1,772	1,751

Source: Authors' compilation based on the Survey of Unemployed Workers in New Jersey.
Note: White and age (over 65) are omitted categories.
*$p < .05$; **$p < .01$; ***$p < .000$

for men and women suggested by tables 8 and 9 are broadly consistent with the pattern observed in our qualitative data, which suggested more marital tensions arising for couples under financial stress with an unemployed male.

Finally, since our findings suggest that a lingering male breadwinner role increases the emotional toll of unemployment for married men, and since according to some existing studies the salience of the male breadwinner role varies by education levels—and specifically has diminished for married college-educated men (for example, Lane 2011)—to explore vari-

ations by levels of education we looked at whether men and women's education level moderates the relationship between unemployment duration and negative mood. Our regression analyses using panel data in tables 8 and 9 show that overall, unemployed college-educated workers (which for purposes of those tables we define as workers with at least some college education) spend significantly less time in a negative mood than unemployed workers who are not college-educated. Prior studies comparing the experiences of college-educated white-collar and blue-collar unemployed work-

Table 9. Random Effects with Longitudinal Data for Time Women Spent in a Negative Mood

	Model 1	Model 2	Model 3	Model 4
Unemployment duration	0.0784***	0.0724***	0.0604**	0.045*
Single	4.728***	2.901*	6.407***	4.062*
Household income		−0.494**		−0.763***
Ethnic or racial background				
Black			−6.897***	−7.960***
Asian			4.408	4.617
American Indian			16.828	14.829
Pacific Islander			16.629	17.945
Hispanic			2.337	1.367
Age				
20–24			17.683**	16.747**
25–29			18.669**	17.479**
30–34			15.970**	15.310**
35–39			18.409**	18.479**
40–44			17.465**	17.692**
45–49			20.573***	20.666***
50–54			17.598**	17.653**
55–59			18.713**	17.892**
60–64			11.388*	11.823*
College			−3.341*	−1.979
Number of children			−0.283	−0.368
Monthly rent or mortgage payment			0.0005	0.000
Extended study			0.213	0.519
Constant	30.152	34.711***	16.889**	23.411***
R²	0.0150	0.0192	0.0448	0.0502
N of observations	14,861	14,310	12,470	12,000
N of groups	2,252	2,181	1,842	1,785

Source: Authors' compilation based on the Survey of Unemployed Workers in New Jersey.
Note: White and age (over 65) are omitted categories.
*$p < .05$; **$p < .01$; ***$p < .000$

ers find that white-collar workers are more likely to experience negative emotions from blaming themselves for their unemployment (Newman 1999; Sharone 2013; but see Chen 2015 finds self-blame among blue-collar workers). However, our findings suggest that when looking more broadly at negative moods, which may be triggered by a variety of sources beyond self-blame, they are more frequently experienced by workers who are not college-educated. The benefit of higher education levels holds for both men and women, but differences emerge between men and women when we control for income and other demographic variables. Among men, after controlling for income and demographic variables, college-educated unemployed workers spent significantly less time in a negative mood than unemployed male workers who did not go to college. By contrast, among women, after controlling for income and demographic variables, college-educated unemployed workers do not significantly differ in time spent in a negative mood from unemployed female workers who did not attend college.

We further examined whether education

Table 10. Random Effects Regression Results for Dependent Variable: Negative Mood

	Only Men	Only Women
Unemployment duration	0.35**	0.14
Education level		
High school diploma or equivalent	5.08	5.98
Some college	−0.12	2.89
College diploma	−2.82	4.29
Some graduate school	9.28	5.61
Graduate degree	4.11	3.82
Education level*unemployment duration		
High school diploma or equivalent	−0.29*	−0.04
Some college	−0.22$^\beta$	−0.04
College diploma	−0.21$^\beta$	−0.08
Some graduate school	−0.44**	−0.09
Graduate degree	−0.39**	−0.07
Constant	31.77***	27.99***
N observations	14,945	14,914
N groups	2,302	2,260
R^2 within	0.0061	0.0015
R^2 between	0.0118	0.0090

Source: Authors' compilation based on the Survey of Unemployed Workers in New Jersey.

Note: Some high school is the reference category.

$^\beta p < .10$; $^*p < .05$; $^{**}p < .01$; $^{***}p < .000$

level moderates the effect of unemployment duration on negative mood for men and women separately. For this analysis, we regressed negative mood on the interaction terms of unemployment duration with education level dummies. As seen in table 10, there is a significant difference for men between the reference category of some high school and the higher education categories. As the education level increases, this difference gets bigger. However, we do not see a similar pattern for women. Figure 1 graphically shows the difference by gender in the time spent in a negative mood as it relates to level of education. The graph shows that for men, but not for women, time spent in negative mood decreases as education level increases. These findings lend some support to claims in the literature that the salience of the male breadwinner role varies by education levels, and specifically, that the male breadwinner expectations, and the emotional toll that accompanies such expectations during times

of unemployment, are less salient for married college-educated men than for men without a college education.

DISCUSSION AND CONCLUSION

Although the Great Recession officially ended in June 2009, its disastrous effects are still with us. Strikingly, the rate of long-term unemployment remains at levels unseen in the postwar era, wreaking havoc on the finances and well-being of millions of American families. Voluminous research has shown that long-term unemployment is associated with a variety of social ills including, among others, job search discouragement leading workers to drop out of the workforce, and deteriorating mental and physical health. As discussed in the introduction to this paper prior research has linked both job search discouragement (Sharone 2013) and the deterioration of health (for example, Rantakeisu, Starrin, and Hagquist 1999; Creed and Bartrum 2007) to the severe and negative emo-

Figure 1. Percentage of Time Spent in Negative Mood

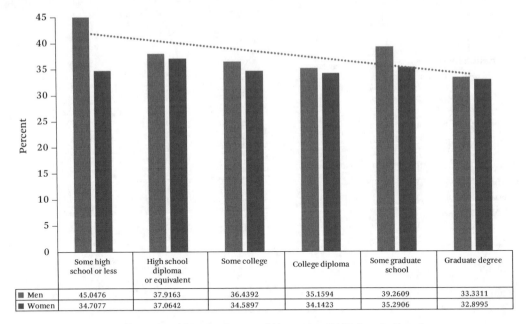

	Some high school or less	High school diploma or equivalent	Some college	College diploma	Some graduate school	Graduate degree
■ Men	45.0476	37.9163	36.4392	35.1594	39.2609	33.3311
■ Women	34.7077	37.0642	34.5897	34.1423	35.2906	32.8995

Source: Authors' compilation based on the Survey of Unemployed Workers in New Jersey.

tional toll of long-term unemployment. Drawing on both qualitative interview data as well as survey data this paper breaks new ground by examining how the negative emotional toll of long-term unemployment is shaped by the interaction of gender and marital status.

A well-established literature shows the salubrious effects of marriage for well-being. Yet, given the ongoing debate in the qualitative literature about the degree to which marriage may in some cases exacerbate the emotional toll of unemployment for married men (for example, Newman 1999) or for married women (Lane 2011), it is surprising that to our knowledge no prior survey study has focused on the interaction of gender and marital status in mediating the emotional toll of long-term unemployment.

Our in-depth interviews with long-term unemployed job seekers in the Boston area reveal a suggestive pattern. As can be expected, given the existing literature on the positive effects of marriage, many interviewees discuss the benefits of marriage. Yet approximately half the interviewees also brought up marital tensions that exacerbated the emotional toll of long-term unemployment. Although both unem-

ployed men and women reported some tensions in their marriages arising from the fact that their spouses had difficulties understanding their prolonged unemployment, it was only men who described a second kind of tension involving spouses who suggested the unemployed male was not doing enough on their search, not doing enough at home, or not looking for the right kind of job. This pattern in the qualitative data, along with prior studies, led us to hypothesize that for unemployed men the generally supportive effects of being married would be counterweighed by marital tensions that tend to intensify the emotional toll of long-term unemployment.

Turning to our analysis of survey data of unemployed job seekers in New Jersey we confirm the immense emotional toll of unemployment, finding large differences in life satisfaction between employed and unemployed individuals, as well as the extent to which negative moods increase over time with prolonged unemployment. How does the interaction of gender and marital status shape this emotional toll? Overall our data suggest that marriages are helpful to the well-being of both unemployed men and women. Yet, an interesting finding emerges when we attempt to understand what it is about being married that is particularly helpful to well-being. Marriages may be helpful in various ways, including as a source of emotional comfort and support and as a form of economic insurance with spousal contributions to household income. It is striking that when we look at the emotional toll of unemployment for men (as measured by time spent in a negative mood) our analysis revealed there were no significant benefits to being married once we controlled for household income. The survey data we analyzed suggest that the main emotional benefit of marriage for unemployed men derives from increased household income. Further research is needed to examine this finding more closely. For unemployed women, by contrast, the benefits of being married for their emotional well-being remained significant even after controlling for household income. These findings are broadly consistent with the pattern in our qualitative data showing heightened marital tensions among married couples with an unemployed male.

This study has important implications for policymakers and practitioners working to respond to the negative consequences of the ongoing crisis of long-term unemployment. In thinking about responses to the negative emotional toll generated by unemployment—which to an important extent underlies issues such as job search discouragement and deteriorating mental and physical health—traditionally available sources of emotional support during times of crisis, most notably spouses, may not be well positioned to provide such support in the specific context of financial stress and long-term unemployment. This points to the importance of policies and practices that bolster public support institutions for long-term-unemployed job seekers and to the need to reverse the trend of defunding public sources of such support (McKenna, McHugh, and Wentworth 2012).

REFERENCES

Bakke, Edward Wight. 1933. *The Unemployed Man: A Social Study*. London: Nibset & Co.

Boyce, Christopher J., Alex M. Wood, Michael Daly, and Constantine Sedikides. 2015. "Personality Change Following Unemployment." *Journal of Applied Psychology* 100(4): 991–1011.

Brand, Jennie E. 2015. "The Far-Reaching Impact of Job Loss and Unemployment." *Annual Review of Sociology* 41: 359–75.

Brief, Arthur P., Mary A. Konovsky, Rik Goodwin, and Karen Link. 1995. "Inferring the Meaning of Work from the Effects of Unemployment." *Journal of Applied Social Psychology* 25(8): 693–711.

Broman, L. Clifford, V. Lee Hamilton, and William S. Hoffman, and Roya Mavaddat. 1995. "Race, Gender, and the Response to Stress: Autoworkers' Vulnerability to Long-Term Unemployment." *American Journal of Community Psychology*, 23(6): 813–42.

Chen, Victor. 2015. *Cut Loose: Jobless and Hopeless in an Unfair Economy*. Berkeley: University of California Press.

Clark, Andrew E. 2006. "A Note on Unhappiness and Unemployment Duration." IZA report 2406. Bonn, Germany: Institute for the Study of Labor.

Clark, Andrew E., and Andrew J. Oswald. 1994. "Unhappiness and Unemployment." *Economic Journal* 104(424): 648–59.

Conger, Rand D., Martha A. Rueter, and Glen H. Elder Jr. 1999. "Couple Resilience to Economic Pressure." *Journal of Personality and Social Psychology* 76(1): 54–71.

Cooke, Robert A., and Denise M. Rousseau. 1984. "Stress and Strain from Family Roles and Work-Role Expectations." *Journal of Applied Psychology* 69(2): 252–60.

Crabtree, Steven. 2014. "In U.S., Depression Rates Higher for Long-Term Unemployed." *Gallup* (website), June 9. Available at: www.gallup.com/poll/171044/depression-rates-higher-among-long-term-unemployed.aspx; accessed August 9, 2016.

Creed, Peter, and Dee Bartrum. 2007. "Explanations for Deteriorating Wellbeing in Unemployed People: Specific Unemployment Theories and Beyond." In *Unemployment and Health: International and Interdisciplinary Perspectives*, edited by Thomas Kieselbach, Anthony Winelield, and Carolyn Boyd. Bowen Hills: Australian Academic Press.

Dettenborn, Lucia, Antje Tietze, Franka Bruckner, and Clemens Kirschbaum. 2010. "Higher Cortisol Content in Hair Among Long-Term Unemployed

Individuals Compared to Controls." *Psychoneuro-endocrinology* 35(9): 1404–9.

Eales M. J. 1989. "Shame Among Unemployed Men." *Social Science and Medicine* 28(8): 783–89.

Elsby, Michael W., Bart Hobijn, and Aysegul Sahin. 2010. "The Labor Market in the Great Recession." *Brookings Papers on Economic Activity* 41(1): 1–69.

Evangelist, Mike, and Anastasia Christman. 2013. "Scarring Effects: Demographics of the Long-Term Unemployed and the Danger of Ignoring the Jobs Deficit." NELP Briefing Paper. Washington, D.C.: National Employment Law Project. Available at: http://nelp.3cdn.net/4821589f87f 6c502e1_nem6b0xjt.pdf; accessed August 9, 2016.

Farber, Henry S. 2011. "Job Loss in the Great Recession: Historical Perspective from the Displaced Workers Survey, 1984–2010" NBER Working Paper No. 17040. Cambridge, Mass.: National Bureau of Economic Research.

Gerson, Kathleen. 2011. *The Unfinished Revolution: Coming of Age in a New Era of Gender, Work, and Family.* New York: Oxford University Press.

Gould, Elise. 2015. "Another Month, Same Story: Job Openings Data; Little Changed in February." Economic Policy Institute, *Working Economics Blog*, April 7. Available at: www.epi.org/blog/another -month-same-story-job-openings-data-little -changed-in-february/; accessed August 9, 2016.

Grusky, David B., Bruce Western, and Christopher Wimer. 2011. "The Consequences of the Great Recession." In *The Great Recession*, edited by David b. Grusky, Bruce Western, and Christopher Wimer. New York: Russell Sage Foundation.

Guyll, Max, Karen A. Matthews, and Joyce T. Bromberger. 2001. "Discrimination and Unfair Treatment: Relationship to Cardiovascular Reactivity Among African American and European American Women." *Health Psychology* 20(5): 315–25.

Hansen, Hans-Tore. 2005. "Unemployment and Marital Dissolution A Panel Data Study of Norway." *European Sociological Review* 21(2): 135–48.

Harrell, Jules P., Sadiki Hall, and James Taliaferro. 2003. "Physiological Responses to Racism and Discrimination: An Assessment of the Evidence." *American Journal of Public Health* 93(2): 243–48.

Hochschild, Arlie. 1989. *The Second Shift: Working Parents and the Revolution at Home.* New York: Viking Penguin.

Hoffman, Saul D., and Greg J. Duncan. 1995. "The Effect of Incomes, Wages, and AFDC Benefits on Marital Disruption." *Journal of Human Resources* 30(1): 19–41.

Jalovaara, Marika. 2003. "The Joint Effects of Marriage Partners' Socioeconomic Positions on the Risk of Divorce." *Demography* 40(1): 67–81.

Jensen, Peter, and Nina Smith. 1990. "Unemployment and Marital Dissolution." *Journal of Population Economics* 3(3): 215–29.

Kahneman, Daniel, Alan B. Krueger, David Schkade, Norbert Schwarz, and Arthur A. Stone. 2006. "Would You Be Happier If You Were Richer? A Focusing Illusion." *Science* 312(5782): 1908–10.

Katz, Lawrence. 2010. "Long-Term Unemployment in the Great Recession. Testimony before the Joint Economic Committee U.S. Congress. Hearing on 'Long-Term Unemployment: Causes, Consequences and Solutions.'" Available at: http://scholar.harvard.edu/lkatz/files/long_term_ unemployment_in_the_great_recession.pdf; accessed August 9, 2016.

Kawachi, Ichiro, and Lisa Berkman. 2001. "Social Ties and Mental Health." *Journal of Urban Health* 78(3): 458–67.

Keating, Daniel. 2009. "Social Interaction in Human Development: Pathway to Health and Capabilities." In *Successful Societies: How Institutions and Culture Affect Health*, edited by Peter Hall and Michele Lamont. New York: Cambridge University Press.

Kinicki, Angelo J., Gregory E. Prussia, and Frances M. McKee-Ryan. 2000. "A Panel Study of Coping with Involuntary Job Loss." *Academy of Management Journal* 43(1): 90–100.

Komarovsky, Mirra. 1940. *The Unemployed Man and His Family.* New York: Octagon Books.

Krueger, Alan B., and Andreas Mueller. 2011. "Job Search, Emotional Well-Being, and Job Finding in a Period of Mass Unemployment: Evidence from High Frequency Longitudinal Data." *Brookings Papers on Economic Activity*, Spring 2011, pp. 1–81. Available at: www.brookings.edu /wp-content/uploads/2011/03/2011a_bpea_ krueger.pdf; accessed August 9, 2016.

Lane, Carrie M. 2011. *A Company of One: Insecurity, Independence, and the New World of White-Collar Unemployment.* Ithaca, N.Y.: Cornell University Press.

Leana, Carrie R., and Daniel C. Feldman. 1991. "Gender Differences in Responses to Unemployment." *Journal of Vocational Behavior* 38(1): 65–77.

Major, Brenda, and Laurie T. O'Brien. 2005. "The Social Psychology of Stigma." *Annual Review of Psychology* 56: 393–421.

McKee-Ryan, Frances, Zhaoli Song, Connie R. Wanberg, and Angelo J. Kinicki. 2005. Psychological and Physical Well-Being During Unemployment: A Meta-analytic Study." *Journal of Applied Psychology* 90(1): 53–76.

McKenna, Claire, Rick McHugh, and George Wentworth. 2012. "Getting Real: Time to Re-invest in the Public Employment Service." NELP Briefing Paper. Washington, D.C.: National Employment Law Project, October. Available at: www.nelp.org/page/-/UI/2012/NELP-Report-Investing-Public-Reemployment-Services.pdf?nocdn=1; accessed August 9, 2016.

McLanahan, Sara, Laura Tach, and Daniel Schneider. 2013. "The Causal Effect of Father Absence." *Annual Review of Sociology* 39: 399–427.

McManus, Patricia A., and Thomas A. DiPrete. 2001. "Losers and Winners: The Financial Consequences of Separation and Divorce for Men." *American Sociological Review* 66(2): 246–68.

Morgan, S. Philip, Erin Cumberworth, and Christopher Wimer. 2011. The Great Recession's Influence on Fertility, Marriage, Divorce, and Cohabitation." In *The Great Recession*, edited by David B. Grusky, Bruce Western, and Christopher Wimer. New York: Russell Sage Foundation.

Newman, Katherine S. 1999. *Falling from Grace: Downward Mobility in the Age of Affluence*. New York: Free Press.

Paul, I. Karsten, and Klaus Moser. 2009. "Unemployment Impairs Mental Health: Meta-analyses." *Journal of Vocational Behavior* 74(3): 264–82.

Rantakeisu, Ulla, Bengt Starrin, and Curt Hagquist. 1999. "Financial Hardship and Shame: A Tentative Model to Understand the Social and Health Effects of Unemployment." *British Journal of Social Work* 29(6): 877–901.

Schneider, Daniel, Kristen Harknett, and Sara McLanahan. 2014. "Intimate Partner Violence in the Great Recession." Paper presented at the Annual Meeting of the American Sociological Association. San Francisco (August 16, 2014).

Schneider, Daniel, and Orestes P. Hastings. 2014. "The Effect of Economic Shocks on Poor Women's Marriage and Non-marital Fertility: Evidence from the Great Recession." Paper presented at the annual meeting of the American Sociological Association. San Francisco (August 16, 2014).

Sharone, Ofer. 2013. *Flawed System/Flawed Self: Job Searching and Unemployment Experiences*. Chicago: University of Chicago Press.

Sharone, Ofer, Rand Ghayad, Gokce Basbug, Alex Vasquez, and Michelle Rosin. 2015. "Supporting Experienced LTU Professionals" In *Transforming U.S. Workforce Development Policies for the 21st Century*, edited by Carl E. Van Horn, Todd Greene, and Tammy Edwards. Kalamazoo, Mich.: W. E. Upjohn Institute Press.

Simon, Robin W. 2002. "Revisiting the Relationships Among Gender, Marital Status, and Mental Health." *American Journal of Sociology* 107(4): 1065–96.

Smith, Vicki. 2001. *Crossing the Great Divide: Worker Risk and Opportunity in the New Economy*. Ithaca, N.Y.: Cornell University Press.

Snyder, Kay A., and Thomas C. Nowak. 1984. "Job Loss and Demoralization: Do Women Fare Better Than Men?" *International Journal of Mental Health* 13(1–2): 92–106.

Sullivan, Daniel, and Till von Wachter. 2009. "Job Displacement and Mortality: An Analysis Using Administrative Data." *Quarterly Journal of Economics* 124(3): 1265–1306.

Sum, Andrew, Ishwar Khatiwada, Joseph McLaughlin, and Sheila Palma. 2009. "The Economic Recession of 2007–2009: A Comparative Perspective on Its Duration and the Severity of Its Labor Market Impacts." Boston: Northeastern University, Center for Labor Market Studies.

Townsend, Sarah S. M., Brenda Major, Cynthia E. Gangi, and Wendy Berry Mendes. 2011. "From 'In the Air' to 'Under the Skin': Cortisol Responses to Social Identity Threat." *Personality and Social Psychology Bulletin* 37(2): 151–64.

Umberson, Debra, Robert Crosnoe, Corinne Reczek. 2010. "Social Relationships and Health Behavior Across the Life Course." *Annual Review of Sociology* 36: 136–57.

Van Horn, E. Carl. 2013. *Working Scared (Or Not at All): The Lost Decade, Great Recession, and Restoring the Shattered American Dream*. Plymouth, U.K.: Rowman & Littlefield.

Vinokur, Amiram D., and Michelle Van Ryn. 1993.

"Social Support and Undermining in Close Relationships: Their Independent Effects on the Mental Health of Unemployed Persons." *Journal of Personality and Social Psychology* 65(2): 350–59.

Wanberg, Connie, Gokce Basbug, Edwin A. J. Van Hooft, and Archana Samtani. 2012. "Navigating the Black Hole: Explicating Layers of Job Search Context and Adaptational Responses." *Personnel Psychology* 65(4): 887–926.

Winkelmann, Liliana, and Rainer Winkelmann. 1998. "Why Are the Unemployed So Unhappy? Evidence from Panel Data." *Economica* 65(257): 1–15.